D0433466

Awakening

The Music Industry
in the Digital Age

by Mark Mulligan

About the author

Mark Mulligan is a music industry analyst and consultant of 15 years standing. Throughout this time has worked with all of the leading companies in the digital music market, right up to the very most senior management, helping them shape their strategy and products. a recording artist, Mark swapped the mixing desk for the analyst's desk just as Napster was beginning to change the music industry for good. For 11 years Mark was a Vice President and Research Director at Jupiter Research and then Forrester Research, where he led research and analysis into how technology shapes media businesses and the consumer. He is now the founder and Research Director of music specialist analyst firm MIDiA Research. Mark also maintains the industry leading blog Music Industry Blog: https://musicindustryblog.wordpress.com

About MIDiA Research

MIDiA Research is a unique syndicated research and analysis service focused on the digital content marketplace. Leveraging proprietary consumer data, market forecasts and indices. MIDiA Research reports provide unrivalled insight into the rapidly changing global music, digital content and technology markets. MIDiA Research makes sense of the disruption and transformation that occurs where technology and the creative industries meet. MIDiA's clients include the leading global media and technology companies as well as small innovative start ups.

http://www.midiaresearch.com

"I live in a strictly rural community, and people here speak of 'The Radio' in the large sense, with an over-meaning. When they say 'The Radio' they don't mean a cabinet, an electrical phenomenon, or a man in a studio; they refer to a pervading and somewhat godlike presence which has come into their lives and homes."
E.B. White 1933

"The future is already here - it's just not yet very evenly distributed."
William Gibson

"The music business is a cruel and shallow money trench, a long plastic hallway where pimps and thieves run free, and good men die like dogs. There's also a negative side."
Attributed apocryphally to Hunter S Thompson

For Chop

Table of Contents

People interviewed for this book

(Job titles may refer to previously held positions)

Adam Kidron	Founder and CEO, Beyond Oblivion
Alexander Jung	Founder and CEO, Soundcloud
Alexander Ross	Partner, Wiggin
Alison Wenham	CEO, AIM
Axel Dauchez	CEO, Deezer
Barney Wragg	SVP Universal Music eLabs / Global Head of Digital, EMI
Ben Drury	Founder and CEO, 7 Digital
Benji Rogers	Founder and CEO, PledgeMusic
Brian Message	Manager, Radiohead, Nick Cave / Chairman MMF
Cary Sherman	CEO, RIAA
Chris Gorman	Founder and CEO, MusicQubed
Cliff Fluet	Partner, Lewis Silkin / Director 11
Daniel Ek	Founder and CEO, Spotify
David Boyle	SVP Insight, EMI
David Byrne	Solo artist / Talking Heads
David Isrealite	CEO, MPAA
David Lowery	Camper van Beethoven / The Trichordist
Edgar Berger	President & CEO International, Sony Music Entertainment
Elio Leoni Sceti	CEO, EMI
Erik Nielsen	Manager, Marillion
Geoff Taylor	CEO, BPI
Gregor Pryor	Partner, Reed Smith
Helienne Lindvall	Award winning songwriter
Ian Hogarth	Founder and CEO, Songkick
Ian Rogers	CEO, Beats Music / CEO TopSpin

Irene B	Artist
Jack Horner	Founder Frukt
Jay Samit	SVP, EMI / EVP & GM, Sony Corp America
Jeremy Silver	VP New Media EMI / Chairman musicmetric
Jim Griffin	CTO Geffen Records / CEO, Cherry Lane Digital
Jon Irwin	President, Rhapsody
Jonathan Grant	Above and Beyond / Founder, Anjunabeats Records
Justin Morey	Senior Lecturer Music Production, Leeds Beckett University
Keith Harris	Manager, Stevie Wonder / GM, Motown
Keith Thomas	Grammy Award Winning Producer and Songwriter
Ken Park	Chief Content Officer, Spotify
Kjartan Slette	Head of Music, WiMP
Larry Miller	COO, a2b Music / President Reciprocal
Liz Schimel	VP Music, Nokia
Lohan Presencer	CEO of Ministry of Sound Group
Mark Kelly	Marillion / CEO, FAC
Mark Knight	Founder and Chief Architect, Omnifone
Martin Goldschmidt	Founder and MD, Cooking Vinyl
Martin Mills	Founder and Chairman, Beggars Group
Michael Robertson	Founder and CEO, MP3.com
Nenad Marovac	Partner, DN Capital
Oleg Fomenko	CEO, Bloom.fm
Paul Hitchman	Founder and Director Playlouder/ MD Kobalt
Paul Myers	Founder and CEO, Wippit
Paul Vidich	EVP, WMG / Director, Reverbnation
Peter Jenner	Manager Pink Floyd, Billy Bragg / MD Sincere Management
Peter Sunde	Founder, The Pirate Bay
Phil Sant	Founder and Chief Engineer, Omnifone
Ralph Simon	EVP Capitol & Blue Note / Founder Yourmobile

Robert Ashcroft	SVP Network Services Europe / CEO PRS for Music
Roger Faxon	CEO, EMI
Scott Cohen	Founder, The Orchard
Simon Wheeler	Director of Strategy, Beggars Group
Sumit Bothra	Manager, The Boxer Rebellion, PJ Harvey
Tim Westergren	Founder and Chief Strategy Officer, Pandora
Tom Frederikse	Partner, Clintons
Tony Wadsworth	Chairman and CEO, EMI Music UK & Ireland / Chairman BPI
Wayne Rosso	President, Grokster
Will Page	Chief Economist, Spotify

Introduction

In June 1999 a software programme developed by a college dropout changed the music industry forever. It triggered a transformation that threw decades' worth of accepted wisdom out of the window and sent the recorded music industry into what at times appeared to be a death spiral. But it was a process that also prompted a crucial era of self-questioning and a reassessment of what the music industry actually is and, most importantly, what it should be. Now, mid way through the second decade of the 21st century, we are witnessing the first stirrings of a new music industry, one that is built on digital foundations rather than bound by the constraints of the CD and physical retail. Without the process of re-examination the business would have been unprepared for the dramatically different realities of the digital era and the demands of the digital consumer. That single piece of software shook the music industry out of the hubris, complacency and arrogance that had come to define during the 1980's and 1990's.

Until that point music executives had enjoyed near absolute control over their highly predictable business and for the previous few decades things had been pretty good. In fact they had been more than just good: since the 1970's record sales had grown at an unprecedented rate, accelerating rapidly since the mid-1980's thanks to the adrenalin shot of the CD. But when Shawn Fanning launched Napster onto the Internet, all of that industry control and power disappeared in an instant. Although the industry would fight a fierce and committed rear guard action for years to come – and indeed still does – the balance of power from record label to music fan had already shifted irrevocably. The music industry's subsequent response gave the impression of a struggle in which the spoils were still up for grabs, but in truth the transformation had already taken place, even though the adversaries did not realize it.

In early 2015, half way through the music industry's second digital decade, there are few who would dispute that complete paradigm shifts in consumer behaviour and business practice took place. There are more than 500 digital music services; Apple had sold more than three quarter quarters of a billion iOS devices with 500 active iTunes accounts; YouTube is streaming 5 billion videos a day; there are 36 million digital music subscribers; and streaming music services Pandora, Spotify and Deezer have more than 200 million active users between them. The music world has changed spectacularly and yet many of the questions Napster posed back in the late nineties remain unanswered today. Since Napster fist raised its head global music revenues have shrunk by 45% and despite the best efforts of those 500+ music services, digital music accounts for just 40% of all recorded music revenues[1]. Tens of millions of people stopped buying music all together rather than go digital while hundreds of millions started streaming music for free online. In the analogue era, whenever the music industry introduced new music formats, periods of unprecedented prosperity followed, in the digital era unparalleled decline ensued.

---

1   IFPI

FIGURE 1

Digital Revenue Has Yet to Offset the Impact of Declining CD Sales

Global Digital Recorded Music Revenue, 2000 to 2013 (Retail Value) (£billions)

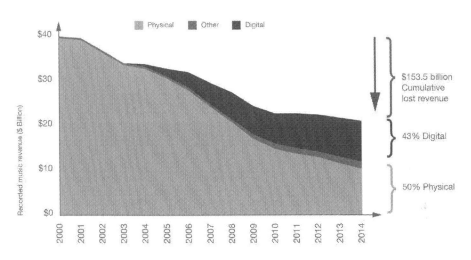

Source: MiDiA Research and IFPI

The most important difference with the digital revolution is that the new format – MP3 – is only partially within the control of the music industry, whereas with vinyl, the compact cassette and the CD it had been able to exercise near total authority over the evolution of these technologies as music formats. Napster wrenched power out of the hands of the record labels, publishers and retailers and thrust it firmly into the hands of consumers. As well as the technology companies that make the software and hardware consumers now use to consume music.

Since that summer of 1999 the music industry has been locked in a battle to wrest some of that control back, a battle that has been fought in the courtroom, in the pressroom and in the boardroom. But despite a few stand out successes like Apple's iTunes Store, Spotify and Pandora, the harsh reality is that the music industry has still not yet found a comprehensive answer to the digital challenge. Piracy continues to boom – albeit in new forms, the CD still remains the bedrock of music sales, licensing and royalty issues bog down legal services and consumer apathy permeates almost as completely as does the contagion of free[2]. Many of the foundations are in place for the next chapter of the music industry but most of the building blocks are yet to be hewn.

---

2   I am indebted to my former JupiterResearch colleague Ian Fogg for this phrase.

FIGURE 2

Recorded Music Formats Have Experienced an Unprecedented Acceleration in Innovation Since the 1990's

Evolution of Key Recorded Music Formats

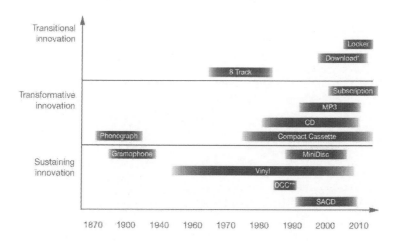

*Paid download
**Digital Compact Cassette

In the heady early days of digital music, the internet appeared to many artists to be a veritable El Dorado of opportunity, and some went as far as contemplating being able to do away with record labels entirely. Many artists were seduced by digital optimism as singer-songwriter David Lowery explained: "In the earlier days of the web many artists started to buy into the disintermediation theory that that maybe the middlemen could be cut out and we could all start selling music directly to our fans and we will make more money." A host of direct-to-fan sites and services emerged to bring artists and fans closer together than had ever been possible in the analogue era. Many artists even saw file sharing as a positive force. But the reality became increasingly dystopian, with artists feeling the harsh effects of shrinking recorded music revenue that even direct-to-fan platforms could not redress. As Lowery concluded: "My digital utopianism started to sour, my thoughts of disintermediation started to fail." Now artists find themselves at a watershed moment, a digital coming of age. Empowered with detailed data about how much they make from music sales online many artists have identified apparent injustices in the digital system and have added their voice to the digital debate. Using social media artists have aired their concerns about issues such as the amount of revenue streaming music services pay back to artists and the perceived lack of transparency between those services and record labels. Part of this assertion process has been a growing realization among artists that the nature of the contracts they have with record labels varies dramatically and thus so does their digital income. Though the signal-to-noise ratio of artist commentary is often compromised by fuzzy data and misinterpretation and discourse often leans towards polemic, there is an inescapable sense that this is the most dramatic change to happen to recording artists since the rise of the seven inch single in the 1950's.

It would be convenient to place the blame for the music industry's malaise entirely on record label greed, pirates' disregard for intellectual property and technology companies' pig headedness. The true story is more complicated and nuanced: it is one of multiple factors, of opposing worldviews, of competing forces and of the irresistible momentum of rapidly changing consumer behaviour. It is a tale of decades' worth of music industry business practice rendered redundant by the emergence of new technology. Of a generation of music executives largely unprepared for the disruptive change that turned their industry upside down, not grasping the gravity of the revolution that had occurred among their customers, right under their noses. Of a new generation of technology-primed music industry executives trying to pull the digital market into the legitimate fold. It is the narrative of a wave of technologists and software entrepreneurs who often ill understood, and sometimes even little cared for, the dynamics and needs of the rights owners whose businesses they were tearing apart, yet had unwavering commitment to delivering to consumers transformational product experiences. Of the paradox of artists being closer to their fans than ever yet struggling to make ends meet like never before.

The music industry's plight is a highly public one: news outlets and broadcasters have run thousands of stories and documentaries; business schools and universities have created countless case studies; books have narrated fragments of the tale, and of course the internet is awash with blogs, forums and comment. Consequently most people have an opinion on the music industry's digital struggle, with many of those opinions deeply entrenched and just as polarized as the extremes of the opposing digital adversaries themselves. Only the news industry can claim to have been as dramatically impacted by the advent of the digital era as the music industry but the tribulations of newspaper editors just do not capture the public imagination in the way the music industry's do. Music is closer to most people's hearts and many feel a sense of personal connection to the music business in a way that they do not to other industries. However, because that connection is with creators of the music, the artists and songwriters themselves, the sentiment usually translates into a mistrust of the actual industry. Perceptions fall into cliché, of fat cigar smoking record label executives and devious accountants determined to squeeze every last penny out of struggling artists. As things transpired, this very caricature became the fig leaf that a generation of music fans hid behind to justify downloading music for free: they were sticking one to 'the industry'. In more recent times that same sense of connection began to spur changing attitudes to free downloading, with a growing understanding that many artists are struggling while big music services and labels are not. But the unifying factor throughout has been the sense that people's personal connection with the music and artists they love has imbued them with something resembling a responsibility to take an interest in the music industry's story.

The media that these interested parties turn to has not always been exactly impartial and objective in its coverage of the rise of digital music. Some of the media, particularly the online portions, often acted as a loose narrative of prevailing opinion, telling the people exactly what they wanted to hear. Some technology news sites and blogs realized early on that playing to the galleries with critical assessments of the music industry's failings was a sure way of generating streams of reader comment and swathes of internet 'eyeballs'. It was a natural transition for these sites to establish ideological opposition to the traditional music industry and in turn polarize the debate even further. The caricature of an out-dated, luddite music industry was the perfect antithesis of progress, the ideal mirror image to contrast with the progressive and innovative character of the technosphere. Of course not every technology news site and blog adopted such a strident approach but those that did tended to have the loudest voice, and their readers have become the loudest voices in online forums, comments and discussion groups. In the intense echo chamber of the internet, the loudest and most impactful voices exercise influence without the need for old world constraints such as qualification or proven expertise. Oft-repeated but misinformed assumptions become fact, wrongly attributed quotes define individuals and misinterpreted strategies permanently tar companies' images.

The music industry has certainly not lacked for coverage in mainstream media either. Broadsheet newspapers, business magazines and TV companies can rarely resist the pull of music industry stories, which so often combine an intoxicating mix of business, larger than life personalities and the epic conflict between the old world of media and the new world of technology. Though much of traditional media's coverage has been balanced and informative, it has also often succumbed to dumbing down complicated issues into banalities, of stereotyping key personalities into wicked villains and brave plucky heroes. But as with any story in the real world, things are never that simple. The role of the media has been further complicated by digital music's various stakeholders increasingly using media to build exposure for their viewpoints. Venture capitalists and entrepreneurs give exclusive interviews to explain that record labels are killing innovation with their financial demands and technology conservatism. Record label executives are quoted explaining how certain services that play ball and are good partners will help build a vibrant future while those that do not are killing the business. Artists appear in documentaries explaining how the old way of doing business is gone for good. Music industry trade associations issue press releases of their latest research that shows how piracy is killing their business while academic institutions counter with their own – sometimes technology funded – research that argues the opposite is true, that file sharers actually spend more. Academics produce literature of varying degrees of quality and authority that provide supporting evidence for virtually every point of view imaginable. The media has become the combat zone of music ideology, where 'fact' is more often used to expound dogma than it is to advance reasoned debate. Genuinely probing analysis and investigative journalism are getting ever more squeezed by adversaries trying to control 'the message'.

It is into this vortex of controversy and agenda that I launch this book. It sets out to give a balanced view of the music industry in the digital era, to let every side of the story have its voice heard, not just the loudest ones. This book is rooted in evidence and research method. The trends and market dynamics that are presented are evidence based, supported by robust statistics and more than 50 interviews with the senior executives who made the decisions that created and contributed to the music industry's digital journey. These decision makers are from across the music industry's various value chains, from record labels to telcos, from trade bodies to consumer electronics companies, lawyers, accountants, agents and of course the artists themselves. In addition I bring to bear the insight and understanding of the market that I have acquired over the course of 15 years working with the key movers and shakers at the heart of the digital music market. In that time I have worked right across the music industry, from being a small time recording artist on an independent label, through to working with all of the major record labels, publishers, rights bodies, telcos, device companies, venture capitalists and the leading music services, often up to chief executive level.

There is no doubt that the record labels made a succession of poor decisions that helped create industry crisis and collapse. Similarly it is abundantly clear that 'piracy' advocates almost always apply an entirely different set of rules to the music industry than they apply to virtually all other non-media industries. But to argue that either of these précis are wholly representative of their respective constituencies or indeed that either party is wholly to blame is both naïve and disingenuous. The single most culpable party of all is us, the consumer, the music fan. Technology enabled change, record labels resisted it. But it is the dramatic way that we changed how we interact with music and the way we transformed our expectations of music as a product that really brought the walls tumbling down. Like revolutionaries throwing a manifesto at the feet of the teetering establishment, 21st century consumers demanded a degree of control and freedom with their music experiences that could not have been imagined in the analogue era. They are 'rights' that are now taken for granted. Watch the incredulity in a young teenager's face when you tell them that in the analogue era they would have had to wait for a song to be available in a shop before they could get it, that they would have had to pay for it, that they would have to buy the entire album just to get the couple of songs they liked, that there was no online video, that there was no easy way to make a high quality copy of a song. It is the new expectations of this empowered generation of young music fans that has most shaken the music industry to its core. Napster lit the fuse on a demographic time-bomb that is now going off in our faces. Each successive technology and business transformation enabled consumer change and was simultaneously driven by it, creating an intricate and interconnected web of cause and effect.

This is why each chapter of the book – following three scene setting chapters – looks at issues from the perspective of one part of the value chain, to give a clear understanding of what makes its stakeholders tick and why they make the decisions they do. But just as with a witness giving evidence in court, each of these chapters also contains a healthy dose of probing cross-examination. With this approach we are able to build an understanding not just of how all the pieces of the story fit together but also we get an appreciation of how little the different sides of the equation often understand each other. The story of digital music is one of exhilarating change, of one person's loss becoming another's gain, of innovation and of fear, uncertainty and doubt. It is a story with profound learnings for all manner of other industries, for in many ways it is the archetype of how disruptive innovation can undo decades of established business practice in just a few years. Wherever your personal views may lie, it is a tale that you neglect at your peril

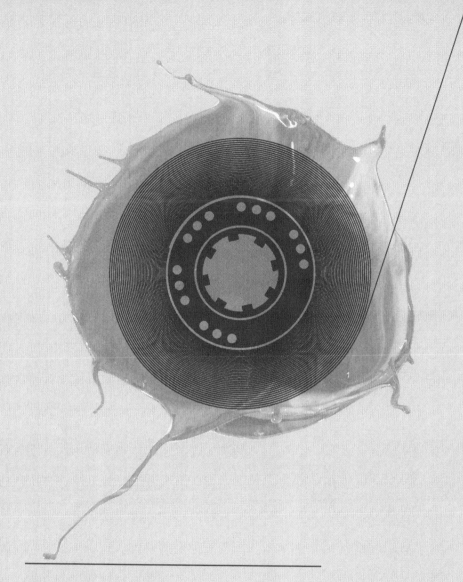

Part 1:
How we got there

Chapter 1: The Rise and Rise of Piracy

June 1999 was where it all started coming undone. It was then that two American teenagers introduced a piece of software to the world that would change the music industry forever. When Shawn Fanning and Sean Parker launched Napster they knew that they were on to something, but they could not even have begun to grasp the seismic, industry changing impact that their creation would have. By the time it closed down in 2001, Napster had become the music industry's public enemy number one, had faced the record labels in court and had even raised the ire of Metallica's Lars Ulrich. But Napster's most significant achievement had far more lasting effect: Napster irrevocably transformed the relationship between music and music fans. Napster gave consumers the previously unimaginable gift of all of the world's music, in one place, at the click of a mouse, and for no cost whatsoever. The music industry's gates were being pulled down by the masses...this was nothing short of revolution.

Napster was not an isolated event though, it was the natural evolutionary output of an acceleration of consumer audio technology in the second half of the 1990's whose roots went back decades. AT&T Labs had started experimenting with perceptual audio coding as early as 1959 but the real origin of species of digital music was the CD itself. With the release of the first commercial CD album in October 1982 - Billy Joel's 52nd Street– the music industry had in its hands a format like no other, before or since. Vinyl has always had its adherents and undoubted qualities, but what marks out the CD is that it is a collection of high quality digital files that can be reproduced without any perceptible quality loss while vinyl is not. As digital music veteran and former CTO of Geffen Records Jim Griffin observed: "We went digital before we went digital. With the advent of the CD suddenly you've got perfect 320 kbps masters propagated into the market." When Sony and Philips were working on creating CD technology in the late 1970's consumer copying technology was still another decade and a half away and their preoccupations were instead creating the original technology and then working towards standards the music industry could get behind. When the labels adopted the resulting Red Book CD standard, they had little concept of just how transformational it would prove to be, of how it would deliver the greatest period of prosperity their industry had ever seen. They had even less idea that in sowing the seeds for the next era of the music industry, they were also inadvertently distributing the pathogen that would bring the walls of that very apogee crashing down around them. Like some over-engineered Genetically Modified crop, the CD drew so heavily on the ground in which it was planted – i.e. consumers' wallets – that after a period of intense yields it left the ground barren and exhausted, unable to sustain the crop any further. As Cooking Vinyl's founder and Managing Director Martin Goldschmidt put it: "Digital started with the CD. No one realized the implications of putting ones and zeros of data on a disc. Vinyl had been the best copy protection technology ever." According to Griffin though, the record labels may have had the opportunity to plot a different path, by adopting a CD standard that baked copy protection into the technology but they opted not to do so: "It's funny, but I think a bit ironic: we got where we are today in part when the music companies chose the Red Book Audio spec for the compact disc, leaving it un-tokenized and relatively unprotected. Had they chosen a conditionality scheme similar to that used for DVD Video, there might have been an additional decade or so where copies were harder to make, the original digits encrypted, their copies interpreted and therefore lower in quality, and so forth. But they chose Red Book for a reason: I am told they liked the idea that it was less susceptible to audits, precisely because it was un-tokenized. Of course they could not imagine a world where the average person could make a disc for pennies, worse still send a perfect copy of a song in an email."

Before that world of ubiquitous homemade digital copies could transpire though, two further sets of technology innovation needed to happen. The first was the advent of digital audio codecs, most notably the International Standards Organization (ISO) ratified MP3, full name MPEG-2 Audio Layer III. In July 1994 German research body the Fraunhofer Society released MP3 to the public with the launch of the world's first MP3 encoding software l3enc. MP3 built upon work from the likes of AT&T and Philip's Musicam and was the result of years of collaborative research and development. MP3 stripped out large portions of the data in audio files to create a much smaller final file. This so called lossy compression method created digital audio files that used less space on computer hard drives and were easier to deliver across internet connections. These were crucial assets in 1994 when computer disc space and internet bandwidth were both scarce commodities. Without the dramatically smaller file sizes that MP3 enabled, the digital revolution would have been still born.

But MP3 itself was only the delivery mechanism, it was an empty vessel without music content itself. Into this vacuum stepped CD-ripping software, the next major step on the road to digital insurrection. A.L. Digital Ltd had created the first CD ripping software CD-GRAB in the early 1990's and by the mid-1990's CD ripping was fast becoming firmly established consumer behaviour. CD-GRAB did what only truly great innovations do: by identifying a truly untapped market need, it created an entire new model of user behaviour. Suddenly consumers could start leveraging the full potential and convenience of their PCs as media devices. No longer would they have to repeatedly take CDs in and out but instead could now have all of their CD collections in one place and all of them immediately playable. But for all of CD-GRAB's first mover pioneer status it took Nullsoft to take CD-ripping to the mainstream with the launch of its seminal combined CD ripping and digital audio player software Winamp. MP3's release to the public was the seed of disruption, Winamp was the killer app that catalysed the rapid dissemination of the file format across the web. Winamp made MP3 ready for primetime.

Up until this point PCs had simply behaved as inferior CD players. The vast majority of PCs were not hooked up to good quality speakers so the playback experience was markedly inferior from the home Hi-Fi or even the car stereo. The only meaningful advantage a PC had was to allow a consumer to play back music in the location their PC happened to be – which at this stage was usually a desktop PC so not a portable device. CD-ripping changed all of that, transforming the PC into a media hub, a digital entertainment powerhouse. CD ripping was the social revolution that underpinned the political revolt Napster would eventually foment.

Despite this innovation the initial effects were still relatively small. With any new technology there is a long flash-to-bang, a gap between its arrival and its transformative impact on consumer behaviour. Technologists may recognize the immediate paradigm-shifting potential of a new technology but consumers typically take years to understand and employ the benefits of it. This is because consumers adopt technology in phases, with distinct consumer groups adopting at different stages (see Figure 3). The first are the most adventurous and technology savvy consumers, the Early Adopters. Early Adopters are usually younger though not necessarily young, often male, and always wanting to be at the forefront of technology. These consumers will willingly tolerate bugs and glitches as part of the price to pay for being ahead of the curve. Though incredibly important, the Early Adopters are only a small share of the total population, typically in the 5% to 10% range, and as a consequence any product that appeals solely to this group will remain confined to niche reach. It is the next wave of consumers, the Early Followers who are in many ways the sternest test of whether a product or service is ever going to break through to the mainstream. These consumers are technology enthusiasts but less willing to endure bugs and glitches, instead they want technology that is exciting and new but that is also ready for prime time. They typically take their lead from the influential voices of Early Adopters, waiting for their affirmation of a technology before adopting it themselves. Slightly more populous than Early Adopters, strong adoption by these consumers will push a product towards 20% to 25% adoption, up to, and perhaps even through, the Critical Mass Threshold. This is the point at which a technology will either push through to the mass market or instead remain tied to the domain of the technology enthusiasts. To date most digital music products have failed to break out of the Critical Mass Threshold, YouTube and Pandora are notable exceptions. Should a technology have truly mainstream appeal, in terms of functionality, ease of use and pricing, then the Early Followers will help drive it to the Mainstream. This is the summit of the ambition of most technologies, but a few will push even further to the Late Adopters and thus onto market saturation. This was the path of PCs, mobile phones, internet access and is where smartphones are tracking towards today. For household technology such as broadband, games consoles and DVDs, adoption follows the same trajectory but at lower penetration rates. Also many technologies can be successful without ever reaching saturation levels because they have a narrower potential reach, such as portable games consoles and e-readers.

FIGURE 3

How Consumers Adopt New Technology

Consumer Technology Adoption Segments and Current Penetration of Key Technologies

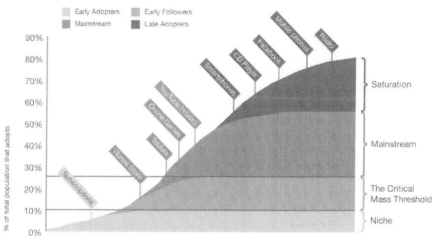

During the early 1990's consumer adoption of emerging digital music technology was stuck in the very earliest and smallest stages of Early Adopter behaviour. Consequently interest within the record labels was understandably limited at best. The labels were in the midst of their most vibrant and successful period ever, powered by the adrenalin shot of the CD replacement cycle: consumers had been convinced, with relative ease, to replace their vinyl and compact cassette albums with high quality CD versions. Demand for buying new music was also at an all time high. In the early 1990's when music sales were booming, the pervasive attitude was that there simply was not any need or time to focus on obscure technologies when the CD was doing so well. This is the classic thinking of incumbent businesses prone to disruption, so spellbound by the success of their products that they cannot imagine the possibility of them not being eternal successes. This is how the railway companies were thinking when Henry Ford's production lines started producing Model-T's and it was Nokia's mindset when Apple launched its first iPhone. Being at the top of your game can all too easily beget hubris, as the record labels found out to their cost. Roger Faxon, the last CEO of an independent EMI, summed up the situation: "The early 1990's was the most profitable the record labels had ever been. [They] were flush with cash and didn't know what to do with the money except buy up every indie in sight. Even after the threat appeared none of those profits was focused on meeting the challenge that digital had unleashed. It was not an issue of resource it was a question of will. The industry to the end and even today believed it would control distribution. They refused to understand how technology would morph and change their business."

As the early nineties progressed and internet penetration increased labels did begin to participate in cautious experiments with technology company partners and to run their own internal initiatives. The prevailing sentiment though was curiosity rather than strategic urgency and most label decision makers expected any output to be focused around how to help the industry sell more CDs. It may have been more than a mere token effort but it was still half hearted as Larry Miller, then COO of AT&T offshoot A2B Music explained: "Labels didn't have their heads in the sand, they could see what was coming but this was the peak of the CD replacement cycle and gigantic profits were still being made. From the mid 1990's there were lots of responsible experiments and every label had its own skunk works and was engaging with tech companies. But these were highly controlled, sponsored by the digital business leaders in labels to learn more about digital and how it could help them sell more CDs." There was a growing body of technology visionaries within the major record labels that began to understand the scale of the coming change but they were small in number and too often had to accept senior management acting as a brake on their innovation efforts.

One of these early pioneers was digital veteran Ralph Simon who in 1993 was brought in by then EMI Chairman Jim Fifield, to reorganize and restructure Capitol Records and Blue Note Records. Simon had spent time in Silicon Valley and his vision was to create a world-wide new media business and a digital music and video operation. Simon was: "looking at getting music into new places, in new ways, with new tech - to reach the obvious new audiences. I said 'Jim all those trucks taking CDs to Tower Records and other stores will soon disappear, and Capitol needs to change and prepare for the future'. He replied 'We'll be first to be second, we don't need to be first to be first'." With hindsight this approach might seem short sighted but was in the context of a time when the internet represented an entirely unproven, nascent set of technologies that as yet had done little to suggest they would do anything meaningful. The risk of failure, of disrupting boom years revenue though was ever present. It also made good strategic sense to let someone else make the first move and learn from their mistakes, let them expend the energies and resources establishing a market. Indeed, in technology most of the time it is the early follower who wins out not the first mover – it is a strategy that has served Apple well throughout its history. Too often, all that bleeding edge innovators do is bleed out.

As nascent as the emerging technology might have been though, it was moving fast and was catching more people's attention and imagination. By 1994, the year after Simon's arrival at EMI, there were already 13.5 million internet users in the US[1] – approximately 80% of the global total – and as Faxon noted: "As early as 1994 it was clear that some form of digital distribution was going to be the future of the music business. The internet had already arrived and it was real." Enough momentum was being gained to nudge some of the first meaningful experiments into motion. Jim Griffin had been hired into Geffen Records as CTO in 1992, two years after the label had been bought by MCA Music Entertainment - MCA was renamed Universal Music Group in 1996. Geffen was still independently run and founder David Geffen and his board prided themselves on their autonomy. In 1994 this approach resulted in Geffen setting a digital milestone as Griffin recalled: "In 1994 at Geffen I was involved in releasing the first commercial full-length song download: Aerosmith's 'Head First'. Geffen was delighted, because as his CFO explained to me 'we budget a quarter of a million dollar loss every time we release a single. The store owners hate them as they take up just as much space as albums so they don't even send us the money they get selling them and we have to pay to get them played on the radio.' The view over at [MCA] was horror, but Geffen and his board were completely behind it." The initiative illustrated that new technology could be used to bring greater efficiencies and effectiveness to established music business practices but it was a drop in the ocean. Record label structures and organizations were still a million miles away from being digitally ready, in no small part because of the physical production and distribution baggage the labels had acquired. This was a period when many big record labels still owned CD warehouses and

---

1   World Bank

CD pressing plants – costly, sizeable operations that through their sheer size could give the impression to some of actually being the core of what the labels were about. For those labels that did not have all of the analogue era organizational baggage though, digital could take root more quickly as Griffin explained: "Other people weren't getting [digital]. Geffen never owned a truck or a warehouse so we didn't measure our strength by our distribution network, so anything that worked around these things was good for us but seen as trouble by others."

Outside of the labels, others too were beginning to test the capabilities of the new platforms and technologies, with 1995 proving to be the year in which momentum really started to build. Scott Cohen, co-founder of digital distributor the Orchard was an artist manager in 1995, breaking new ground running online artist campaigns: "We had a row of PCs on dial-up modems staffed with interns from NYU, each of whom we got an AOL account. We ran a campaign for godhead and got the interns to go on to AOL message boards to look for anyone talking about related bands. Back in those days there were no pictures or music and people were anonymous online. But we realized we could click on the username and email them directly telling them about the band. We got a 100% response rate. As much as anything I think people were just amazed to be getting people emailing them about music they might like. It was a completely new concept back then." Some artists were also getting their first taste of digital music, as Camper van Beethoven and Cracker's David Lowery recalled: "I remember in 1995 my bassist sent me a rough mix of a one of our demos in MP3 format and I was 'holy shit, this is going to be a game changer'." In the technology space too, change was accelerating with an increasing number of bulky hardware prototypes beginning to be put together. Miller's fellow A2B co-founder Howie Singer at that time: "was walking around with a prototype device the size of a shoebox that played AAC files." But despite all the developments in music technology internet speeds remained a major brake on consumer adoption as Miller explained: "We take bandwidth for granted now but back then it was a scarce resource. Imagine trying sipping a McDonalds thick shake through a small cocktail straw, that is what music downloading was like back then." Cohen was also coming up against the constraints of slow dial-up internet access with his prototype online artist campaigns: "Sending an MP3 took an hour and many attempts. The reality was it took all day to send out music on connections that were on a per minute charge by AOL and phone companies, and that you had to disconnect your phone to do so. Everyone forgets we didn't always have mobile phones or always-on internet access."

Internet speeds did increase year on year though and the cost of bandwidth and storage came tumbling down, edging digital music ever closer towards its mainstream possibilities. By 1997 momentum was building both among consumers and within the business.. Miller recalled a meeting from that year: "I was in EMI's London headquarters with their Head of New Media Jeremy Silver. I showed him a prototype of a solid-state drive music player that used AAC and stored the files on a PCMIA card. He took it out of my hands and ran down the hall shouting for other people to come out of their offices to look at it, saying 'this is going to change the business!'" Far from everyone was convinced though, as Cohen learned when in 1997 he co-founded the Orchard with Richard Gotterher. Though now a firm staple of the digital landscape the concept of a digital distributor that supplied music files from labels to services was an alien one in the late nineties: "When we started the Orchard in 1997 people said 'no one wants a digital file, they want the tactile feel of the CD'. I said 'no they want the song', but I was vilified, it was sacrilegious, blasphemous to say these things. By the time of Napster in 1999 these same people were saying stop these guys stealing my stuff."

Some forward thinking independent labels though were beginning to sense that digital might allow them to open up opportunities previously inaccessible to them. UK independent label group Beggars Banquet was one such company and its Head of Strategy Simon Wheeler was involved in its very earliest forays into digital: "We had a real belief that the music was interesting and good enough and there was a global audience out there, but we weren't about to reach them via traditional distributor arrangements." In 1997 Wheeler went to the annual music industry conference Midem in Cannes, France with Beggars founder and label head Martin Mills: "A couple of companies wanted to meet us - Amplified.com and Liquid Audio - and Martin said 'come along and see what they want to say'. We came out of the meetings, looked at each other and thought 'this could change everything'." Beggars did deals with both Liquid Audio and Amplified.com but with no precedents or established business practices to work to there was a lot of learning to be done on both sides: "Metadata wasn't in our lexicon, we were sending CDs to everyone. Once we'd done the deal we sent a box of CDs and an Excel spread sheet including identifiers – we had just about created a database." However Beggars were astute enough to recognise the potential long-term ramifications of some key decisions: "Back then we didn't have any rights, we realised that we needed to be supplying to the world rather than licensing them to others. We decided to explicitly exclude digital rights from licensing deals. To this day we don't license digital rights so we can manage our global rights from the UK." Despite the brave new world of innovation though, this was still a proto-market in its very earliest phase as Wheeler soon discovered: "When we got our first cheque it was $25 for worldwide sales for the first quarter." The future was not here yet but the pieces were beginning to fall into place and the next piece that did would have the greatest immediate impact yet.

Barney Wragg, former SVP Universal Music eLabs and Global Head of Digital EMI

Jay Sammit, former SVP EMI and EVP & GM Sony Corp America

Paul Vidich, former EVP Warner Music, now Director Reverbnation

MP3.com, Breaking the Mould

In November 1997 a service finally arrived that gave consumers the ability to search for and download MP3s free of charge and in doing so changed the face of music: MP3.com. Founded by Michael Robertson and Greg Flores MP3.com was the first digital music service of scale and was the starting point for the market we have today. As Cohen put it: "Everything started with MP3.com". Robertson and Flores had not in fact set out to create a music site and their business interests lay elsewhere until Robertson started to see some unusual spikes in behaviour on their search engine Filez.com: "I always tracked what people were searching for and then in 1997 I noticed something appear, people were searching for something called 'MP3'. I did some quick investigation and I discovered it was an unknown audio compression technology that was below the radar." This was a time when encoding MP3s was a complex procedure and encoding tools were scarce. Robertson saw the opportunity to meet the needs of a nascent and underserved community. He decided to build an MP3 site as a traffic generator for Filez.com, buying the MP3.com domain registration for $1,000 from someone who had registered it because MP3 was his online user name. Robertson was about to find out quite how big an opportunity he had unearthed: "On the first day we turned the site on we got 10,000 unique visitors. Filez.com had been online for two years with a marketing effort behind it and we only had 35,000 unique visitors. That was the first indication I had that this was something really big."

Initially Robertson populated MP3.com with lists of MP3 encoders, music news and links to music sites but it wasn't enough: "I kept getting user feedback like 'your site sucks, I looked for music but there's no music there'. There were a lot of music sites on the net but none had music." So Robertson decided to try to make happen what he thought would be the logical next step in this quickly emerging opportunity: the record labels making their music available online. Any early hopes were quickly extinguished though: "I got in my beaten up old 1987 Honda Accord and drove to LA from San Diego to talk to the labels to explain how there was this great opportunity to market their music. They did not believe that the PC world would become the hub of people's music experiences. Their view was that PCs didn't have speakers and they were for doing word processing on. No amount of evangelizing from me was going to help them see that the music experience was going to move from the Hi-Fi to the PC. I quickly realized that the labels were not going to help. So I scoured the web for bands giving away MP3s." Robertson's search turned up a dozen bands but as soon as MP3.com linked through to them the volume of traffic crashed GeoCities, the site where most of their band pages were hosted. With the cost of storage and bandwidth coming down virtually every day Robertson quickly realized that the most practicable solution was to actually host band pages themselves. After a brief period of building custom band sites MP3.com introduced a self-publishing solution for artists that swiftly proved to be as successful as it was ahead of its time. Robertson recounted that: "we started with 5 bands a day, then 20, then it exploded. It might seem obvious now but it wasn't then. By the time we sold MP3.com we had 200 bands a day signing up." For many artists MP3.com was their first experience of digital music and, crucially, being able to communicate with their fans at scale. Bands started to mention MP3.com at concerts and in posters, and gave away on average five free tracks on the site. It was an early digital virtuous circle in which bands got exposure, consumers got music and MP3.com got traffic. MP3.com's marketing acumen and consumer-centric user experience delivered success metrics that set a dauntingly high standard for subsequent digital music services: MP3.com peaked at 25 million registered users and its 1999 IPO, at the peak of the dot com bubble, raised a cool $370 million. MP3.

com was the record labels' wake-up call to the immensity of disruptive force the internet could wield. Although online destinations such as warez sites and FTP servers had already been enabling people to find and swap music files for years they remained the niche domain of tech savvy geeks. MP3.com took the concept of online music to the mainstream consumer.

Even as MP3.com was reaching its zenith the rot had already set in and many of those newly acquired millions of dollars would soon disappear defending a lawsuit brought by Universal Music.[2] The case centred around MyMP3.com, a new service Robertson and Flores launched at the start of 2000. MyMP3.com let users access their music collection online as long as they could prove they owned the original CD albums by placing them in their PCs' CD players. It was an early predecessor of contemporary cloud locker services from the likes of Apple and Amazon, but in 2000 it was navigating unchartered legal territory. The business and product strategy were natural next steps for MP3.com whose burgeoning audience was quickly outgrowing the limited catalogue of predominately small up and coming bands. Robertson explained the rationale and their approach: "With MyMP3.com we thought 'how can we get people's music collections up into the cloud?' We quickly realized that all CDs were identical so that all we needed was a system that ID matches the CD with proof of ownership and then allow access to a central cloud copy. We could already see that unbundling from downloads would drive music revenue collapse so we thought it would be better to extend the life of the CD by making it relevant in the digital age. We spent a million dollars on CDs and digitized them."

The music industry however did not buy into the vision. Robertson and Flores argued that MyMP3.com fell under the provisions of 'fair use' legislation designed to protect consumers' rights to make personal copies of their purchased music. The big record labels saw things very differently and feared that MyMP3.com would set a dangerous business precedent that could undermine the ability to build licensed services business models in the future. Cary Sherman CEO of the labels' US trade body Recording Industry Association of America (RIAA) described the industry position: "What Michael Robertson did with MyMP3.com was create his own database of recordings which he was planning to stream to consumers. He was going into business as a digital music service without any licences. It would have set a terrible precedent, it would have transformed digital distribution from opportunity to risk. We sued him on a very basic point, not whether he was making unauthorized public performances, but instead that he had made unauthorized reproductions of CDs." It was classic disruption meets incumbent protectionism. To MP3.com this was an entirely natural next step, an elegantly simple solution to a clear consumer need – so much so in fact that global tech superpowers Amazon, Google and Apple all launched similar services in the 2010's. But to the labels this was a clear case of an uninvited guest strolling into the bedroom, getting under the covers and nestling up close. The entire basis of the record labels' business was built on control of distribution and MyMP3.com threatened to turn the internet into a lawless wild west, from which point lawlessness would undoubtedly seep ever outwards. Thus the labels opened up the first real engagement in the control wars that would define the recorded music industry's relationship with online music for years to come.

Universal Music eventually won the case, successfully arguing that MyMP3.com was not protected by fair use because it was a commercial venture that had created its own central library of CD copies rather than allowing users to create their own copies.[3] This latter technicality was as much a consequence of the limits of available technology as it was of MyMP3.com's

2   The legal costs for the case exceeded $53 million.
3   Though subscribers did not have to pay for the service. MyMP3.com generated revenue from sales of online advertising inventory.

business model: home internet upload speeds in 2000 were far too slow to make uploading CD collections a realistic option. [4] But the detail nonetheless proved pivotal. Robertson remains adamant that it was the wrong decision: "The industry sued us, they said 'the database isn't licensed and therefore you are infringing our copyright'. The fact we were tarred with the same brush as the pirates shows how irrational the labels were. I defy anyone to look at what we built and say it wasn't a valid system that could have been hugely valuable to the industry."

The UMG vs MyMP3.com ruling proved to be a landmark, defining some of the first clear and tested legal operating parameters for digital music by drawing a clear distinction between time shifting - recording music to listen back to later - and place shifting - creating a copy to access from another location. As important as the ruling had been however, it revealed that cracks were appearing in analogue-era music business practices as they buckled under the weight of digital-era dynamics. This was a case of cobbling together old frameworks with sticky tape rather than building a new set of parameters tailor-made for the digital-age. MP3.com had hammered home an uncomfortable truth: the music industry was simply not ready for the digital era. The advent of internet music services had caught the industry unawares and it was utterly incapable of responding in an effective and appropriate manner. Record labels, publishers and collection societies alike were just not geared for the digital revolution. They were not ready commercially, legally, organizationally and most importantly they were not equipped ideologically. The music industry's prevailing worldview was still light years away from that of the pioneering digital entrepreneurs.

Throughout the analogue era of the recorded music business the labels had exercised near absolute control across virtually all of the value chain. The record labels had had a monopoly on control of supply. As a consumer, if you wanted to own music you had to buy it from a record shop, which in turn had to get its stock from a record label or a record label-approved distributor. As an artist, if you wanted your fans to get your music you signed a deal with a record label. If you wanted to be played on the radio or on TV you signed with a record label. The model was predictable, highly repeatable and completely secure, so much so that it provided the foundation with ever accelerating revenue growth throughout much of the post-war period, right up until the emergence of the internet. Controlled and predictable businesses get used to feeling immune from disruption and quick unexpected change, so when it does eventually come – as of course it does always come eventually - they are caught entirely off guard. The systems and process the music industry had evolved were well suited for oiling the wheels of the analogue machine but ill-equipped for responding to digital disruption. In the analogue-era music sales, technology and behaviour were constants carved into solid stone. The music business's legal principles were designed for static and tangible traditional distribution models, they did not have to accommodate theoretical use cases or hypothetical business practices. So when MyMP3.com came along, the ensuing court case was as much a test of whether music industry law was up to the needs of the digital era as it was of the legality of the service itself.

In the end MP3.com was sold to Vivendi Universal, the parent company of the very same record label attempting to sue them out of existence. The irony was not lost on Robertson: "UMG were the ones who sued us most and they went on to buy us for $372 million in cash and stock in 2001. [5] I was later told 'you know why we sued you? Because you were getting too powerful.'" This plaintiff-turned-buyer situation may have appeared cynical to some, but it was an acceptance among the management of Vivendi Universal – UMG's French parent company -

4   Upload speeds on dial-up internet connections were typically about 6 kbps, against an average download speed of 64 kbps.
5   The effective purchase price was more than this; Universal had also agreed to take on other liabilities.

that they had to play a rapid game of digital catch-up. MP3.com represented, in theory at least, a short-cut to pole position. At the helm of Vivendi Universal was the diminutive but charismatic and hugely ambitious Jean Marie Messier. Messier was on a mission to transform Vivendi from a traditional French utilities conglomerate into a global media and telecommunications powerhouse. This meant putting internet services at the heart of the business, even if it meant going against the wishes of some Universal Music executives. Ultimately though, MP3.com went the way of most vibrant start ups acquired by big traditional companies: withering steadily on the vine into insignificance. Vivendi Universal learned the hard way that you cannot simply buy digital transformation, it requires much more organic and far reaching organizational change, something for which UMG to its credit was already beginning to set the wheels in motion. Meanwhile the epicentre of the nascent digital music market had already shifted from MP3.com, indeed it has done so even before the MyMP3.com case had hit the courts. The digital baton had been passed: just as MP3.com hit the crest of its wave, Napster began its rocket-propelled ascent in the stratosphere, taking digital music into an entirely new realm.

The Napster Effect

MP3.com set the rules and standards for online music experiences by bringing the best practices of online marketing and consumer websites to music downloading. It was an innovative and disruptive evolution, but an evolution nonetheless. Napster wrote an entirely new rulebook. Shawn Fanning and his business partner Sean Parker chose a fundamentally different path: instead of trying to surgically layer a website on top of music downloading, they went back to digital music's warez sites and FTP origins and started afresh.

Fanning was a 'code head' who had spent much of his childhood at his uncle's internet company Chess.Net before going on to college and then dropping out to focus on the development of his creation Napster. He recognized that if music downloading harnessed the scale potential of the internet, it could far exceed the reach of a single website such as MP3.com. So Fanning created a software application that sat on a network formed by each downloaded copy of the application. He created the world's first purpose-built, global scale peer-to-peer (P2P), music file sharing network. Unlike MP3.com, Napster depended upon individuals using the network and the music that they shared: their music collections collectively became Napster's music library. As the application became more widely used the network became larger and more robust and the catalogue of music more comprehensive. For sites like MP3.com more users simply meant more bandwidth capacity was needed, but as Napster got bigger it got better.

Napster was a labour of love for Fanning who stayed up 60 hours straight finishing the code, embedding robust search, sharing and chat functionality into an application that at its peak would give consumers access to 80 million different tracks. Even though a large chunk of that 80 million comprised poorly tagged duplicates, never had such a massive library of music been presented to anyone, anywhere in the world, ever before. This was nothing less than an entire new paradigm for recorded music. Napster turned on the tap to the world's entire catalogue of recorded music in a way that no high street store, radio station or TV channel could ever have dreamed of doing. Napster users did not have to worry about whether a song was still available in the stores, or even whether it had actually been officially released. Its servers quickly filled up with not only virtually every album available, but also deleted releases, live recordings, bootlegs, unreleased gems, disregarded remixes. Music fans now had instant access to an effectively infinite amount of music: it would have taken 533 years to listen to every single track available on Napster.[6] No previous generation of music fan had ever had this sort of choice before. The rules of engagement had changed too. From here on in music services would have to measure their catalogues in millions not thousands. As Spotify's Chief Content Officer Ken Park put it: "Napster was instant access at the speed of light, it created a generation of music fans accustomed to speed of light consumption."

To anyone who used Napster it was immediately apparent just how transformative its impact was going to be. One of those people whose imagination Napster had caught was a then young digital executive at a major label who preferred to remain anonymous. He could see the huge potential of the Napster model if it could be harnessed by the music industry, but he quickly learned his enthusiasm was not widely shared. He demonstrated Napster to the label's management: "I was a long haired upstart, punky looking kid heavily into music. I was really excited by the fact I could get access to stuff and discover new music. In my head I could see the revolution happening. There had an all hands meeting. I was intended to be the light relief at the end of the meeting. I booted up my Napster client and I asked for someone to pick an artist. One senior executive picked out an obscure band he'd signed years before and results started cascading down the screen. Everyone's expressions changed, there was a cacophony of 'oh fuck's. One lawyer said 'we're so fucked. Who can we sue?' I remember my face dropping and thinking 'oh shit, this has gone the wrong way.'"

From an early stage Napster had established a cordial enough dialogue with record labels but even then it was far from clear whether Napster was going to be able to build productive relationships with content owners. Jay Samit was President of Digital Distribution for EMI between 1999 and 2003 and recalled an early meeting with Fanning: "I had an office at the top of Capitol Tower in LA with the Hollywood sign over my shoulder out of the window. Shawn came into see me. I asked him 'What's your business model' to which he said 'I don't have one yet' so I replied 'Come back when you do.'" Pretty quickly though it became apparent that Napster did not have serious intentions of acquiring licenses, as Cary Sherman explained: "We reached out to Napster very early on. It was pretty clear this was not going to be someone schooled in copyright law. So we reached out saying 'this is a clear violation so stop what you're doing but talk to the labels, what you've got is very interesting.' Their CEO Eileen Richardson clearly had no interest in doing anything with the labels, she was stalling while they built their business. There were efforts to license Napster between record company CEOs and the VCs that were operating Napster. But they were offering a billion dollars to a 15 billion dollar industry. What they were offering made no economic sense."

As Napster gained scale the strategic permutations were still not widely understood, but with hindsight the significance is hard to overstate. Napster not only threw the record labels' monopoly of supply out of the window, the window was instantaneously bricked up behind it. The genie was out of the bottle and there was no going back. No longer did music fans have to wait for record labels, retailers and radio stations to tell them what music to listen to and when and where they could get it. The implications were seismic even if they were not all immediately apparent. This was suddenly the age of the empowered music consumer and the music industry was quickly going to realize it needed to learn how to understand and meet his needs and wants. As Roger Faxon put it: "The music business never cared what consumers thought, it cared instead what retailers and radio thought." But most importantly, this new celestial jukebox was completely and utterly free. Until then,

---

6   Calculation based on three and half minutes average track length and a catalogue of 80 million tracks.

music fans' ability to sample new music had been constrained by how much music they could afford to buy and how much radio they wanted to sit through until the DJ played a new song that they liked. Removing pricing from the equation changed everything. Now people could try out music on a whim and they could build music collections that would have filled their houses to bursting if they had been CDs rather than digital files.

Even at this stage some senior record executives still genuinely believed that Napster and online music as a whole were minor irritations that would eventually go away, so that everyone could get back to using the internet for what it was best at: selling CDs in online stores. Napster though quickly did more than enough to disabuse any record label executive of the idea that it was a mere flash in the pan. Whereas MP3.com had peaked at about 25 million registered users, Napster reached 60 million, with a high of 26.4 million of them active in February 2001.[7] This was online music at an absolutely unprecedented scale. And with things moving at such electrifying pace, there was considerable debate over exactly what impact Napster would have on the music industry. There were some artists that began to see Napster as a useful promotional tool, with Limp Bizkit going as far as having Napster sponsor one of its tours. Some observers even somewhat tenuously argued that 'The Bends' became Radiohead's first ever US number 1 album because it had been download for free millions of times on Napster.

Other artists however saw things in more monochrome tones. David Lowery remarked that: "there has always been a certain amount of informal piracy, friends dubbing tapes etc. but Napster was totally different, it was mass scale infringement." Napster also created the new phenomenon of online pre-release leaks, something that veteran heavy metal band Metallica found out to their significant displeasure. When Metallica learned that their track 'I Disappear' was being downloaded on Napster before it had been released – along of course with their entire back catalogue – the band swiftly filed suit against Napster in April 2000 for copyright infringement, seeking $10 million in damages. Metallica went as far as to hire web agency NetPD to compile a 60,000 page long list of 335,435 names of individuals who they believed had illegally downloaded Metallica content. Pioneering hip hop artist Dr Dre launched a similar case in May, though the announcement ironically came the day after Limp Bizkit had announced their Napster sponsored tour. If anything was clear it was that the artist community was far from speaking with one voice. No one seemed to really quite know what to do with this internet thing.

What was happening, even if it was not yet fully understood, was that the domino effect of the CD, MP3, Winamp and Napster was creating a new music ecosystem that was entirely out of the traditional industry's control despite already having impact on every part of its value chain. Unlike the incumbent ecosystem of the CD, radio and high street this new challenger system emerged without either the approval or participation of the music industry. This was a new internet-era music ecosystem that threatened the traditional structure to the core (see Figure 4):

- MP3 was the new format

- Napster was the new distribution channel

- Winamp was the new playback technology

---

7   JupiterMedia Metrix

FIGURE 4

Napster Was The Core Of An Entirely New Music Ecosystem

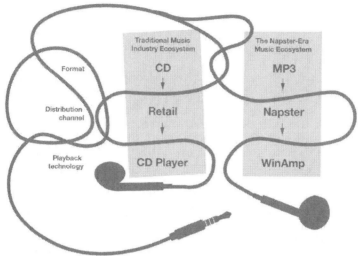

It was hardly surprising that the industry viewed this new upstart ecosystem with intense distrust and distaste. This new set of technologies and relationships had been built solely around consumer behaviour with no thought given whatsoever to how the owners of the music upon which it intimately depended might be compensated. The digital pioneers like Fanning saw themselves as bringing long overdue change to out-dated business models, to which record labels simply had to learn to adapt. But of course Fanning and his investors would have viewed things very differently if their business was being threatened to the core by a disruptive new entrant that had built its business using Napster's source code. It was a myopic and inherently inconsistent worldview of source code and technology patents being considered as valuable intellectual property while music copyright was not. It is a recurring theme alive and well today, with technology companies aggressively lobbying for radical copyright on the one hand but spending billions to acquire patents on the other. The conception that somehow the intellectual property of digital era companies should be treated entirely differently from the intellectual property of the analogue era companies remains a defining characteristic of the clash of media and technology ideologies in digital music. Thus we currently have Google lobbying for copyright reform on the one hand while simultaneously spending billions of dollars acquiring, protecting and enforcing technology patents. This is just one example of how the events of the early years of digital music were setting a script for media company and technology company dialogue that remains effectively unchanged in substance today.

Napster in the Courts

Once it became clear that Napster had no intention of seeking out record label licenses on terms that the record labels would countenance, the music industry swiftly formed a largely united position against Napster. According to the RIAA's Sherman: "We had to bring the Napster case because you could not stand by and let this sort of music service come to market without a license. We had to establish a clear rule of law for future music services." Napster had thrust the record labels onto the defensive. What had been a novel if somewhat undervalued area had suddenly mutated into truly dramatic risk, as EMI's Faxon explained: "Back then, when digital was not a threat, the labels were actively thinking about using it as a tool. However once innovators the likes of Michael Robertson appeared, who had no respect for copyright, fear overtook the industry. The threat of disintermediation changed everything. Fear ran through the industry in a very visceral way. Piracy was the only topic from the late 1990's to early 2000's. We were trying to put the genie back in the bottle. What had started out as an interesting opportunity turned into a massive threat."

The record labels channelled their legal attack under the auspices of the RIAA, which had been quick off the bat, filing suit against Napster as early as December 1999.[8] It proved to be a watershed moment for the music industry but the prevailing popular sentiment was on the side of Napster not the labels as Sherman recalled: "It was abundantly clear to us that Napster was infringing, but it wasn't so clear to the public or to the media. The media coverage wasn't from the music feature writers, the Napster story was covered by the tech beat and they had a very specific view point." The case went through numerous twists and turns, each of which were excitedly reported on by a media that were quickly realising that decades' worth of music business practice were being challenged to the core. As the RIAA, Metallica and Dr Dre cases all slowly worked their way through the courts, Napster's user base continued to grow at a rapid pace, aided of course by the publicity surrounding the very court cases designed to stymie Napster's advance. In the courtroom, the core focus was to attribute legal responsibility for copyright infringement to Napster itself, which was progressively achieved with a tortuous back and forth, but the going was slow.

Presiding Judge Marilyn Hall Patel soon became a familiar name in music industry circles while the publicity storm whipped up by the frenzied media attention helped push Napster ever further into popular consciousness. The case also tested music law to the limit, including the recently enacted Digital Millennium Copyright Act (DMCA). The DMCA essentially provided the legal grounding for the music industry in the digital era and passed into US law two international treaties on copyright that the World Intellectual Property Organization (WIPO) had passed in 1996. Among the core focuses of the bill was the criminalization of creation and distribution technology designed to circumvent measures for protecting and restricting the use of copyrighted materials. The DMCA was unanimously voted through the US Senate and then signed into law by President Bill Clinton in October 1998 and remains the key legislative reference point for digital content even today.[9] The music industry did not get it all its own way however, as another central tenet of the DMCA was to enshrine into statute the exemption of Internet Service Providers (ISPs) and other technology company intermediaries from direct and indirect liability of copyright infringement. Napster's legal team wasted no time in integrating this Net Neutrality position into their defence but Judge Patel ruled that the defendants had 'constructive knowledge' of Napster users' copyright infringement and were thus not protected under this DMCA provision.

For a while, in addition to successfully arguing that it could not be held responsible for identifying infringed copyrighted works on its network, Napster also contended that its meta data was so messy that it made identification of infringement nigh on impossible. Though Napster did not realize it, it had overplayed its hand: by effectively arguing that the service was inherently too

---

8   The ensuing case became known as A&M Records Inc. v. Napster Inc. but was in fact on behalf of 18 record labels and coordinated by the RIAA.
9   The European Union later passed two parallel directives: the European Electronic Commerce Directive in 2000 and the European Copyright Directive 2001.

flawed to police, Napster pushed the RIAA closer towards the nuclear option of closing the service down entirely. Napster's less-than-committed approach to even attempting to police copyright infringement only compounded matters and even prompted Judge Patel to refer to its efforts as "disgraceful". Napster was eventually compelled to implement a technology solution to a technology problem: namely implementing audio fingerprinting technology to analyse the sonic characteristics of files and cross reference them against a central database of record label works. Even though Napster achieved a 99.4% effectiveness rate, Judge Patel almost inevitably – given Napster's prior bad faith behaviour - ruled that Napster would have to be closed down until it could achieve the, obviously impossible, 100% accuracy standard. The final ruling also importantly established once and for all that home copying and fair use – the right to make copies for private use - provisions did not apply to file sharing services. Now established, these principles would form the legal foundations the future 'war on piracy'. The fact that the case had massive legal precedent potential was something that Judge Patel was keenly aware of and she had taken it upon herself to fully understand what Napster was about as Sherman explained: "Judge Patel was a very smart woman. She actually went online and used Napster. She experienced it first hand and saw what the implications were, and then delivered a very strong opinion. It was reinforced by the court of appeals."

Both Napster and the RIAA had embarked on all-or-nothing legal campaigns and their respective positions had become so entrenched that final ruling was always likely to be utter defeat for one side and absolute victory for the other, this was total war. The opposing parties had established themselves as ideological opposites, caricaturing each other as technophobe label fat cats on the one hand, and reckless criminals on the other. The music industry was determined to make an example of these new internet music sites in order to act as a deterrent for other would-be entrants. And it looked like the industry was winning – in the courtroom at least – with victories against MP3.com, Napster and also another file sharing service, Scour.

Napster went off-line in July 2001 and finally filed for bankruptcy protection in September 2002, but not before German media powerhouse Bertelsmann tried and failed to buy Napster. Bertelsmann was the parent company of major record label BMG, one of the plaintiffs in the case against Napster. That this plaintiff-turned-buyer may seem eerily reminiscent of Vivendi Universal's decision to buy MP3.com is no coincidence. Bertelsmann was Germany's answer to Vivendi Universal. At the helm of Bertelsmann was Thomas Middelhoff, every bit as ambitious as Vivendi's Messier and with the same vision of creating a global media and telecommunications super power. Like a modern day, corporate re-run of the Napoleonic Wars the two media conglomerates locked horns on multiple fronts with the French and German generals leading each other's vast forces into battle. Napster was Bertelsmann's direct response to Vivendi's acquisition of MP3.com. Both companies had gone through the knee-jerk pivot motion of zealously attacking to enthusiastically embracing disruptive threats. As early as 2000 Bertelsmann had started pumping money into Napster in the shape of loans to the tune of $85 million, and in 2001 placed BMG executive Konrad Hilbers in the role of Napster CEO. When Bertelsmann made a formal bid for Napster the shock and derision from executives in other record labels was palpable. Judge Patel blocked the sale to Bertelsmann but this did not prevent the other major record labels – and some independents – turning their legal attentions to Bertelsmann itself and suing it directly for its support of Napster and, in turn, copyright violation. From fighting a common enemy the record labels effortlessly slipped into internecine conflict, and while the music industry was busy suing itself illegal music services boomed like never before. The piracy problem had moved on but the label legal teams were not going to let Bertelsmann off the hook until they had got their pound of flesh. The protracted legal conflict lasted until 2007 by which stage Bertelsmann had spent more than $60 million in paying off the other labels even though they had never even successfully acquired Napster.[10] This brought Bertelsmann's total Napster outlay in to the region of $150 million yet it had nothing to show for it other than a gaping hole in its finances. Napster itself went into bankruptcy protection in May 2002 and in November, in a move dripping with karma, Napster's assets were bought for $5 million by Roxio, a maker of CD burning software.

The A&M Records Inc. v. Napster Inc. case was on paper a victory for the music industry, but it quickly became apparent that it had just been a small battle in a much bigger war, and perhaps even that context only a pyrrhic victory. Just as had been the case with MP3.com, the digital baton had been passed once again. What was different this time though was that there was not just one heir apparent but multiple ones, including:

- Audio Galaxy: a newly launched P2P app that had started life in 1998 as an FTP search engine

- Gnutella: a decentralized P2P network originally developed by AOL-owned Nullsoft. The company quickly distanced itself from the software after which it went open source

- eDonkey2000: a P2P protocol that supported 'swarming' where users could download parts of single files simultaneously from multiple locations

The War on Piracy

By the time Judge Patel was making her ruling, digital music technology had long since moved on, but more than that it had explicitly evolved in response to the case. The truly definitive judgement against Napster was not read out in court because it was a business conclusion rather than an explicitly legal one, namely the overriding lesson that technology moves far more swiftly than judicial process. Judge Patel was able to order the closure of Napster because it ran its network from a collection of central computer servers that could quite literally have their power turned off. But the emerging next generation of file sharing networks solved this problem by being de-centralized, relying on the connectivity of each user's computer within the network. Without a central server of content these new networks were organic entities with a life of their own, beyond the complete control even of their original programmers. Like a vaccine-resistant virus, file sharing had just mutated, out-evolving the music industry's counter measures. The music industry had used the slow moving and, in this context, blunt tool of legal process to tackle technology. The newly constituted file sharing community had simply responded with better technology. The template for future clashes was set, a pattern that repeated throughout the 'war on piracy' with countless heirs apparent challenging for the throne of whichever file sharing network had found itself fixed in the music industry's cross hairs. Henceforth the music industry would find itself engaged in an enervating game of whack-a-mole, with a new network or application popping up as soon another had been knocked down. Eventually the music industry would turn to technology solutions such as filtering and deep packet inspection to supplement legal action but it was not enough to break the cycle. Instead, the piracy landscape was about to get even more difficult to police.

---

10 EMI, Universal Music and several independent publishers filed suit against Bertelsmann in 2003 for contributing to copyright infringement by financially and strategically supporting Napster.

Chapter 2: Digital's Stuttering Start

The emergence of the new wave of P2P destinations made it abundantly clear that the piracy genie was not going to get back into his bottle. What few had realized at this stage was that this was not down to business strategy or even because of technology but because a fundamental behavioural change had taken place: an entire new paradigm in consumer behaviour had come into existence. Downloading music from an apparently infinite celestial jukebox was a radical new chapter in the history of music consumption and consumers were not about to let the clock be turned back on them. Even if the music industry had for some fleeting moment managed to close down all piracy destinations, the demand vacuum would have been quickly filled.

Whether the industry liked it or not, the internet had quickly become established as a digital discovery and distribution platform. Embracing the internet was no longer a matter of choice, it had become a point of necessity. The labels started to build upon their earliest moves by hiring the first generation of digital business experts, one of these was Jay Samit. Samit had developed a career in multimedia and gaming, and in 1999 got a call from then EMI CEO Ken Berry. Berry had been encouraged by the initial success of EMI's nascent New Media team and was early to recognize the truly important disruptive impact digital was going to have. Samit described the call from Berry: "I told him 'I'm not a music guy' to which he responded 'I have 11,000 music guys, what I don't have is a future'. He was one of the best guys I have ever worked for. There was no fear of letting go of the past. Every time I hit a wall of resistance Ken would brainstorm with me how to get beyond it." But Berry's approach was not typical of senior major label executives at the time, nor even indeed of contemporary senior EMI decision makers as Samit recalled: "EMI had a board which didn't even dictate email let alone use it themselves. Most didn't even have a PC."[11]

By the late nineties digital was causing more headaches for the record labels than it was benefits. Not only was it disrupting distribution and consumption it was beginning to force labels to change how they marketed music as illustrated by an anecdote from Jim Griffin: "One day I'd been for lunch with Mo Austin (long term industry veteran and then head of Dreamworks Records) and he was driving me back, we pulled up to a red light and he asked me 'What's the world's favourite form of transport?' I replied 'walking?' The light turned green, he hit the gas and said 'no it's the bandwagon! People want to be part of the next big thing. Now you digital guys are coming along and tracking everything, it's harder for us start that buzz by gaming the charts.'"

Digital was also revealing major cracks in record labels' contracts with artists. Nowadays contracts are designed to be as future proof as possible for the labels, with sufficiently far reaching and broad terms to ensure that future business models will be covered in a manner that sufficiently protects their margins. Many analogue-era artist contracts had not been designed with such prescience. This meant that in many instances record labels did not have the rights to sell their artists' music digitally, while in others the contracts committed the labels paying higher royalty rates to artists than they wanted to. Samit described the situation: "Back

---

11 In a similar vein the author recalls sending an email to a senior music executive in the early 2000's and getting a reply in the post, hand written on a print out of his original email.

then the labels didn't have the digital rights to 99% of their catalogue. In the early 1970's an 'uncoupling' clause started making its way into artist contracts which stated that if a label wanted to strip out individual tracks from the album they had to ask the artists for permission. The clause was designed to prevent labels from releasing compilation and greatest hits albums [without permission]." Tensions began to emerge between record label digital teams that wanted to strike deals and in house legal teams that wanted to prevent dangerous precedents being set as Jeremy Silver, then a member of Samit's team, explained: "Our main opponents were business affairs, their number one concern was setting a precedent that would trigger wholesale renegotiation of artist contracts and make the whole model unravel." Samit hit upon a novel solution: "I created a list of every EMI artist that had sued us in the last 3 years, which came to 93 artists, and put them in a separate bucket while for the rest I didn't ask for their permission. And that list of 93 became 4 by the time I had left EMI. The sell was pretty straight forward to them 'this is how much of your catalogue has been stolen in the last 24 months, now do you want to license.'" Sometimes however, labels took a more Machiavellian approach as Alexander Ross, partner at law firm Wiggin explained: "One major label came to us some years ago and said 'tell us what we should be paying this artist for downloads'. I looked at the recording contract which was from 8 years earlier and I said '50% of revenue'. They replied 'that's what we thought'. I asked them what they were going to do and they said 'Not sell downloads until the artist comes begging us to sell. At which point we'll say we don't have to sell downloads, but we will if the artist re-negotiates'."

The need to license to legal services was clear: the longer that the legal market was underserved, the more that illegal alternatives filled the void, but therein lay the problem. Most major record labels, whose catalogues accounted for approximately four fifths of all the music sold, were not yet ready to license fully to digital music services. Many independent labels were more willing to do so, but despite accounting for approximately half of all catalogue released their 20% market share of music sales limited their potential impact. Without most of the best selling music available for sale online the legitimate digital music market was not so much stuck on the starting blocks as having its feet nailed to them.

Music services that wanted to play by the rules had to be creative to break the Catch 22 of launching a music service without music. In the US CD retailer eMusic and Nordic Music created a joint venture to become one of the first online retailers of record label MP3s in 1998, stocking a small catalogue of independent label music.[12] CDNow, another early online CD retailer, swiftly followed suit, launching its own digital download store stocked of course with only independent label catalogue.[13] eMusic would go onto enjoy sustained success on a much larger scale in later year years, but in the late 1990's eMusic and CDNow were isolated pioneers. For the majority of the first wave of legal digital music services the experience would prove fruitless, frustrating and ultimately futile.

One of the challenges that digital music's early innovators faced in trying to convince record companies to work with them was the contrast in quality between the CD and compressed digital audio files. The previous two decades had all been about improving

12 eMusic had started out as MP3 download site MP3 downloads on music site Goodnoise and in 1998 acquired another pioneering music site, the Internet Underground Music Archive (IUMA) which had been set up in 1993 using FTP and Gopher sites before the world wide web had taken hold. The IUMA had been set up allow unsigned bands share music and had aspired to become an alternative to record labels.
13 CDNow remained focused on its CD retailing business but found itself increasingly unable to compete with the rapidly growing Amazon. CDNow ultimately followed the classic dot.com bubble template, peaking at 500 employees and $130 million annual revenues before falling into a spiral of layoffs and other cost-reduction methods as it frantically attempted to transition from revenue to profit. The efforts proved fruitless and in the summer of 2000 CDNow sold to the burgeoning Bertelsmann for its new BeMusic Internet music division. Bertelsmann had planned for BeMusic to become an internet music powerhouse built around CDNow, BMG Direct (a CD music club) and Napster. But the writing was on the wall for BeMusic as soon as Judge Patel scuppered Bertelsmann's attempts to buy Napster and so in 2011 the CDNow story ended somewhat poignantly with its sale from Bertelsmann to its old sparring partner Amazon.

the quality of the music listening experience. The CD was a high quality audio product that did not suffer from physical degradation in the way that the compact cassette or vinyl had done.[14] The music audio equipment business had also experienced unprecedented success meeting an apparently endless growth in consumer appetite for better quality audio. This thirst for quality had even helped the audio separates business connect with an eager mainstream market. So the concept of a digital audio file that put convenience ahead of quality was never going to be an easy sell to record labels. Codecs such as MP3 and AAC had the potential to deliver high quality audio files but the prevalence of slow home download speeds meant that the best opportunity for these lossy audio formats was to deliver small files that traded optimum quality for optimum accessibility.[15]

When the audio quality issue was combined with the lexicon of technology company business strategy, many traditional record label executives were quite simply incredulous. Up until this point record labels and the technology sectors had had remarkably little interaction and they poorly understood each other's worldviews. Moviso founder and former EMI exec Ralph Simon had gained first hand experience of the gulf in understanding between the music business and technology companies. Having moved to San Francisco in 1991 he: "came to the realization that there was a clear synthesis between music and the emerging technology world – and recognised that we in music didn't understand technology and that they in technology didn't quite get us." The language of business was also very different between the two sectors. As a creative industry the music business had always relied heavily on gut instinct rather than the process heavy research and development approach of the technology and Consumer Electronics (CE) businesses of the 1990's. This contrast was compounded by a very different approach to management. Whereas technology and CE companies tended to have a professional manager class and to hire people with MBA's, up until the 2000's many record label executives had worked their way up through the business often from A&R roles. This gave them a keen understanding of how their businesses worked from the bottom up but it also meant that they were less exposed to emerging contemporary business thinking and vocabulary. The culture chasm is illustrated by an encounter that A2B Music's Larry Miller recounted: "I [was] in the boardroom of one major label to explain our model and playing a compressed 128bps music file using AT&T's AAC codec. The major exec said 'I don't understand a fucking word you're saying. What do you mean by disintermediation? No one will ever fucking pay for music that sounds like that'. Obviously he was very wrong about that." Although with the perspective of 15 subsequent years of digital music such an attitude may appear narrow minded it was illustrative of just how alien a proposition digital music was to many record label executives, particularly when it came to audio quality. It is a point emphasized by the RIAA's Cary Sherman: "Record labels spent their lives trying to improve sound quality and the internet came along and reversed that. All the original digital music innovators, such as AT&T Labs and Liquid Audio, were working with compressed sound. The labels saw the potential of digital distribution, but not in that format; MP3 was regarded as a low quality format. It has taken 15 years to get to the point that people have started seriously thinking about restoring the quality that has been lost."

The music industry had not however stood still and in late 1998, sandwiched between the launch

---

14 Some earlier CDs were of a lower quality and were susceptible to degraded playback over time but these teething problems in pre-recorded CDs were largely fixed over time.
15 Lossy audio compression creates digital files by compressing the original audio through removing elements of the sound that are less obvious to the human ear. When a file is only moderately compressed most of the lost audio will be inaudible to most people, but when a file is more heavily compressed it will be of a noticeably lower quality, often including unusual audio artefacts that might give the impression of a song sounding like it is being played underwater. Multiple additional factors impact the quality of a digital file, including sample rate, type of codec used, quality of the original file and quality of the encoding software.

of MP3.com and Napster, the Secure Digital Music Initiative (SDMI) had been set up. SDMI was a forum of record labels, consumer electronic companies, technology companies and ISPs with the overarching aim of creating a secure standard for digital music distribution. SDMI created an early venue for collaboration between the music industry and the burgeoning technology sector as Sherman explained: "CD ripping was starting and it was clear that litigation would have taken years and the result was uncertain. So SDMI was a platform for working together with technology companies to deliver value to the consumer. We had 200 companies attending, with meetings every two months and then every month. The technology sector saw true potential." The vision was to create an entire vertically integrated ecosystem that would encompass digital music hardware, software and retail. This would be achieved by creating an undetectable and irremovable digital watermark on all audio files along with a series of approved software players and portable media players that would prevent playback of any watermarked file that the user had not purchased a license to play. It was a strategy that might just have worked in the analogue era when it was possible to exercise total control of channels and dictate which platforms consumers would use. But in the age of the internet the consumer had choice and therefore ultimate control. SDMI attempted to create a police state in the wild west. Even if it had been built, consumers would have been easily able to circumnavigate it. Record labels' obsession with wrapping their music in cumbersome Digital Rights Management (DRM) that controlled what a user could and could not do was an understandable echo of their era of control but in practice it simply disadvantaged legally retailed files against unlicensed free MP3s. Locking the gate only makes sense if you actually have a wall. Wimamp, MP3.com and soon Napster ensured that there was no wall for music file security on the web. As Cliff Fluet, now partner at law firm Lewis Silkin but then Business Affairs Director at Warner Music UK, put it: "SDMI was born out of an absolute belief that the internet was simply a 'new format' that could become controlled."

SDMI's control culture also manifested itself in some of its dealings with the technology community. In September 2000 SDMI published an Open Letter to the Digital Community inviting hackers and others to find and remove from audio files the watermark that it had spent the last couple of years developing. A cash prize was offered to participants who succeeded in the task as long as they signed an NDA to ensure that hack instructions did not leak onto the open web. One academic, Ed Felten, succeeded in removing the watermark and because he had opted not to sign the NDA he wrote an academic paper on the SDMI technology and how he and his team found and removed the watermark. Horrified, SDMI and the RIAA attempted to prevent publication of the paper under the auspices of the Digital Millennium Copyright Act (DMCA) before the US Department of Justice ruled that the act could not be used to stifle legitimate research.

The focus on control often got in the way of more constructive aspirations as Barney Wragg, a participant in SDMI and at the time SVP of Universal Music's eLabs Division recalled: "SDMI was a group to get a standard set of content usage rules and watermarking that might lead to some interoperability between technologies. The focus on watermarking to stop the "analogue hole" was unhelpful and undid what could have been a useful forum." One important role that SDMI played was enabling the record labels to work collaboratively on an industry-wide challenge when anti-trust regulations would otherwise prevent them from doing so as Wragg explained: "Critically anti-trust legislation meant that the industry couldn't work together to create a single consumer standard to combat the tidal wave, it was absolutely bonkers." It is a view echoed by Fluet: "Despite all of the conspiracy theories, the prevailing attitude amongst the labels was to ensure non-collusion for fear of being perceived as acting in a cartel-like manner and thus falling foul of anti-trust and competition authorities. This contributed to the labels failing to take a consistent view on digital."

One of the consequences of the lack of unified strategy among the labels was market fragmentation and the growing problem of interoperability. Without any single industry approved standard the licensed digital music market was a complex web of proprietary formats, codecs, rights protection and players that entirely lacked compatibility and interoperability. A song downloaded from one service would typically only work in the proprietary player of that service and most often not in a 'standard' player like Winamp, Real Player or Windows Media Player. The situation was far from ideal for any of the involved parties as Wragg explained: "UMG would say 'we have done all the assessments and decided on this codec, DRM and file format.' They had to do that in isolation as each piece of technology had to be licensed from the developer on stand alone commercial terms. You couldn't go to other labels and tell them what we had chosen and why. So UMG would announce in the press it was using AAC, Interturst and Caraf and then Sony, EMI, BMG or Warner's would announce something different. There was zero interoperability and thus zero value to the consumer who was struggling to avoid being caught up in a format war. As an industry we tried everything to try to promote interoperability. We went to ISO standards groups to help create machine readable formats that included description of the content, rights management systems and what features hardware would need to use that content. I spent two years writing a rights expression language to express what permissions a creator/distributor had assigned to their content. We developed a full XML schema and a reference dictionary for digital media distribution. This was just to express usage rights and it's an ISO standard now, but as far as I know never used by the music industry."

One of SDMI's strengths would also prove to be its Achilles Heel: with over 200 members the forum was unable to make quick decisions in a market that was transforming at the speed of light. It is an observation made by Paul Vidich, then EVP at Warner Music: "It was really hard to create standards in real time in a market that was moving quickly. With SDMI there was a push to create a copy protection regime around the digital distribution of music. The early conversations with the likes of Sony and Philips were focused on building a system with rights protection. Dutifully these companies would go off and build stuff but invariably the user experience just wasn't very good." In practice the efforts of participating companies were doomed with SDMI effectively becoming obsolete before it had even had a chance to create a standard. A little over six months after SDMI had been launched Napster crashed onto the scene. Sherman described the impact: "Napster changed everything. Suddenly the question became 'why did technology companies need to work on standards for interoperability and protection when all the music was already there?' A lot of the motivation evaporated." Participating technology companies realized that they would be able to achieve many of their music product aspirations without having to go through the tortuous process of creating industry standards resulting in rights protection-shackled products. What had been cordial and productive inter-industry relationships began to fracture, with lasting repercussions as Geoff Taylor, Chief Executive of the UK record label trade body the BPI explained: "SDMI revealed a fundamental lack of alignment between technology companies and content creators. Although creators and tech came together to try to develop an ecosystem that would allow content to be monetised, it broke down because tech companies decided it wasn't their responsibility to protect creators and they could make money from content without doing so. This breakdown laid the foundations for 15 years of struggle between technology companies and content creators." And this was not a case of divisions just appearing between the labels and technology companies, for cracks of seismic proportions were forming actually within the latter group. This was a time of the rise of PC and internet companies, and the decline of the traditional CE companies. The latter had been solid, slow moving, predictable organizations that the music industry had been able to do business with comfortably and fruitfully for decades, the most profitable result of which had been the CD. But the new PC and internet companies played by different rules and operated in fundamentally different ways, both of which had direct bearing on their approach to music according to Sherman: "The fundamental difference between CE and IT industries is that the CE sector was all about standards. Their approach was to pool technology, agree on standards and then compete on implementation. The IT industry rarely agrees on standards, they fight it out. So there was a built-in conflict."

Once SDMI had lost the confidence of some of its key participants it quickly became a lame duck organization and both technology and music industry companies started looking for alternatives including IBM's Project Madison. Launched in early 1999 Project Madison was a digital music delivery system that was aimed at creating a standard for the music industry called the Electronic Music Management System (EMMS). With all of the major labels on board – Sony, EMI, Bertelsmann, Time-Warner and Universal – it was interpreted by some as a direct challenge to SDMI. However the label partners were keen to stress that EMMS would sit on top of whatever SDMI eventually came up with. Acronym overdose aside, it was clear that the efforts to solve fragmentation were, well, suffering from fragmentation. Sherman explained the rationale for working with IBM: "There was a serious question about who to work with. Liquid Audio and so many of the other companies there at the start were small, and the labels needed to find reliable partners with sufficient capital and technology credentials. Also the labels' ability to work together on a project was limited by anti-trust laws. Ultimately the labels decided to work with IBM on the "Madison Project" going into trial offering full album downloads." However the labels were moving with extreme caution even with Project Madison, offering only a couple of thousand albums via the platform. Caution and fragmentation were becoming the defining characteristics of the major labels' approach to digital, which stood in stark contrast to the bold unity of Napster.

SDMI's uncomfortable mix of lofty ideals and cynical business aspirations were never the best recipe for success but ultimately the speed of change catalysed by the arrival of Napster doomed the cross industry effort to failure. SDMI stuttered on for a couple more years before accepting the inevitable and calling it a day in May 2001. SDMI's preoccupation with control acted as a blinker on its strategic vision, stymying its ability to both see and address the bigger picture. As such it was emblematic of much of the major record labels' approach to digital at the time as Roger Faxon argued: "The music industry did not understand the technology, the consumer, nor how to evolve the business model to take advantage." Perhaps SDMI's most important legacy was to shine a light on the true scale of the problem the music industry was facing as Barney Wragg noted: "The combination of the effects of anti-trust legislation, the power of tech companies, and the rise of easy file sharing was a perfect storm for the music business."

Swimming Against the Tide

With projects like SDMI and Project Madison the major labels were putting all of their money on black and spinning the roulette wheel. In doing so they were effectively putting their digital strategy on hold: they were betting big, on being able to exercise influence across a tightly vertically integrated ecosystem. The irony is that such a system would evolve in the coming years and change the digital market forever, but it would be one that would be outside of their direct control. Meanwhile the first generation of ground-breaking digital music services was paying the price of first-mover disadvantage, unable to secure the content required to breathe life in to their propositions. Independent label catalogue was becoming more prevalent with many indies more willing to take risk in order to take advantage of the opportunity presented by the major label content vacuum. One such example was Rykodisc, making a small selection of tracks available for sale at $0.99.

The dotcom bubble which was financing so many of the first wave of digital music technology companies was about to burst but few foresaw the coming crash and until it came there was a pervasive sense that the Internet needed to be a priority for all kinds of businesses. Lohan Presencer had recently left Warner Music to become CEO of Ministry of Sound and was concerned that for all the digital hype there was very little evidence of a consumer market for paid digital music: "When I went to Midem in 2000 it was already as much about technology as it was music but almost all of the tech was premature. Consumers and the market weren't ready yet. We did a deal with OD2 to put downloads on the website. Nobody was downloading them though." The market was still missing many key components, most important of which was deep major label content.

Liz Schimel, former VP Nokia

Ralph Simon, former EVP Capitol & Blue Note / Founder Yourmobile

Martin Goldschmidt, founder and MD Cooking Vinyl

Most services knew that they needed major label content if they were ever going to be able to appeal to mainstream audiences. Additionally securing partial catalogue from countless small independent labels was a sizeable effort that did not guarantee comparable returns. Some services decided to taken an entirely different approach, bypassing record labels entirely and going for unsigned artists. One such example was Peoplesound.com from the UK, launching in late 1999. Peoplesound had the bold idea of replacing A&R executives at record labels, believing that they could remove all of the risk of discovering new artists by providing comprehensive regional, demographic and behavioural data of music listeners. Record labels' scepticism of

Peoplesound's data charts and spread sheets was partly borne of unfamiliarity but also of a keen understanding that the ineffable essence of good A&R might be helped by data, but could never be wholly replaced by it. In the end, instead of delivering a wave of internet-tested hit acts, Peoplesound had to content itself with launching the career of UK urban pop act Mis-Teeq who went on to sign with Telstar and reach number 2 in the UK singles charts.[16]

Another digital pioneer that had opted for the unsigned artist route was Italian company Vitaminic, setting up business in April 1999. As Vitaminic's founder and CEO Gianluca Dettori explained, artists had always been at the core of the idea: "We wanted to open up the channel for the artists. We knew it was going to be difficult with the labels but we always wanted to work with them." The fact that unsigned artists were the core of the content offering hinted at just how difficult it would prove to make progress with the labels.

Indeed selling unsigned music was a necessity of circumstance rather than strategic preference. Vitaminic had its sights set firmly on selling music downloads of major record labels and Dettori worked tirelessly on the task of trying to secure the requisite licenses. But try as he might, he just could not get labels to sign the deals. Vitaminic paid the price for being too early for most labels and found themselves on the receiving end of either apathetic disinterest or downright disdain. Dettori recalled one label encounter in particular that illustrated the scale of the challenge he faced: "I went to London to meet with a major. They said 'our terms are 90% for us, 10% for you and you have to pay the publishers. Pricing has to be the same as the CD, with no unbundling [of individual tracks] and we want 20% equity'. The message was very clearly 'we don't want to get involved in this. Not a single one our competitors from that period survived."

Fortunately for Vitaminic the buoyancy of the dotcom bubble enabled the company to achieve a successful stock market flotation but without major licenses the company was stuck in neutral. Vitaminic acquired struggling Peoplesound in 2001 but by 2003 Dettori and co admitted defeat and merged Vitaminic with emerging mobile content company Buongiorno. Enough time has passed for Dettori to be able to reflect on the experience philosophically: "Not being able to get the licenses we needed to make Vitaminic a success was a pretty big loss but those are the times your grow most and learn most. As things turned out I was very proud to see Buongiorno [the company that Vitaminic merged with in 2003] sell for $300 million [to NTT Docomo in May 2012]."

In 2000 internet entrepreneur Paul Myers embarked on a similar journey, launching a legal P2P service called Wippit. Paul would go on to spend the next nine years using every ounce of his renowned charm struggling to get the major labels to license to his service. Playlouder, another early pioneer, succeeded in securing content from big independent Beggars Banquet Group - which shared a similarly strong appetite for experimentation – but it too faltered when it came to the major labels. Other services, such as iCrunch, NetBeat and Freetrax, did not even bother trying to go down the major route, focusing instead on providing distribution for independent labels. The failure to secure licenses doomed so many of the first wave of music services to failure. There were some notable survivors of the cull, including eMusic, Spinner.com and Pandora, all of whom went on to enjoy long-term success.

Inevitably, cautious experimentation was all too little. In the US digital music only managed to

---

16 Peoplesound got a share of Mis-Teeq's early publishing revenue as part of its end user agreement with the group. For artists who wanted to sign with Peoplesound's record label the site offered 50% of net receipts. Mis-Teeq disbanded in 2005 though one member of the trio, Alesha Dixon, went onto to become a successful solo artist and TV presenter, including a stint as a judge on the BBC's 'Strictly Come Dancing'.

account for a measly 0.1% of total music sales in 1999 while in Europe it did not even register on the scale. Despite the valiant efforts of digital music's first generation of entrepreneurs, the lack of major label support sealed their collective fate and the damage that was done in those early days would have much more far reaching impact than just stunting the growth of a few music start ups. The major record labels' early reluctance to embrace digital was an own goal of epic proportions. By May 1999 'MP3' had become the most searched for word on the web. The digital music revolution was not waiting for the music industry to get its house in order but was instead forging ahead at full steam. While the major record labels' dithering consigned the nascent legitimate sector to irrelevance, illegal services boomed. Consumer expectations had changed forever and the paucity of legal digital music meant that the first generation of digital music consumers were cutting their digital teeth on illegal services.

Without doubt there had been a crucial window of opportunity for the record labels to seize, that instead had been left begging. This has led many to argue ad infinitum that the record labels could have nipped piracy in the bud should they have chosen to license to Napster rather than sue it out of existence. There can be little doubt that the legitimate market would have got off to a dramatically faster start but it is naïve to suggest that it would have stopped piracy in its tracks. As we have seen, pretenders to Napster's throne were already emerging from the wings long before Napster went offline. New unlicensed P2P sites, networks and applications would have continued to proliferate no matter what number of legal services record labels might have managed to license to. That said, there is no doubt that the major labels should have licensed to the nascent legal services in that first window. And even when the labels did finally lumber into action they started off by pursuing a conservative and timid strategy that would continue to give piracy a free run around the track while the legitimate market limped around with its starting blocks still dangling from its bloodied feet.

A Stuttering Start to the Music Industry's First Digital Decade

By the later part of 2000 each of the major labels had started to make tentative steps into the digital waters. Unfortunately for the pioneering digital music entrepreneurs struggling for licenses this often only stretched as far as each label striking individual exclusive deals with single outlets, and even then only with miniscule catalogues. In September Warner signed a deal with Real Networks to sell a small catalogue of downloads on Amazon.com and Walmart. com. BMG meanwhile was pursuing a number of digital deals under the auspices of the Bertelsmann eCommerce division that was headed up by Thomas Middlehoff's fast rising star Andreas Schmidt. In October Schmidt finalized a deal with internet portal Lycos that gave BMG its first foray into selling music downloads, but it was a deal defined by conservatism. A paltry 100 BMG singles and albums were licensed to Lycos' Premium Download store, though they did at least feature big name artists such as Whitney Houston and Christina Aguilera. The contrast with Napster was again stark and it is little wonder that the store made no meaningful impact (see Figure 5). Any single one of limited geographic availability, tiny catalogue and excessive pricing would have been enough to consign Lycos' music store to miserable underperformance, all three guaranteed abject failure. But the biggest shackle that Lycos had to bear was the major labels' control culture manifest as technology: rights protection. It was an innovation tailor made for the record label's caution-first approach but ultimately proved to be hugely counter productive as Faxon observed: "The music industry imposed a huge number of restraints on the innovators, the most damaging of which proved to be DRM, which was meant as a means of regaining control of the distribution and did the opposite."

FIGURE 5

Tentative First Steps by Major Labels Were Hardly Even
Drops in the Ocean Compared to Napster
Comparison of Key Licensed and Unlicensed Music Service Catalogues in 2000

80m
Napster
Including wrongly tagged duplicates

10,000
Wallmart/Amazon

100
Lycos

Although MP3.com and Napster had let their users download music with no restrictions, the record labels were convinced that when they sold music downloads they needed to be wrapped with rights protection technology that dictated how and where consumers could listen to them. Digital Rights Management had initially been intended, as the name suggests, to help rights owners manage their digital content assets but it soon found its true vocation as digital rights protection. A host of technology companies including InterTrust, Liquid Audio and Microsoft were quick to recognize a business opportunity in the music industry's digital hang up. These companies pitched their wares as a way of enabling the labels and publishers to protect their content online. In practice this meant that any consumer who had paid to download an authorized record label music file was not able to transfer it from the PC on to which they had downloaded, nor were they able to make a CD copy. In an age when the vast majority of music listening was done on a CD player, not being able to make a CD copy was a distinctly draconian measure. If long-term vision had prevailed over short-term caution, labels would have recognized the importance of CD burning as a tool for transitioning consumers from analogue to digital consumption patterns. But of course that was the opposite of what most senior major label executives wanted at this stage; their belief was still firmly that the internet's key role would be marketing and selling CDs. Meanwhile of those who did begin to contemplate a possibility that digital distribution may come to define their future, many became preoccupied with how to slow the cannibalization of CD sales. The outcome of the labels projecting their strategic confusion onto the digital music marketplace was a complex and fragmented collection of sub par consumer experiences. The fact that DRM was also predominately used to tether music downloads to PCs also ensured any early adopters of MP3 players had to forget any crazy ideas they might have had of being able to play legal digital music downloads on their new purpose built digital music devices.

If major label rights protected downloads had been launched into virgin digital territory these restrictions would have still been bothersome but at least they would have been the standard. But they were not introduced into an undiscovered realm, they were launched into an already established marketplace. The fact that it was an illegitimate one that existed without the major labels' and publishers' consent did not matter because the new, and now established, digital generation of music fans expected digital music to be MP3. They understood digital as a highly convenient and flexible environment that supported all of their key use cases. An environment that allowed them to play their music downloads whenever and wherever they wanted, to make CD copies if they wanted, to transfer them to any of their PCs and to put them on their new MP3 players. In short, Napster and MP3.com enabled their users to believe that they owned their music in the fullest of senses. This was in the sharpest of contrasts to the major label stores that had made it abundantly clear to their customers that they had simply paid for the privilege of being able to do whatever the labels and their technology partners told them they could do.[17]

The bitter irony of the situation was that the music industry was effectively penalizing its most loyal customers: anyone who decided they wanted to do the right thing and buy music from a legal store had to pay over the odds, choose from a trifling catalogue and then on top of all that, tolerate excessive restrictions. It was nigh on impossible to build a consumer experience case for using legal services over illegal ones. Business decisions were overriding consumer preferences and until this balance could be fixed – and thankfully it would at least improve relatively soon – the scales remained definitively tilted in favour of the illegitimate sector. The music industry, by ensuring licensed services were so poor was again giving piracy a free hand. Which meant that the technology companies' assurances that rights protection technology would protect the labels' and publishers' content online rang fatally hollow. It was digital snake oil, a solution that would have struggled to work before the piracy genie was out of the bottle but was now entirely incapable of delivering on its promise. The major labels' caution did not stop with rights protection, some elements also tried to push a pricing strategy that, if it had been the long term blue print for digital, would have stifled growth dramatically. Paul Vidich remembered the approach: "The thinking of many label execs was that 'if we unbundle the song from the album we're only going to sell two or three tracks off every album so we need to ensure they make us the same money as the album, so tracks need to be $2.45, or $2.99 each.'"

One of the problems facing major label digital strategy in the late 1990's and early 2000's was that decision making was limited to a relatively small number of executives as Vidich explained: "What you have to realize is that back then it wasn't an industry making decisions, it was 15 people across the five majors making decisions." The recently formed digital and new media departments of labels were still relatively junior within the corporate hierarchies and also comparatively lightly staffed, so their voices were usually not part of the decision making process. The author remembers a meeting with a group of senior executives and a handful of new media staff at one major label in 2000. The executives were middle aged, mostly men, and intensely anti-digital with the exception of the two young people from the new media team who appeared to be there because someone had – only just – won the argument 'that we should have someone from new media along if we're going to discuss our business future'. The two hour meeting quickly degenerated into a verbal duel, with the author and the two 'new media' people making a valiant but ultimately futile, defence of digital.

---

17 Consumers never actually own music files, whether they buy them on CD or as downloads. Record labels merely sell music buyers a license to play the music within clearly set parameters. But with the standard CD and with MP3 downloads consumers never have bumped into this restriction and thus the music effectively feels truly owned.

At best digital was at the time an entirely unproven platform, at worst it could be the death of the CD. In such a context it took an incredibly brave person to build a case for digital, a point made by Vidich: "Nobody succeeds in business by saying 'I'm going to shrink the business and my boss will get a smaller bonus.'" Digital was also in the difficult position of both being a very small revenue source and having the potential to turn the main revenue sources on their heads. With so little existing upside and so much potential downside it is no surprise that there was frequent resistance further up the label organizational structures to the deals that the digital teams were bringing in. Fluet recalled the challenges trying to support digital business in Warner's UK efforts: "In the UK, Sony, BMG and Warner's were all affiliates of major corporations based overseas. All deals slightly out of the norm had to go 'head office' for sign off. EMI could walk first because they were the only ones who had the decision making power to do so in the 'home' territory. New media deals were getting killed with HQ saying "kill this deal because we don't understand it". In my exit interview I said 'I have to go on the other side and get some rights from you or we are all finished.' I left Warner's in 2001 very disappointed." There was also a growing sense of disparity between the intense scrutiny placed on the emerging digital businesses and the much lighter touch applied to other parts of the business, especially A&R. Fluet described the dynamic: "My impression was that the A&R were seen as untouchable alchemists – sometimes I felt they were indulged. The rationale for signing an act appeared to be on gut instinct and sales assumptions were never really challenged." Perceptions of imparity could lead to simmering resentment, especially in an environment of shrinking budgets and teams as overall revenues plummeted. These were the first symptoms of the stress fractures that would appear across record label businesses as digital become an ever bigger part of their operations. Whereas many of the traditional functions of record labels, A&R in particular, were rooted in creativity and instinct digital was grounded in data and process. The digitization of the record labels would prove to be as much about adapting the ways the companies did business in a larger sense as it would be transitioning revenue.

First Hints of the Future

Despite the clear failings of DRM, fear of the unknown ensured the major labels persisted with it, and by the turn of the new millennium there was a new wave of eager digital music start ups willing to accept that it was the price that need paying to get major label content on their services. Without catalogue from the majors the last generation of digital music services had fallen by the wayside, doomed to inevitable failure. Now the labels were at last willing to license limited portions of their content and this new set of music entrepreneurs were not going to let the opportunity go begging, even if the technology IQ within record labels was not always as high as might have been hoped. Gregor Pryor, now a Partner at law firm Reed Smith but then head of legal and business affairs at Music Choice, remembered a frustrating encounter with one major label executive: "We presented the beta version of our new music download product to a digital executive at one of the majors and he asked 'Where's the one-click purchase button? We're not interested if there's no one-click button' To which we replied 'You mean the exclusive patented product that Amazon owns?' 'Yes that one'. So we said 'Ok, we'll see what we can do' and my boss slammed his laptop shut and stormed out of the meeting."

Over at EMI Jay Samit refined a commercial approach that the label had been developing over the last few years in which music services paid advances and gave equity stakes as part of the licensing deal, a blue print for the approach of current major label licensing strategy. EMI's then VP of New Media Jeremy Silver explained the approach: "We defined a clear digital deal structure based around content for equity and advances. Our opening gambit for equity was 25% and we'd negotiate down from there. With some companies it was 50%." In a comparatively short period of time EMI struck a large number of deals as Silver's then boss Samit recalled: "Over 18 months I moved content to 70 different companies. My mantra was make it easier to buy and more difficult to pirate." In 2000 at UMG Barney Wragg joined from technology company ARM to head up its eLabs division, which Wragg described as having been: "born out of the dot com days when labels believed that they needed to build the whole encoding and delivery architecture."

Gianluca Dettori, former founder and CEO Vitaminic

Gregor Pryor, Partner, Reed Smith

Elio Leoni Sceti, former CEO EMI

One of the first companies to build a comprehensive offering around rights protection-wrapped major label content was European start up On Demand Distribution (OD2). Founded in 1999 by prog-rocker Peter Gabriel and Charles Grimsdale, OD2 had the forward looking vision of providing white labelled music services to ISPs and other such companies wanting to get into the digital game. The white label model would go on to become a mainstay of the digital music ecosystem. Even though OD2 were wrapping all their content in rights protection technology the labels were still reluctant to license meaningful amounts of music and OD2 had to go to market with a modest catalogue of 200,000 tracks from 8,500 artists. OD2's business model was different to most of the first generation of digital music start ups, allowing third parties to launch their own music services by licensing OD2's technology and content on a white label service basis. Though the catalogue was small it was pretty much as good as it got in 2001 and in November that year OD2 announced its first partnership with Italian ISP Tiscali. Individual tracks were available for between £0.99 and £2.00 and OD2's pricing also had an innovative twist up its sleeve: instead of just buying individual downloads consumers could pay a monthly fee for an allowance of downloads, £5.00 for 20 tracks and £9.99 for 60.

Underneath the novel pricing lurked the now familiar face of rights protection technology. All OD2 tracks were downloaded in rights protected Microsoft Windows Media Audio (WMA) format, restricting OD2 customers to only play their music downloads on a PC. Transferring onto MP3 players was forbidden as was CD burning. This was of course entirely at the behest of the major record labels but regardless piracy was once again the winner. Nonetheless, because DRM was the only game in town for major label content, and also as OD2 had done the hard work of striking the licensing deals – no mean feat – a host of other partners soon jumped on board the OD2 bandwagon, including the big catch of Microsoft's MSN Music. Another OD2 partner was Dotmusic, using OD2's technology to power an innovative subscription service but as Ben Drury, then at Dotmusic and now CEO of 7Digital recalled, rights protection planted itself firmly in the way of a compelling user experience: "We launched Dotmusic On Demand, an unlimited music download and streaming subscription service with OD2 in 2002 and in doing so learned how not to do it. It was crippled by horrible DRM and it was too early." OD2 established an impressive footprint, providing services across Europe for many leading ISPs and portals before selling to Loudeye in 2004 and then finally to Nokia in 2006 where it would form the basis for the ill-fated Comes With Music.

Across the Atlantic an even more innovative US service was making its first tentative steps on what would prove to be a long and fruitful path. In December 2001 Rhapsody became the first ever streaming music subscription service. The concept of paying a flat monthly fee for unlimited streaming music access was a radical game changer. Unfortunately it was too revolutionary for the record labels and Rhapsody was initially unable to secure either major label content or indeed even much in the way of independent label music. Over time though the labels were progressively sold on Rhapsody's story and by July 2002 all of the majors had licensed to the service that would evolve into what would be for some years the most sophisticated digital music service in the market. In 2003 Rhapsody and its owner Listen. com was bought by the increasingly ambitious RealNetworks, keen to diversify away from its audio codec and rights protection focus. Set up in 1996 by former Microsoft executive Rob Glaser, RealNetworks had become one of the key technology players in the nascent digital music market. But locked in a DRM arms race with Microsoft and Intertrust, RealNetworks and its competitors were creating a complex and confusing morass of proprietary audio codecs. Consumers had to navigate through a bewildering array of file formats such as .wma, .rm and .saf each of which locked the music files to its own exclusive software player. These fiercely competitive companies managed to exploit the labels' fears to bisect the digital landscape with a mass of impenetrable technology walls. Some companies tried to solve the growing interoperability problem including Microsoft-backed digital content service provider Reciprocal. In 1999 Reciprocal had acquired AT&T's A2B Music including its co-founders Howie Singer and Larry Miller, with Miller serving as president of the newly formed Reciprocal Music division. Miller explained that Reciprocal aimed to act as a service layer across all digital music technologies: "a clearing house for rights and transactions for digital music, like a credit card clearing house." It enjoyed solid success, but gaining large market share of a niche DRM-shackled digital music business inevitably proved to be too little as Miller recounted: "By mid 2001 Reciprocal was managing 70% of the secure transactions in the digital music business but the business just wasn't scaling quickly enough so we sold to Microsoft in an asset sale."

The core legacy of rights protection technology was not curtailing piracy, but instead stunting the growth of the infant legitimate market by carving it up into technology siloes, locking consumers into the products of the DRM providers. It did little to protect intellectual property from the impact of piracy but was a highly effective consumer lock-in tool for the technology companies. If a consumer had built a .wma music collection he was locked into that format, player and store and therefore the services selling music in that format. If he wanted to take that music elsewhere or combine it with digital music he had purchased elsewhere he had to buy it all over again in a new format. Also if that music service went out of business, as they often eventually did, the rights technology server would usually be turned off and the user would no longer be able to play his music but instead have a hard drive full of redundant, inaccessible files. The much simpler option of course was to go to download the music for free in MP3 format from a P2P network. Once again piracy was the winner.

Moving Up The Value Chain

As if fighting against restrictive rights protection technology, pitifully small catalogues and the onslaught of piracy was not enough for new emerging music services, they soon found themselves competing with a new competitor: the record labels themselves. In 2001 the major labels launched two music services of their own, Pressplay and MusicNet. The major labels had decided that the internet was an opportunity for them to turn decades of music retailing practice on its head. In the physical world record labels relied upon retailers to sell their music to the public, which of course came at the price of a substantial share of the sale price going to the retailer. 'What if', the thinking went, 'we become the retailers ourselves online, imagine how much more profitable we will be and how much more control we will have over our destinies'. The labels' thinking had certainly come on a long way since they had first starting grappling with MP3.com and Napster, or perhaps not. In the closing stages of the Napster trial, Napster's legal team had argued that the record labels were seeking to take the P2P service out of the market because the labels wanted to have the market to themselves to launch their new services. Indeed Pressplay had first been formed in 1999, in the earlier stages of the Napster case. However the record labels' core concern at that stage had been removing an unlicensed threat to their core business: selling CDs. Planning for creating a legitimate market afterwards was a natural extension of the strategic thought process but not the motivating factor. Even if it had been, the record labels were still within their legal, commercial and moral rights to prevent illegal sale of their product by an unauthorised retailer. Just as a car dealer would have been had a competitor stolen his stock of new cars, opened up a shop next door and then started giving all of that stock away for free. The 'suing a competitor out of existence' argument in itself was tenuous. Where there was room for debate though, was whether the services the labels were willing to license to were in fact genuinely compelling alternatives, and now the newly emerged question of whether the labels were hurting other legal services' ability to compete by launching their own services.

Anti-trust investigations inevitably followed, but as it transpired the digital music ecosystem had little to worry about. The two services split the majors down the middle, with Universal and Sony forming Pressplay and the remaining majors backing MusicNet, though eventually all of the majors would cross license both sets of services. MusicNet and Pressplay were the product of a curious mix of compromise and overreaching ambition. On the one hand the vision of the labels' digital executives had been watered down into insignificance by the ultra-conservative leanings of their bosses. While on the other those same bosses also saw digital as a perfect opportunity for them to extend their reach, power and influence. Instead of settling for simply licensing their content to digital music services, the major labels wanted to become the services too. Throughout the analogue era they had surrendered their relationship with the consumer to retailers – a few music club experiments excepted. The internet now presented the chance for record labels to sell directly to consumers, giving them a direct relationship with their end customers, and in the process cutting out the middleman to enable better profit margins. That was the theory, the practice turned out to be quite different. The labels learned the harsh lesson that they simply did not have the retailing expertise necessary to succeed, that they were not going to catch up with their retail partners' decades of retailing expertise in a few short months. Both services were inevitably fatally hamstrung by excessively restrictive usage terms, inadequate pricing, poor user experience and inter-label bickering. PC Magazine famously labelled the services as 'brain-dead' technology. Even the fact that there were two competing label-backed services illustrated the challenges the major labels' short lived initial foray into direct-to-consumer digital retail strategy would face.

MusicNet and Pressplay essentially offered the same subscription value proposition with minor differences. Pressplay charged $15 for 500 streams, 50 downloads and 10 CD burns, though only a small subset of the catalogue was available for download and burning. MusicNet was $10 a month for 100 streams and 100 downloads. MusicNet's downloads came with a catch though: each download expired after 30 days and renewing it counted against the next month's allowance of downloads. Pressplay and MusicNet were tour-de-forces in music DRM but at least they finally supported the right to burn music to CDs. Though even this move was laced with irony as the major labels were simultaneously bringing CDs to market with technology built in to prevent CD ripping. In the face of near non-existent consumer demand and overall marketplace disinterest Pressplay and MusicNet swiftly went through a series of service updates. Portability, or rather lack of it, was a key issue for both services. By 2002 it was clear that digital music consumers wanted to be able to listen to their downloads on MP3 players. But because both Pressplay and MusicNet's rights technology was proprietary it was not supported on the majority of MP3 players in the market, which meant that their customers could not play their purchased music on the go while P2P users could. So once again piracy had the advantage – you should be spotting a recurring theme by now. Pressplay's 'solution' to this was to instruct their customers that all they needed to do was use their CD-burn allowance to copy songs onto CD and then to rip them again to strip them of protection technology so that they could then put them onto their MP3 players. This convoluted work-around failed on three counts:

1. It was a terrible user-journey.

2. It encouraged customers to break copy-protection, raising the question of why it should be there in the first place.

3. It revealed DRM to be the farce that it had become. Not only was it limiting the behaviour of the most honest and willing digital music customers, it was now only affecting a subset of those consumers, namely those who did not have the technology wherewithal to break the technology by burning and then ripping. So rights protection technology was now limited to policing the less-technology literate subset of honest music fans. The rest could do as they pleased.

Pressplay and MusicNet soldiered bravely on for a while longer, striking up channel partnerships with the likes of Yahoo! but the writing had been on the wall from the word 'go'. MusicNet and Pressplay limped on in a few different guises but by 2003 the major labels collaborative retailing experiment was over.[18] Pressplay closed down and MusicNet

---

18 Pressplay, which had started out as Duet – reflecting the partnership of Universal Music and Sony Music, was later acquired by Roxio and went on to power much of the discovery and curation elements of music subscription service Rhapsody. MusicNet pivoted into a white label music service company, providing the back end for digital music stores and services for the likes of HMV and Virgin. It rebranded to MediaNet and continues to operate today.

switched strategy to an OD2-like model of providing white label services before being sold in 2005.[19] The BPI's Geoff Taylor succinctly sums up the legacy of the two failed major label services: "My view is that the industry lost a couple of years developing Pressplay and MusicNet. The idea of trying to extend into retail/distribution as well as the creation of content was too ambitious. It wasn't that the industry didn't try to grasp the opportunities that digital offered – but we backed the wrong horses. There was no road map to the future".

Pressplay and MusicNet had been born out of a combination of desire for control and a general mistrust of the digital marketplace. By the early 2000's this mistrust still bubbled close to the surface. Ian Rogers was then VP and General Manager of Music at Yahoo! and recalled an incident with Warner Music: "When [I was] handed the reigns I was told 'the first thing you need to do is make things right with Warner. I fixed things with Lyor [Cohen, former North American Chairman and CEO of Recorded Music for Warner], or at least I thought I had. He pulled the rights at the last minute and, I'm told, at a company offsite. He had said to me 'I can't believe all our music videos are only worth $1 million a year.' I said 'Look man, I am paying you 60% of our revenues, I wish it was bigger too. Show me someone of our size paying higher CPM's." Underpinning Warner's approach was an overestimation of the value of music to Yahoo's business. In the early 2000's Yahoo! was one of the most valuable digital assets that the record labels had. By 2004 it was – in the US – the #1 music video service, the #1 radio service and the #1 music website (according to ComScore). But as Rogers explained, it was a costly business: "The CFO said 'this is crazy, the more Yahoo! Music makes the worse our margins are. To do a music video deal we had to pay the labels big advances. Yahoo! News and Yahoo! Music had similar gross revenue but Yahoo! Music employed 100 people and carried a 75% royalty burden while Yahoo! News employed 5 with a 5% royalty burn. By comparison music was a crappy business. There was a prevailing attitude that Yahoo! was using music to drive people to its properties to drive its core business. But the reality was that there were only five of us in management who cared about music and the rest couldn't give a damn. I would say to labels 'I'm not trying to steal your business, I'm trying to help. Why am I getting beaten up all the time?'"

The over estimation of the importance of music to Yahoo's business was not an isolated event, in fact it is just one example of a trend that has perpetuated throughout the entire history of digital music, namely that rights owners tend to over estimate the value of music to their partners. The flipside is also true, namely that partners tend to underestimate the value of music, and there is no doubt that music was an important part of Yahoo's business that delivered significant revenue. But it was not crucial and outside of the relatively small circle of internal advocates, there was a tendency to view music as a high cost, high-risk investment that simply was not worth the hassle of demanding content partners. It is a view that persists today within the management of many digital music partners as illustrated by a senior executive at a telco who wished to remain anonymous: "The simple fact is that music just doesn't matter to us that much. We have many other revenue streams and products that it is much easier for us to make money on and that our customers more readily understand the value of." Luckily for the record labels, the abject failures of Pressplay and MusicNet, and partner spats were about to be entirely overshadowed by a new entrant to the market that would change the face of digital music forever and, for the better.

---

19 MusicNet eventually became a successful digital content services company under the guise MediaNet.

The Future Arrives

In 2003 a small computer manufacturer from California launched its own music download service: the iTunes Music Store. Apple succeeded where no other licensed digital music service had: it created a compelling consumer use case for paid downloads. Heck it even managed to create a compelling use case for paid rights protected downloads. The reason Apple managed to do so was because it had a unique asset that none of its competitors had: a device ecosystem. With iTunes and the iPod, Apple formed a tightly integrated system that guaranteed a quality of experience to its users. The iPod became the emblem of Apple's 21st century resurgence and also that of its charismatic CEO Steve Jobs. The iPod's success story also laid out the blueprint for the early follower approach Apple would hone to excellence to deliver even more stellar success throughout the following decade. The iPod was far from the first MP3 player, that had been SaeHan Information Systems Eiger Labs' MPMan in 1997. The second _ Diamond Multimedia's Rio PMP3000 – had found itself the subject of a Temporary Restraining Order brought by the RIAA to prevent sales of the device. The RIAA saw the MP3 player as a piracy device that breached the 1992 US Audio Home Recording Act. Thankfully the RIAA eventually saw the positive potential of MP3 players, ultimately paving the way for the arrival of the iPod.

MP3 players had been firmly on the record labels' radar for years but the disruptive threat had thus far remained unrealized. Lohan Presencer remembered an early encounter with MP3 players when he was Marketing Director Warner Music UK: "One day in 1999 this guy from AMX Digital came into the office holding up an MP3 player saying 'this is going to fuck up your business, especially your [compilation] business.'" But the flash-to-bang consumer adoption delay ensured that nothing much actually happened for the next few years. The iPod however transformed theoretical possibility into market reality. It combined elegant design with user experience simplicity, but its real ace was seamless integration with the iTunes music management software. Combined, the two delivered a best-in-class user experience that was the foundation for success. A great MP3 player was close to useless if the software it depended upon was unwieldy, and vice versa. Apple let the likes of Rio and RealNetworks haemorrhage on the bleeding edge of digital innovation, priming the markets for a more mainstream player, all the while learning from their mistakes. The iPod launched into a market that had been polluted with competing DRM systems, one in which the typical use case involved consumers not expecting their music software to talk to their MP3 player and vice versa. Apple's iTunes and iPod combination showed the world what a digital music experience could, and should look like.

Nowadays, in a world of high capacity touch screen iOS devices, music inherently matters less to Apple, but in the days of the early iPods music was the killer app. With just 5GB of memory and a monochrome screen, music was pretty much all the first generation iPod did when it was released in October 2001. And yet when the iPod first launched, there was no music store to accompany it. Instead Apple relied upon the far from music industry friendly marketing tag line: Rip Mix Burn. Jobs though was a music man at heart and he recognized the value an integrated music store would deliver to the iPod and iTunes value proposition. Indeed, early on the iPod was far from a runaway success and by the end of 2002 the iPod had still only sold 625,000 units. Jobs knew that the potential of the iPod was so much greater, but he also keenly understood that launching a music service that played by the Pressplay and MusicNet rules would not only be still born, it would likely kill off the iPod too. Following the failure of SDMI, Apple had been involved in a spin off standardization initiative called DMX that was also doomed to be similarly unproductive. Apple learned a priceless lesson from the continued failed efforts to reach workable consensus despite the willing participation of all the key industry players: the need to bypass industry standards. Wragg explained Apple's 'eureka' moment: "In many ways [the DMX] work begat iTunes because Apple realised there was no standard in sight, and that they could create a really valuable user experience as they had control of the hardware and software from start to finish."

Jobs set out on little short of a crusade to persuade the record labels that they needed to do things differently, very differently. His starting premise was that digital music needed to be portable to be mainstream, that portability is where the true advantages of digital over physical could begin to be enjoyed by music fans. Jobs identified Warner Music as the best label to start working with. Warner had been acquired by the telco giant AOL in the late 90's and as Wragg put it: "were in the belly of a technology company." Warner's then EVP Paul Vidich explained that: "part of the justification of AOL's acquisition of [Warner Music parent company] Time Warner was 'we can now be smart with digital music.'' Jobs also knew the then AOL Chairman and CEO Barry Schuler and reached out to him in early 2002 to sound him out about building a music service. Vidich found himself at the centre of the ensuing discussions: "Steve Jobs put a call into Barry Schuler and Schuler put him onto me. I flew out with Roger Ames [the then Warner Music CEO] to California and we discussed what it would take to make an Apple music service a success. We told them that we would work with them devising a user experience and setting commercial terms that will work for us and therefore probably for the other labels too." Both sides wanted to make something happen but they also each had certain non-negotiable positions. For Apple the simplicity of user experience and pricing were absolutely key as Vidich noted: "Steve was very clear about what the proposition should be: 'one product, one price.'" Meanwhile Warner were adamant that Apple could not launch a music service without, you guessed it, rights protection technology, as Vidich recounted: "One thing we were clear about was that tracks should not be able to easily make their way onto P2P networks so we ensured they were locked to the computer." EMI's Samit also emphasised the importance of rights protection: "The turning point of these negotiations was could we get them to put DRM files to slow piracy."

Up to this point DRM had been a byword for poor quality user experiences and with a less determined negotiator than Jobs, iTunes might have ended being forced down the same strategic dead end its contemporaries had been pushed into. But Jobs and Apple were unwavering in their vision of a seamless user experience even if that might mean compromising on other aspects of the proposition. Robert Ashcroft, now CEO of the PRS for Music, was SVP for Sony Network Services Europe and conveyed an illustration of this approach: "At one point Apple sounded out Sony for possibly licensing ATRAC [Sony's proprietary audio codec] for the iPod – it would have given the iPod double the battery life out of the gate compared to AAC [the codec that Apple eventually licensed instead]. But Sony was unwilling to separate ATRAC from Open MagicGate [DRM] and Steve Jobs refused to take the combined offering as he knew that the three check in/out process was a poor user experience."

After extensive negotiations and deliberations Apple hit upon a way to play the DRM game but with its own rulebook. All iTunes downloads were to be wrapped in Apple's proprietary Fairplay technology with a quota for CD copies, though unlike other DRM systems Fairplay permitted use of 5 computers and, crucially, unlimited iPods. Apple's DRM did what all other DRM should have done but did not: it put restrictions one step away from the typical use case of its consumers. Which meant that most iTunes customers never actually felt the limits of the rights technology, something that could not be said of a typical Pressplay or MusicNet customer. As Beggars' Simon Wheeler observed: "Apple's system worked so well, in those early days so much else was hampered by DRM. If you used Apple devices you didn't know it was there." Crucially, listening to music on iPods was the core use case for iTunes customers and Jobs had managed to wangle a complete lack of restriction on this from the record labels. But even this DRM coup would have failed to deliver if it had not been for Apple's vertically integrated ecosystem. Because every iPod was linked to a users' iTunes account that in turn was linked to their iTunes Store account the rights technology was effectively invisible. Without this seamless integration users would have had to authorize each device individually with the library management software, and then with the download store, and as always happens in such scenarios, faults and compatibility issues would have been routine. It was the combination of Jobs' astute negotiation strategy and the iTunes ecosystem that provided the platform for the iPod to become the truly transformational device that it became.

It took time though to win the labels over to what was a radically different approach to digital music and Jobs himself could be a divisive figure, inspiring some, aggravating others. From the viewpoint of some label executives here was an overly confident technology guy who was telling them to throw a central tenet of their safety-first digital strategy out of the window, all to help the sales of a modestly selling little white MP3 player. But Jobs' argument and the sheer strength of his personality won through as Faxon observed: "It took Steve Jobs to show the industry that there was a genuine business opportunity to deliver to consumers what they wanted. Only someone with Steve's grit had the ability to pull it off. How do you convince the labels to give up their assets when under threat? Even still, the industry imposed pretty strict restrictions on the iTunes model."

Negotiations with the other major labels went through successive twists and turns, with scepticism and caution frequently prevailing. Though it was the labels themselves that would soon pay the commercial price for continued digital conservatism, as Vidich explained: "The other music companies in the most part were cautious but they didn't have any alternatives, so they struck one year trial deals. And because iTunes proved to be so successful this ensured that Apple had all the leverage at the renegotiation stage." One crucially important card that Apple played to win the labels over was a massive commitment to marketing. At that time the majority of digital music services did not even register on mainstream traditional media. Digital music start ups could ill afford TV ad spots and most promotion was limited to online advertising and direct marketing. Apple though came to the negotiation table with a marketing spend commitment that had the majors salivating, if not necessarily for the right reasons as Wragg explained: "Apple was the only company that really applied a consumer marketing approach to digital music. They said 'we spend $25 million a quarter on advertising, we'll put all of our marketing budget into iTunes, iPod and music for a year. They pitched a commercial reason to labels why they should license. Steve Jobs blew away the whole restrictive minutiae by focusing on 'let's get a great consumer service in place'. I think it's fair to say that many of the senior execs that Steve spoke to, really didn't think that music would ever be sold via computers, but they did think that if Apple spent $100 million on marketing 'music' they'd sell a lot more CDs."

With the balance beginning to tilt but still refusing to tip, Jobs played a strategic masterstroke: he suggested that the labels let him run a live 'experiment' on the safe and small control group of Macintosh computer users. Mac users were a group of engaged, loyal, high value, early adopter technology aficionados – the perfect group for delivering positive product test results. The Apple Mac iTunes Music Store 'beta' exceeded even Apple's expectations, with paid download rates going through the roof in comparison to other contemporary services. From there it was a relatively easy sell to the labels to extend the iTunes Music Store model to PC users. The iTunes Music Store promptly started delivering paid download milestones at a simply unprecedented rate and it had the competition running scared as Gregor Pryor, then at Music Choice, recalled: "When Eddie Cue presented at the first MidemNet and said that iTunes had hit 1 million downloads, I looked across at our Head of Marketing and said 'we're fucked'." By July 2004 Apple had sold 100 million downloads, by December this had doubled to 200 million, by May it had doubled again and by January Apple was well on course for its one billionth download, having reached the 850 million point. Apple had shown that the paid download model could actually work and as a consequence the digital music market would never be the same again. The labels also quickly realized the scale of impact Apple was going to have on their digital business and started making important changes to the way that they operated. Wragg, who'd been part of Universal's negotiating team explained the impact at Universal: "When Doug Morris [then CEO of Universal] said he was going to do the deal with Steve he ensured that from the top down management got behind it. It was a turning point for the business. We changed everything including senior executive bonus structures. Digital changed from being at the periphery to being deeply integrated right across the business." The impact on the digital business of record labels of all shapes and sizes was transformational as illustrated by Wheeler's account of the iTunes effect at Beggars: "iTunes changed everything. Apple entering the market turned the market from peanuts to very quickly becoming a major income stream, and Apple marketed digital music when no one else was."

However early on Apple's relationship with the independent sector was far from smooth, having opted to launch only with major label content. Ministry of Sound's Presencer described the situation when Apple launched the iTunes Music Store in the UK: "We were keen to get on iTunes but it proved difficult. iTunes was understaffed in the UK and the legal team in Cupertino didn't want to deal with a UK indie. Our thinking was that if this is going to affect the chart and we are not able to get our content onto iTunes quickly enough then that is not fair." Wheeler detailed a comparable situation for Beggars: "We weren't the first on the service because we had a clear idea of what our rights needed to be. We'd been in the digital business for a while and had a view that we should be given the same terms as the majors. Apple was always aware of what we were and wanted our business. They knew our content was a key part of what would drive early adopters. We stood our ground and I think earned a bit of respect from them for doing so." Alison Wenham, CEO of the UK's Association of Independent Music made a similar observation about Apple's early dealings with independent record labels: "We had an unfortunate opening skirmish but the relationship is very good now. iTunes are [now] a very fair partner."

It is difficult to overstate the importance of the iTunes Store to the digital music market. It was a clear turning point and was also a dramatic contrast to Pressplay and MusicNet. But even if the major labels had been able to put their lessons learned there into practice it is highly unlikely that competition authorities on either side of the Atlantic would have allowed a single, fully major label backed, service get to market. It is a point made by industry veteran and artist manager Keith Harris: "The received wisdom has been that it took Apple to come along and show the music business how to create a music service. But if the labels had tried to create iTunes themselves the competition authorities would have come down on them like a ton of lead." What is clear though is that Apple opened the record labels' eyes to the importance of user experience in the post-scarcity age. In the analogue era user experience had been a much lesser priority because of how much control the labels had exercised: if consumers wanted music they either bought it or tolerated sub standard audio experiences. With content scarcity gone consumers now would pay for music if it was a high quality, compelling user experience but otherwise they had no need to do so. It was a reality that Vidich recognised the gravity of: "Music executives traditionally believe that they sell music, but consumers actually buy experiences. The whole purchase and consumption experience of iTunes was core to why it was so successful." A similar view was expounded by the BPI's Geoff Taylor: "We didn't grasp well enough back then that what counts is the quality of the consumer experience, in particular the integration of device and music service. That was Steve Jobs' lasting gift to the music industry." But the secret to the success of the iTunes experience was that it straddled store, music management software and device, so that music purchasing became a natural extension of a fully integrated experience. As Orchard founder Scott Cohen identified, this was the exception not the norm: "iTunes solved customers' problems, if you plugged in the device it was smart enough to know you wanted to synch. People forget this isn't how devices used to work."

FIGURE 6

The iPod Needed the iTunes Music Store Just
As Much As The Record Labels Did

Cumulative Full Year Sales Figures for iPods

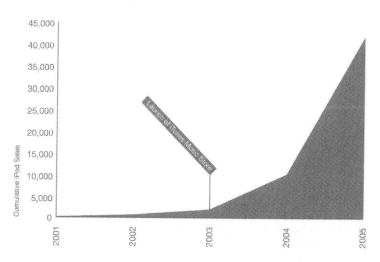

Source: Apple reported numbers

If the record labels were beginning to feel some sense of gratitude for someone finally having hit upon a solution to the awkward challenge that digital posed, then Apple had good reason to be casting reciprocal appreciative glances their way too. After the first full year of the iTunes Music Store sales of the iPod had quintupled from 2 million to 10 million, and one year later they surpassed 40 million (see Figure 6). In those early days of the iPod, Apple needed the music industry more than the music industry needed Apple. Over the course of the rest of the decade however, the dynamics of that relationship would change beyond recognition. In the late 1990's the record labels had been shocked into action by a fear that they were losing control of a new emerging channel, by the early 2000's they believed they were finally taking control of the wheel. Apple was about to show them that they had never even got into the driving seat. The digital music market was finally getting out of first gear but if anyone was hoping that the dysfunctional relationships, conflicting strategies and recurring mistakes that had characterized the early days of digital were over then they were going to be sorely disappointed.

Chapter 3: Competition

Up until the emergence of Apple's iTunes Music Store, there was a fundamental problem with legal online music services: there was just no compelling reason to use them. It was something of a miracle that anybody opted to pay for low quality audio files that could only be played in a proprietary piece of software, were locked to a single PC, could not be burned onto CD and could not be transferred onto an MP3 player. Particularly when Napster allowed consumers to do all of those things but for absolutely no cost. A pattern was becoming established that continues to define the digital music market even today, namely that paying for music online was becoming a lifestyle choice, an honesty box for the conscientious music fan. In the analogue era paying for music was an inherent component of being a music fan. Sure some people got by with buying little or nothing, relying solely on poor quality dubbed cassette mix tapes or album copies from friends, but most people who considered themselves to be a music fan routinely bought music. Some might have only ever bought records in second hand / used music stores, others might only have bought occasionally, but the underlying principle was the same for all music consumers: buying music was at the heart of being a music fan. Then Napster arrived and suddenly you didn't need to buy music anymore to have a great music collection. The majority of the music buying population however were not yet using the internet for listening to or acquiring music so the impact of piracy was progressive rather than immediate for the mainstream. And of this small but growing base of online music consumers only a tiny minority had made the proactive decision to tolerate DRM bloatware in order to pay for digital music. On the internet buying music had changed from being an opt-out decision to an opt-in one, and the contagion of free spread like wildfire over the coming years.

The Four Columns of Competition

Napster's meteoric rise to success did not however happen in a consumer behaviour vacuum. People had already started to change the way they interacted with music and how they identified with it. Consumers were evolving highly disruptive behaviours that were pulling them away from traditional music industry channels and partners. The music industry found its relationship with its consumers threatened by the simultaneous advance of Four Columns of Competition (see Figure 7):

- Identity: consumers defining themselves culturally by more than just music.
- Attention: the rise of lean-forward interactive media pushing music into the background.
- Scarcity: consumers valuing experiences which remain scarce.
- Wallet Share: multiple additional ways for consumers to spend their disposable income.

FIGURE 7
The Four Columns of Music Competition
Columns of Competition: Identity

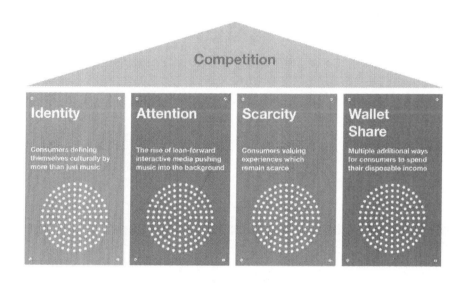

The history of modern popular music right up until the 1990's was defined by the rise and fall of scenes and movements, with the associated imagery and fashion culturally every bit as important as the music itself. Music fans identified themselves with, and defined themselves by, association with genres of music. They wore the clothes and hairstyles of the bands and singers of their scenes as a stamp of identity, membership of a club of culture and youth. In a virtuous circle of influence, music scenes emerged out of changes in social and cultural behaviour, eventually becoming their manifestation and in turn projecting back onto them the cultural reference points that further honed and defined them. People followed music scenes with which they identified and wanted to be identified by. From the 1950's up until the early 1990's it was usually possible to know what kind of music someone liked by the clothes they wore and the hairstyle they sported. In the 1950's gelled back quiffs identified the rock 'n' rollers; in the 1960's leather jackets and sharp suits separated the mods from the rockers; in the 1970's denim jackets and long shaggy hair divided the heavy rockers from the glittery disco crowds; in the 1980's heavy metallers sported big hair while ravers wore baggy jeans and hooded tops. Music was the most common way in which people defined themselves culturally; it was a short cut to personal identity. Music performed the dual role of cultural tribalism and social reference point. Because music was the core popular culture reference point the average level of engagement with music relative to other media was higher and thus the definition of a casual music fan was much higher than today. In the 1980's a casual music fan might buy a seven inch single every week, now they will likely buy nothing but instead voraciously consume programmes like the X Factor and America's Got Talent.

By the mid 1990's things were beginning to change. Music still mattered deeply to people, but it no longer had the stage to itself. Younger people had an increasingly wide and diverse range of media choices and lifestyle options to identify themselves with:

- Interactive media such as console gaming, which lifted off to the mainstream with the launch of the Playstation (1994) and the Nintendo 64 (1996).

- Teen focused TV programming, which was kick started with a slew of MTV reality shows from the mid 1990's such as 'Singled Out' and 'The Real World'.

- The rise of strong youth focused clothing and footwear brands.

- Internet sites and online chat.

- Extreme sports.

Music was becoming just one part of how young people defined themselves. According to Peter Jenner, an artist manager who in his time has managed artists such as Pink Floyd, the Clash and Billy Bragg: "Music is less important to us culturally than it was." At the same time music genres were beginning to bleed into each other with cross over-genres such as Nu-Metal and Indie Dance, and more niche genres were getting repackaged for the mainstream. By the end of the 1990's terms like 'Indie' and 'R 'n' B' were becoming replaced with broad brush mainstream terms like 'guitar rock' and 'urban'.[20] They were beginning to come down and mass media was the hammer smashing at the stonework. With the advent of round-the-clock music TV, a golden era for music magazines and the rise of online music destinations, more people were getting exposed to more music than ever before. The distinct genres of previous decades were fusing into an MTV-friendly mainstream whole. People started to answer the question 'What kind of music are you into?' with 'I like a bit of everything'. People's music tastes moved from set menu to the all-you-can-eat buffet. As the 1990's progressed, outside of some of notable sub-genre holdouts, it was no longer easy to know what music someone listened to just by looking at them.[21] Napster was in the right place at the right time. It was the technology solution for the music culture zeitgeist. People now wanted to immerse themselves in masses of music, not be limited to one or two collections of a dozen songs on a shiny disc every month or so. Inherently this meant that consumers often did not develop deep relationships with individual albums or artists in the way that had been the norm during the age of scarcity. Napster was the music platform of the mass media age. Music marketers had sought to make more music more accessible to wider audiences by pulling more genres towards the mainstream. Little could they have realised that in doing so they were helping create the perfect cultural foundations for the Napster generation.

Columns of Competition: Attention

Right up until the 1990's music had faced comparatively little direct competition for consumers' attention. Listening to an album for the first time often entailed ritualistic behaviour, with the consumer sitting, listening to the music play in its entirety, looking at the artwork and reading

20 Somewhat paradoxically, for the musos genres got more specific not less, with the emergence of micro genres like Nu-Skool Breaks and Dirty South. What has emerged is a 'genre ladder' where the broad brush categories are used for the mainstream and the further up the sophistication ladder you go, the more detailed the genre classifications become. E.g. at the bottom of the ladder is 'Rock', then for those with more than a passing interest there is 'Metal Core', 'Heavy Rock', 'Alternative Rock' etc, while at the top the rock aficionado may choose between 'Metal', 'Shoegaze', Classic Rock' etc. Ironically, the further up the genre ladder one goes, the more tribal the divisions become. Thus a mass market rock fan might be as partial to a little Bon Jovi as he is Coldplay, but a Bring Me the Horizon fan is unlikely to be seen dead listening to Nickleback.
21 Fans of more tribal sub genres such as Psy-Trance and Screamo remain more likely to gravitate towards a specific dress code.

the lyrics. The listener leant back to listen to the album, letting the music wash over them. It was both lean back and an immersive experience. For youth in the 1950', 1960's and 1970's a record player and a radio were most often the only entertainment sources they had in their bedrooms, while the TV in the living room had a limited number of channels and even less programming that would interest them. By the 1980's TVs and computers began to enter many teenagers' bedrooms and by the mid 1990's the seeds had been sown for a media landscape that would push music into the role of supporting actor in youth entertainment. The new computer games and youth orientated TV shows that were ever more shaping teenagers' identity were also soaking up their attention on a growing number of devices they personally owned, including TVs, portable music players, games consoles and personal computers. And of course it was not just teenagers' attention that was getting swept up by the onrushing entertainment tidal wave. All people were spending more time with more media across more platforms than ever before, a trend that continues to accelerate today.

More people now listen to more music than ever before, but it competes much more fiercely with other forms of entertainment. Just as the iPod evolved from a monochrome screen device that only played music into the multi-media, colour screen iPad, so consumers' personal entertainment has become equally diverse. People always had access to different forms of entertainment around the home, but the increase in personal technology ownership since the mid 1990's has transformed consumers' personal entertainment mix. The computer, TV, games console and phone all evolved from household devices to personal devices. Smartphones, tablets and laptops all enabled consumers to build rich personal entertainment experiences that are no longer tied to the household technology. Crucially, from the music industry's perspective, these devices have enabled audiences to access entertainment that differs fundamentally from music: namely lean-forward experiences whereas music is still inherently a lean-back experience. PC and console games, the internet, smartphone apps, connected TVs all deliver entertainment that demands consumers' full attention while music does not. Instead music can just play in the background to these activities. Thus music has become relegated to the role of backing track to our modern digital lives. The proliferation of devices we can listen to music on has helped music become the soundtrack to the gym, work, travel, reading, to browsing the web on our PCs, playing games on our consoles, to messaging on our phones.

Columns of Competition: Scarcity

With music downgrading to a second tier entertainment format, consumers began to question whether it should therefore cost less, or even nothing at all. After all if it is just there to be played in the background, why should it be a premium product? This was the crucible into which Napster had arrived, giving real word substance to esoteric considerations about whether music should be paid for anymore. To the consumer, the change was virtually all upside: Napster had an infinitely larger catalogue than any record store could stock, the music was delivered instantly without having to leave home and it was totally free. Sure the audio quality was often not great but this was the birth of the generation for whom convenience quickly trumped all else. Napster's unprecedented user experience created a new type of music consumer, characterised by two key behaviours:

- Sampling: with the price tag removed, consumers were no longer limited by their level of disposable income. P2P users started downloading much larger quantities of music than they could ever have paid for. Initially slower home internet speeds meant that most of the downloads were single tracks or albums, but nowadays, with most homes in major music markets having high speed broadband, P2P users will often download an artist's entire back catalogue as a single download. File sharing is the manifestation of base human instinct. If the shop doors on the high street and mall were flung open for people to take whatever they want for free, people would fill their trollies to bursting point. The same happened with music piracy as Roger Faxon observed: "Piracy is an expression of hoarding, we have grown up to perceive music as a scarce good. The whole psychology of music consumption has changed." Hoarding in turn accelerated the diversification of musical tastes because music fans are able to sample so much more music so easily. Some P2P users use file sharing to filter out what they will then go on to buy, but many more simply use it instead of purchasing. Whatever the net impact on music sales though, what is inarguable is that file sharing exposed more people to more music than had ever been the case before.

- Cherry picking: from the late 1950's record labels had progressively shifted their business from one built around singles to one based upon album sales. Over time artists quickly came to recognize the album as a creative construct, and so today most artists and record labels alike still consider the album as the beating heart of the music business. The problem is that most digital consumers no longer feel the same. File sharing gave consumers the ability to disassemble an album, skipping the filler tracks and heading straight for the killer tracks they actually wanted. In the CD era albums had become bloated with the average number of tracks simply reflecting how much music could physically be squeezed onto a CD. In the vinyl era artists had settled for four or five tracks per side of an LP because that is what the physical capacity of vinyl enabled. But with CDs suddenly track listings stretched to 14, 15, 16 songs per album because the format could accommodate the additional tracks, and inevitably this rush to fill space resulted in a dilution in the quality of music. Quantity trumped quality, ironically at the exact same time quality of audio fidelity was in the ascendency so that the rising curve of one passed the curve of the other as it plummeted earthwards. File sharing, and later legitimate download stores like iTunes, put power into the hand of the consumer and allowed them to push aside the carefully constructed filler tracks. The album had become the dominant format because in a wholly controlled, scarcity-based market the record labels and retailers could determine it to be so. In the digital era, scarcity and control fell away to leave the album exposed and vulnerable like a carcass in a desert, to be picked away at.

Piracy's utter desecration of recorded music scarcity compounded the effects of Identity Competition and Attention Competition to send music's perceived monetary value plunging to the bottom. Music still matters, it still helps define who we are and we still spend lots of time listening to it, but because it is now so easily available the sense that it should be free spreads like an infection. When a consumer chooses between a $0.99 single track download and a free single track download, the free one will always win the value-for-money argument hands down. The static audio file is no longer scarce and therefore no longer has inherent monetary value. The consumers who do choose to pay $0.99 may do so for a multitude of reasons, such as: wanting to do the right thing, for the convenience of it working seamlessly on their device, for fear of getting a virus from P2P networks etc. But it is no longer because they have to.

Music has become utterly ubiquitous with the contagion of free achieving truly epidemic proportions. Charging consumers for a product that they can get just as easily, even sometimes more easily, for free is a hard sell in anyone's book. Many other media industries though have either found their scarcity less directly impacted by piracy or are doing a better job of learning how to protect it. The movie theatre experience with all of its popcorn and soda trappings and inherently social character continues to be scarce despite P2P networks filling up with movie downloads. Games consoles with their closed operating systems and proprietary controllers remain the only place consumers can actually play console games, even though consumers can easily find pirated games online. So although piracy meant the death of scarcity for recorded music products it has not been so for all other forms of media, at least not yet.

None of this though should be mistaken as a collapse in the emotional worth of music, after all some of the most valuable things in life are often free at point of consumption: water, air etc. This point is well illustrated by the comments of a young teenager who was interviewed as part of a UK Music focus group on file sharing. The teenager was asked why he was downloading music free, whether that meant that he didn't care about music, whether music did not really matter to him. His response was: "If I could download my Nike then I would pay for my music."[22] Thus music often emotionally matters more than other products but because it can be free, so many consumers decide that it will be free.

This disconnect between the fan's emotional attachment to music and the willingness to pay is one of the key paradoxes of the digital era and it is a problem that the business is yet to truly crack. It is a point made by Elio Leoni Sceti who was CEO of EMI between 2008 and 2010: "The music industry never made the link between excitement and intention to purchase. They did not know how to turn good fans into consumers. Purchase intent is just not in the lingo of the industry. They know how to excite and engage but not how to drive purchase."

Columns of Competition: Wallet Share

Competition for Attention from other products and services still protected by scarcity, and therefore that must be paid for, conspired to create a perfect storm for music spending. The net result of this is people spending less of their disposable income on music, this is the fourth column of competition: Wallet Share.

People are not spending less money on music because they can no longer afford it, quite the contrary. In the US total consumer expenditure on entertainment rose by 89% between 1990 and 2009.[23] Nor is it that youth cannot afford to buy music anymore. Young people now have more disposable income than was the case for any previous generation. In Sweden for example, under 20's had 34% more disposable income in 2010 than they did in 1991.[24] In fact it is not even that people are not spending money on music either: global live music and music merchandise revenues grew by 358% between 1990 and 2012.[25] People are spending less money on recorded music because they can do so without impacting their ability to get music and they are spending the money they save on other media and lifestyle expenditure choices. Consumers' wallets are getting bigger but there are more demands on them, and thus music's share gets smaller. Music now has to compete against broadband and cell phone charges, Pay TV, mobile apps and countless other new and emerging regular expenditure. Add this to the rise in consumer spending on personal technology such as laptops, smartphones and tablets and the room left for music spending is narrow at the extreme. Expenditure on recorded music has declined both in real terms and relative to other forms of entertainment spending. In the US, music sales decreased by 1.1% between 2010 and 2012, while total entertainment expenditure

22 As quoted by then UK Music CEO Feargal Sharkey speaking on a panel at music industry conference London Calling in 2008.
23 US Census Bureau.
24 Statistics Sweden.
25 Pollstar, IFPI, MIDiA Research estimates.

increased by 4% over the same period, so in relative terms music lost revenue and share.[26] Music has not kept up with changing media expenditure trends where others have managed to fare much more favourably. Declining wallet share is both the symptom and the effect of the competing combination of Identity, Attention and Scarcity. Music matters to people, but its role in their lives has changed immutably as has their perception of it as a paid for commodity.

Competing for the Consumer

Changing consumer behaviour transformed recorded music from premium product to free utility. But the transformation would not have occurred at anything like such a destructive pace if it had not been for the rise of piracy to meet the sea change in consumer demand. The epithet 'being in the right place at the right time' does not come close to describing the supreme serendipity of online piracy's perfect timing. But as fortuitously timed as piracy's arrival was, the role it acquired was far from accidental. In a continual circle of influence and influenced, piracy became the manifestation of rapidly changing cultural and consumption patterns, simultaneously shaping and responding to consumer demand. Piracy was an accelerant sprayed on the already furiously burning blaze, the catalyst for consumers' changing relationship with music. By destroying Scarcity, piracy enables consumers to move seamlessly from Attention competition to Wallet Share competition. Because piracy removes the need to buy, consumers can shift their entertainment spend elsewhere and still get all the music they want, and in fact usually get more, much more. Thus while some engaged music fans learned to appreciate file sharing as a discovery complement to music spending, the Wallet Share shift for many file sharers was absolute, with music spending going from full to zero. This in turn means that recorded music's ever diminishing share of consumer spending has actually helped drive the boom in other content types: because consumers are spending less on music, they have more money to spend on other media. Instead of just being a symptom of changing consumer preferences, Wallet Share competition has become a direct output of the rise of piracy. The music industry's loss has been other media industries' gain. Also it is important to note that not all the lost spend has disappeared out of the music business, with some of it simply shifting to scarce music products like live and merchandize. In fact between 2008 and 2013 global live revenues grew by 10%.[27] Why? Because live remains a truly scarce experience.

Though it is too simplistic to argue that piracy is the sole cause of declining music spending, it has played a central role throughout. While piracy went from strength to strength music sales fell year by year. All of the Four Columns of Competition have driven the process but piracy has been the fuel in the engine.

---

26 Music spending (IFPI) refers to actual spending on music products i.e. exclusive of synchronization revenues. Entertainment expenditure refers to average annual consumer expenditure on entertainment (US Bureau of Labor Statistics).
27 Informa Media and Telecoms.

Music Everywhere But Nowhere

Piracy is not the only source of free music that has been consistently placing downward pressure on music spending. Free music from legal sources played an even more pervasive role in the deterioration of music spending. The rise in legal free music mirrors that of online piracy, surging since the early 1990's. It comes from multiple sources:

- Synchronization strategies: While recorded music revenues plummeted, publishing revenues – the income from the songwriters' rights – prospered. Music publishing's boom has been driven by synchronization strategies, namely licensing music to be played in different media, such as adverts, TV shows, movies and console games. It is an act that the record labels have been quick to get into too, culminating in global record label revenues of $300 million in 2013.[28] Music Supervisors – the people at games companies, TV shows and movie companies who select music for their media –have quickly become the new A&R guys of the 21st century music business. But the result of the synchronisation strategy is that there is much more music around us much more of the time and in many more places. Though the fact these revenues represent just 2% of recorded music income raises the question of whether the detrimental impact on music spending is justified by the comparatively modest revenue. For publishers it was for a long time a much more robust business case, with synchronization revenue representing a core direct revenue stream in which they were not subject to the whims of record label sales performance. In more recent years though they also have seen reason to question the strategy as they feel the effects of declining mechanical royalties due to the fall in music sales.

- Digital radio: With the advent of satellite radio in the US, Digital Audio Broadcast (DAB) in Europe and internet radio across the globe, it is far easier for audiences to find radio stations that play more music that is more suited to their tastes more of the time. Traditional radio broadcasters always had to sacrifice targeting, instead pumping the same music to all of their audiences at once. Digital broadcasters have no such problem. The costs of launching highly targeted online-only radio stations can be a tiny fraction of the cost of building an analogue terrestrial station. And though the infrastructure costs of other digital platforms such as satellite radio and DAB are significant, they give broadcasters far greater targeting capabilities than terrestrial broadcasting. No longer do broadcasters have to play a 'safe' selection of songs to keep a majority of listeners content, instead they can build genre and culture specialized stations to reach specific audiences. Whereas terrestrial radio programming leaves most listeners happy some of the time, digital radio can keep most of the people happy most of the time. Personalized radio services like Pandora take the equation to another level, allowing the listener to actually shape what they get to hear.[29] Interestingly the music industry has a conflicted view on the impact of radio on music sales. Half of a typical label's staff will argue that without the promotional power of radio fewer people would discover and buy music while the other half will argue that they lose sales to people who simply listen to music radio instead of purchasing. The issue is so complex because both sides of the argument are true.

---

28 IFPI Recording Industry in Numbers 2013.
29 An often cited counter argument to the user benefits of personalized radio stations is that such a high degree of tailoring the music to the listener's taste weakens the serendipitous discovery value that programmed radio can deliver. That the listener effectively narrows his listening horizons.

- Music TV channels: Most leading music markets now have mature multichannel pay TV sectors and also strong free-to-air multichannel TV offerings. A consequence of this is that the majority of homes in these countries have one or more dedicated music TV channels, often with a range of genre choices to select from. These are typically programmed by genre, providing audiences with music video that closely matches their tastes, free at point of consumption.

- Music TV shows: One of the success stories of the music industry in recent years has been the rise of TV talent shows such as the X Factor, Incroyable Talent and American Idol. These shows have done a fantastic job of building communities around the featured acts and even driving music sales and establishing artist careers thereafter. They create deep emotional ties between the audience and the artists, often resulting in mass market music audiences feeling more engaged with music than they ever did in the CD era. But while doing so, these shows also deliver yet more free music straight into people's homes. Although for some shows such as the X Factor this is partially compensated with a music sales push at the end of the series, this remains a relatively small component of what can be a 30 episode season of shows.[30] In fact there is so much music content concentrated over a show's season that for the mainstream audiences that watch them there is little appetite left for any further music. They glut on such shows and then top up with radio.

- Online services: In addition to all of these sources, music fans can now access vast catalogues of free music legally online from YouTube and Vevo primarily, but also from the free tiers of services like Spotify, Deezer and Rdio. YouTube in particular has become the world's most popular digital music service, used frequently by hundreds of millions. Perhaps even more importantly, YouTube presents a discovery and consumption safety net: even the most mainstream of consumers know that if they want to find a song it will be on YouTube. It is the fall back option for most of the world's connected music fans. Before YouTube P2P was the safety net for digital music consumers, so at least the transition has been from free and no industry income, to free and modest industry income.

For the more engaged music fan, some or all of these free music alternatives are used in addition to music buying, and in the best case scenario they even help them discover new music that they pay for. But for the more passive music fans the cumulative effect of this spread of legal free music is to give them fewer reasons to buy music because all of these are enough in themselves. In the analogue era passive music fans would have bought a couple of albums a year, often on impulse. The Four Columns of Competition have weakened passive music fans' relationship with music spending, to the extent that the ubiquity of legal free music has become the perfect music consumption fit for these consumers. The definition of a casual music consumer has changed forever. In some ways the effects of legal free music are farther reaching than online piracy. Whereas the latter is largely the domain of the tech savvy and the young, legal free music permeates all consumers' lives and affects the mainstream the most.

---

30 X Factor UK had 31 main shows in 2012 in addition to companion programmes on sister channels.

CONCLUSION: After the High Water Mark

In the 1980's and 1990's music reached a high water mark, an apogee. But while music sales continued to boom in the 1990's the decline had already started in the part of the equation that really mattered: audiences' engagement with music. By then the competition for time, money and attention was in full swing, so that when piracy and synchronization strategies came to the fore, they accelerated nascent trends that were already bubbling furiously just beneath the surface. The boom years of music sales pushed up the average level of music IQ and engagement, now paradoxically as more people are exposed to more music than ever before, it is creeping back down again. Scarcity of music is gone for good, as is the dominant share of cultural identity that music once claimed. But neither of these need represent a death knell for recorded music, instead they provide the context for creating the next era of the music business. One that must be built on entirely different assumptions and precepts. The rest of this book looks at how the music industry has begun to learn and accept this reality, and how in the words of science fiction author William Gibson: "The future is already here, it's just not very evenly distributed."

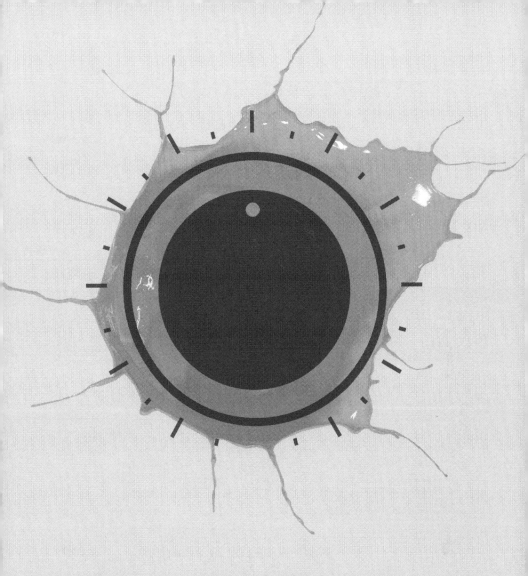

Part 2:
The Digital Era

Awakening by Mark Mulligan

Chapter 4: The Consumer's Story

The Transition Generation

Napster's users were at the vanguard of change. They carved out new territory and established new rules as they went along, but their worldview was inexorably shaped by the physical era. They had grown up buying CDs in high street stores and playing those CDs in Hi-Fis and boom boxes. Even though they quickly learned new behaviours and rapidly evolved their outlook, these were Digital Immigrants and as such fundamentally they were a Transition Generation. For these consumers the journey from physical to digital was an inherently progressive one, tempered by the process of comprehending new concepts, most notably the shift from tangible ownership to a more ethereal notion of access. The Transition Generation's shift to digital is thus peppered with analogue artefacts. The vast majority of them have not yet been able to make the complete break from physical: nearly half of digital music buyers still regularly buy CDs.[1]   Going completely digital is clearly still something of a daunting prospect even for digital music buyers. There remains something important to these consumers about the tangible presence of the CD and indeed of vinyl, despite the obvious benefits of digital. There is also an argument to be had that the very fact these 20 and 30 somethings make up the majority of digital music buyers is an indication of transitional behaviour, that buying music is still the natural reference point of music fans who grew up in the analogue era. Moreover, the digital technology that was being built in the 1990's and the 2000's, and to a large degree today also, is built by that self same Transition Generation. Thus digital music has been shaped by the Transition Generation on both the supply and on the demand side.

The technology this Transition Generation adopted was, although ground-breaking, nonetheless transition technology. Napster, MP3.com, MusicNet were all transition technologies that helped bridge the divide between analogue and digital, with an eye on the digital future but a foot firmly planted in the analogue past. Even the iTunes Store, and the music download more generally, is a transition technology, combining the solid and reassuring analogue era concept of ownership with the convenience and immediacy of digital. In many respects the download is little more than e-commerce with a twist: just like the CD, it is an example of the transactional ownership model, and thus it is a natural product evolution path for Transition Generation consumers. It is a point made by Spotify's Ken Park: "iTunes was the first great user experience that had been sold but it was the old product in a new bottle: selling units" and supported by Roger Faxon's observation: "I do not believe we have yet crossed the digital border. iTunes is a duplicate of the physical business, the behavior and economics are the same, but disembodied." To be clear, the tag 'transition' is neither a derogatory nor a demeaning one, it is simply placing the appropriate historical context on events. All new technology looks more like what came before than it does what will come. The first cars were steam-powered carriages, entirely similar in design to horse drawn carriages except for the absence of the horse. Henry Ford's

---

[1]   MIDiA Research Consumer Survey December 2013, UK only.

Model T was the first mass produced car but it too looked much more similar to a horse drawn carriage than a modern car. By the 1930's some of the more expensive cars started to sport the luxurious, elegant lines of the modern automotive aesthetic. But it was not until the 1950's that truly modern, aerodynamic curves and lines began to appear. In contemporary cars the transformation is complete, with the four wheels and seats being the only fixed link with their equine powered past. This is how technology evolves and digital music technology is no different. The $0.99 download is the 1930's luxury car on the evolution path: it is forward looking, with a firm foothold in the past and is fundamentally niche in appeal. By 2013 only 26% of global recorded music revenue came from download sales,[2] with digital download buyers as just 17% of all consumers.[3] Thus the digital download is a transition product that only appeals to a small subset of consumers and even for the vast majority of them it is not good enough to convince them to ditch CD buying entirely. Little wonder then that digital music revenues continue to grow more slowly than CD sales contract in most global music markets.

The Post-CD Collapse

The situation is further complicated by the fact that Transition Generation consumers are beginning to run out of places to play their little shiny discs. Car manufacturers such as Ford have already started phasing CD players out of their cars and the fastest growing part of the personal computer market – the tablet – does not have a CD player, nor do many newer laptops such as Ultrabooks. In the living room, consumer expenditure has shifted firmly from audio to video. This contrasts starkly with the 1980's and much of the 1990's when consumers would replace their Hi-Fi simply because the manufacturers had changed the colour scheme of their product ranges. By the 2000's the home Hi-Fi market was in tatters.[4] Yet during the same period the TV market enjoyed a period of unprecedented prosperity. As consumers were scaling back their spending on Hi-Fi equipment, the TV got progressively bigger and more expensive, and the pile of devices underneath it – which confusingly continue to be called 'set-top boxes' even though no TV now is wide enough to balance much more than a pen on top of it – grew and grew. As a direct corollary of the Four Columns of Competition, entertainment hardware expenditure has shifted firmly from the Hi-Fi to the TV. Now the average living room has a large wide screen TV with multiple boxes. But where a shiny new Hi-Fi once sat as the pride of the living room, there now sits either a dusty old midi system, a docking station or worse still an empty space because the stereo has gone into the bin or into storage. Added to this mix is the fact that music retailers have all but disappeared from the mall and the high street in many cities in the US and Europe. Bit by bit the CD is disappearing out of people's lives.

---

2 IFPI Recording Industry in Numbers 2013.
3 Average aggregate figure from various consumer surveys including NPD, Kantar and MIDiA Research.
4 During the 1980's and 1990's consumer electronics companies went through a series of home audio replacement cycles with colour being a key component of the transition, changing from chrome, to black, briefly to white and then back to chrome. Other factors did of course play a role: such as moving from the flat 'sound system' design to the vertical 'stacking Hi-Fi' tower approach; twin cassette decks; and CD players. The late 1980's and early 1990's also saw a boom in the audio separates business, with manufacturers selling higher spec, more expensive individual Hi-Fi units such as CD players and amplifiers. This model still exists in the super high-end audio-file segment, but as the mainstream separates market slowed, mass market manufacturers soon returned to the all-in-one approach with 'midi' systems, which remain in market today alongside docking stations.

But as foreboding the impact of this change on the Transition Generation might be, there is another group of consumers that is much more immediately vulnerable: the Fading Buyers. At least Transition Generation consumers are on the digital path, they know where to go and how to get there when the CD disappears out of their lives. But they are not the mass market; the vast majority of consumers however have not gone digital at all in terms of music buying with more than fourth fifths of all consumers not buying digital music.[5] Though there are some ardent CD aficionados among these consumers, the lion's share of them are passive buyers who are becoming increasingly disengaged from music purchasing. Though they represent the majority of music buyers they massively under perform in terms of spend. For example in the UK the bottom 60% of music buyers account for just 20% of music spending.[6] On average these consumers only buy a CD or two a year and are already teetering on the brink of not buying at all. Many have already fallen out of the habit of buying music entirely and these Fading Buyers have shown little or no interest in starting to buy digital music and much more typically stop buying music entirely rather than transition from the CD. The passive music consumer typically used to still be a music buyer, but that is no longer necessarily the case.

The cumulative effect is that we are sat on the verge of a Post-CD Collapse. For the Transition Generation who have already started to go digital, the growing inconvenience of being a CD user will help nudge them more quickly to going entirely digital. But for the Fading Buyers, the next stage of this digitization process, the route is as inevitable as it is obvious: the majority of music buyers will simply stop buying because there is no simple, convenient transition path for them. This does not mean that the majority of music revenues will disappear with them – they are after all low value customers – nor does it mean that all of them will be lost for good. There is even an argument that the music industry may be better off without these expensive to reach, low value customers. But make no mistake, their departure will be a massive speed bump for the music industry, and even those customers who have the potential to start buying again will not be won back easily. Besides the sizeable challenge of convincing them of the virtues of digital, the effects of the Four Columns of Competition will ensure that most of these newly lost music buyers will hardly even notice a change in their lives. They will still get most of the music they want without needing to buy the occasional CD nor even listen to one. Stopping buying will not be a dramatic life style decision, instead one day they will simply realize that they just do not buy CDs anymore. The next inevitable step is to question why they even have that dusty old Hi-Fi in the living room anymore, and once that is gone, the music industry will have, for the first time since the advent of the gramophone, lost its foothold in the living room.

The Demographic Pincer Movement

As if grappling with its older customers disappearing was not enough for the music industry, it has found itself simultaneously under attack from the opposite demographic direction. While the Transition Generation were furiously immersing themselves in the internet and learning entirely new ways to consume music, a new generation was emerging that had none of the analogue trappings of those transition consumers. Consumers born from the late 1990's onwards are truly children of the digital era. Their cultural and lifestyle reference points are shaped and defined by digital technology. These Digital Natives have not known a world without high speed broad band, mobile data, touch screen devices and unlimited on-demand access to virtually every piece of media on the planet for no cost whatsoever. Whereas the Transition Generation – both consumers and technologists – rooted all of its behaviours and

5   MIDIA Research Consumer Survey November 2013, UK only
6   MIDIA Research from Kantar World Panel / BPI.

expectations in analogue era reference points, the Digital Natives have no such baggage. The consequence of this is that these young consumers' digital expectations are markedly higher; technology that is greeted enthusiastically by Transition Generation consumers may not even pass muster for the Digital Natives.[7] As a consumer force Digital Natives act as a catalyst for accelerated change, and increasingly many are becoming active participants across music technology value chains as young entrepreneurs and developers. The problem for the music industry though, is that these new emerging behaviours and expectations also lack a crucial tenet of the analogue era: namely that recorded music is something to be paid for.

Whereas previous generations of youth developed a keen sense of the monetary value of music, saving their pocket money to buy singles and albums, music has always been both ubiquitous and free for Digital Natives. While older music fans who stopped buying music or buy less changed their habits, these younger consumers never had to rely upon paying for music to get it. This does not mean that Digital Natives do not pay for music at all, indeed a solid share of them do, what it does mean though is that their perceptions of music as a paid for commodity are dramatically different. Those Digital Natives who do want to buy music find themselves stranded between product choices: on the one hand the CD is yesterday's product but on the other buying digital downloads requires a credit card, something which youth typically do not have. Access to parents' iTunes accounts and digital music gift cards have helped soften the blow but the fundamental dynamic remains. Faced with the combination of ubiquitous free music and poorly accessible paid music it is not surprising that Digital Natives have proven to be relatively disinterested music buyers. The potential consequences for the music industry are clear: unless the Digital Natives start to develop a heritage of paying for music by the time their spending power increases then there will be a gaping hole in music spending that will make the current downturn in music sales look like a mere blip. In essence a demographic time bomb is ticking for recorded music revenues: as Fading Buyers seep out of the market, Digital Natives are not coming 'on stream' in order to offset the decline. The net result of which is to leave recorded music revenues overly dependent on the remaining rump of music buyers: the Transition Generation. This is the demographic pincer movement that threatens to envelop the music industry (see Figure 8).

---

7   An interesting illustration of how the expectations of even the youngest Digital Natives outpace the product development capabilities of technology companies is found with TV retailers. Many of whom now keep extra stocks of screen cleaners to wipe off the TV screens the fingerprints of young children who expect the picture to swoosh across in response to a swipe of their fingers. For the Transition Generation improvements in touch screen technology are greeted with appreciation, but for many Digital Natives the worldview is that devices which do not have touch screens are simply outdated and inferior. Indeed the TV itself is no longer the video consumption device of choice for Digital Natives, that is a role now performed by tablets and laptops which give them the power to watch what they want, when they want, without restrictions and limits on their behaviour.

FIGURE 8

Music Spending is Buckling Under a Demographic Pincer Movement

Music Spending

Digital Natives are growing up without a heritage of buying music

Older consumers are stopping buying music as the CD dies

The Digital Natives are post-scarcity consumers who do not see the Four Columns of Competition as competition but instead simply as facets of everyday life. While Transition Generation consumers grapple with the move from ownership to access, these young consumers have very different concepts of ownership and value. Access and convenience are more valuable to them than ownership and quality, a point made by Keith Harris: "Too much emphasis in the piracy debate was put on people getting music simply because they could, rather than on the fact that it was far more convenient."

During the 1980's and 1990's music consumers were collectively educated in the value of audio quality with the shift from compact cassette to CD and higher spec Hi-Fis. Digital Natives though have grown up listening to often poor quality digital music on headphones, a listening environment where many of the audio artefacts of poor quality audio are often less apparent. [8] It would be inaccurate to suggest that ownership of music does not matter to them, but their sense of ownership is distinct from that of previous generations. Ownership for them is not measured in terms of rows of CDs or LPs on a shelf that have been slowly acquired over many years, but instead digital files on their hard drives or in the cloud. Files that have been

8   Lossy audio codecs such as MP3 and ACC compress audio using a process called perceptual coding that removes portions of the sound that are not as easily heard by the human ear. Often these occur at frequencies that are outside of, or at the limits of, the frequency response of low and mid price range headphones.

downloaded in an instant and that can be deleted just as quickly to make way for a new batch of music files. As Oleg Fomenko, CEO of streaming service Bloom.FM, put it: "I used to measure my music collection in terms of Roubles but digital pirates measure it in terms of gigabytes and now terabytes." And because all the music in the world is instantly available, the only consequence of deleting tranches of music is the slight inconvenience of having to download it again. For many Digital Natives even having files reside on a hard drive is an increasingly bygone concept, gauging ownership instead in terms of playlists, bookmarks and access to thousands of digital music files. In these digital contexts of ownership there is no monetary concern or risk of unavailability. Because purchasing has become decoupled from ownership for Digital Natives it is hardly surprising that as the cloud becomes more robust and reliable the majority of them do not pay for subscription services but instead have YouTube as their music app of choice, with 64% of them now using it to listen to music.[9] While Transition Generation consumers spend $9.99 a month to listen to streaming audio from Spotify et al, the Digital Natives have gone the whole post-scarcity distance, accessing a vastly bigger catalogue for absolutely no monetary cost whatsoever. Of course the diminished spending power of Digital Natives plays some role but it is not just the absence of cost that makes YouTube so appealing to them: it is a truly digital era product, with video and social functionality that allows them to dive into sight and sound in a way that they simply cannot on audio-only streaming services. Digital Natives have already voted with their feet: video must be at the core of future music product experiences.

The impact on the evolution of music format adoption is stark: while all previous music formats have heralded an unprecedented surge in recorded music revenue digital has instead overseen a revenue drain (see Figure 9). With each previous major music format the successor format was fully in the ascendency by the time its predecessor was in its death throes. No such succession path ensued for digital, at least not for the part which consumers pay for. Instead the demise of the CD has been painfully prolonged while paid for digital products have only managed to capture a fragment of consumers' digital music activity. While previous music formats drove genuine format replacement cycles at scale, digital has presided over a death of mass-market music formats.

FIGURE 9

CDs Continue To Dominate Music Sales Due To Digital's Failure To Drive A Format Replacement Cycle

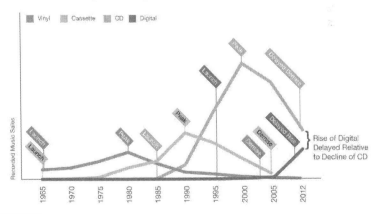

Convenience and the Age of the Empowered Consumer

The product attributes that were used to sell music in the analogue era – audio quality, reliability, trustworthiness etc. – are still cited as reasons to use legal services over unlicensed alternatives. Consumers are reminded that music from the likes of Apple, Deezer and Amazon are high quality files with no risk of a virus, unlike online piracy. The problem is that those factors are incontrovertibly trumped by the convenience factor. Convenience has been the unifying character trait of the digital revolutionaries. Whether it be downloading an entire artist's musical history in one file; having virtually every music video ever made at the swipe of a finger; skipping the filler tracks from an album; or creating a playlist from tens of millions of songs, convenience is the key. Paid music services play the convenience card too, but while that card may trump products, it rarely matches the convenience factor of that ace in the convenience pack: free.[10] Convenience has empowered music fans in the digital era, putting them in charge while music industry control ebbs away. The value of digital music destinations, particularly illegal ones, has become measured in convenience rather than quality, and as a consequence digital music has too often become highly convenient but devoid of monetary value.

CONCLUSION: Digital Era Consumers Demand Digital Era Experiences

The Transition Generation were both the fuel and the engine of the first phase of the music industry's digital transition. But the growing influence and scale of the Digital Natives create an entirely different set of parameters within which the digital market must grow. These consumers have not learned digital freedom of choice, they were born into it and their power and influence is increasingly pervasive. A certain type of company culture puts the customer first, and builds everything around the customer's need. That has not been the cultural heritage of the music industry but it will increasingly need to become it. When the baseline is competing against free, the legal alternatives have to be as convenient as they possibly can be with as few steps to meet a consumer's needs as possible. When digital music products are not convenient, the empowered digital consumers simply stay away, forcing them out of the market. This is what happened to DRM, it is what happened to Pressplay and MusicNet, and it is what is ultimately going to happen to the CD because the demise of the playback technology will render the format inconvenient for the masses. Currently there is still too much distance between emerging consumer behaviour and emerging digital music services. That gap needs bridging with haste. Digital era consumers expect digital era experiences, not analogue era products squeezed into digital wrappers.

---

10 I am indebted to my former Forrester colleague James McQuivey who pioneered research and analysis around the impact of convenience on digital products and services, creating a concept called the Convenience Quotient published in various Forrester Research reports. The Convenience Quotient measures the appeal of a product using the formula that the Convenience Quotient = benefits minus barriers. This analysis provides the grounding for this subsection.

Chapter 5: The Record Labels' Story

Turning the Oil Tanker

While Napster was transforming consumers' relationships with music consumption, the business of selling music remained all but intact. In 2003 Peter Jamieson, then chairman of the UK music industry body the BPI, argued that the record labels understood that change was necessary but they needed time to adapt. He likened the labels to an oil tanker, a vast craft with such inherent momentum that it requires a mile's notice to be able to turn to change course. The observation was accurate and prophetic in equal measure. This was a business that was full of analogue era anomalies and was ripe for disruption with implications right across the value chain. One such factor was the labels' obsession with market share, a preoccupation that Cliff Fluet suggested was often counter productive: "When execs became compensated by reference to market share the behaviour appeared to change. The mentality became about creating the biggest splash or creating blockbusters. So we ended up with £1m videos for records that cost £250,000 to make. We appeared to be paying so much money to get our music in the stores, costs for creating megahits became gargantuan. The superstars paid for everyone else." This focus on market share over profitability and overall revenue was the product of a highly predictable market enjoying long-term growth. Risk could always be taken today because tomorrow would pay back at twice the rate. Though not exactly the most responsible of business models it could nonetheless operate reasonably well in a bull market and the labels keenly understood that the walls would quickly come tumbling down if the music business transformed into a bear market.

Thus the labels became locked into a process of fighting to retain control, with the legal action against Napster and MyMP3.com focused on preventing digital copyright precedents that would have threatened that control. Roger Faxon described the worldview: "The music industry is based upon exclusive rights of distribution which created an extremely profitable business. The loss of control over the distribution of the content threatened the foundation of the industry." Underpinning the control of distribution was control of copyright. In the finite confines of the analogue era, copyright could be enforced highly effectively but in the boundless expanse of the digital world true control of copyright was gone for good even if the labels' business models did not recognize the fact. According to Fluet: "Copyright creates an illusion of control. Record labels' obsession with ownership of the master recordings was akin to the veneration of the Ark of the Covenant." The fight to regain control continues to be fought keenly even now but as Elio Leoni Sceti observed it is ultimately a futile one: "The old model was to push product to the channel but piracy got in the way. The digital channel is not a channel. It is a place. Consumers define and change their preferences there. There is no chance of controlling the channel, instead you influence consumers' decisions by putting relevant products into that space."

The record labels nonetheless remain convinced that it was a battle that could be won and the control culture strategy all too easily created the pantomime villain against which the emerging digital innovators could pit themselves. Napster and MP3.com saw themselves freeing music from the archaic chains of a Jurassic industry that was best hastened into hyper-evolution, or failing that, extinction. Their ideological goading inevitably succeeded in hardening the position of the labels and confirming the assumptions of the digital sceptics within them. It also defined the terms of the marketplace dialogue, casting Napster et al as Robin Hood characters and the labels as the malevolent Sherriff of Nottingham. Because the digital upstarts were part of the internet world it was only logical that internet media coverage biased strongly to their position. It was a dynamic that remains true today, with blogs, forums and the online tech press viewing the music industry debate through the Robin Hood prism. By contrast the record labels had virtually no online voice and still have little of one now. This left the record labels with antagonistic adversaries with the full weight of internet propaganda and bias behind them. This was the emergence of the free-economy bias of the web.

These factors alone would have been basis enough for digital deadlock, but coupled with the analogue-only worldview of senior label executives the digital market was doomed to have its early days defined by legal conflict and recrimination. Even in the early days of digital though, a change in outlook was emerging, thanks in large part to the parent companies of many of the majors. This was particularly true for UMG and BMG, where the parent company chief executives Jean-Marie Messier and Thomas Middlehoff were embarking on bold digital strategies for their media and technology powerhouses in which music was expected to play a key role. The fact that Messier and Middlehoff's vision and decisions were shaped by the needs of multiple business types, including pure internet businesses, gave their vision a digital edge that most traditional label executives did not have at that time. Similarly AOL's acquisition of Warner had given that major a distinctly digital agenda, while Sony Music was owned by the CE giant Sony Electronics. Thus by the turn of the millennium one could have been forgiven for thinking that the corporate ownership of most of the major record labels augured well for a vibrant epoch of digital renewal. But the theory did not translate into practice. Instead, the dominance of the CD business model would neuter major digital strategy for the next five years.

The Ringtone Boom and Bust

While online was proving to be an epically proportioned thorn in the side of the labels, one part of digital opened up new opportunities for music publishers: mobile ring tones. The first generation of ringtones, so called monophonic and polyphonic ringtones,[11] were synthesized versions of songs rather than the original song itself. This was crucial from a record label perspective because it meant that no royalty was due to them as owners of the recorded work, instead of music publishers, the owners of the rights to the underlying composition, were due royalty payments. However the publishers initially did not exactly welcome ringtones with open arms and the companies pioneering the new market quickly found that the music publishers were just as sceptical of digital as their label counterparts. Arguably the founding father of the global ringtones business was Ralph Simon. Looking at the growing popularity of the emerging un-licensed ring tone sector and the early success of ringtones in South Korea, Simon started Yourmobile [later renamed Moviso] in 1999. The company went onto become the first ever commercial ringtone business outside of South Korea but only after having first navigated treacherous licensing waters as Simon explained: "Trying to get publishing rights was very difficult, if not impossible. We approached all the music publishers in the USA, but none would give us a licence. Shaun Fanning had appeared on the cover of Time Magazine heralding the birth of Napster, so music publishers were spooked and worried about the piracy that Fanning had unleashed. Everyone had views on digital and the threat of piracy - the response was,

11 Monophonic refers to the sound generator only being able to play a single note at any one time, polyphonic refers to being able to play multiple note simultaneously.

lock the doors, don't let them in. We got comments like 'there's so much piracy that we're not going to license to you. We're going to wait to see how the market develops.'" Simon kept on in the hunt around for licenses from the major publishers but the pattern of rejection continued until he finally made headway with Sony ATV: "Sony ATV was the only publisher who said 'yes, OK, we want to license ring tones, this is the future'. After getting Sony ATV, which included the Beatles, we got the other publishers - but it took nearly two years. Most of the holdouts were old school publishers who just didn't listen to their digital teams, or were fearful of what ringtones might be." While he was struggling to license the major publishers Simon also hit upon an ingenious licensing work around, acquiring a 12 month trial license for copyright usage for all major publishers through the Australian rights body APRA. Unfortunately for Simon the publishers were not impressed: "Soon afterwards, we got cease and desist notices from EMI Music Publishers telling us unless we removed their copyrights from the service they would sue us for being pirates. They warned: 'you'll hear from our solicitors in the morning'. We got served with a writ - to me in my personal capacity and to our company separately, each for $45 million. I called my mother and told her. She said: "Are you crazy, sort this out, otherwise EMI Music will ruin our family." After some high level, high tension negotiations Simon received a call from his lawyer telling him: "'we have good and bad news. The good news is that they will settle, which is definitely good news as you can't afford to go to court. The bad news is that they want $150,000.'" Simon successfully used his Errors and Omissions insurance that he had taken for inadvertent use of copyright[12] to settle the lawsuit paving the way to secure a license from EMI.

Once Simon had finished his icebreaker role for the ringtone sector, the market erupted into growth, generating an estimated $6.6 billion in global revenues by the end of 2006.[13] One of the more controversial ring tone companies was German outfit Jamba. In addition to being the home of the ringtone sensation the Crazy Frog, Jamba gained notoriety for a misleading subscription proposition that resulted in customers racking up big monthly bills while thinking they had only bought an individual ringtone. The confusion was intentional and at one point Jamba did not even publish the SMS code for cancelling subscriptions on its FAQ page. Jamba's mobile subscriptions included a range of mobile content including ring tones and wallpapers and the company invested heavily in marketing the service at the youth market. In 2004 VeriSign bought Jamba for $270 million, apparently unconcerned with how the company's shady product practices might reflect on its core role as a security and authentication business. The acquisition nonetheless proved commercially astute, with Jamba's revenues reaching $600 million in 2005. In the same year, in an ironic 'pop will eat itself' turn of events Jamba's Crazy Frog signed a record deal with the UK's Ministry of Sound and went onto release a number of singles and albums.

As the ring tone market went from strength to strength the labels finally got their opportunity to get a seat at the table. Improvements in mobile phone technology created a new ringtone format: the truetone or mastertone. Because these ringtones used a sample of the actual audio recording of the original song, the record labels became the main royalty beneficiary, with a markedly smaller share allocated for the publishers. Not that the labels were immediately enamoured with the concept as Ralph Simon recounted: "When the market moved onto truetones, there were major label executives who were genuinely horrified at the prospect of putting ringtones into the market place without DRM." Eventually the labels were convinced and the truetone business accelerated into growth, booming at the

12 Errors and Omissions Insurance is a form of professional liability insurance that protects companies against claims made for, among other things, negligent actions.
13 JupiterResearch

direct expense of monophonic and polyphonic ringtones, resulting in more than a little antipathy with the music publishers who were seeing their newly found digital gravy train culled almost as quickly as it had arisen. However the labels' moment in the ringtone sun was also short lived. Truetones peaked at an impressive 31% of global digital recorded music revenue in 2006 but fell quickly to 25% in 2007[14] and by 2012 was into single digit percentage points. Improvements in mobile technology had created the truetone market opportunity but it also killed it off: mobile phone functionality started enabling consumers to easily create their own ringtones from their own music collection without having to pay a penny. Video might have killed the radio star but the smartphone killed the ringtone star.[15]

The labels thought they had a natural truetone successor in the shape of ring back tones, a format that plays music to the caller instead of a dial tone. The format had been successful in South Korea and the expectation was that this testing bed of mobile music content had created another global hit. Unfortunately lightning did not strike twice, with the ring back tone never truly getting established globally and already losing share of digital revenue in South Korea by 2007. Unsurprisingly the ring back tone caused huge consumer confusion in Europe and the US, with countless accounts of consumers hanging up thinking they had got through to a wrong number or hold music. Some mobile carriers tried to solve the problem by superimposing a dial tone on top of the song that only resulted in creating a clumsy worst-of-both-worlds experience.

David Boyle, former SVP Insight EMI

Simon Wheeler, Director Strategy Beggars Group

Cliff Fluet, Partner, Lewis Silkin / Director 11

Who Wants to Kill A Golden Goose?

The ringtone market had burned furiously bright for a relatively short period and did not leave much of a lasting legacy. But ringtones did perform a crucial role of educating large swathes of publisher and label executives that digital could create new revenue opportunities rather than just eat away at existing income. Napster and MP3.com had pushed the record labels

14 IFPI Recording Industry in Numbers 2008
15 Because this also helped ensure the untimely demise of the Crazy Frog one could be tempted to argue that every cloud has its silver lining.

onto the back foot, making the priority retaining the strategic initiative through quashing a small group of disruptive upstarts that showed little or no interest in respecting their rules and commercial practices. A charitable counter-factual analysis might conclude that, had the labels been successful in nipping digital piracy in the bud, they would then have gone on to devise assertive and innovative digital strategies that would have incubated a vibrant and dynamic digital music market. More realistically, the labels – the majors at least – at this stage would have battened down the hatches and slowed the digital market's evolution even more than actually transpired. The label decision makers were not yet the growing body of forward looking digital staff but instead seasoned executives whose reference points and success metrics were firmly rooted in the analogue era. They had helped create the most successful years the record labels had ever known and in the process they had earned robust reputations for success. What reason should there have been to doubt that the music industry's most successful generation of managers ever seen would be anything other than best placed to deal with this latest troublesome, but still relatively minor challenge? Of course with hindsight we can see that the very fact that their success was rooted in the success of the CD would also prove to be the reason that they were the least well equipped to address digital. As the saying goes, if you are a hammer then everything looks like a nail. The CD generation of senior record label executives were quite simply too heavily burdened with analogue era baggage to have the strategic agility and fearless appetite for innovation necessary to meet the digital challenge head on.[16] They were not able to think out of the CD box. Even by the mid-noughties though the digital market was puny enough to reassure digital sceptics that perhaps they might not need to throw away their CD worldview after all.

Although global recorded music sales had been declining since 1999, by 2004, five years on from the launch of Napster digital revenues still only accounted for just 1.8% of global recorded music revenues.[17] Digital thinking was not only irrelevant to the majority of the contemporary business, its goals and bonuses were not geared towards making it a success. Digital was a quirky little appendix humoured by some, derided by others but effectively ignored by most because it simply did not figure prominently in their daily business lives. The CD was where the money was even if it had experienced a few years of decline. In fact there was a genuine expectation that the sales downturn would bottom out soon and the industry could then return to growth, with the CD its beating heart. The viewpoint is less naïve than subsequent events suggest. There had been no precedent of digital's impact on the media industries, just the most pessimistic within the labels thought that they were only at the start of what was nothing short of an utter decimation of their industry. Record labels, along with newspapers, were indeed just at the start of a painful journey that other media industries would find themselves progressively sucked into as the 2000's progressed.

---

16   The CD is of course technically a digital format but for the purposes of this book we use the term digital to refer
to music services and products which depend upon digital technology for delivery and consumption.
17   IFPI Recording Industry in Numbers 2006

FIGURE 10

Digital Has Not Yet Got a Firm Foothold on a Global Revenue Basis
Distribution of Music Revenue of Selected Music Markets, 2013

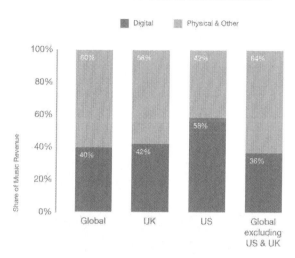

Source: MIDiA Research

Nor was the assumption that the CD would remain the core product exactly fanciful. As we have seen, at the end of 2013, when the US and UK are taken out of the equation, digital accounted for just 36% of global recorded music revenues (see Figure 10).[18] On a fully global basis physical music revenues accounted for 60% of all revenues,[19] with most labels still earning more from physical than digital. The Anglo-American bias of the global music industry can give a misleading impression of just how much digital progress has actually been made. Especially so when it is considered that the US and UK only account for 38% of the global music market while the other 8 top 10 music markets collectively account for 51%. The US and UK's impact on the digital market is inversely disproportionate, with the two accounting for 55% of the global digital music market in 2013. But even in the US, CD albums' unit sales of 193 million in 2013 outnumbered the 118 million digital albums sold so even though the US crossed over the 50% digital threshold in 2011 the CD remains the number one album product.[20] Moreover, the CD still dominates many important music markets in the world. In Japan, the second largest music market in the world, digital represented just 14% of recorded music income in 2013 and actually declined 61% from a 2008 high.[21] Similarly in Germany, the third largest global music market, digital represented just 19% of sales.[22] All of which contrasts sharply with the situation in Sweden where 70% of revenues were digital in 2013. If one thing is clear about the evolution of the digital music market across the globe, it is that there is no single clear trend, it is a picture of diverse growth rates and revenue shares. The only unifying factor is that in most markets the CD remains the bedrock of music sales.

18   MIDiA Research Music Global Music Forecasts 2014 to 2019: The Shift To The Consumption Era
19   IFPI Recording Industry in Numbers 2013
20   Nielsen
21   MIDiA Research and Recording Industry Association of Japan (RIAJ)
22   MIDiA Research and German Federal Music Industry Association (BVMI)

FIGURE 11

The Global Footprint of Streaming Is Highly Diverse

Digital Music Revenue Distribution of Selected Music Markets, 2013

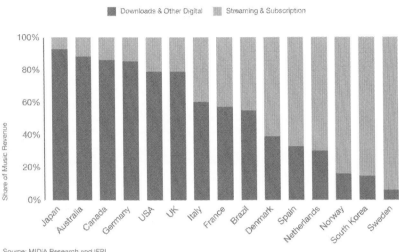

Source: MIDiA Research and IFPI

CD buyers thus remain crucially important to the future of the music industry just as they did in 2004. Unfortunately this consideration often curtailed labels' digital ambition, with a recognition that getting the digital migration strategy wrong could result in accelerating the rate of their decline rather than establish long-term growth. As the RIAA's Carey Sherman observed: "You had an obligation to customers and to your artists to continue to sell CDs while licensing new business models." It is a point also made by Roger Faxon: "The old CD model still works even at half the volume. The impetus to change is therefore not great."

As much as the labels had been subjected to transformational change, their fortunes remained intimately tied to the lingering embrace of the CD. Catering for the CD market quite simply impaired the labels' ability to deliver on digital strategy. Digital and physical music strategy are effectively a conflict of interests that beget strategic paralysis: the labels know they need to change their product mix but dare not change too quickly for fear of killing off a vast chunk of their business. This dilemma breeds caution and conservatism. A digital service that looks exciting to a technology company and to an investor may resemble disruptive threat to core CD revenues for a label. And although the record labels may have lost their monopoly of control of content, from a consumer perspective they still retain absolute control over the flow of content to legal digital music services. Thus CD-bred caution not only holds back the labels it also hinders the growth of the digital marketplace. This strategic conservatism created fault lines within record labels, as Jeremy Silver recalled: "There was a lot of tension internally. As the new media guys we wanted to do the deals but we'd then have to fight internal battles." These sorts of internal divisions remain an important part of the mix but have lessened over the years. Similarly attitudes to the importance of the CD are changing too, with some label executives even going as far as to comment in private that they want to hasten the decline of the CD, so that they can put that chapter behind them and focus on the future. It is a brave stance with significant risk but one that needs taking if record labels want to regain some control of their destiny. It is not however yet a mainstream label management view.

As the 2000's progressed digital continued to present more risk than it did upside, and analogue-era executives retained a robust degree of scepticism. In 2007 the then CEO of Universal Music Doug Morris was asked by Wired magazine why the major labels had responded so slowly to digital. His response was: "There's no one in the record company that's a technologist...It's like if you were suddenly asked to operate on your dog to remove his kidney. What would you do?" The interviewer responded: "Personally I would hire a vet".[23] Morris' comments were widely viewed as luddite, but they were steeped in realism and also the worldview of the CD addict. Morris was at the head of the world's largest music company with digital at that time still only a minor revenue source. His prime responsibility to his artists, employees and shareholders was to protect and nurture their core source of income: the CD. In 2011 Morris was replaced by the more digitally inclined Lucian Grainge but Morris and his strategic outlook were still in demand, with Sony Music appointing Morris as CEO in July 2011 just six months after his Universal exit.

The CD habit will die hard and the after effects will be keenly felt because it still constitutes the record labels' killer product, a product with far more universal appeal and reach than any premium digital product. This is why record labels cannot yet throw off yesterday's clothes with wanton abandon and fully embrace the digital era. Their customers are not ready, their retail partners are not ready, their own organizations are not ready and the revenue is not yet there. Despite vast digital progress in terms of organization, process and strategy major record labels, and many independent labels, are in many respects still not set up for digital success. This might sound like a strategic failing but it is simply a structural manifestation of the income supremacy of that little shiny disc. After all, who wants to kill a golden goose?

The CD is the dirty habit that record labels cannot kick. They know that as a product it is on life support and that their future depends upon successfully migrating consumers away from it, but equally they cannot bring themselves to turn off the respirator. The CD's tendrils continue to stretch into virtually every aspect of a label's business, from retail to marketing, from A&R to commercial affairs. In many respects the CD's impact on how the major record labels in particular work is still as pronounced now as it was in the mid 2000's, despite a marked increase in digital revenue, as described by EMI's former SVP of Insight David Boyle: "The prevailing attitude was 'yes it is going to be all about digital but right now where all our revenues are and what we control is all physical'. People were too busy surviving to focus on a bigger picture." The CD album as a concept still shapes the majority of label thinking, from actually creating an album, through artist marketing campaign budgets to product decisions. All record labels now have large swathes of highly skilled, technologically savvy, digital era personnel who totally 'get digital'. But so much of record label organizations are geared around the sale of CDs, with teams goaled and rewarded accordingly.

The CD will fade away as a mainstream product – that much is certain. What is at stake is how much of the record labels' revenue it will take with it.[24] The challenge for the labels is to know

---

23 Wired November 2007 http://www.wired.com/entertainment/music/magazine/15-12/mf_morris
24 Through the 2010's the CD market will polarize between the low end and the high end, with the majority of the middle segment migrating to digital or disappearing from music spending. The low end will coalesce around lowest common denominator mainstream pop music and discount compilations and catalogue releases. The high end will come to resemble the current high end vinyl market, only on a larger scale. Just as the CD is entering its death spiral, the high spending audiophiles have finally come round to the CD. With most audiophiles now adding high specification CD players to their audio set ups a market for high-end, luxury CD box sets is emerging and will become a mainstay of the future CD market.

when to jump off the merry-go-round. Jump too soon and they'll miss out on some of the ride, jump too late and they will hit the ground hard. Until that decision point is reached record labels are stuck in music product limbo. The change that is required cannot come at an organic rate though, if it does, then it will simply be a process of managing decline rather than proactively driving revenue success. Teams need new goals, business units need new objectives and the companies need new strategic priorities. Record labels must bite the bullet and support their ambitious digital revenue targets by not just targeting their digital teams to succeed, but also, in effect targeting their physical teams to fail. The physical focused parts of the business need digital goals too, else the main revenue generating parts of label businesses will continue to push in the opposite direction of digital teams. Numerous legacy business practices that keep label teams thinking in analogue era terms also need sun setting, such as archaic 'breakages' clauses in digital contracts.[25] Digital transition strategy, and by implication the way in which record label businesses are set up to energize the entire process, is more important than digital growth strategy. Without the former, the latter will struggle, as has been the case in Japan. All this will of course change and most labels and major music markets are nearing the digital tipping point. But even when they do so the CD will remain a crucially important part of their business.

Often the necessary change is not as black and white as digital versus physical. For example, marketing teams working on a new release still rely upon CD-era reference points with everything gearing towards an album release even though digital consumers will usually buy or stream just a few tracks from the album. Singles are given to radio stations to play weeks before they are released even though digital consumers expect to be able to access new music immediately instead of having it artificially held back. Thankfully there is growing appetite for challenging the accepted practices of the analogue era music business as illustrated by this comment from Edgar Berger, the CEO and President of International at Sony Music: "Day and date will eventually go. From a consumer perspective it is absolutely crazy to put a song on the radio and say you can't buy it. We will also get to the stage where we have a global release date, one day for all countries, as the web has no borders."

In addition to the protectionist view of radio play that remains prevalent today, there are multiple other label marketing practices that have the trappings of digital – social media, Instagram content etc. – but that are at heart still the old model in new clothes. For example, label marketing teams routinely create an increasingly rich mix of digital content assets for media partners to help promote an album release. This 'marketing content' includes items such as backstage footage, acoustic sessions and video interviews. Though these are typically populated to digital 'marketing' channels, the omnipresent CD worldview means that these assets are simply viewed as tools for helping sell the album. In a digital context though these assets can be just as valuable as the album itself for many audiences, in fact they should be every bit as much of the product as the music itself. None of these practices are explicitly geared towards supporting the CD yet perpetuate its legacy by being deeply rooted in analogue era thinking. The digital transition is not just about supporting digital teams but implementing an all-encompassing change in both thinking and doing. As important as the process is though, the digital transition will, if done properly, likely hasten the demise of the CD at a quicker rate than digital revenue will pick up the slack. The unavoidable consequence of which is that labels will be staring at bigger losses for a while, at just the time they are beginning to see revenues rebound, albeit gently. For publically traded labels, such as Universal and Warners, that is a pretty tough story to sell to investors, but it is one that needs telling regardless.

25 Breakages used to refer to physical damage of CDs in the retail and distribution stages and were often abused as part of a creative accounting process. Breakages clauses still exist in digital contracts even though there is obviously no physical product that can be damaged. Breakage clauses are often used in digital contracts to account for underuse of services compared to expected levels.

Becoming Digital Businesses

One of the many reasons that the record labels, big and small, found it difficult to adapt to digital was that it was not enough to just license to digital services, they had to digitize their businesses also. Even the comparatively routine task of converting their vast catalogues of music into digital files was a massive undertaking and often far from straight forward for older tracks. Just finding the original master recordings could prove a challenge, lost in dusty old storage rooms or sometimes even deleted from the archives. In other instances original master tapes had actually started to corrode and degrade, requiring painstaking restoration to get them ready for digitization.

The record labels also needed to develop new skillsets and acquire new expertise in order to 'go digital'. Many of the essentials of the analogue business, such as how to get CDs pressed and onto retailers' shelves, simply did not translate to digital. Once the labels stepped up their licensing efforts the demands on record label technology and infrastructure intensified markedly so the labels had to respond quickly as Barney Wragg explained: "The big change came in 2000/01 when the labels moved away from using in-house systems to licensing to 3rd parties. This allowed music services to begin to build cross label catalogues around one technology and set of usage rules. Internally this meant we not only had to create and manage the commercial deals with these 3rd parties, but we also had to set up all the processes for digital asset management, distributing and accounting to support multiple licensees." It was clear at a very early stage that digital business processes were going to move at a much quicker rate than their analogue predecessors and generate a much greater volume of data. The old record label procedures were simply not fit for purpose. It took large scale investments in technology architecture and the implementation of entirely different ways of doing business for the record labels to be organizationally prepared to support the new digital music economy. Systems needed to be built from scratch to support new supply chains in which digital assets could be created, catalogued and delivered in an instant rather than the days or weeks common in the physical market. Without the requisite supporting infrastructure labels simply could not support their new digital business partners.

Universal Music recognized particularly early the significance of structural re-organization and undertook a major project of building technology infrastructure that later led to a best-in-class eCRM system unifying multiple fan and consumer databases to support targeted artist marketing. Developing back-end systems may not exactly have been the sexiest of topics but it was just as important as the digital deals themselves. Unfortunately not all the majors were as forward looking as early as Universal was, as Jeremy Silver recalled: "EMI was just putting all the money straight onto its bottom line. What Sony were doing and what Larry Kensal at Universal was doing was much more sophisticated. We looked like the go-to guys for digital but we didn't have anything to back it up."

As more and more of the record labels' business became focused on licensing to new music services, a marked shift in the internal balances of power in record labels began to occur. The digital business and commercial affairs teams quickly rose in terms of both prominence and importance. These were the teams who were responsible for shaping and closing the deals that were finally coming to be seen as crucial to the future of record label revenue. With the shift to digital gaining so much momentum, senior digital business executives eventually rose up the ranks so that they were no longer just senior digital executives but top label executives in their own right. Unlike the first wave of digital executives who had been pioneering niche models with limited revenue impact, this second generation of digital executives were driving revenue and partnerships that were both meaningful in the present and core to the future. It was now inconceivable to think of digital not being a central part of record label strategy. Digital had come a long way, and the tanker was certainly beginning to be turned.

Renewal

Despite the overarching influence of the CD within the record labels' businesses, a vast amount of digital progress has been made. Though the labels, particularly the majors, can be justifiably criticized for having stunted the early stages of digital growth with their initial conservatism and caution, all that began to change from the mid 2000's. By this stage the digital executives were becoming firmly established in the mid-to-upper echelons of label management hierarchies. Similarly digital teams were beginning to become central components of record label organizations rather the relatively inconsequential novelties many 'new media' divisions had been in the early days. Organizationally digital had come a long way in the record labels. Though there remained many doubters and the long and enveloping shadow of the CD, there were nonetheless few people in the record labels who any longer doubted that their businesses were going to go digital eventually. It was now a question of 'when?' not 'if?'

The technology market had come round to this way of thinking too. Back in the early 2000's there had only been a handful of digital music companies knocking on the doors of the record labels for licenses for their services. By the 2005 there were dozens. By 2007 there were 285 licensed music services in Europe alone.[26] The growing number of digital deals ensured the commercial affairs divisions of record labels became even busier and progressively larger. But there was a problem, for all of the choice of music services there was in practice actually very little choice at all. With the notable exceptions of a handful of pioneering subscription services, the vast majority offered the same rights protected $/€/£0.99 download as iTunes, but with one crucial difference: no iPod. Without being able to sell music to the cream of digital music consumers, who were of course in the main iPod owners, there was a very limited market opportunity for music stores that used the by now industry standard Windows DRM. Apple's digital music market share in key territories like the US and UK hovered somewhere round the 70% mark. This meant in Europe that the best part of 285 music services were chasing far less than half of the market's revenue in 2007. This translated into just $2 million of download revenue opportunity per service, and a paltry $470,000 of post-rights costs margin opportunity from which all other costs then had to be deducted (see Figure 12).[27] But even that overstates the case due to the dominant share of the iTunes Store in European music downloads in 2007. Once Apple's market share had been accounted for the total revenue per service opportunity was in fact $160,000 a year. It did not exactly make for a compelling business case.

---

26 Promusic.org
27 Net operating margin uses the following post-sales tax cost base assumptions of 65% label licenses and 12% publishing. Calculation based on 275 European music services and $580 million download revenues.

FIGURE 12

Average Revenue Per European Digital Music Service in 2007

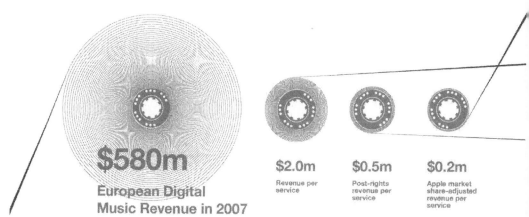

$580m

European Digital
Music Revenue in 2007

$2.0m

Revenue per
service

$0.5m

Post-rights
revenue per
service

$0.2m

Apple market
share-adjusted
revenue per
service

iTunes' rise to dominant player status resulted in a conflicted outlook within the labels. On the one hand iTunes was so dominant that it was dangerously powerful, on the other so much depended on Apple that the labels had to be cautious about potentially killing the new digital golden goose by licensing to disruptive alternatives. Both concerns manifested themselves in business strategy. Many label executives were preoccupied that they appeared to have 'done another MTV'. In the 1980's the record labels had let MTV build a media powerhouse off the back of content the true value of which they had not recognized. By the time they did, MTV was too powerful and too important a part of their business for them to do anything about it. Now history appeared to be repeating itself with Apple and there were concerted efforts among major labels to 'level the playing field', to try to give non-Apple services a head start into the market. Lacking the iPod / iTunes ecosystem most of these services would already have been doomed at best to also-ran mediocrity. But when the other side of the labels' conflicted Apple strategy – supreme caution – was added into the mix, many of these services were signing license deals that doomed them to failure.

What iTunes competitors needed most was to not be iTunes competitors. They needed to have business models and consumer value propositions that competed around Apple, not with it. They needed to not be $/€/£ 0.99 download stores. Yet to not be a download store typically implied a new model that could potentially disrupt the iTunes revenue predictability that the labels had quickly grown to rely upon. Thus the labels got themselves caught in a trap of strategic conservatism and in doing so pulled the rest of the digital music market in with them. Although piracy was still on the rise, the labels were beginning to feel that they had at least finally got a handle on the licensed part of the digital market. In reality more risk needed to be taken and the existing mix of music services was not driving the digital transition quickly enough.

Telco Tensions

Elsewhere telcos started taking a more serious look at how they might play a role. Most telcos had been burnt by investing heavily in poorly performing fixed line music services years before, paying the price for either being too early, or later not being able to compete with Apple. Telcos saw themselves as the natural conduit for digital music as they were providing the data networks upon which the files were being delivered. It seemed like a natural fit but the opportunity too often failed to translate into reality. The fixed line ISPs also had an internal conflict of interests: in the early 2000's file sharing was one of the most frequently cited reasons consumers gave for upgrading from dial-up to broadband. Nor were telcos exactly shy of promoting music downloading as a key use case for broadband, with incumbent telcos such as British Telecom running TV ads for broadband as a great way to download music even though the ISP itself had no music service. Broadband ISPs were faced with the choice of prioritizing clunky download stores that had limited catalogue, restrictive rights technology and pitifully small numbers of customers or instead allowing file sharing to continue to be a key driver of adoption of their core product. Matters were compounded by the fact that telcos had little way of competing with Apple because they had no way of breaking into the iTunes ecosystem and getting onto iPods, the digital music consumer's device of choice in the 2000's. Prioritizing between miniscule digital music revenue potential and making file sharing as frictionless as possible hardly warranted a second's consideration but unsurprisingly created tensions between ISPs and the record labels, tensions that persist today. The BPI's Geoff Taylor described the labels' perspective in the 2000's: "We felt that ISPs should be obvious business partners. After all, without-content networks are a commoditized business. But the opportunity didn't translate because broadband providers made so much more money from data than they would have with music services, and because music services take real expertise to retail." ISPs were happy enough to settle for file sharing to be a zero-investment means of harnessing online music to drive broadband uptake. But before long the broadband gold rush was replaced by a race to the bottom with fierce price wars, commoditization of internet access and networks increasingly congested by file sharing and video consumption. Suddenly ISPs wanted to get into the Value Added Services (VAS) game, bundling content and services in with broadband subscriptions. Music was seen as the low hanging fruit but ISPs quickly learned that they faced two insurmountable hurdles:

1. ISP customers who had been marketed broadband as a great way of downloading free music from file sharing networks and had got used to downloading all their music for free, were not particularly receptive to suddenly being asked to pay for it

2. Those of their customers who were willing to pay for digital music usually already had an iPod and were buying their digital music from Apple

The ISPs had attempted to sink the digital music boat and then missed it when it passed them by, un-sunk. As the decade progressed there was growing unease among telcos that they were being left behind in the digital content revolution, that they were being relegated to the role of dumb pipes. This, coupled with the growth in consumer mobile data adoption, sowed the seeds for a new wave of telco music service strategy, with subscriptions replacing download stores as the central strategic thrust. In the UK Omnifone set up to help telcos launch music services without having to build the infrastructure themselves and quickly secured some early wins, as Chief Engineer and Co-Founder Phil Sant recounted: "Telenor was our first customer in June 2007, with the Telenor Music Station. We went for global mobile licenses and ended up with the 1st global major label licensed unlimited music service." Another Omnifone powered service was Vodafone's UK MusicStation, also launched in November 2007. According to Sant the influence of Apple was key: "Vodafone threw resources and cash at this because O2 had the iPhone on exclusive so they needed to respond…. within eight weeks [MusicStation] had 100,000 subscribers paying £1.99 a week." The strategic imperative of having a speedy response to O2's iPhone partnership meant that Omnifone had to deliver the service at breakneck pace as, Co-Founder and Chief Architect Mark Knight recalled: "It took us just 12 weeks to go from signing the deal with Vodafone to getting MusicStation into market for them, including being totally integrated into their billing system." In Denmark 24-7 Entertainment powered a ground breaking hard bundled unlimited music service with incumbent telco TDC, free for large swathes of TDC's customer base. The new telco enthusiasm for music services was not constrained to Europe, with mobile carrier 3 in Hong Kong launching an Omnifone powered service in November 2007 that according to Sant was: "the first APAC subscription service, with 90,000 tracks."

The white label music servicer provider model was not new of course, with OD2 and MusicNet having helped create the market half a decade earlier, but the market was mature enough in the late 2000's to see at least some telcos getting significant consumer traction. The labels realized that there needed to be more experimentation beyond the telco sector and so began to license to a new generation of edgier, new model services. These included advertising supported download services from Q-Trax and Spiral Frog. Both in their own ways made a splash: Spiral Frog got high profile Financial Times coverage at launch while Q-Trax infamously announced their launch with major label content at Midem even though, as the labels were quick to remind them, they had not yet secured the licenses! Both services were short lived, encumbered with rights technology that had to be even more heavy handed than standard download services. In many respects both were ahead of their time, cutting the path through the ad supported music service undergrowth that Spotify would soon follow. Despite their failings though, both services were pushing the music service envelope. The labels would have clearly liked them to be successes but even in failure they provided them with invaluable insight into what would and would not work outside of the download store straight jacket. The most significant of the new wave of services that the labels licensed to in this period though was both edgy and from a telco: Nokia's Comes With Music.

Comes With Music was a frustrating mix of a highly innovative concept far ahead of its time, and poor execution. Comes With Music was an All You Can Eat (AYCE) service hard bundled into the cost of the device, with the original deal struck directly with Universal Music in 2007. Lucian Grainge - then Chairman of UMG International - and Anssi Vanjoki – EVP and General Manager of Multimedia at Nokia – led the negotiations and in 2008 Nokia brought in telco music executive Liz Schimel to head up the service. Schimel recalled that the service was a good strategic fit for the labels, presenting them with the opportunity to both drive market innovation and clip Apple's wings: "[It] fitted into the labels' holy war against Apple. It was a mutual win for Nokia and the labels. Everyone in the music industry was in the moment of maximum pain of realizing that Apple had built a huge device business off their content and that they had not seen any benefits from it." Comes With Music was built upon the highly prescient assumption that mobile devices would become the main point of consumption but it swiftly became clear that Nokia was not going to be able to deliver upon its bold vision. Although it was shackled with fiercer rights protection technology than most music services had to endure Comes With Music's biggest failings were strategic and commercial. Comes With Music was part of Nokia's bigger vision to become a content and services company, a strategy that effectively bypassed mobile carriers even though it depended upon them to get their handsets into consumers' hands. Unsurprisingly the carriers were not overly enamoured with the idea of subsidizing handsets that would create additional revenues they had no part in and that directly competed with their own costly digital music services. Without the carriers being willing to help finance their own disintermediation Nokia was left with a high compromised route to market. Nokia did not help itself, launching the service on a number of existing handsets instead of building a new dedicated music handset, despite Universal having prodded them to do exactly that. The result was a sub par user experience that most consumers never even knew existed.

The nail in Comes With Music's coffin was Nokia's fall from grace. Comes With Music suffered from bad timing, coming to market just as Nokia's era as the preeminent smartphone manufacturer was coming to an end. Apple had launched its iPhone in 2007 and was quickly setting the pace in the smartphone market. As Schimel put it: "Nokia's OS problems completely submerged everything else, with a device portfolio that was declining in desirability and unprecedented competition and disruption. Nokia saw their business in similar terms to how a mobile carrier would: a steady predictable customer base. But in actual fact the mobile phone business is very much like the music business: it is hit driven. Unfortunately Nokia learned this the hard way."

Even without all of these factors there is a question whether Comes With Music could ever have been financially viable due to the costs structure of the service and the commercial terms with the labels. Nokia had agreed to revenue thresholds that proved wholly unrealistic and soon found itself burdened with a very costly, miserably performing music service whose brand equity was increasingly toxic to the company. As Schimel observed: "There were some really deep flaws in the original structure [that] began to become clear as the project progressed." The fact that Nokia had signed first with Universal was highly significant. Nokia knew that if it could convince the world's largest record label to sign a deal with them that the other majors would eventually follow, and Universal knew it too. It was an approach that Spiral Frog had already used, getting the Universal deal signed first and then seeing the other labels follow suit. In both circumstances Universal made it clear that the services understood just how much value there was in having the world's biggest label take a punt on their risky services, and this was reflected in the deal terms. In effect Universal was setting itself up as the majors' risk taker and unsurprisingly this resulted in discord among the other labels. As Schimel explained: "There was a lot of frustration among the labels that UMG was rumoured to have got preferential deal terms. We [later] renegotiated because it was clear that we could not get the device pricing and operator alignment needed otherwise. There were advances and revenue terms that were very favourable for the labels. We were injecting very welcome capital into the industry when it was needed."

DRM RIP

Even with the likes of Comes With Music, Spiral Frog, Qtrax and, by 2008 Spotify pushing the accepted parameters of what a digital music service should look like, Apple's market dominance remained largely unchanged in the latter part of the 2000's. For companies trying to break into the download market the challenges were often insurmountable. Ministry of Sound's Lohan Presencer recalled the company's ultimately doomed efforts at building out a digital store: "We launched Ministry of Sounds Downloads in late 2006. The first compilation on the site was only 8 tracks – we could only use tracks we owned publishing and recordings rights for – no third party would license content to a digital compilation. We sold

25 copies. The margins just weren't there when we were selling third party content: we were on a 3% net margin. Even with massive scale you were not going to make money. iTunes was a Trojan Horse for selling iPods and so could afford to swallow negligible margins."

By now a growing body of major label executives had begun to realize that if they wanted the digital market to grow beyond the Apple beachhead then sooner or later they would have to follow the lead of many of their independent label peers and drop Digital Rights Management. It was both fragmenting the market and stubbornly ignoring the reality that the installed base of iPod and now iPhone customers effectively were the addressable market for all digital music services. DRM-free files were the only way most music services could have any hope of selling to these invaluable consumers. However opposition to MP3 downloads remained a deeply entrenched point of view among many label executives. The author remembers recommending MP3 download strategies to record label clients in 2006 and being given incredibly short shrift, in one instance being called 'naïve'. Going DRM-free was of course an anathema to the control culture and it was also perceived as being high risk. Risk, and the mitigation of it, had been the unifying threads running through record label digital licensing strategy. Up until this point risk mitigation manifested itself as the rights technology that shackled licensed music services into gloomy pens while MP3s from illegal services frolicked free in the hills. File sharing had gone from strength to strength but the number of truly successful licensed paid music services, including iTunes, could be counted on one hand. With the standout exception of iTunes, rights protection technology was invariably a poor quality user experience. It was a manifestation of the major labels' digital fears: they still did not trust digital and with protections they showed it. The combination of licensing too little catalogue and wrapping it in restrictive technology put the legitimate sector at an absolute disadvantage to online piracy. Yet by letting their anxieties get the better of them the record labels actually helped those fears come into being. Label conservatism held the digital market back at exactly the time it needed liberating and empowering. When digital revenues should have been booming along with the upsurge in broadband and MP3 player adoption, it remained stuck in a niche while piracy flourished. Once again it would take Steve Jobs to get the music industry out of a hole.

In April 2007 Apple and EMI partnered to create the first ever complete major label catalogue available for sale DRM-free. It was a coming together of two companies with a common objective. The rest of the labels were not yet ready but EMI was prepared to lead the way. Leading the push was Barney Wragg who had left his position heading up Universal's eLabs to become EMI's Global Head of Digital. Wragg had been a key force in industry standards including DMX and the ill fated SDMI but the experience had ultimately made him realize the Quixotic futility of the strategy, particularly in the face of the increasing ubiquity of MP3. Wragg's realization had come to him in Californian sunshine: "I left UMG and spent six months by a pool in California and I realized how huge the interoperability problem was and how much it held back consumer adoption of digital music. MP3 was already a standard that every single device played. The CD had no rights protection technology and the entire industry's catalogue was available in that format with no sign of stopping. It was bonkers to assume there would ever be an interoperable DRM and thus to ignore MP3. As soon as I started at EMI I went to Eddie Cue and proposed doing DRM free downloads. He said 'we only did DRM because the labels wanted us to'. We spent 6-8 months negotiating internally inside EMI. The final turning point was Amazon. Jeff Bezos [Amazon's CEO] point blank refused to open a digital music store unless the files he sold worked on all devices. My gamble was opening the market to people like Amazon would grow the overall business. At EMI we did the deal first with Apple who had always been the digital leader, and then we licensed Amazon."

It was a hugely important step but the majors were simply playing catch up with the independents, the majority of whom had been licensing catalogue DRM-free to the likes of eMusic for years. The dominant attitude towards rights protection technology among the indies had been ambivalent at best for some time as Presencer's comments illustrate: "My view on DRM has always been: what is the point of making a rights protected digital file when you are creating unprotected digital files every day in CDs." But the majors owned the rights to the majority of the content that mainstream consumers wanted, which is why the EMI / Apple deal was so significant and the effects were so keenly felt across the competitive marketplace. In many respects other digital music services benefited more from Apple's push for DRM-free than Apple did itself. For Apple it was both the removal of a user experience speed bump that few consumers ever actually came up against and a useful tool for demonstrating to increasingly critical consumer advocacy groups that it was committed to opening up the consumer journey. But the actual practical impact on its business and value proposition was modest. After all Apple customers could already move purchased music to whichever Apple device they chose and they could already burn copies onto CD. But for the chasing pack it changed everything. Up until that point competing music services could not sell major label content that could be played on Apple devices, and because Apple device owners represented the majority of the high value digital music customer base, this meant they had been fighting over scraps. Now with major label MP3 and DRM-free AAC catalogue Apple customers were suddenly a directly addressable audience. One early beneficiary was the UK's 7Digital and according to CEO Ben Drury: "Going DRM-free was [a] big game changer for us. EMI chose us alongside Apple as the launch partner for the first ever provider of full, major label DRM-free catalogue. We were chosen because we were powering much of EMI's other stuff and Apple didn't much like having us there! We beat Amazon to being the first DRM-free store in Europe, launching in September 2008 and were the first service globally to get WMG catalogue in MP3 format. Sales went up massively after launching MP3 sales and customer satisfaction rates rose massively too. Making catalogue available DRM-free has helped the world move away from being a download monopoly."

The overdue demise of Digital Rights Management was if not too little, certainly too late. Apple had already established an imperious market lead and because of its iTunes ecosystem consumer lock-in, any erosion of its market share would be a process of steadily chipping away rather than rapidly carving out wholesale chunks. The ability to sell directly to iPod customers was clearly hugely advantageous for Apple's competitors, but for the Apple customer there was comparatively little reason for switching from iTunes. After all that is where all of an Apple customer's music collection resided and the store was an integral extension of that experience. Added to that the iPhone now delivered the ability to buy straight from the phone, without any need to resort to re-entering credit card details or fussing with some clumsy micro payments solution. Even Amazon, who had – and indeed still has – active billing relationships with a huge swathe of Apple's customers struggled to convince those consumers that there was any good reason for buying from them the same music they could get on iTunes. And that was with seamless iTunes integration and highly competitive pricing – so competitive in fact that the labels were unhappy with Amazon taking a loss to sell music for so little.

None of this is to say going DRM-free should not have happened and that it did not have a meaningful impact. On both counts there is an indisputable case in favour: it finally set the download market up for success by giving the consumer the same freedom of control that he could get from piracy sites. In doing so stores like 7Digital could finally reach previously inaccessible, super valuable customers. But if all this had happened five years earlier then the results would have been far more meaningful. In 2007 though the only company that was going to have dramatic impact on Apple's digital music business was Apple.

Lohan Presencer, CEO Ministry of Sound Group

Scott Cohen, Founder The Orchard

Martin Mills, Founder and MD Beggars Group

Feeling the Pinch

With the launch of the iPhone in 2007 Apple had already found its new love and she was getting all the attention. By the end of 2009 Apple had sold 42.5 million iPhones while App Store downloads had hit 3 billion. Meanwhile year-on-year iPod sales had declined for the first time in history. The record labels were about to realize that when Apple sneezes, the music industry catches a cold. With Apple still accounting for the majority of digital music sales, the iPod slowdown inevitably translated into an iTunes music sales slowdown too. In 2009 global digital music growth collapsed from 43% in 2008 to just 7%. The slowdown sent shockwaves throughout the labels. Digital was meant to be the industry's route out of an increasingly dire situation, this was not supposed to have happened. Over the previous ten years global CD revenues had fallen by 55% dragging total revenues down by 36%.[28] The music industry was locked firmly in recession, years before the global economy followed suit. Retailers were disappearing from the high street and labels were cutting costs and scaling down their operations. Nowhere was this felt more keenly than at EMI. Throughout the decade EMI had seen repeated attempts to merge with other labels rebuffed by the European Commission on grounds of being anti-competitive. EMI had identified that its small US footprint and lack of a technology or media powerhouse parent company left it unable to compete on the global stage. The regulatory authorities saw things differently so that all EMI succeeded in doing was expending millions of dollars and crucial management expertise on failed corporate deals when it needed most to be focusing all of its efforts on the consumer. After successive rounds of cut

28 IFPI Recording Industry in Numbers 2011

backs EMI was finally bought by private equity firm Terra Firma in 2007. Terra Firma had been convinced that they were buying into the music market just as it was about to tip into recovery. They very quickly realized, to their great financial cost, just how wrong that advice had been.

Terra Firma attempted to bring modern business practices to the music industry. It was a strategy with broadly sound intent but ultimately doomed to failure, foundering on the clash of opposing worldviews and mutual mistrust. It was a rude awakening for Terra Firma boss Guy Hands who came up against oddities such as large bills for 'candles and flowers' that in fact were euphemisms for drugs and escort girls. Hands appointed experienced FMCG executive Elio Leoni Sceti as EMI CEO, a move intended to drive change in the business and to bring a fresh approach. Sceti recalled the environment he entered into and his vision for product strategy: "A very large percentage of energy in the industry was spent between labels, managers and industry bodies arguing how to share what little share of value digital left at the table. The discussion was always 'digital has robbed us all'. Everyone was measuring value but piracy made that irrelevant, so we made products that were relevant to their preferences. We tried to not look at digital as an alternative channel but instead as a digital space. We moved from a desire to control to an approach of change and development." Sceti discovered that his bold attempt to apply FMCG product principles to music product strategy was alien to many in the business: "The music industry does not have a culture of innovation, the concept that you can deliver music in multiple ways is alien. The concept of adapting and repackaging the same track is not in the music industry's DNA." The approach was out of the comfort zone of many executives and artists alike and a pattern began to emerge of those who got behind the new vision and those who began to work against it: "Artists who understood it, like Coldplay, Katy Perry, Damon Albarn, embraced it and were excited by it. Other artists who didn't believe as much in IP were against it. Those who had the intellectual capacity to understand the concept that it was not compromising the content, got it. Those without the intellectual capacity resisted because they misunderstood the threat."

For all of Terra Firma's bold vision their years at EMI developed into a catalogue of struggles and division. A number of high profile artists jumped ship including Radiohead and the Rolling Stones, while others such as Coldplay publically voiced their concerns. All the while Terra Firma's investment dwindled in value, which in turn put immense pressure on the vast debt the company had acquired to buy EMI. The pressure began to show and as one anonymous former EMI executive explained: "Terra Firma people didn't respect the people and the skills they did have and instead focused on skills they didn't have. They too quickly tried to implement what they had seen work elsewhere. Many of their plans looked good on paper but didn't apply to the music business. As a consequence they lost the respect of EMI employees." The writing was on the wall for Terra Firma and eventually its main backer Citigroup, which owned $4bn of the debt, assumed control of EMI. Management of the company passed to a 'music business guy', Roger Faxon, a long-term EMI executive. David Boyle, who had been brought in to head up EMI's new Insight division observed: "EMI staff had been through so much, and they were often bruised from the experience." Following a series of notable turnarounds Citigroup eventually sold much of EMI to Universal Music in 2012, with the remainder of the company broken up and sold elsewhere at the behest of the European Commission.

Time for Plan B

EMI's plight, though extreme and unique, was nonetheless the music industry's problems in microcosm. It was a clash of ideology between the old and new worlds, of instinct versus rigid process, of digital's Dr Jekyll and Mr Hyde role simultaneously instilling fear and excitement. Whatever the prospects might have been for the Terra Firma vision in better times, what did for it in the late 2000's was the continued failure of digital to offset the effect of declining CD sales. That had been the story for the first half of the decade and it remained true for the remainder. Apple had been the music industry's only knight in shining armour but the sheen on its breastplate was beginning to dull, at least from the music industry's perspective. Apple was casting ever more covetous glances over to the worlds of games, books, video and mobile apps yet despite download sales slowing it remained the only force of scale. The flurry of failed experiments with edgier services had little discernible impact by the late 2000's. Apple remained the only serious game in town but although it was clear that it would not be enough on its own no one else was likely to make the 99 cents download model work at scale. Consequently the late 2000's were essentially wilderness years for digital music. Paul Vidich went as far to argue that: "Between 2004 and 2010 not much else very interesting happened in the digital music market other than YouTube, which came along just as MTV had pretty much abandoned music videos, and Pandora, which was a by-product of the DMCA." The record labels needed a Plan B and they needed it fast.

By the start of the 2010's the labels had established strong digital expertise throughout their organizations, from highly effective marketing teams that pioneered new digital tactics through to highly effective commercial teams. The labels were also presiding over a shift to a digital business with much lower fixed costs than the dying physical business, with hefty analogue era costs such as pressing plants, cover art print runs and CD distribution having no role in the digital business. The labels had needed new skillsets right across their businesses and in the main they now had them. Although the omnipresent spectre of the CD album continued to shape so much of business strategy there was a new freedom of thinking as Boyle described: "Even in 2009 there were some big digital debates, such as considering stopping wasting time focusing on the CD."

The digital world had changed dramatically in the decade since Napster's rude awakening for the labels. Broadband connectivity was becoming ubiquitous and mobile internet adoption was accelerating. The foundational pieces were falling into place for the access age. Streaming had been a part of the business since Launchcast but now technology and consumer behaviour made it ready for prime time and a host of new music services were lining up to seize the opportunity. It was serendipitous timing for the record labels with plan B effectively falling into their laps. A slew of streaming services such as Spotify, Deezer, MOG and Rdio had started to emerge in the late 2000's and by the start of the 2010's they were ready to pick up the digital baton. Whereas Apple had helped consumers transition from the physical era by using an ownership model, these new services instead provided consumers with access to music, throwing the ownership paradigm out of the window. It was an alien and somewhat ethereal concept for most music fans to get their heads around and consequently growth progressed more slowly than download revenue growth did in the mid 2000's. Taking the launch of the iTunes Store in 2003 and the launch of Spotify in 2008 as the starting points for each market, download revenue growth far exceeded that of subscriptions and streaming, reaching $1.5 billion compared to $0.7 billion (see Figure 13). In fact this analysis is if anything too biased in favour of subscriptions as Spotify et al launched into an already well-established subscriptions market. Record labels have become increasingly enthusiastic advocates for the subscription services because of all of the clear business benefits such as increased Average Revenue Per User (ARPU) and predictable revenue. But the numbers clearly show that they neglect the importance of downloads at their peril.

FIGURE 13

In The First Five Years Of Growth The Apple-Driven Download Market Far Outpaced The Spotify-Driven Streaming Market

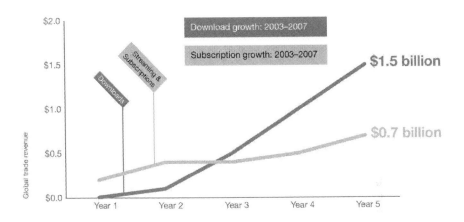

Source: IFPI, RIAA

By the end of 2013 streaming and subscriptions accounted for 28% of digital revenues and their impact on digital growth was crucial.[29] Already by 2012 these services were pulling their own weight in the digital music economy, adding $0.5 billion in revenue compared to just $0.1 billion for downloads, growing the digital music market more than downloads did that year.[30] By 2013 streaming was growing at the direct expense of download revenue, with the latter shrinking by 4%. The effect has been felt most keenly in the US where downloads are eating directly into download revenue by converting the most valuable download buyers into subscribers. 23% of music streamers used to buy more than an album a month but no longer do (see Figure 14). Thus an average spend of $20 or more is becoming $9.99. It was not meant to be this way. Streaming was meant to be the high tide that would rise all boats. In the first six months of 2013, downloads accounted for 69% of digital revenue, by the same period in 2014 the share had fallen to 60%.[31] Apple is seeing Spotify poach its most valuable customers but it still rules the roost, the largest player in the largest segment of digital revenue, but at least now there is a brood of new challengers that are competing around Apple rather than with it.

29 MIDiA Research Music Global Music Forecasts 2014 to 2019: The Shift To The Consumption Era and IFPI Digital Music Report 2012
30 IFPI Recording Industry In Numbers 2012
31 Nielsen Soundcan, via New York Times

FIGURE 14

Streaming Impacts Consumers' Wider Music Consumption But
Further Growth Potential Remains

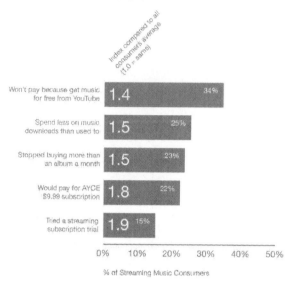

Index compared to all
consumers average
(1.0 = same)

Won't pay because get music for free from YouTube	1.4 34%
Spend less on music downloads than used to	1.5 25%
Stopped buying more than an album a month	1.5 23%
Would pay for AYCE $9.99 subscription	1.8 22%
Tried a streaming subscription trial	1.9 15%

0%   10%   20%   30%   40%   50%

% of Streaming Music Consumers

MIDiA Research Consumer Survey 06/14 (UK and US) n = 2,000

Following the late 2000's lull another strategy the labels started doubling down on was focusing on partners with the potential to bring large reach and scale, companies like Google, Facebook and Amazon, top tier players with vast customer bases. In part the approach emerged as a reaction to labels tiring of investing time and effort developing relationships with small start ups that quickly ran out of money, leaving little or nothing to show to for their efforts. Labels began to recognize the advantages of working with partners that had tens of millions of customers to whom music services could be sold, and that had large marketing budgets with which to reach them. The logic of the strategy is to separate the wheat from the chaff, whittling down would-be music services to those with serious ambition and the ability to go the distance. But the strategy has had the unintended effect of skewing the market towards companies with the deepest pockets, companies that are not always those that are the most innovative nor that always have the music industry's interests closest to heart. As Larry Miller put it: "History has shown us that this industry only respected scale, rapid growth, traction and a strong balance sheet." Big telcos and Consumer Electronic (CE) companies tick the boxes of scale and capital but for them music is simply a means of selling data and hardware. The concern is that bigger companies with ulterior motives for selling music can easily unbalance markets by undercutting pure-play music services, willingly loss leading with music in order to achieve their core product aims. Matters become even more complicated when these companies switch their priorities away from music to focus on other ways to sell their core products, having left the digital music market disrupted by their short-term pricing and product strategy. It is a risk highlighted by Axel Dauchez, former CEO of streaming music service Deezer: "If the long term future of the music industry is in the hands of non-music companies rather than pure-play music services then the future of the labels is at risk. The record labels realize this in their hearts but not their heads."

The Digital Revenue Target Effect

Arguably the most significant strand of label strategy evolution has been the approach to risk and licensing. Although revenue guarantees, equity stakes and non-repayable advance payments charged against anticipated earnings had always had a role in label licensing from the late 2000's they have taken centre stage in discussions and remain controversial deal components even today. Confidentiality clauses ensure that these are shrouded in mystery and questions remain over whether the full amount of all of these advances are treated as true digital income and therefore eligible for sharing with the artists.[32] Recognising the bad image of advances one major label started telling licensees that it will waive its five-to-six figure advances but instead insists upon a $0.10 'set up fee' for every track within in its catalogue. The net impact for the licensee is effectively unchanged: a large up front payment is required to secure the content from that record label while the label gets to say it's no longer demanding advances from start ups.

The rationale beyond label advances is relatively sound, namely that the labels need to mitigate the risk potential of music services by taking upfront payments, rather than having services disrupt the market but then fold, unable to build a sustainable business. Over time though the tactic has become relied upon on too heavily as a predictable income source. However Faxon believes the advance strategy was both founded on shaky foundations and became misused: "The labels saw their best answer was to take as big an advance as possible and pray that the service fails so that they could keep all of the advance and not share it with their artists. It was not a progressive view of the world. It was not trying to advance the market." Nonetheless, over time labels have been able to replace the world of highly unpredictable revenue from early stage music services with highly predictable advanced payments. Risk tomorrow is paid off with cash today. Suddenly digital music revenue forecasting has become much more predictable and far less risky. Each new service immediately delivers a guaranteed amount of income regardless of how many consumers do, or do not, adopt.

Depending on the perceived risk quotient of the licensee's service record label advances can comfortably reach into the tens of millions of dollars per label per service. For example, bankruptcy filings of now-defunct music service Beyond Oblivion in 2012 revealed that it owed a combined $100 million of unpaid fees to Warner Music and to Sony Music without the service ever having reached a single consumer. The riskier the service to the record labels' established business models, the larger the required advance. This front-loading of label digital income is both a product of, and drives a short-term focus on quarterly digital revenue targets. It is no coincidence that the nitty gritty of digital deals with major labels is done by relatively junior digital executives who have aggressive quarterly digital revenue targets while the senior team leaders step back. Thus the executives with the strategic vision and a remit for taking the long view extricate themselves from the actual deal making at the stage when the resulting terms place commercial burdens on music start ups that threaten their sustainability. The consequence is that the long-term strategic vision being built by the management teams of major labels has become increasingly disconnected from the near term outlook of digital deal teams, but with the express consent of the same management teams. They do so because their boards and shareholders demand and expect strong digital revenue and this approach is the most reliable way of delivering it, even if that means that

32 One lawyer, speaking on grounds of anonymity claimed that portions of advances are actually treated as 'signing-on bonuses' for the labels and are therefore not subject to being shared with artists. 'Administration fees' and 'set up fees' are a common component of label licenses and as the names suggest are not royalty related and therefore are also not inherently due for sharing with artists.

long term vision is compromised in the pursuit of quarterly and annual revenue targets.

While the revenue risk is reduced for the labels it remains high for the services themselves as they are compelled to commit larger shares of their income earlier to rights costs instead of spending it on marketing or product development. Meanwhile labels complain that digital music services do not spend enough money on marketing their wares. The alternative, at least for those services that are able, is to secure greater amounts of investment, but according to Beyond Oblivion's former founder and CEO Adam Kidron that route can be even riskier: "All that labels are worried about is what it does to their existing customers. At the beginning of Beyond Oblivion the labels were saying it was really risky and that we had to pay all this money to take away the risk. We had to pay the labels so much insurance that we had to bring in so much external capital that it destabilized the business." In effect the labels have reduced their risk but doubled that of the music services. It is a direct transference of economic risk: the labels transfer the music services' risk protection - i.e. their investment - directly into their business to become the labels' risk protection. If the services succeed but cannibalize existing revenue the labels have revenue protection and can still pull the plug if they wish, if the music services fail the labels still bank the money. Kidron believes the approach originates in the labels' financial footing: "The labels are under capitalized, they can't be players in distribution because they don't have the money to participate so they use copyrights as ransom."

Equity stakes are another integral part of the licensing process. For cash-starved early stage start ups that can ill afford to pay big advances, weighting deal terms towards equity can certainly be a lesser of two evils. Equity plays also make strong strategic sense for labels. After all the roadmap of a typical digital music service is: get investment, get licenses, launch, get market traction and then sell for many multiples of the original investment. The record labels, and indeed publishers and rights bodies, saw that it was their content fuelling the acceleration in value, so they saw it only fit that they should be able to participate in some of that multiple increased value opportunity. All of the theory is perfectly defensible, but the practice does not always live up to the same standards. The advance and equity strategy is not inherently flawed as long as it is pursued properly and aligned with the appropriate degree of effort required to service a deal. Which infers labels taking their equity stakes seriously by becoming active participants in the businesses they take stakes in, effectively treating their investment with the same respect any other investor would. But at times cynicism overrides commercial pragmatism as illustrated by an experience recounted by music business lawyer Gregor Pryor: "I went into a licensing meeting with a technology company client and a major record label. The label exec said 'we really like your company, so much so in fact that we'd like to take a stake in it'. To which my client replied 'that's great. Our company is valued at x so the market rate would be x for 5%. We've just closed a round but we would even be prepared to give you the investment at the now discounted rate.' To which the label exec replied 'No, we're not going to pay you for the stake - it's part of the price of getting a licence from us. We do this sort of deal all the time.' My client quickly understood the reality of the situation and said 'Look, it's clear that this particular conversation isn't going to bear fruit, so let's move onto the terms of the licence'. Then, mid way through the licensing discussions, the label exec said 'look, we think your model is really risky, so we're going to have to charge you a premium on the standard licence rate.' This of course shocked my client who replied 'But I thought you just said you really liked our company, now you're telling us that you view it as being risky'. It was clear that the label was simply looking for ways to increase the deal value, so we walked away from the negotiation and didn't sign a deal with that particular label for over a year." Some investors grew tired of seeing sizeable portions of their investments going straight onto the bottom line of record labels in the form of advances and simply decided to stop investing in the space. Wiggin's Alexander Ross recalled one such conversation with a major VC: "[he] told me 'it's pretty easy for us: if the service requires licences then forget it. We're for services that piggyback legitimately on other companies' licences or that have found an ingenious business model that doesn't need them."

On top of advances, guarantees and equity give-aways music services have also had to accommodate Most Favoured Nation (MFN) clauses guaranteeing the signatory label the same best deal terms of all other labels the service licensed to. Thus while a label is able to license competitively, striking different terms with different services, a music service is not allowed to. The balance of power is clear. Favoured nation clauses are a natural product of risk mitigation strategy, but they are a misuse of power, not so much any single label's market share power, but of labels as a body.[33] The labels may have lost their monopoly on control of the consumer with the rise of Napster, but they retain near absolute authority over the legitimate digital music market. With a few notable exceptions, such as online interactive radio in the US which is licensed by statutory rates, the record labels decide what does and does not get licensed and at what rate. This has often culminated in risk aversion distorting the digital licensing landscape. It also means that the licensee-licensor relationship is a far from even one as illustrated by what happened to another of Gregor Pyror's clients: "In one deal the label almost doubled the previously agreed advance during a conference call, saying 'this is the only amount the board will accept. The deal can't go ahead unless we go with this amount. This was the first my client had heard that the advance was again up for debate." The licensee thus had to accept the new terms at metaphorical gunpoint or not get the license.

The final set of commercial licensing levers that labels pull are revenue guarantees which bind licensees to paying minimum amounts of revenue however poorly their service may fare. As if that was not enough these 'floors' are usually combined with 'ceiling' commitments that commit a service to paying fees that are the higher of one or more variables, normally a fixed rate or a percentage of revenues. Thus if a service does badly the label gets guaranteed revenue and if a service does better than expected the label does even better. The label gets to double dip while the service has to grapple with how to hit the middle ground with a sizeable chunk of its working capital tied to licence fee costs rather than being available for marketing, development or sales support.

The situation has intensified as the major label landscape has consolidated. At the start of the 2000's there were five major labels, by 2013 there were just three. Because of the labels' monopoly of supply of content this concentration of power has important implications for music services as Martin Mills, head of independent label group Beggars argued: "There is quite an uneven balance of power: someone at UMG is now in a position to deny a service's existence." Thus the greatest power that a major label now has in the digital arena is the power of 'no', the ability to ensure a service either evolves its strategy to meet that of the label, or else to simply ensure it never gets to market with a full quota of major label content. To get around this roadblock some digital services have walked away from major label discussions to build an audience around independent catalogue and then returned to the negotiating table with the majors with the invaluable asset of 'traction' under their belt. It is a strategy that is becoming increasingly appealing to many smaller music start ups.

33 Part of the terms that UMG agreed with regulatory authorities to push through its acquisition of EMI, and largely as a consequence of lobbying from IMPALA, included not being permitted to use MFNs in digital deals.

The Independent View

The major record labels may account for approximately 75% of all music sales across the globe but thousands of independent record labels make up the remainder. These independents range from being so large in some markets that they resemble major labels, right down to little more than a self-published artist. But as diverse as the independent sector is, it has acquired a broad reputation for bold innovation in the digital space. As far back as the mid 1990's some independent record labels were licensing their content to digital music services long before the majors were countenancing the possibility. Similarly independent labels were the first to license to Rhapsody and to the first large scale licensed MP3 download service, eMusic. While major record labels' approach to digital has often been conservative and cautious, the independent sector has continually pushed the envelope.

They have done so because they have less to lose and much more to gain. Independent record label A&R budgets, marketing resources and influence on retailers are so much smaller than those of major labels that experimentation and innovation is a routine necessity in order to just level the playfield a little. Even the biggest independent labels have only low single digital percentage point global market shares and though there is some high level industry collaboration between independents – such as the licensing body Merlin and the trade bodies AIM, A2IM and IMPALA – ultimately each independent is a direct competitor. There are comparatively few commercial opportunities to unite against a common 'foe' so their modus operandi is continually looking for a way to even the odds, to find a way to get an advantage and to punch above their weight. Putting their content on music services that the major labels are not yet on has been an effective means of achieving this. Once the majors get their content onto digital services however independent labels swiftly find their artists lost under a barrage of major label artists on the home screens of services like iTunes and Amazon. Even though independent record labels account for the majority of all releases they only drive a quarter of total sales.[34] Small labels simply do not have the marketing muscle and influence on most music services that their major label peers have. Even with this inbuilt handicap many independent labels have succeeded in making digital work for them. Such an example is the roll out of iTunes to new markets, as Beggars' Simon Wheeler explained: "The extension of territory doesn't matter as much for majors but had a much bigger effect on our business. Because we have all our digital rights, Apple turning on markets like Mexico was immediate new free revenue for us." Whereas many independent labels in the analogue era were super local, digital platforms opened niche local audiences but on a global scale. Without needing to deal with the complications of pressing and physical distribution smaller independent labels have been able to carve out successful niches for themselves in the digital marketplace. It is an observation made by AIM's Alison Wenham: "Many of our member labels started in the digital era and have worked out how to make it work for their businesses." 78% of AIM's membership of UK independent record labels were formed in the 2000's i.e. exactly in the midst of the period when music sales went into a tailspin.[35] What is clear is the changing rules of engagement have created new opportunities for small independent labels, opportunities that were not necessarily present in the CD era.

Independents have always had markedly different approaches to the majors, culturally and in business terms. Throughout the digital era, with margins ever tighter and sales dwindling, these differences have become more pronounced with independent labels focusing on building

34 It should however be noted however that the market share figure, as reported by the IFPI, likely underestimates the global independent label share as it attributes independent releases distributed in other territories by major labels as major label revenue.
35 AIM Membership Survey 2011 Results

commercially prudent businesses. Whereas majors have the scale and financial reserves to be able to take big bets on a large number of acts, independent labels typically focus on a small number, often working with them over a longer period of time and more tolerant of a more modest start to their careers. Major record labels have always leaned towards pursuing big successes and while revenues have been in decline this has often translated into taking a more measured approach to risk. As Sony's Edgar Berger explained, major labels have in many respects raised their ambitions: "We are in the business of using our muscle to create global superstars and I want to see us creating more global superstars." The greater focus on big bets by majors has meant that many artists who would have once been candidates for a major label deal have instead become independent artists. Measures of success have also changed. In the 1980's a major label artist who sold a few hundred thousand copies of an album would no longer be considered an achievement, but now this can easily constitute success. The reduced levels of sales also translate directly into the amount of money invested into recording and promoting artists. Major labels have generally operated on a principle of only one out of ten artists turning a profit for the label, but the success of that artist being so big that it comfortably pays for the rest.[36] Independent labels though often cannot afford to operate on this basis as Martin Goldschmidt, founder and MD of Cooking Vinyl explained: "There is a big margin difference between independents and majors. We don't have mega executive salaries and we're not using one successful artist to fund 20 failures. This enables [us] to pay through more to artists."

Robert Ashcroft, CEO PRS for Music, former SVP Network Services Europe Sony

Alison Wenham, CEO AIM

Larry Miller, former COO, a2b Music / President Reciprocal

Transparency of reporting and payments to artists, always contentious issues, is another area where digital has emphasised the differences between majors and indies. In the digital era, with such an increase in both the volume and granularity of data from retailers, the issue of transparency should have lessened but has paradoxically become more intense than ever.

---

36   The veracity of the 1-in-10 principle has been called into question by some on the grounds that this is as much of a reflection of record label accounting procedures as it is actual profitability, that there is a vested interest for labels to keep a release out of profitability as this means that income does not then need to be shared with the recording artist. (Artists only get paid royalties from a record label when they are 'recouped', namely that the record label's costs associated with the release have been covered by sales income.)

This is because the greater the depth of data that artists get from other sources (web site and Facebook analytics, CD Baby reports etc) often contrasts strongly with the level of detail they get from rights owner accounting. In addition to contractual and accounting issues that blight some artist relationship, many labels - some independents included - can pay as little as 15% royalties to artists for streaming. So many independent labels have seized upon the opportunity to differentiate further from the majors, paying artists 50% streaming royalty rates and being more transparent with their reporting structures. It is a point made by Martin Goldschmidt: "If you are not earning you can clearly understand why you are not earning and you have been part of the discussions and decision making, then it is much easier to accept the situation than if it is hidden behind obscure accounting." This sort of approach sits more naturally with smaller organizations that are built upon more intimate working relationships and underpins the culture of labels and label groups such as Beggars, as Beggars' Martin Mills described: "We do things for the right reasons. Financial reasons are virtually always the wrong ones. We are an old fashioned cottage industry working in a modern way." It is a view echoed by Jonathan Grant of dance act Above and Beyond and co-founder of UK dance indie Anjunabeats: "We have turned down so much stuff that would have been great commercially speaking but not something we wanted to do. It is about doing the right things for the right reasons. We want a long-term future, a legacy."

The digital market's unique characteristics have enabled independent labels to both succeed where previously they may not have, and to forge distinct paths from majors. Being forced to think more carefully about how they make their investments and how they run their businesses has helped create the foundations for a more effective and efficient music business. Goldschmidt believes that these new operating principles should also be reflected in different measures of success for the industry: "People underestimate how well the business is doing. All the focus is on revenue but if you look at margin there is a different story. Margins (before marketing and promotion) in physical are 50%, in digital they are 75%. So even if revenues remain flat but transition to digital then we will have a very healthy music business. The gross margin (profit) in the business has improved massively."

FIGURE 15

The Decline and Fall of the Top 10

Percentage of US Top 10 Album Sales by Genre

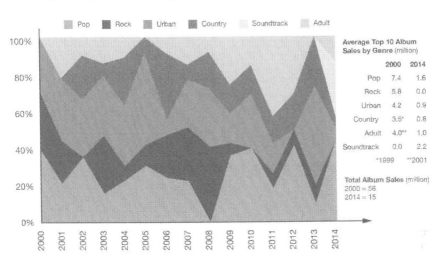

Sources: Nielsen Soundscan via Wikipedia, MIDiA Research

Another consequence of the fight to survive is an increasingly stark contrast between the A&R strategies of major labels and independents. Although majors always veered towards the bigger bets, declining music sales forced them to be less risk averse and focus energies around mainstream pop acts. This is not to say that independents have not also been guilty of playing the safe-bet card themselves, and they have also been able to sign a larger amount of commercial but slightly left of centre acts that in previous years would have found a home at a major. The implications of this are that major labels risk becoming viewed purely as the territory of the American Idol / XFactor generation of manufactured pop artist. It is an observation made by Paul Vidich: "I continue to see a big place for the major record labels as marketing partners for celebrity musicians, but their roles have changed markedly. They are taking bigger risks on fewer bands, and there has been huge growth in a whole layer of activity below them."

Some industry executives have suggested that the major record labels' more cautious approach to A&R strategy has resulted in a deterioration in quality of output, with a pronounced focus on 'safe' pop music. Alison Wenham argued that there is an inherent structural conflict at majors: "There is a dilemma at major record labels: their corporate structure hampers creativity, making it more difficult for them to avoid derivative and mediocre music."

Whatever the cause, there has been a gravitation towards the mainstream in the top end of music sales. Looking at the US Top 10 selling albums from 2000 to 2012 there is a clear trend away from rock and alternative music, with pop now more pervasive than ever representing 41% of top 10 album sales (see Figure 15). Underpinning the shift to the mainstream is a concerted effort to minimize risk as sales tumble: the top 10 albums accounted for 56.4 million unit sales in 2000, by 2012 this had dropped by 38.7 million to 17.7 million, a 69% drop. Thus even for top 10 pop acts sales pale in comparison with those of the 2000 peak. One Direction's 1.6 million and 1.3 million sales and Justin Bieber's 1.3 million in 2012 compare miserably with 'N Sync's 9.9 million, Britney Spears' 7.9 million and the Backstreet Boys' 4.3 million in 2000. Urban has also steadily declined over the period, from a high of 50% of top 10 sales in 2005 to zero in 2012, while Country has steadily grown its share from zero in 2000 and 2001 to 19% in 2012. Rock, following a few strong years from 2006 to 2008, has been relegated to a niche of no more than 8% every year since, disappearing entirely in 2010. The average number of sales per top 10 album for Rock, Pop, and Urban all fell by 75% between 2000 and 2012. Country only fell by 66% and Adult by just 30%. Adult, with artists like Michael Bublé, Adele, Susan Boyle and Josh Groban represent the new 'safe' market for album sales, particularly because the average age of music buyers has increased steadily throughout the 2000's. These artists appeal to older music buyers who still predominately buy CDs and often rely upon mainstream outlets like Walmart. The top 10 album sales are not the whole music market, but that is sort of the point: the top 10 is becoming ever less a gauge of music buyer tastes and even further from the tastes of more engaged music fans. Instead it is becoming a measure of the safety-first, mainstream consumer focused A&R strategy. Meanwhile streaming and a la carte digital services are empowering the music aficionados to deep dive, if not into the long tail, then certainly into the full torso of music, bypassing the short head of the top 10, which leaves the top 10 as the pulse of the dwindling mainstream.

The contrast with the prevailing A&R strategies of the independent sector is pronounced but also has an impact on sales as Martin Mills explained: "The music we make is much more fan based so buying is a big part of the equation." The contrast in music strategy has also helped the independent sector be less heavily pulled towards the single dominated consumption patterns of digital as Alison Wenham argued: "It has become a digital singles market in the Rihanna world but it's not in the Bon Iver and Queens of the Stone Age world."

Changing Sales Cycles

The decline in album sales has turned many of the fundamentals of record label business practices on their heads. Because label operating practices still revolve around album releases, particularly so but not exclusively so in majors, chart positions and units sales are still the most important currency for recorded music – though streams are becoming an important part of the picture too. Good chart positions have long been a springboard for success, with a good first week chart showing opening up radio play, TV appearances and driving consumer awareness and in turn sales. In the analogue era record labels would over supply retailers, at their own cost, because chart positions were based on units shipped, rather than units sold. Now with sales falling so quickly labels have started to focus efforts on ensuring the first week of sales packs a punch. This was done to great effect in December 2013 with the release of Beyoncé's eponymous fifth studio album that was launched directly onto an iTunes one week exclusive with no pre-release marketing. The ensuing media coverage created a level of buzz that no traditional music marketing campaign would have been able to achieve and resulted in 600,000 first week sales, a record for the artist (see Figure 16). Prior to the release of this album Beyoncé's sales were in sharp decline, from a peak of 4.9 million US sales for 'Dangerously in Love' in 2003 to just 1.4 million for '4' in 2011. The total market decline in album sales was clearly a mitigating factor but the rate at which the top 10 album sales declined over the same period – 50% – was significantly less than the 71% by which her album sales declined. The 'Beyoncé' first week success followed on the heels of two other notable first week successes for Daft Punk and for Taylor Swift. Daft Punk secured first week sales of 339,000 for 'Random Access Memories' representing 44% of all US sales to date. By contrast their previous album 'Human After All' sold just 127,000 in the US. But it was Taylor Swift's 2012 'Red' that set the bar for first week sales with an impressive 1.2 million. The fact that these sales represented 31% of the entire sales for the album, which were down on her previous two, illustrates the growing importance of first week sales pushes for the record label release teams behind global front line artists. As music sales continue to dwindle artists' release teams have to get increasingly creative about how they get the most bang for their marketing buck. The focus on first week sales with only further sharpen.

FIGURE 16

The Growing Importance of First Week Sales

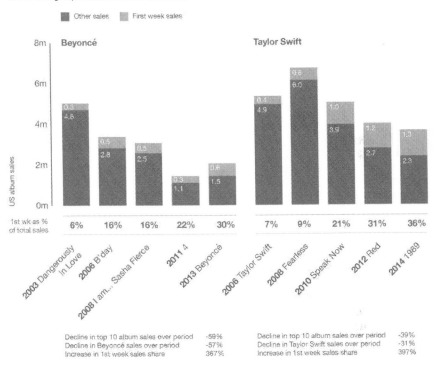

Decline in top 10 album sales over period	-59%	
Decline in Beyoncé sales over period	-57%	
Increase in 1st week sales share	367%	

Decline in top 10 album sales over period	-39%	
Decline in Taylor Swift sales over period	-31%	
Increase in 1st week sales share	397%	

Source: Nielsen Soundscan via Wikipedia

In many respects first week exclusives are the music industry's answer to the movie industry's release windows. With a typical movie release there are clearly delineated windows of release going from theatrical to Video On Demand (VoD), DVD, linear Pay TV, terrestrial TV etc. With each window the sphere of exclusivity expands and a different commercial model is applied in order to maximize revenue among largely distinct consumer segments. The movie industry has been fortunate enough to be able to retain a degree of scarcity because of:

- Effective counter-piracy measures e.g. cracking down on covert in-theatre filming by audience members

- Shifting value to where digital change creates it e.g. DVD and BluRay sales are dwindling but Netflix and Pay TV VoD have become core revenue sources

- Maintaining scarce experiences e.g. however good home entertainment systems may become the trip to the movie theatre remains a scarce and sought after experience

Though content scarcity cannot be recreated for music, or for any content type for that matters, the movie release window shows us that the appearance of scarcity in specific contexts can prove highly effective with consumers who do not have the will or the inclination to search out free alternatives. A high spending cable subscriber will happily pay to watch a new movie on demand even though it is also available on Torrents. An iTunes one week exclusive plays the same role for music, mobilizing the core fan base of an artist within an environment where convenience and quality are motive enough to pay. This is the first release window for digital music. Determining where streaming fits into the equation requires a little ingenuity: free tiers clearly have no place in the first window, in fact they should come last in the line as these are the destinations for the lowest spending, lowest value music consumers. Although 10% or so of these consumers will eventually pay for premium tiers, the inconvenience of having to wait for the latest releases will act as a further spur to converting to paid for them. Where the premium subscribers themselves fit is less straightforward. Streaming services make the case that if they limit the choice on their free tiers then they will convert fewer people to paid tiers. However sooner or later this will have to happen.

In November 2014 Taylor Swift sent shockwaves through the music industry with her label Big Machine's decision to withhold her album '1989' from Spotify and to also pull all her back catalogue. '1989' went on to sell 1.3 million copies in its first week of sale in the US, a record for first week sales by a female artist, just beating Britney Spear's 2000 record set for 'Oops!...I Did It Again'. Until the album '1989' 2014 was on track to become the first year in decades without a million selling album. Though windowing is not about to turn back the clock on album sales, it undoubtedly helped shore up sales for Swift's release. In doing so it intensified the case for premium tiers to be treated as separate tiers from free ones. Spotify's insistence on treating them the same way saw it lose on an 'all or nothing' tactical battle but with its eyes set firmly on the longer term strategy.

FIGURE 17

Streaming and Subscriptions Are Growing But Downloads Remain The Core

Global Digital Recorded Music Revenue 2004 – 2013 (Retail Values)

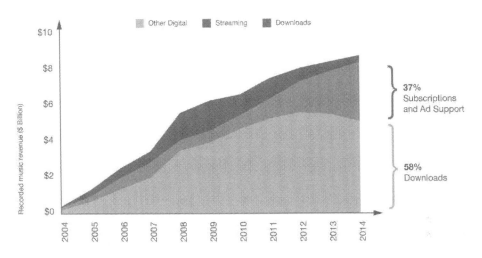

Source: MIDiA Research

The record labels have had to deal with simultaneous disruptions across multiple parts of their business, encompassing their customers, their business partners and their products. Once they had got over the initial resist-reflex the labels embarked on a path of better understanding their business partners and their consumers, and listening to what telcos and brands want out of music rather than assuming they already know. The tired badge of dinosaur hardly fits on the labels anymore. By the end of 2013 digital music accounted for 40% of recorded music revenue and within that digital segment streaming and subscriptions generated 37% of revenues (see Figure 17). This is a market that is both delivering genuine scale and that is also becoming increasingly sophisticated. It is not a stretch to say that a digital corner has been turned.

And yet despite all of the change and the increased profitability of digital, the labels continue to struggle to get back on a stable footing. The BPI's Geoff Taylor summed up the change: "We have been on a fifteen year journey: in the mid 90's, the accepted wisdom was that networks and instantaneous distribution would mean exponential growth in consumption and therefore increase the value of content. Content was King. Napster changed it all, reversing the polarity of the debate, pushing it to the other extreme that content was tending to a value of zero. Both extremes were wrong and the pendulum is now swinging back. Content creators and technology companies now understand that they can create partnerships where both benefit from content."

Access based models - Digital Plan B - have clear promise but are some way off being a proven quantity yet, and all the while the CD continues to refuse to die, creating conflicts of interest across the labels' businesses. The net result is that by the end of 2013 combined income from the CD and downloads – the clear winner of Digital Plan A - accounted for

79% of total recorded music revenue globally.[37] The labels' business is thus skewered on a single CE company with slackening interest in music, and an un-dead music format that continues to drag itself through the marketplace in zombie-like fashion.

However the record labels, big and small, are increasingly prepared for the digital transition, to migrate over the rest of world revenues to digital. The back end systems and processes are in place as Beggars' Simon Wheeler noted: "As new services are switched on there is comparatively little additional effort for us compared to the earlier days of digital." So what is required more than anything is for labels to ensure the digital cultural shift permeates wide and deep, far beyond the confines of the digital teams. Throughout the 2010's the situation will further improve for the record labels but if they are to thrive rather than just survive they must intensify their innovation efforts, both in terms of their business and the products they sell to consumers. They must also do more to establish the right kind of dialogue with partners, to understand how to best balance their needs with the labels' own. With that sort of change record labels can be better prepared to deal with a decade that will continue to be highly challenging and to throw up as many new problems as it will solutions.

CONCLUSION: On the Right Path But Plenty More Journeying Ahead

The pervasive narrative of the music industry's digital travails is of monolithic record labels resisting change and stumbling myopically towards oblivion. That the record labels are essentially the authors of their own demise. It is an analysis that is as lazy as it is clichéd. Of course where there is smoke there is often fire and in this instance there is certainly more than just the glowing embers of a metaphorical blaze. Yet the situation is much more nuanced than the pervasive superficial narrative suggests. The record labels – and the majors in particular, but not only them – undoubtedly started slowly out of the blocks, unable to see the opportunity beyond the disruptive threat. Their initial actions and reactions clearly stymied the growth of the early digital market, but over time they progressively embraced change and addressed the challenges facing them. This digitization of strategy has not always had the right objectives however. It is a trend observed by Beggars' Martin Mills: "The major record labels in the last 14 years have been undeniably luddite, only in the last three to four years have they relaxed. They are now clearly in a process of trying to get control back, though they will only get a portion of it back, if at all."

---

37 MIDIA Research

Chapter 6: The Innovator's Story

The Decline and Fall of Music Tech Invention

The music industry's fate has always been firmly shaped by technology innovators. The big step changes in its fortunes were driven by inventions built by technology companies, not record labels or publishers. Right from Thomas Edison's invention of the Phonograph in 1877, through Philips' Compact Cassette in 1962, Sony and Philips' introduction of the CD in 1982 to the Fraunhofer Institute's MP3 format in 1993, it is technology innovators who have effectively plotted the music industry's path. In the analogue era the music industry was usually able to exercise a fair degree of control and influence over this process, due to its monopoly of supply of the content that these inventions played. A liberal dose of failed formats aside – 8-Track, MiniDisc, Digital Compact Cassette to name but a few – the music industry was able to build global revenue success using these new technologies.

Digital era technologies such as A.L. Digital's CD-GRAB CD ripping software, Sahen's MP3 Player and Fraunhofer's MP3 format changed all of that by shattering the content supply monopoly (see Figure 18). The accepted wisdom is that this heralded an unprecedented phase of innovation, a Renaissance for technology innovators. However the picture is not quite so black and white. There is undoubtedly a greater number of new music inventions and innovations coming to market than at any previous period, and it is inarguably the case that this is delivering consumers more choice and control than ever before. But the last great music technology invention that has had proven global impact was the MP3 Player in 1997. With the possible exception of BitTorrent there has not yet been a great 21st century music technology invention, something that has truly transformed the music industry on a global scale. 21st century music innovation has busied itself with riffing off the last great 20th century inventions, rather than doing what those great 20th century inventions did: creating entirely new music industry paradigms.[38]

---

38 It is important to distinguish between 'invention' (namely a new creation) and 'innovation' (doing something new and novel with existing technology).

FIGURE 18

Music Technology Innovation Milestones

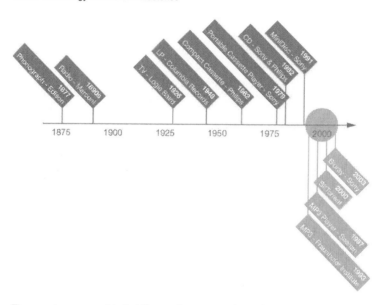

The counter argument is that the previous generations of inventions are artefacts of an era when music consumption was format based, that in the digital era it is digital experiences that shape the music industry, not formats. Though this argument has foundation it also misses a crucial change in dynamics: every one of the music technology inventions up to, and including, the introduction of the MP3 generated decades of global revenue for the inventors via license payments. Each one of these inventions served as the platform for a new music industry epoch, upon which supporting hardware was built and sold, and music was encoded and sold. Digital era innovation, thus far at least, has been more modest in scope and remit, solving specific problems in a focused enough manner to appeal to investors, without whose money the vast majority of digital era innovators would not have had any meaningful success. In the world of start ups this approach is termed the Minimum Variable Product (MVP) strategy, namely creating a product that focuses on doing just a couple of things very well in order to get to market, rather than trying to launch with a full feature set. For entrepreneurs and investors it is a smart, focused approach that helps protect against an early stage company failing due to trying to do too many things too early. But for the music industry it has the unfortunate effect of a predominance of venture and angel funded start ups creating features rather than products. In truth, the MVP strategy most often becomes in practice the Minimum Viable Feature strategy. Again for starts up and investors this is no bad thing, as it actually makes it easier for a bigger established company to assimilate their technology into their broader product set which in turn makes them a more appealing acquisition. But for the music industry it creates an undulating mass of successive adrenaline fuelled micro-innovations that burn furiously bright for a few years and then fade into the obscurity of being acquired by a bigger company, or of course the oblivion of failure. The consequence is that the average life span of digital music services is just 5.5 years (see Figure 19).

FIGURE 19

The Lifespan of Key Digital Music Services

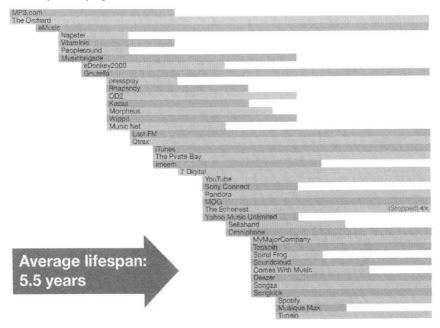

Throughout this process of Digital Darwinism the industry wide innovation needle is nudged along in infinitesimally smaller increments than it should be when measured against the amount of investment poured into music technology companies since the late 1990's. Consumer experiences changed dramatically and music industry business models and revenues were turned upside down, but fundamental music technology remained relatively constant. Part of the problem is that so much of the inward investment goes not into product development, but into other costs such as marketing, operations and, crucially, rights. Investment is effectively supercharging mini-innovations. The music industry is still waiting for its first great 21st invention, but it may find its arrival as elusive as Godot's. The revenue promise that the music industry was able deliver upon for 20th century inventions can no longer be guaranteed, making it much harder to justify the requisite research and development investment. Instead technology inventions and innovations are becoming media-agnostic, not dependent on the fortunes of any single troubled media industry, let alone the music business. Arguably the most important consumer product of the 21st century so far – the tablet – is an enabler of multiple content experiences.[39] It does not tie itself to any single media industry or its preferred technology. There may yet be one last great music technology invention, but this generalist content technology innovation path is the one that the music industry is ultimately going to have to get used to. The remit of music innovation has become to build within the confines of other technology and platforms rather than to become the technology platform itself.

Even with this caveat considered, clear progress has been made. Back in 2002 when there

39 Even the tablet is more innovation than invention. Advocates of the tablet position it as the pioneering technology of the post-PC age, but it is of course simply a computer with a new form factor.

were few compelling licensed music services to talk of, piracy sites dominated and generated an average of 30.3 million monthly active users at their peak (see Figure 20). In 2009 the picture was not particularly encouraging with licensed music services generating less than half that figure – 12.9 million – at their peak but the situation now is dramatically different, with licensed services generating an average of 60.8 million monthly active users, compared to just 5 million for The Pirate Bay, the stand out pirate destination. The licensed sector finally appears to be wining out against piracy. There are mitigating factors, such as the fact that Soundcloud skews the numbers high and that overall consumer digital sophistication has increased, but both of these can reasonably be considered facets of the new opportunity rather than exceptions to be discounted. YouTube and Soundcloud have managed to absorb a lot piracy's heat. Across the 40 main music services – including YouTube and other free services – the combined total users is 2.4 billion.[40] Among free digital music destinations at least, the legitimate market has reached its prime time audience. Though this creates the paradoxical situation of premium music services still having to figure out how to compete against free, only this time round legal free is their foe.

FIGURE 20

Music Services Are More Successful Than They Have Ever Been

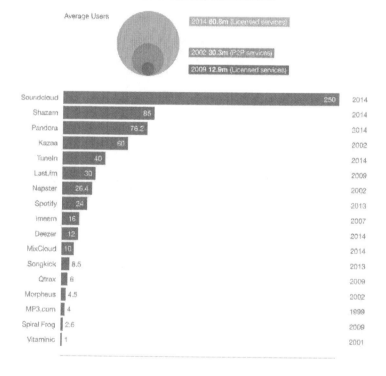

40 MIDiA Research 'Global Digital Music Services Benchmark'

Worlds in Collision

The music industry cannot though cast itself as innocent victim, having played a very active role in limiting the impact of digital era music technology innovation. Record label decisions about what innovation gets licensed and what does not, determine whether an innovation ever makes it to market – by legitimate means at least. It does not matter how well a technology has been built or marketed, how good the management team is or how bold the vision is, if record labels do not license to it, it will simply not make it to market. An innovation that requires music content and that wants to operate legally but that lacks record label supported is doomed to a stillbirth. It is here, at the sharp end of digital innovation that entrepreneurs and rights owners clash most spectacularly.

But the conflagration is most often a collision of worldviews rather than a waging of war. Rights owners naturally have an essentially defensive and conservative outlook: they have everything to lose and the vast majority of digital innovations have historically either failed to deliver on their promise or have been hugely disruptive. They are also naturally slower moving and their prime motive is to protect their assets and to retain the status quo. Digital innovators however have, by nature, an almost polar opposite viewpoint: their challenge is to push boundaries, to push into the unknown and to move quickly, with little regard for tradition. As Ralph Simon observed: "In Silicon Valley failure is simply scar tissue." Start ups are agile, have few corporate constraints and are concerned most with disrupting the status quo. This divergence of ideology alone would be a potent enough mix, but the 'go big or go home' mentality instilled by venture capital typically pushes the digital innovators further towards bold, disruptive ambition and thus even further from rights owners' comfort zones.

Not all digital innovators are the same though. In fact they typically fall into one of three camps:

- Rights Ally: these innovators work closely with rights holders from an early stage, working hard to get their services fully licensed. Successful examples include Spotify and Apple. These innovators pursue a cooperate strategy.

- Rights Frenemy: these innovators strike a careful balance between maintaining good relations with rights holders on one side of their business but testing the limits on the other side. Successful examples include YouTube, Google and Amazon.[41] These innovators pursue a do first, ask forgiveness later strategy.

- Rights Refusenik: these innovators rail against copyright and often see themselves as waging war against copyright. They typically show little or no interest in licensing their services and will happily take their fight to court. Successful examples include Napster, the Pirate Bay and Megaupload. These innovators pursue a push on regardless strategy.

---

41 Google's business is riven with conflicting approaches to rights holders. For example it is an active licensor with the Google Play download store but it is a relatively reluctant enforcer of copyright on its Google search and YouTube properties, where rights holders routinely complain that Google makes it difficult for them to get infringed works removed. Google even posts a link to a 'ChillingEffects.org' website for each DMCA removed link that points to the censorship issues surrounding DMCA takedowns. Google also opted not to license a 'point and play' music locker service from the labels, choosing instead to implement a license-free DMCA compliant 'upload' locker service. In a similar manner, Amazon also chose the 'upload' locker option despite also having a fully licensed download store. In both locker instances, the license fee demands from the labels were cited as being prohibitively expensive. Apple launched a fully licensed 'point and play' locker service, though as a premium offering.

The volatile mix these parties and their competing strategies create has defined the shape and pace of digital music innovation, and indeed of digital content as a whole. Ironically it is the digital innovators who do the least to work with rights holders – the Rights Refusniks and the Rights Frenemies –who achieve most from an innovation perspective. These innovators go straight to market without licenses, either intending never to acquire them, or to negotiate from a position of power when they have millions of users. Larry Miller suggested this approach is a recurring success: "If you think of the world as divided into those who ask for permission and those who ask for forgiveness, by any measure those who have created the greatest wealth for themselves and for their investors are those that asked for forgiveness. History has shown us that the path is littered with the husks of well-intended start ups who played by the rules. Vevo, founded by Sony and Universal, and Spotify, are notable exceptions that prove the rule."

The Refusnik and Frenemy approached arose as a direct result of label and publisher digital conservatism in the late 1990's and early 2000's. But while the Refusniks rose as revolutionaries, bent on overthrowing the music industry establishment, the Frenemies learned from the experience of the early digital music services that they would not get what they needed from rights owners at a quick enough pace. While most Refusniks have found themselves eventually thwarted by music industry counter action such as protracted legal proceedings, the Frenemies often achieved more than the Allies. YouTube's success in signing deals with the major record labels on the eve of its acquisition by Google, but a year after launching, is the most significant and successful example to date of the do first, ask forgiveness later strategy. David Israelite, President and CEO of the US music publishers trade body the NMPA, described the impact of YouTube's approach: "YouTube is the most important music venue in the world and it is a synch site. It was a rough route and we had to sue them for a few years but we have now got to a good place." Meanwhile innovators who have played strictly by the rulebook have often found themselves having to launch with products that fall far short of consumer expectations. In the mid to late 2000's many big and otherwise successful companies attempted to replicate the success of iTunes but failed miserably because they adhered too closely to the Rights Ally model. Lewis Silkin's Cliff Fluet recalled such a case: "I took an exciting new digital proposition with a healthy seven figure sum to the labels, but after two meetings all the USP and excitement had been completely squeezed out of it. The power of 'no' is a negative veto." Another example was British satellite TV broadcaster Sky who meticulously built a music subscription service around the record labels' preferred model of PC tethered streaming with a small monthly allowance of downloads. Despite Sky's considerable marketing efforts the service promptly flopped because it met rights owner needs rather than consumer needs. Paul Hitchman suggested that Rights Allies have routinely paid the price for playing by the rules: "Companies trying to do things in a legal way got battered but those who didn't, like Last.FM and YouTube sailed by to success."

Sony's Fall From Grace

One of the companies that was most affected by its failed attempts to make digital work was Sony. Before the rise of iTunes Sony held most of the aces in the pack for music technology: it was the co-founder of the Red-Book CD; it was the world leader in portable audio with its Walkman brand; it was a leader in home audio; and of course it numbered Sony Music among its corporate entities. If anyone was expected to be a digital music success story it was Sony, with its unique blend of technology innovation and music expertise and focus. The way that things panned out though was very different indeed. Instead of embracing the change wrought by the rise of the internet Sony found itself stuck in the role of slow moving incumbent, unable to grasp the dynamics and implications of disruptive, digital era innovation. The Walkman should have been the preeminent digital music brand but it remained glued to the side-lines, helplessly watching the inexorable rise of the iPod. It was a bitter pill to swallow for the proud Japanese company that prided itself on decades of high quality, elegantly designed products that consumers around the world once aspired to. Sony could have been forgiven for feeling that Apple had stolen its clothes. It was not that Sony had simply sat back and done nothing. Rather it stuck with its analogue era modus operandi and consequently ended up with a rude awakening. Apple prospered exactly because it did not play by the old rulebook. As Warner's former EVP Paul Vidich noted: "There were no other companies that were going to be able to do what Apple did. Microsoft didn't have its own devices and it was always going to struggle to join the dots across all of its business units. Microsoft and Sony both listened too much to what the labels said and not enough to the consumer. Jobs was focused on the consumer." Apple stole Sony's clothes and ran.

On the surface it simply looked like Apple had built a better music player, but something much more fundamental had taken place. Building CE products in the 1980's and much of the 1990's had been all about hardware, but the internet changed all of that. The software experience that a product delivered became just as important as the hardware, an inextricable extension of the device experience. Sony continued to build exemplary devices but failed to deliver the same level of quality to the software component. Robert Ashcroft, who served in various senior roles at Sony between 1999 and 2007 including as SVP Network Services Europe, described the situation: "The key thing that underpinned Sony's difficulties was not fully grasping the fundamental shift from hardware to software. It just didn't have the insight into the mind of the empowered consumer that relied upon software to achieve usage goals, and this manifested itself in products. For example Sony Vaio laptops were widely recognized as fantastic pieces of hardware with quirky software. Sony was trying to replicate old world functionality in digital contexts rather than supporting new behaviours." Throughout the 2000's Sony digital music devices out performed competitor products across a broad range of specifications such as battery life, build quality and audio fidelity. But where they fell down, and crucially so, was in the user experience. Ashcroft recalled one user post on the MiniDisc user website that said "this product is amazing: the hardware is amazingly good, the software is amazingly bad."

Sony was famed for encouraging internal competition and during its peak years this model begat some of the most important CE innovations and inventions there have ever been. But it also resulted in a lack of homogeneity among its various product portfolios. In the 1980's and the 1990's this had been a minor fissure but by the 2000's it had developed into major fault lines as Ashcroft explained: "The culture of Sony was focused on individual products rather than platform technologies. There was also a prevailing idea, carried over from hardware design, that good application software needed one-touch features. I remember a highly respected engineer enthusiastically telling me how he had improved the Open MagicGate Jukebox [Sony's Music Player software] by removing the playlist function and making the burning of CDs 'one touch'". Sony's product siloes manifested themselves in a disjointed user journey from the outset. While Steve Jobs concentrated Apple's energies on ensuring there were as few user speed bumps as possible in a single unified product experience, Sony allowed product fiefdoms to arise that paid scant attention to the priorities of the macro user experience they contributed to. Jay Samit, who spent four years as EVP and GM at Sony Corporation of America after having left EMI ran up against these internal divisions as he tried to help Sony address Apple's challenge: "If I'd had all the pieces then things could have got done. But Sony was so siloed. If a product had a spinning disc it had to be made in the Vaio team, if it had physical media it had to be made in the Walkman team. Neither group could come up with an iPod challenger."

Sony remained stubbornly committed to its design and technology principles even if this meant flying in the face of consumer behaviour and demand. The 'Sony's way or the highway' mentality resulted in Sony digital music players only supporting its proprietary ATRAC audio codec and pointedly not the dominant MP3 format. For all those digital music consumers with MP3 files – i.e. nearly all of them – they had to individually transcode each MP3 file into ATRAC if they wanted to be able to play them on a Sony digital music player. Sony compounded issues further with a quasi ideological commitment to its proprietary DRM system Open MagicGate as Ashcroft recalled: "Sony absolutely saw DRM as useful tool, not just something forced upon them by the music industry. Open MagicGate was widely considered internally to be the jewel in the crown." While most digital music services were doing all they could to break free from the constraints of DRM Sony was a loyal adherent.

Sony did not however give up the fight, and continued to try to establish a footprint into the digital marketplace, including the launch of the pioneering but ultimately doomed subscription service StreamMan. According to Ashcroft Sony was: "…way too early with the StreamMan subscription streaming service for lots of business, technology and infrastructure reasons. We were even too early from a rights management perspective because the labels had no benchmark against which to value the rights we needed." By the late 2000's Sony reignited its interest in subscriptions, initially focused on mobile but soon widening the scope of its ambition to multiple platforms. The first step was the launch of Play Now Plus in September 2008 via its mobile phone joint venture Sony Ericsson. Play Now Plus started cautiously however, launching with Telenor, not in the incumbent telco's home market Norway but instead in Sweden where it was a small challenger carrier. Play Now Plus was Sony's take on Nokia's Comes With Music and it turned to UK music services provider Omniphone to build the service for them. Omniphone Chief Engineer and Co-Founder Phil Sant explained that: "Sony Ericsson wanted to respond to Nokia, and Sony Play Now Plus on Sony Ericsson devices was it." Play Now Plus eventually launched in 18 countries but failed to set the world alight.

Sony's appetite though was not dimmed and instead returned with a far bolder vision. Sony still had a strong and diverse portfolio of CE products across TV, games, phones, computers and music players, with ever more of them becoming 'smart' with interactivity and internet connectivity at their core. What Sony needed was a content 'glue' to bind them together and it opted for a multiplatform subscription service curiously named Qriocity. Given Sony's organizational siloes, the challenge of pulling together a service that worked across devices as diverse as the PlayStation, Sony Bravia TVs and Sony Ericsson phones was no small task. Omniphone was again chosen to build the service for Sony and Sant recalled that it "was a monster deal that took 18 months of negotiating, it was the first scan and match service with the majors." Qriocity did not get off to the best of starts, first of all rebranding to the rather more conventional but hardly imaginative brand name Sony Music Unlimited, and then facing the far more serious challenge of a security breach with thousands of Sony Music Unlimited subscribers' payment details being hacked. Sony Music Unlimited eventually overcame these hurdles to become established as a respectably successful global digital content service passing the one million subscriber mark in January 2012. But for a company of Sony's scale and ambition, this was at best a modest return and did little to change the underlying situation that Sony was no longer anything more than a bit player in the digital music economy.

Although the rapid rise of Samsung provided Sony with more serious competition across a larger swathe of its product portfolio, Apple was the company that hit Sony where it hurt most, usurping Sony's role as the leading aspirational, premium quality device brand. Also Samsung, though a fierce competitor, competed on terms that Sony understood: it was one CE heavyweight slogging it out with another. Apple on the other hand reversed into the CE business from its position as a PC and software company, using music to establish the beachhead from which it rapidly expanded. Thus Samsung found itself as equally powerless as Sony to build a compelling content and services strategy, despite establishing sales leadership in smartphones and tablets. Though many more units of Samsung smartphones may have been shipped than the iPhone, its failed Music Hub service did not even get out of the starting blocks, let alone pose any meaningful challenge to iTunes. Thus Sony's travails are, rather than unique, a macro illustration of how traditional CE companies failed to understand how to adapt to internet-era company competition and disruption. As Adam Kidron succinctly put it: "Most CE companies are fragile because they have been brutalized by Apple."

The Innovator Ascendency

Sony's fall from grace was just one part of a wholesale changing of the guard, a passing of the baton from 20th century CE companies to 21st century software companies, with digital music the defining battleground. Whereas CE companies spent decades nurturing reciprocal relationships with media companies the modus operandi of this new wave of companies was to push technology to consumers first and then pursue content strategy. Although the technology space is characterized by a plethora of hungry young start ups, it has come to be dominated by a few key players in just the same way the CE space was. Whereas the old CE companies exercised control through retail and distribution relationships, these new companies do so by controlling the platforms through which labels, artists and technology companies alike reach consumers.

Three technology companies have come to dominate the digital music economy, and digital content more broadly: Amazon, Apple and Google. Each company's business model is highly distinct and each has different strategic objectives, but all three have become established as clear control points in the consumer music journey. Amazon for online CD buying, and increasingly MP3s; Apple for downloads, apps and devices; Google for search, video, via YouTube, and devices via Android and Motorola. With these combined assets of hardware, software, discovery, consumption, data, payment and fulfilment, they are the dominant platforms for digital music. Each has become a control point, or number of control points, so powerful that the labels and publishers are effectively no longer masters of their own destinies, relying on the platforms and devices of these technology companies to connect fans with their artists. It is a reversal of roles from analogue era innovation.

When one of these new control points starts to behave as a Rights Frenemy, or worse as a Rights Refusnik, things get really bad for the music industry. While Apple in the main adhered to the Rights Ally role, Google's position oscillated between ambiguous and outright anti-copyright, often simultaneously. Nowhere is this conflicted approach illustrated better than in Google's takedown procedure: on request from rights holders Google removes links to copyright infringing sites – so far so good – but then tags each affected search result with a link to a site called 'chillingeffects.org', a site with the stated aim of countering "the chilling effects of overreaching 'cease and desist' notices of intellectual property infringement." Not exactly the actions one would expect of a company that claims to be committed to working with rights owners. Google is carefully portraying itself in the role of unwilling partner, being forced to work within a system it does not agree with.

The contrast with Apple is abundantly clear as Geoff Taylor pointed out: "There is a sense that Google is slowly moving in the right direction but they do not yet have the same appetite as Apple to promote and value content." Nonetheless Google is probably the single most important technology company for the music industry, with its vast array of assets that spread across music discovery, consumption and acquisition, including Google search, YouTube, Android, Play Store and even its music subscription service Google Play Music All Access. Google is an end-to-end music ecosystem that dwarfs iTunes in terms of reach but delivers far less direct music revenue. Google is in fact a collection of interconnecting self-contained ecosystems, some with devices, some without, but coalescing to form the biggest gatekeeper of them all.

Many internet thinkers had expected the web to do away with the 'gatekeepers' – a role most often performed by traditional media companies in the analogue era – but what has happened instead is the emergence of a new generation of gatekeepers. The disruptive technology companies that had promised to change the world realized that the clothes of the previous incumbents fitted them pretty well too. Algorithms replaced human editors, one set of gatekeepers effectively replaced another, the revolutionaries became the new establishment. Power shifted seamlessly from old gatekeeper to new as David Lowery observed: "Whoever has the biggest aggregated audience becomes the new intermediary."

Alongside Google, Facebook stands out as one of the most significant new intermediaries of the early 2010's, establishing itself as an entry point to the wider web for more than a billion internet users without spending a penny on content licenses. This is part of Facebook's Integrated Web Strategy, placing itself at the centre of as much of as many consumers' digital lives as it possibly can and in doing so creating as many consumer lock-ins as it can.[42] Content is one of those lock-ins, with music at the core. Facebook is reinventing itself as a 21st century portal, a destination that aggregates consumers' content rather than expensively creating and licensing the content in the traditional media company way that the 20th century portals like AOL, MSN and Yahoo! did.[43] Facebook lets music services like Spotify, Rhapsody, Deezer and Rdio expensively acquire music rights and instead allows those services to pipe music into the Facebook timeline. Facebook gets free music and increased audience time – read 'increased advertising revenue' – while the music services, in theory, get increased exposure. In practice most see much more in the way of additional cost than they do benefit.

Facebook has another strand to its content strategy bow: the artists. Apple used music downloads to establish iTunes, YouTube music videos and Amazon CDs, Facebook leveraged the artists themselves. With more than one billion users Facebook has virtually every type of fan for virtually every type of artist among its installed base, and in most cases it has all or

---

42 The Socially Integrated Web is a strategic necessity for Facebook. Mark Zuckerberg knows all too well that no company is invincible in the face of competition, there was after all a time when MySpace had the social networking world at its feet and almost overnight crumbled into a curious footnote. The odds of Facebook following such a rapid path to obscurity are small, but it will some time or another face a serious challenge from a would-be Facebook killer. Google+ might yet prove to be that challenger. That is why Facebook needs to deeply embed itself in as much of its users' digital lives as it can, to make it as difficult as possible for them to want to leave. Without those foundations any amount of advertising business model innovation is an exercise in futility. Currently Facebook has a great communication lock in (for how many of our outer circle of friends have we lost phone numbers and emails,so that Facebook is our only means of contacting them?). But Facebook wants to have similar lock-ins across our digital lives, especially our content experiences. It is pulling more of our content experiences into Facebook and simultaneously pushing itself outwards into more of our content experiences that happen in the outside web.
43 I am indebted to my former JupiterResearch colleague David Card for the perceptive term '21st Century Portal'.

most of their entire active fan bases. Little wonder then that artists flocked to Facebook to create artist pages, mainly a MySpace exodus, but also from their own websites. Then, just as with the other technology super powers, once Facebook had established itself as a control point it started changing the rules of engagement. Artists learned how true rang the old adage 'there's no such thing as a free lunch'. Instead of being some sort of altruistic fan engagement platform for artists, Facebook is of course an audience acquisition business and artists are simply one type of fuel for that engine. More than that, artists have had to start paying their way as David Lowery explained: "As artists we collected all of our fans to our Facebook pages to interact with them. Then Facebook changed the rules and so our fans now don't see our posts unless a fan shares them or we pay $49 to $100 per post to promote them. That is a process of reintermediation, but it is more than that, it is pay to play and it is exploitative."

The Innovator Hegemony

Facebook, Apple, Google and Amazon all in differing ways used music as a stepping stone towards achieving global scale that, once gained, let them change the nature of their interactions with the music industry's various stakeholders. Once respective goals were achieved, the balance of power shifted and the technology 'good cop' was usurped by 'bad cop'. Labels and artists suddenly found themselves beholden to companies they helped succeed and that success was now used against them.

Although the sheer global reach and influence of these companies was largely out of the control of the labels, they played a significant role in the rise of each. At times the record labels were out manoeuvred by technology companies that over played their hand early on but got away with the bluff. There were many stages on the road to innovator hegemony at which labels could have acted to balance the interplay of power but did not. As David Boyle put it: "The industry was not bold enough in dealing with the big digital partners. We should have had an evidenced based conversation with Apple." Early on in the road to hegemony the technology companies needed music more than vice versa and as Cary Sherman argued music and content are usually at the centre of the use cases for digital technology: "The excitement is not just about the technology in the device, but the content that the device can deliver. Content is being seen as a driver of technology innovation." Unfortunately for the music industry the fact that music can so easily be acquired for free means that music can still be at the core of device experiences without a penny being spent on content licenses.

The record labels' growing obsession with working with global companies that brought 'scale' to the table helped consolidate the dominant positions of these technology powerhouses. In the cases of Apple and YouTube, music was instrumental in their respective ascendencies. Roger Faxon suggested that this has led to an environment of mutual distrust: "The relationship between most of the music industry and Apple, Amazon and Google is anything but a partnership. There is a huge amount of mistrust." The objective of working with partners with long term plans rather than riskier start ups with a three year window before their investors want an 'exit' is understandable. But it has had the inadvertent effects of skewing the market towards companies with financial muscle and slowing innovation. Because music is a means to an end for these technology superpowers rather than the objective itself, they pursue the good enough method of innovation rather than pushing the user experience envelope. They get sufficient benefit to their core businesses from good enough innovation, leaving little business rationale for investing heavily in developing cutting edge features for modest additional return. If a comparatively low-cost, DMCA-compliant digital locker is enough for your customers why spend millions building something more complex?

Thus innovation has slowed, not just because of the rights holders but because of the technology companies too. Rights owners recognize that their long-term future depends on ambitious innovation but lack the innovation heritage and resources to drive it so are dependent upon technology company partners. Yet the big three technology companies have slowed their rate of innovation because they do not need to do more. Instead Amazon sticks with static eBooks and Google launches an unlicensed DMCA music locker service.[44] Features that are good enough to help sell more devices but that do not move the innovation needle too often result in digital products that are not fit for purpose. They are products that are good enough for the technology companies but not good enough for media companies, nor often are they good enough for consumers. There is however a growing, if cautious, sense that change is beginning to occur. The fact that Apple continues to generate so much more value from its customers than any Android ecosystem is able to, continues to spur Google and others towards more ambitious content strategies. One label executive went as far as to say that: "Google is chasing Apple's tailpipe."

However the counter argument is that Google gets everything it needs from music already. Google is in the business of creating and collating user data in order to generate advertising revenue. YouTube is undeniably Google's best music asset for user data creation and it is far more successful as a free service than any licensed Google service could dream of being. Google's launch of two subscription services - the clumsily named Google Play Music All Access and YouTube Music Key – both feel more like attempts to portray the image of being the 'good partner' to labels than they do a burning desire to be a premium music service success story. A cynic might suggest that Google will willingly support both efforts for a finite period of time before shuttering both and turning to labels with a 'see we tried it but it didn't work, now let us get back to doing what we know works.' The fact Google secured on demand album 'playlists' as part of its main YouTube offering even while Music Key was in invite only Beta illustrates where Google's priorities lie. It also shows just how shrewd a negotiator the company is.

But the predominant focus of digital music service strategy has become driving down the cost of the rights, with the big technology companies simultaneously playing a short game and a long game. The short game takes the shape of fiercely contested licensing negotiations – especially in the case of Google, while the long game involves the technology companies trying to change the very foundations of copyright itself through lobbying and influencing efforts. The tactics include Google sponsoring academic papers that question issues such as whether piracy hurts music sales as well as direct lobbying efforts. After years of label lobbying ascendancy, the balance has begun to swing towards the technology companies, winning over key influencers such as the European Commissioner Neelie Kroes. It is a trend picked up by Martin Mills: "In the legislative arena technology companies have a consistently louder voice" and by Alison Wenham: "Governments have been persuaded by technology and search companies to devalue copyright." Sherman believes that the big

---

44 While Apple needs digital content to help sell iOS devices, Google to help drive Android adoption and ad revenue, Amazon needs to ensure that books and music remain part of the first rung on the purchase ladder for their customers. Amazon's model works on the basis that new customers come to Amazon through lower consideration purchases such as books, CDs and DVDs. Over time customers become more comfortable with Amazon's platform and migrate to higher consideration purchases such as PCs and TVs. The risk for Amazon is that digital companies like Apple cannibalize this market with paid content sales which is why the retailer is aggressively pursuing its own digital content strategy.

technology companies are often far from transparent in their lobbying efforts: "We have witnessed the growth of super-powerful technology companies that have huge online reach and have used their influence to shape views on copyright. They should be honest that their stances on copyright are defined by their business interests, not by principles or ideals." In other words commercial and business strategy is being disguised as copyright ideology.

The balance of power of influence is also distorted by anti-trust and competition legislation. Dating back to the analogue era when media companies were all powerful, anti-trust legislation was designed to prevent media companies colluding and entering into monopolistic behaviour. But now that technology companies own the platform control points that media companies depend upon in the digital realm, anti-trust and competition legislation has the unintended consequence of consolidating the power of the technology monopolies by neutering the media companies. Record labels are prevented from working together to establish unified positions so each of the big technology companies can pick off the labels one by one in licensing discussions. Many record label executives observe that there is often an implicit, and sometimes explicit, threat that their content could be pulled from a service at the drop of a hat. This pervasive fear can often distort business strategy as David Boyle observed of EMI: "People were too busy surviving to focus on a bigger picture. We felt helpless trying to shape digital, it was all about influencing the likes of iTunes and Spotify. There was a fear of the partner, of always wanting to be the good partner."

Anti-trust legislation plays a crucial role in ensuring record labels do not abuse their oligopolistic positions, but it does not sufficiently cater for the realities of the adjacent markets that emerge out of digital business models. The three big technology companies have a greater concentration of influence and market share in paid content than any of the labels or publisher. Amazon, Apple and Google have become a single, effective monopoly in each of their respective marketplaces. Thus anti-trust legislation currently appears to have the unintended consequence of reinforcing market concentration in the digital content marketplaces. It is a point made by Sherman: "Anti-trust has been an impediment for media companies growing into the digital age. You have issues going well beyond pricing, which you cannot do together, but [also] of much bigger, fundamental changes to business that would benefit from collective thinking and approaches."

The big technology companies use their dominant power and influence to pick off rights owners one at a time while record labels are prevented by law from being able to coordinate a response. For example if Apple or Amazon feel that the other is being given an advantage by a specific record label they will not hesitate to threaten to pull that label's content from their service unless the situation is rectified. One major label digital executive explained: "We are really limited in what we can do with the big partners. It is difficult to build something that will work for all of them, but if we try to do something with just one of them the other will threaten to pull all of our digital catalogue from their store, immediately. And that phone call has happened before. They're not afraid to play that card." This dynamic effectively forces labels into choosing between doing something resource intensive with all major partners, or nothing at all.

The tension between rights owner protectionism and innovator disruption is immutable and has too often slowed the rate of innovation in the legitimate marketplace. All the while the informal, unlicensed sector flourishes with no such shackles. But it is also a dynamic that, when correctly balanced, acts as a crucial innovation catalyst, ensuring that innovation drives value right across the value chain and not just to rights holders or to digital innovators. While the type of innovation that delivers prolonged prosperity for all parties, that characterised 20th century music technology invention may be a thing of the past, innovation can and should drive mutual benefit in the digital age. As Geoff Taylor observed "in the last three years technology companies and content creators have been on the path towards becoming partners." It is however a long path, fraught with difficulty. One music service more than any other has exemplified the tensions and continual flux, YouTube.

YouTube Changes Everything

In February 2005 three former PayPal employees launched a video sharing web site that has done more than any other single web property to change the way in which consumers interact with content online. Until the advent of YouTube, online video was a market waiting to come into being. Home broadband adoption was only just beginning to take off, with total household penetration still averaging below 30% across European and the US. Those more sophisticated internet users who did have fast connections and spent time hunting out online video had to search far and wide for it, with only a few key video destinations. A number of technology companies foresaw the opportunities that a couple of years of rapid broadband growth would bring but because the first wave of broadband connections were still relatively slow, with many users on 256 kpbs connections and with data usage caps, short form video worked far better than mid and long form video.

Music video was the perfect fit. Music video start up Musicbrigade, coming out Sweden – the country with among the highest western world broadband penetration rates in the early 2000's – had been among the first to attempt to capitalize, forming the company in 1999 and acquiring some rights from all majors.[45] By 2005 the online video sector was accelerating with two US based companies in particular pushing music video to the fore. One was social network MySpace, which became established as the de facto social destination for artists and fans and identified music video as a natural extension of its music platform strategy. Another was Yahoo!, the leading music video destination online, which despite its licensing troubles with Warner acquired an impressive 24 million US unique visitors by the end of 2005.[46] YouTube though was about to show that these metrics were merely an appetiser for what was just becoming the online video revolution.

Following a beta launch in May 2005 YouTube went to public launch the following November and usage accelerated rapidly, to such an extent that the site reached 12.6 million unique US users by May 2006[47] and hit 100 million monthly video views by that July. In June 2006 YouTube broke into the top 50 most visited web properties in the US with 16 million unique users, though still behind MySpace Video and Yahoo! Video which had 21 million unique users.[48] Within a few months YouTube had surpassed both on its path to becoming the leading global video destination and the catalyst for online video adoption across the globe. In YouTube, online video found its killer app and its killer content was music: by 2007 music was by the most popular category of video on YouTube, accounting for 23% of all videos.[49]

---

45 Musicbrigade proved to be too far ahead of its time, struggling to gain consumer traction and ultimately being disrupted out of the market by YouTube, finally going into administration in February 2008.
46 Comscore Media Metrix, via http://www.imediaconnection.com/printpage/printpage.aspx?id=7803
47 Comscore Media Metrix, via http://readwrite.com/2006/06/27/youtube_nearly#awesm=~oh2zAL5241auKt
48 Comscore Media Metrix http://files.shareholder.com/downloads/SCOR/2677587020x0x102108/63
4a5c23-1ec8-47dd-828f-2487557f395f/SCOR_News_2006_8_15_General_Releases.pdf
49 Statistics and Social Network of YouTube Videos. Xu Cheng, Cameron Dale, Jiangchuan Liu,
School of Computing Science Simon Fraser University, Burnaby, BC, Canada 2007

YouTube's rapid ascent as the global consumption point for music video was a clear case of a vacuum being filled, coming at a time when MTV was moving away from music video towards reality TV shows such as the Osbournes, Laguna Beach, Punk'd and the Ashlee Simpson Show. MTV's transition had left music fans without a standout music video destination, a supply and demand side hole that YouTube filled effortlessly. Despite the labels' obsession with not doing another MTV they let YouTube did exactly that, and with exactly the same content. Everything had happened before and was happening again.

Unsurprisingly YouTube did not have an easy ride with content owners, in large part because the company allowed users to upload content rather than seeking out licenses for them. Seeing the surge in popularity of music video but no license income, the labels started to apply pressure on YouTube, with Universal even hinting that it would consider legal action. YouTube made commitments to remove infringing works and started to explore revenue sharing agreements with the majors, however they were largely unimpressed due to YouTube's relative lack of proven revenue streams at that stage. This was classic Rights Frenemy strategy. The situation changed in an instant once Google entered into negotiations with YouTube to acquire it and allocated a portion of the acquisition fee towards paying rights holders.

Now that YouTube could start offering sizeable upfront payments the labels began to play ball. In an ingenious ploy YouTube gave each of the major labels an equity stake in the company the day before Google bought it for $1.6 billion in November 2006. Then Google promptly paid each of the labels $50 million for their shares ensuring that the labels could treat their income as returns from investments and therefore not subject to being shared with their artists. Almost immediately after the labels' deal had been struck Universal Music promptly sued two YouTube clones – Bolt and Grouper – for copyright infringement. The message was clear: YouTube was from there on the record labels' platform of choice for music video and no one else was invited. YouTube had transformed from unlicensed irritant into a formal appendage of major label digital strategy.[50] It was a resounding endorsement for the 'do now, ask for forgiveness later' approach.

YouTube went from strength to strength and as of November 2013 YouTube had 1 billion unique users viewing 6 billion hours of video every month and uploading 100 hours of video a minute.[51] Since its acquisition by Google, YouTube has become a crucially important part of the digital music landscape, perhaps even the single most important destination of all. It has become a standard component of any artist's digital marketing strategy and the world's single most popular digital music app, bar none. The percentage of consumers who watch music videos on YouTube at least monthly is 40%, rising to 59% among 18-24 year olds, and 18-34 year olds account for 50% of all YouTube music consumers (see Figure 21). For youth, YouTube is most often the music app of choice and its universal availability across PCs, smartphones and tablets for no cost to the consumer ensures it has unrivalled reach and influence.

---

50 Once Google had completed its acquisition of YouTube various content owners decided to try to tap into its deep pockets by filing suit for copyright infringement. This resulted in a series of high profile legal cases, most notably with Viacom, parent of MTV who had quickly recognized that not so much were its clothes getting stolen but its entire wardrobe was being taken. Viacom filed a $1 billion lawsuit in 2007 for copyright infringement of shows such as SpongeBob SquarePants and the Daily Show, but did not achieve the quick success it had expected – so much so in fact that as of August 2013 the action is still on going.
51 Google: https://www.youtube.com/yt/press/en-GB/statistics.html

FIGURE 21

YouTube Is The Destination Of Choice For Young Music Fans

Distribution Of YouTube Music Video Viewers By Age

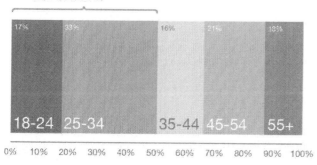

50% YouTube music video
users are under 35

17%　33%　16%　21%　15%

18-24　25-34　　35-44　45-54　　55+

0%　10%　20%　30%　40%　50%　60%　70%　80%　90%　100%

% of YouTube Video Users

Source: MIDiA Research Consumer Survey 06/14 (UK and US) n = 2,000

Purists argue that audio quality on YouTube videos is poor, however over recent years there has been a marked improvement in YouTube audio quality, often leaving little to distinguish itself from Spotify's standard steam quality. But focusing on audio quality almost misses the point, YouTube's strength lies in: the depth of the catalogue; the fact it has video; the fact it is free and mobile; and that it simply works. YouTube is a truly digital-era music product that leverages interactivity, social functionality and video to create an immersive music experience. For Digital Native teens YouTube is digital music. And therein lies the music industry's YouTube Quandary: YouTube is simply so good that it leaves little oxygen for other music services to breathe. Whereas a consumer has to pay $9.99 to get streaming music onto their smartphone with a service like Spotify, YouTube is instantly accessible for absolutely nothing. And because so much of YouTube's music catalogue comes from users uploading their own music collections rather than being seeded by labels, the breadth and depth of catalogue is far superior to any traditionally licensed music service. All of those deleted tracks, unreleased bootlegs, live performance, rare cover versions, un-digitized independent catalogues can be found on YouTube even though they are not available elsewhere. Google has spent recent years honing its takedown process to help rights owners ensure that rights infringing files are removed but the process is far from perfect, with factors such as caps on how many takedown requests can be submitted per rights owner. More recently Google introduced its Content ID system enabling rights owners to identify unlicensed version of their music but instead of removing it opt to earn income from it. While this has the undoubted benefit of allowing rights owners to generate extra income - found money, if you like - it also has the added benefit of legitimizing more of YouTube's informal, 'unlicensed' music catalogue. An opportunity not open to other music services that instead have to depend solely on what tracks the labels make available to them.

The reason why one rule appears to apply to YouTube and another to the rest is because it is simply so big, so powerful and so influential that the labels dare not do without it. Labels big and small bemoan the relatively poor level of income in relation to number of plays and have limited ability to attribute its specific impact on sales, yet rarely contemplate removing their content. It is no different for artists who save their ire for Spotify which pays much higher per stream rates. Because the music industry still views YouTube as a marketing channel rather than a consumption channel it is measured by different standards. Deezer's former CEO Axel Dauchez went as far as to call YouTube the 'licensed pirate'.

Labels and artists alike are conflicted over YouTube because it has the ability to make or break an artist. In 2012 Psy's ubiquitous 'Gangnam Style' became the first ever YouTube video to receive one billion views, by 2014 it had racked up 2 billion. This is the age of the YouTube star, artists such as Justin Bieber who shot to prominence on YouTube while others such as Rihanna and Lady Gaga rely upon it for global reach and impact. YouTube's importance is underscored by the way in which big established major label stars practically fall over each other to boast of their YouTube success. Rihanna's PR team were eager to point out that the singer surpassed Justin Bieber to become the most watched artist on YouTube in June 2013 when she hit 3.8 billion YouTube views. Then in September 2013 Miley Cyrus challenged her fan base to make the pseudo-controversial video for her single 'Wrecking Ball' the most watched Vevo video in history. The potent combination of a super engaged fan base and shameless promotion ensured it promptly became just that, and by November 2013 the video had a staggering 327 million views.

The fact that Cyrus' label and management had channelled fan activity through Vevo rather than YouTube was no accident. Launched in December 2009, Vevo is the labels' attempt to regain some degree of control from YouTube. Jointly owned by Universal Music and Sony Music – among others – Vevo's strategy is to create a licensed, official home for music video that sits on top of YouTube. In many respects Vevo can be viewed as a parasite, feeding off YouTube's audience, but YouTube had little choice other than to welcome it because Vevo's backers controlled the rights to the majority of its most viewed music videos. Vevo has gone on to enjoy significant success, reaching 243 million monthly unique viewers in February 2014. However the majority of these views came from YouTube with many of those viewers not even realising that they were not viewing YouTube content. Vevo is a highly effective channel that helps protect the labels against YouTube becoming even more powerful but it is long way yet from being able to stand on its own two feet. Indeed it may never be able to, but that says more about the ubiquity of YouTube's reach than it does about the relative merits of Vevo.

YouTube's vast marketing value is clear and the divided opinion it inspires is highly similar to that of radio: walk into most record labels and you will find executives who say that they simply cannot get people to discover music without radio but you will also find those who believe that many radio listeners buy less music because they get so much for free on the radio. Both perspectives are true, which is why the issue will remain unresolved in perpetuity. But whereas for radio there is an ultra clear delineation between marketing platform and acquisition channel, for YouTube the demarcation blurs to irrelevance. For many consumers YouTube is the destination. It is simply so good a user experience that journey and destination have become one, yet music marketing professionals continue to treat it in the same way they have always treated radio, with the underlying assumption it will help sell the core music product. So if whole swathes of music consumers only ever engage with an artist via YouTube the question becomes whether it is sustainable for that engagement to generate so much less income for rights owners relative to that from the core digital 'destinations' such as iTunes and Spotify. When a discovery platform does not predominately lead to sales anymore can it really still be called 'discovery'?

Scale is YouTube's biggest ally. It is this crucial asset that has been almost solely responsible for it navigating the notoriously choppy waters of rights holder negotiations and coming out largely unscathed. But 25% of consumers (rising to 33% of 18-24 year olds) say YouTube is just so good that they feel they have no need to pay for a streaming service. YouTube takes away more from the streaming market than it contributes. Even discounting the 25% and adding in approximately half a billion of potential YouTube subscription revenue, the net impact of YouTube on the streaming subscriptions market would still be net negative to the tune of $2.3 billion a year in the US and UK alone.

YouTube is more important than ever as a promotional platform to labels and artists. But this role was established when there was still a clear demarcation between discovery and consumption, and thus a clear argument for YouTube acting as a driver of sales. Now though, in the midst of the transition to the consumption era where access models dominate, it is no longer clear what the promotional end game is. The objective of selling tracks and albums does not apply to subscribers or to the most active free streamers. And if the aim is to drive stream count on higher revenue services, like Spotify, then driving free streams on YouTube is wholly counterproductive. Too often there is an organizational disconnect within labels, with release teams focused on YouTube play count goals that are unrelated to company level business strategy. Too many label executives have not woken up to the fact that their advert is now actually the product too.

CONCLUSION: Innovation and Investment in the 2010's

Record labels undoubtedly upped their innovation game over the course of the last decade but it is not their core remit. Instead start ups and technology companies will continue to be the key source of innovation as these are the companies whose organizational structures, skillsets and business models are built around innovation. They have the capabilities and the resources to drive it. The role of record labels and other rights owners is to provide the content and support that enables innovators to be a success. Throughout the 2000's there were far too many examples of this model not working sufficiently well, of rights owner conservatism and, at times cynicism, stifling innovation and growth. Since the latter part of the last decade this has begun to change, with labels leading the charge of licensing to an increasingly diverse range of music services. What the music industry has not yet been able to master however is to manage the transition from rapidly growing, exciting new service to dominant, overweening tech super power. The relations rights owners establish with small start ups at the earliest stages of their lives are crucial because any misplaced arrogance and intransigence there will come back at them with interest if that company becomes powerful enough to start calling the shots in the way Google et al can now do. The technology superpowers may appear to represent the best route to scale for rights owners, but that potential does not always realize, for example what has Samsung done of meaningful note? The bog technology companies do however represent a fantastic asset for the music industry, if they can be engaged as innovation partners not simply dumb licensees.

Chapter 7: The Entrepreneur's Story

Getting Out Of The Gate

Big technology and CE companies provide most of the momentum and scale of the digital music ecosystem but the innovation lifeblood is small start ups. Unlike their corporate peers these smaller companies have to deal with a much broader set of business challenges than just trying to convince rights owners to play ball. For many music start up founders their company is their first experience of running a business and thus the history of digital music technology start ups is as much about young entrepreneurs learning to do business as it is music industry problem solving. This brings both benefits and problems to the market. On the positive side of the equation the sheer hunger to succeed among young innovators often sees problems identified and solved far more quickly than they would be in bigger, corporate entities. In established companies long hours are typically the domain of ambitious management executives, but in small start ups there is most often a collective ethos than engenders superhuman efforts and excessively long working days across all staff members. There is a clear sense of everyone working towards a common purpose, often underpinned by a keen understanding of exactly what impact each other's work will have on others. Whereas an employee in a larger organization usually has little direct sense of what his colleague's work contributes to that of another, the simple fact of being small, tightly knit entities means that start up teams are closely intertwined. Start up employees are also usually free of big company processes, instead of spending endless hours in meetings about meetings and pushing virtual paper around, there is a laser focus on product and growth. This can be both exhilarating and terrifying, often at the same time, but it also stimulates free flowing creative thought. This was something that Jeremy Silver learned first hand when he left EMI to become a co-founder at Uplister in 2001: "I learned more in my two years at Uplister than I had in the previous 10 years. It was hugely liberating to be able to think so freely. You don't realize when you are inside a corporate organization just how constrained you are in your thinking."

Right from the start of the music industry's digital era, start ups played a pivotal role in identifying problems and creating solutions at a far faster rate than would have been achieved organically by incumbent companies. Many of the more successful ones have grown out of innovators not seeking out problems to solve but instead building solutions for problems that founders personally faced in their everyday lives.

One such example was the pioneering digital music distributor the Orchard which emerged as a solution to challenges co-founder Scott Cohen experienced as a music manager: "With so many of the indie bands we were pushing we couldn't get press, we couldn't get radio and we realised that if we were having all those problems surely most other indie acts were too, that the problem was not being able to reach your audience." Cohen was an early digital innovator, experimenting with new digital marketing tactics but in doing so his outlook was almost too far ahead of most of his peers. His business idea had to have contemporary relevance if it was to be accepted: "Our early experience of the internet had made it clear where things were going to go. But that future was still a way off. Richard [Gottehrer, Orchard co-founder] said 'if you want to offer something in the future you need to promise something in the present'. So we became the exclusive supplier of [CDs and vinyl of] indies to CDNow and Music Boulevard and we ensured that the first line of the contract with each label was 'you grant us the digital rights."

The Orchard launched in 1997 but even with this dual 'present and future' approach the concept was still too early for most of the market and the company proceeded to haemorrhage cash. Because Cohen and Gottehrer had funded the company themselves all of the ensuing financial losses were deeply personal in a very real sense: "After a few years I was painfully in debt, I'd lost everything, my house, my car, my apartment and I was considering permanently sleeping in the office. Because we had never been cash positive and because we'd taken no investment we had accumulated a debt of over $3 million. It was pretty brutal but still exciting because we had the absolute certainty that this was the way it was going to go. Then in 2003 right before the iTunes Music Store launched I got a call from Danny Stein, the head of a private equity firm. He said 'you need to sell. People are going to enter this space fully funded and kick your ass.' We had 300,000 songs, the largest single digital catalogue there was at that time but we needed growth capital. So we sold 70% of the company. It felt so good to start writing cheques to everyone we owed money and to start drawing a salary. It was a weight lifted." The Orchard so nearly did not make it but emerged from the jaws of oblivion to become a crucial component of today's global digital music economy.

Another example of a now highly successful digital music company with a long and difficult path to success is US based personalized radio service Pandora. In October 2013 Pandora accounted for 8.06% of all US radio listening time with 1.47 billion listening hours in that month alone, but there had been little in the earlier days of Pandora's life to suggest such massive success lay in the future. As with the Orchard, Pandora arose out of everyday life in the traditional music industry just when digital was taking its first steps. In the late 1990's Pandora founder and Chief Strategy Officer Tim Westergren was eking out a career as a professional musician and composing film scores. It was whilst doing this that Westergren first started to develop an idea that would become the foundation stone for Pandora: "While composing film scores, I learned about the musicology of composition. My job first and foremost was to understand the music tastes of directors. I would play them songs and gauge what interested them. This led to the genesis of the Music Genome Project. It took me a few months to go from 'oh cool idea' to acting on it. It hadn't occurred to me that I could start a company. It was the heyday of the dotcom boom and it was the right sort of environment to do something. I shared the idea with a college friend, we wrote a business plan and raised $1.5 million in 2000." The Music Genome Project was an ambitious project to classify music, one song at a time across more than 400 variables and now drives the music programming in the Pandora radio service.

Back in 2000 though, Westergren and his colleagues had built a different business around the Music Genome Project, licensing the technology as Savage Beast Technologies to drive music recommendation engines for music services. Unfortunately the business model proved to be less compelling than the technology itself: "We tried building a B2B business licensing recommendation technology but despite having big clients like AOL there just wasn't enough money in it. We had some lean years and at times had to go without salaries." Just as the Orchard's Scott Cohen had done, Westergren managed to weather the storm and end up stronger for having done so: "But by dint of just surviving by 2004 we had a really valuable IP asset and we hit upon the idea of personalized radio. Whereas in 2000 we'd suffered from bad timing, in 2004 it was great timing." Holding on by the fingertips for so long leaves a start up in a highly fragile state and that Pandora was able to become a success from such a compromised position was due to a new injection of capital, again as happened with the Orchard. Taking new investment when at rock bottom though is never an optimum situation for a start up as the hand is heavily stacked towards the investor. So it is crucial for the entrepreneur that any potential investor has the right vision and does not simply want to pick up assets on the cheap and then potentially get rid of the founding team – a not infrequent occurrence. Pandora and the Orchard were both fortunate to get the right sort of investor to come on board at just the right time. According to Cohen in the case of the Orchard the investor could see the long-term opportunity and the need to grow the business organically: "Our investors [Dimensional Associates] were in it for the long term as were we. The fact we're all still involved in the company now, ten years after the investment shows that." At Pandora Westergren was able to convince his new investors to clean the slate of the struggling company: "We had a really generous set of investors who paid everyone back. It is very rare that new money is used to pay off old money debts but I'd made a pact with my team that if we every managed to raise more money that I'd see everyone who was owed money made good." In 2005 Savage Beast Technology was renamed Pandora Media and Pandora Radio was launched on July 21st that year. The service got off to a solid if unspectacular start, clocking up more than 3 million users by the end of 2006, but Pandora did not really come of age until the launch of its iPhone app in mid 2008. Pandora was one of the early success stories of Apple's App Store, with the app bringing Pandora to life as a personal radio service. Prior to the app launch Pandora had 15 million users, less than a year later that number had doubled. Westergren described the iPhone app effect: "It is hard to overstate how important the iPhone app was. Until then virtually all of listening was in the office so we were missing out on the majority of radio listening. We grew as the iPhone did. We grabbed onto their coattails and held on! [In doing so] we redefined the category from PC radio to personalized radio." Pandora's consumer adoption trend was a classic consumer adoption S-Curve (see Figure 22) with the iPhone App acting as the catalyst to spur penetration beyond the Critical Mass Threshold.

FIGURE 22

Pandora and the Consumer Adoption Curve

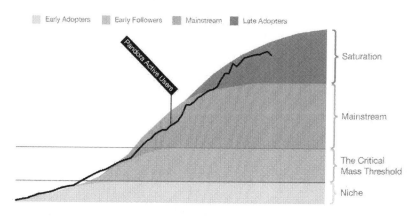

Ralph Simon's ring tone company Moviso was another digital music success story that nearly did not make it. Following his protracted licensing adventures Simon was struggling to drive enough revenue to keep the company afloat when a serendipitously timed phone call came in: "We had 12 days of money left and we got a call from Atlanta, from a senior executive at Cingular, the largest telco in the USA. He said 'we've spent the last nine months looking at your ideas, we have done the due diligence and want to licence your platform exclusively'. I said 'Well it would be two million dollars' to which he replied 'No problem'. I jumped for joy, as not only was the company saved, but we had a contract with the biggest telco in North America. I put down the phone and told one of the team to go down to the corner shop to get 6 bottles of champagne for our team to celebrate." Simon had previously tried to get extra investment once his seed funding had run out but he had been unable to get any investor to put in further substantial investment. The Cingular deal though proved to be a turning point and in 2003 he sold Moviso to Vivendi Universal in 2003 for close to $20 million.

Pandora and the Orchard were both slow burn success stories, a contrast to many of the more rapid rises to prominence, and often equally swift demises, of many digital music services. Both also had the common denominator of Apple spurring rapid growth following a long incubation period. A third digital music company to follow this same model was music identification service Shazam. Founded in 1999 Shazam's product enables people to identify music by capturing a clip of the audio on their phone. It was a piece of technology that worked as flawlessly then as it does now but it took many quiet years before Shazam started to enjoy any meaningful success. As with the Orchard and Pandora, it took an extra injection of capital to get Shazam through to when the market was ready for it to be a success. That investment came from venture capital firm DN Capital. DN Capital's founder and Managing Partner Nenad Marovac recounted the chance encounter with Shazam that ultimately led making the investment: "I shared a cab at a conference with Chris Barton [Shazam co-founder] and he asked the cab driver to turn the radio up. He then held up his phone to the music and within seconds he'd got the name of the track delivered to him on his phone. I was blown away and thought 'wow that's really fucking cool'. "But at the time they had no business model and too few users."

Marovac brought in a new CEO – Andrew Fisher – and "introduced the company to their first US employee who then got Shazam into AT&T and Verizon, which proved to be the single biggest shift in the company at that time: "Our usage started to rocket and we started to make some money." But it was the advent of Apple's App Store that was once again the real growth inflection point. Prior to the iPhone app Shazam had relied upon clunky implementations such as users dialling a short code number that hung up after 30 seconds, before then sending an automated SMS. The iPhone app format though was a previously unachievable self-contained, elegant user experience. Marovac recalled how the iPhone app came into being: "Apple contacted us about launching the store for the new iPhone. We had to move quickly and Rahul Powar the then top engineer at the company built the app in a weekend and it was an instant hit on the App Store, our tag volume went through the roof. It transformed a doldrum investment that was starting to look dire into a very exciting one. At that point Kleiner Perkins started knocking on our door." Once again the potent mix of perseverance, new investment and an Apple-driven technology leap transformed a struggling business into one of the cornerstones of the digital music marketplace. As of 2013 Shazam numbered 300 million users of which 70 million were active. No mean feat for an app that almost did not make it.

Another entrepreneur who was active in the earlier days of digital music was 7Digital CEO and founder Ben Drury. Drury was one of the first team members of the pioneering music

Tim Westergren, Founder Pandora   Nenad Marovac, Managing Partner   Ben Drury, founder 7Digital
DN Capital

site Dot Music: "I went in to learn as intern but ended up building the website, and then worked through my third year of university doing the charts for Dot Music on Sundays." Dot Music hit one million users in 1997, no small achievement in those early days of the internet and Drury recalled that: "The parent company pumped in more money and McKinsey built a business case saying that we would be a $100 million business." In those days of the dotcom bubble a number of respected financial institutions played a highly active role in creating the over heated financial environment that would soon turn boom into inevitable bust.

One entrepreneur recalled that a leading financial institution would have 'start up days' where a succession of companies were paraded into a meeting room, told that their company could be worth x million dollars and then presented an IPO strategy, from which of course the financial institution would pocket a healthy transactional fee. It was a cynical production line that cared little or nought for sustainable commercial models nor indeed for the long-term plight of the start ups or the market. In the case of Dot Music, as with so many dotcom era start ups, the valuation was too high, even before the dotcom crash sucked out much of the actual commercial value. In 2002 Drury led British Telecom (BT)'s acquisition of Dotmusic for just £200,000. Drury joined BT in 2000 to help drive its music strategy but within a few years the company opted to pull out of its content business as part of a strategic tie up with Yahoo!. Drury decided it was the right time to strike out on his own: "I convinced my Dotmusic colleague James Kane to co-found 7Digital. We self funded the set up with £6,000 and secured WMG, EMI, UMG as clients in 2004, building artist and label stores." 7Digital went on to build a global business as a digital services provider for the likes of Samsung and Blackberry, and Drury has revelled in the company's role of plucky small British tech company: "At Live 8 we were selected with Apple to try to set the world record for the fastest time for releasing a digital song for sale from a live performance. We were sat in Universal Music's Piccadilly offices waiting for someone to run across from Hyde Park with the audio file. When they arrived they gave it to Apple first who had a huge team and equipment, while from 7Digital it was just myself and James, and a laptop. Apple took 4 hours from the live performance to sale, we did it in 46 minutes. We had already sold thousands of copies by the time Apple had gone live."

Adjacent Innovation

2007 saw one of the landmark digital music acquisitions when CBS paid $280 million for music discovery site Last.FM. Following hot on the heels of Google's YouTube acquisition the Last.FM sale appeared to indicate the start of a digital music gold rush. In reality it proved to be more of a high water mark, with few digital music companies since having come close to achieving such top level sales. Last.FM was launched in 2002 and, after merging with Audioscrobbler – a tool for scanning users' music collections in order to make tailored recommendations – became a unique element of the digital music landscape with a fiercely loyal user base that at one point numbered 30 million. Combining crowd sourced artist information and personalized radio stations based on users tastes Last.FM was by the mid-2000's being seen by some as the future of digital music. Last.FM was the fairy tale success story of a small start up founded by young technology entrepreneurs becoming the market zeitgeist and then achieving a big exit with a traditional media company.

Reed Smith's Gregor Pryor represented Last.FM and recalled the first impressions made by founders Martin Stiksel and Jonas Woost: "[They] turned up on a scooter, with open-faced helmets, jeans and a battered laptop. My law firm partners asked 'who are these people, and why are we doing business with them?'" Unfortunately for Last.FM their archetypal start up trajectory also saw, following the CBS acquisition, the inevitable slow, steady descent into terminal decay within the confines of their new corporate paymasters. CBS simply did not know quite what to do with Last.FM and despite some initial success, once the founders had parted following the expiration of their contractual lock-in periods, the service slowly withered on the vine. Today it retains a significant loyal audience, but any aspirations of being the future of digital music are long gone. CBS bought Last.FM at the peak of its hype cycle and believed it was buying itself a seat at digital music's top table. Last.FM's early growth was impressive and when mapped against other current and past darlings of the digital music market – Spotify, Pandora and imeem – outperformed all three over the first 42 weeks in market (see Figure 23). Despite Last.FM's stellar start CBS realised that it was shouldered with a costly acquisition that had a challenged business model and the company ended with little to show for its money other than some expert music recommendations for its US HD radio channels. After an encouraging post-acquisition 20% audience growth CBS progressively turned off more and more of Last.FM's free content in a bid to push the service towards operational profitability. In doing so it neutered the service's value proposition. Instead of betting big to push Last. FM to the centre of the global stage CBS clipped its wings so far down they bled. Last.FM had meant to be exactly that, the 'last FM', the last radio that would ever be needed. Instead it saw itself passed by the likes of Pandora, Slacker and Songza. Last.FM became Past.FM.

FIGURE 23
Growth of Four Key Streaming Music Services
Over the First 42 Months in Market

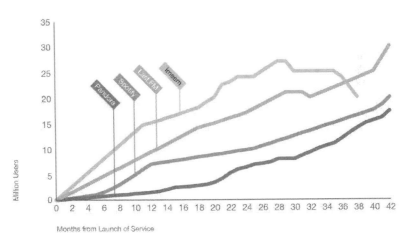

Source: Company Reported Numbers

It was a textbook case of a traditional, incumbent company having bold vision but mistaking acquiring a disruptive company for embracing disruption. If CBS had been willing to pivot its organizational structure, content programming and audience strategies around Last.FM then it might have been able to extract some significant lasting value, but it was just too big a gamble to take. Perhaps the greatest compliment paid to Last.FM was Apple's addition of the Genius feature to iTunes 8 in 2008, a clear mimicking of Audiscrobbling. Unfortunately it also meant that Apple had effectively boiled down Last.FM's entire business legacy into a single product feature.

CBS's misfortune would also prove to be that of the digital music market's: rights owners looked at the YouTube and Last.FM sales as the benchmarks for digital music exits and wanted a bigger part of the action. The author recalls presenting to the board members of one rights holder soon after the Last.FM and YouTube sales and being told that they needed to work out how to make money fast out of digital music start ups because if they did not they would miss out on the opportunity to earn what they considered their 'fair share'. Their view was that a digital music start up had a relatively short period that it would license from them before being bought and that despite the financial upside being squarely built upon the foundations of music content, they would not benefit from the sale. YouTube and Last.FM had made the digital start up market look like an economic hothouse and many rights holders felt they were getting severely short changed. The irony is that even today YouTube and Last.FM were digital music exit high water marks, and YouTube was about a lot more than just music even in 2006. With these two companies accounted for, the digital music investment-to-exit-value ratio – i.e. the collective amount music start ups have sold for versus their collective level of investment – is 7.0 but without them it is a far more modest 1.4 (see Figure 24).

FIGURE 24

Despite a High Failure Rate a Few Big Successes Have Ensured
Digital Music Has Delivered a Strong Return on Investment
Total Investment in 10 Digital Music Start Ups and Total Value of Exit

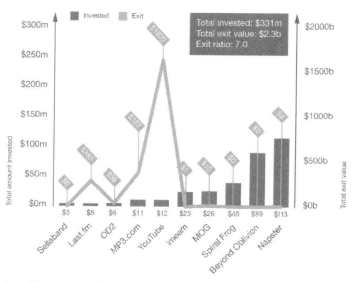

Source: MIDiA Research and IFPI

The effect of rights holders increasing their financial demands combined with a growing sense that Last.FM had actually been over valued nipped a digital music start up boom in the bud. With investors tiring of seeing large chunks of their investments disappearing onto record labels' bottom lines in license fee advances, would be entrepreneurs found it increasingly difficult to convince investors to put money into music services. So it was entirely logical that from the late 2000's many digital innovators started to 'de-risk' their propositions by innovating around rights rather than with them directly. In doing so they remained Digital Allies but effectively by inaction. This was the advent of Adjacent Innovation: innovating around the edges of the digital music market, to make the ancillary components work better rather than try to reengineer the beating heart itself.

Adjacent Innovation was both a strategic and a commercial decision: on the one hand entrepreneurs were realizing that there were plenty of digital music problems that needed solving that did not require record label licenses; while on the other it was far easier to get investors to part with their cash. The strategic shift could easily have foreshadowed a dramatic innovation hiatus but instead it produced a renaissance in digital music technology creativity. 2007 saw the launch of a slew of a new wave of start ups that innovated around rights, rather than directly with them. One of these was streaming audio site Soundcloud.

Soundcloud became a top tier player in the digital music arena with 250 million users as of October 2013 which is no mean feat for a service that is built largely around music content, is not fully licensed and yet is more than tolerated by record labels. Soundcloud was able to strike this rare balance in large part because it helped solve a record label – and artist – problem, establishing itself as the digital replacement for the clunky demo CD, and thus always had large contingents of supporters in both constituencies. Soundcloud founder and CEO Alexander Ljung recalled the genesis of the service: "We built a platform for Eric [Wahlforss, Soundcloud co-founder and CTO] and I to send files to each other of songs we were working on. Up to then the process for sharing audio was very clunky. We knew we wanted a smooth process for uploading, a visualization of the wave form and the ability to comment." Ljung and Wahlforss also recognized the importance of the social element of the Soundcloud experience: "Our starting point was trying to be social around a piece of sound. We knew that was important to all people and yet not really served yet online. The web wouldn't be complete without it. That's when we felt our sense of purpose, that we had to build it and that it could have hundreds of millions of users. Once you have got that sense of purpose there is no point in resisting it!" The pair started developing Soundcloud in their native Stockholm but moved to Berlin to launch the service in 2007 and then came out of beta in late 2008. Berlin was developing a strong reputation as a hub for the European technology sector, with a compelling combination of cheap real estate and access to a rich seam of talented but cheap Eastern European developers, coupled with a vibrant music scene. It was a perfect fit for a young, hungry digital music start up.

One element of Soundcloud's strategy that set it apart in its earlier years was a highly liberal API strategy. Ljung and Wahlforss effectively used the Soundcloud API as a technology manifestation of their massively-social-audio strategy, making it as easy as possible for people to port Soundcloud audio across the web via embeds and links. The API strategy also had the added benefit of allowing Soundcloud to focus on their core competencies and not allow their product focus to get distracted by feature creep as Ljung explained: "With the API we're just taking inspiration from the internet as a network of distributed nodes. It is like Lego pieces that all have consistent format and can build amazing things. It has helped us keep things simple and allow third parties to develop some of the more sophisticated stuff that isn't so core to our strategy." Coupled with a near obsessive focus on a simple user experience, Soundcloud's API strategy fuelled astronomic growth, to the extent that by August 2013 the service had 12 hours of audio uploaded every minute though as Ljung noted: "We need to keep working on ways of making sense of that audio."

Soundcloud's growth brought challenges too. In Soundcloud's earlier days its user base was concentrated in the music industry itself, ensuring that it developed more than its fair share of advocates within labels and the artist community, thus helping it keep licensing discussions at a comfortably safe distance. But as Soundcloud took on further investment investors were looking for a bigger growth opportunity than the comparatively narrow confines of the music industry's inner workings. Soundcloud proved eminently capable of delivering the massive base of consumers, and in doing so moving towards its founders' original world domination vision, but each extra ten million users made rights owners wonder that bit more why they were not licensed like any other music service.

Ian Hogarth, founder and CEO Songkick

Alexander Ljung, founder and CEO Soundcloud

Daniel Ek, founder and CEO Spotify

Another of the Adjacent Innovation Class of '07 was live music community and news site Songkick. Songkick's origins lay in its founders attempting to solve a music fan problem as founder and CEO Ian Hogarth explained: "We all thought that the thing we were most excited about is seeing bands live and yet technology hadn't caught up yet. General access to recorded music had lifted off but not to live music." They also recognised that the live ecosystem was ripe for disruption, with so many extra layers of profit making having evolved around a product that has been shielded from disruption for so long: "Many fans hate the secondary market, and lack of transparency around booking fees. With Songkick and Detour [Songkick's crowd funded touring side project] we are trying to make booking fees transparent and upfront."

So Hogarth and his colleagues set out on a mission to 'make live music as accessible as possible' and got up and running with a $15,000 investment from US seed accelerator Y Combinator. Songkick went from strength to strength, benefiting both from being an early mover in an underserved space and from a Soundcloud-like open API strategy that enabled it to quickly permeate throughout the wider social web. A $4 million Series A investment from Index Partners followed in 2008. Just as with Soundcloud, Songkick understood the core value of empowering music fans to connect and to share, as Ian Hogarth stated: "There has been a complete paradigm shift in how fans and artists connect via social networks and in the accessibility of recorded music. Live is the missing bit that hasn't really changed." Songick's momentum accelerated into the 2010's with Index Partners and Sequoia Capital investing $10 million in 2012 and being one of the few partners selected by Spotify at the launch of its app platform the same year. By November 2013 Songkick had 8.5 million active users, making it the second largest concert site behind Ticketmaster US.

Yet another class of 2007 graduate was music analytics company Musicmetric, providing record labels and others with detailed analytics via a comprehensive 'Artist Dashboard' web interface. In a similar way to Soundcloud, Musicmetric set about solving a music industry business problem rather than a consumer one. Adjacent innovation momentum continued with the launch in 2008 of start ups such as RJDJ – a reactive music app; MXP4 – a multi-track digital audio app; and Next Big Sound – an analytics company that tracks social mentions of artists. The preeminent start up of 2008 however was a welcome return to focus on music services, namely a little start up from Sweden called Spotify.

Spotify was launched into the record labels' digital wilderness years with iTunes' dominance clear for all to see and the Spiral Frog and Comes With Music led Plan B stumbling at the starting blocks. Founded by Daniel Ek and Martin Lorentzon, Spotify followed a smart strategy of understanding what the labels wanted music services to deliver and doing what they could to help make their story fit those expectations. As Spotify CEO Ek recalled it was not always an easy sell, requiring patience and determined persistence: "We went on a pretty long journey over the first couple of years. I was some young Swedish guy knocking on record label doors all over the world and I was asking them to license their music to us to give away for free; it's understandable that it took them a little while to come round to the idea. But, I practically slept on their doorsteps for those two years, and eventually, slowly, they began to understand that Spotify just might be part of the solution to the woes of the music industry at that time, and they believed in us enough to take a chance on us."

In October 2008 Spotify launched an invite only beta version of its free product and established momentum quickly, seeding influencers and tastemakers with batches of five invites they could share with others. These invites quickly became a highly sought after commodity within music influencer and digerati circles as word spread of a cool new music service that let you stream all the music in the world, instantly, with no buffering and for free. The 9.99 subscription product was available to anyone but it was the free offering that caught the imagination of a quickly growing body of enthusiastic early adopters. As with all great innovations, Spotify did a couple of things really well:

1) offering a vast catalogue of free music

2) consigning stream buffering to the history books with its use
   of P2P distribution and progressive downloads.[52]

By targeting the influencers with a high quality product Spotify could almost sit back and watch the marketplace market its service for it. Ek remembered the feeling of excited pride as Spotify first started to lift off: "Having worked so hard to get to that point, when Spotify launched it was the most fantastic feeling. Of course, we launched with an invitation-only system, and we didn't know how that would be received, so when we started to see hundreds, then thousands of music fans signing up for invites, it was the best feeling in the world. And that feeling has never really gone away."

Next, in 2009 another batch of adjacent innovations came to market including SoundHound – a music identification app similar to Shazam but that enables users to hum or sing songs;

[52] Spotify's progressive downloading predicts which tracks a user is likely to want to stream soon (e.g. remainder of an album or a playlist from which one song has been played) and starts to download them in advance so that when the tracks start playing they do so instantly. Spotify also used to leverage peer-to-peer distribution to speed up streaming, using the network of its user base to distribute files rather than only stream directly from central servers. These two technologies often required the Spotify client to create large file caches on a user's PC hard drive. There is of course a poetic symmetry to the fact a service heralded as a tool with which the industry can fight piracy depended upon that foundational piracy technology P2P.

Mixcloud – a user uploaded audio destination with a focus on DJ mixes; and We Are Hunted – a music discovery site that was acquired by Twitter in 2012 to become the basis for Twitter Music in 2013. A stand out member of the Adjacent Innovation Class of '09 was PledgeMusic, a fan funding platform for artists. While labels and music services had been struggling to get to grips with digital, artists had seen their world change beyond recognition. They felt closer to their fans than ever before yet at the same time were watching their recorded music income plummet. This was the paradox that PledgeMusic sought to address.

PledgeMusic was the brainchild of Benji Rogers who in the 2000's was a gigging and recording artist struggling to make ends meet: "I was touring for 9 to 10 years and had a couple of indie deals but I just couldn't make it work, I was sleeping on an air mattress on my mum's floor with my wife at 34 years old. Then one night before I was due to play a gig in Amsterdam I had this idea. Artists, fans and charities! I ran downstairs and started to work on my mum's kitchen table and the idea evolved." There were already a number of sites that had started to tap into the crowd funding for artists opportunity including Sellaband, Slice The Pie and MyMajorCompany but Rogers saw the missing part as being behind the scenes updates, creating a special exclusive bond between artist and fan. Next Rogers: "found that the pledgemusic.com url was available and bought it immediately with the last money in my account. After the show in Amsterdam I was drinking many whiskeys with a fan who turned out to be a lawyer and when I told him about the idea he said 'get an NDA and don't tell anyone about the idea until you've done so. I want in.'" Rogers set about drawing up a business plan but had no formal business background: "I'd left school at 15, I had no idea what a Swot analysis or Gant charts were. But I quickly realized that it's not about setting your sights too high and missing your mark, it is about setting them too low." Rogers found that people were receptive to his idea and secured funding to launch the business. In July 2009 Rogers launched the first Pledge campaign for one of his own E.P.s. PledgeMusic's beginnings were typically frenetic for a start up: "The early days were chaotic, payments didn't work because we couldn't get anyone to let us transact and our offices were in a basement in Covent Garden with the Guillemots rehearsing in the room next to us." As PledgeMusic began to scale it became clear that the company needed some more formal business structure, which included the appointment of A&R veteran Malcolm Dunbar as managing director. When one of Rogers' contacts first suggested introducing him to Dunbar he was sceptical of what value he would bring to the business but when they met he understood just how little of the total opportunity PledgeMusic was currently targeting: "He shared his vision that PledgeMusic wasn't going to just be for small artists but for big established acts also and said he wanted to run the company with us. And of course his vision was totally right." Dunbar also quickly demonstrated the value his A&R contacts could bring the business as Rogers recalled: "During the [same] meeting I said I liked 'Count to Ten' by Tina Dico, and he had her in our office within a week. I thought 'wow this guy is good!'" Pledge has gone onto enjoy considerable success and to demonstrate clear value for artists such as Ben Folds Five, Slash and Sandi Thom, with an average campaign success rate of 86% and $55 average spend among Pledgers.

Thus by 2010 a vibrant sphere of digital music innovation was emerging, a refreshing contrast to the preceding wilderness years, even if much of it was still on the periphery of digital music. The message was becoming clear: it was easier and more effective to launch music start ups that dealt with the wider digital music journey than it was to try to deal with the heart of the matter. Licensed music services were looking like an increasingly shaky investment proposition with high risk and modest returns, whereas ancillary music services presented the opportunity to invest in the music space without licensing baggage such as advances and minimum guarantees. It was a trend observed by Larry Miller: "Investors do not want substantial quantities of their money going to content companies in the form of advances. They also want venture-like growth rates, the potential for 25-40% CAGR over a five year period. There is a mismatch between the risk and the potential return of digital music businesses. But hope continues to spring eternal because music is everywhere and matters to all of us."

The music industry had come a long way since its digital beginnings but it had been a costly journey with successive generations of start ups paying a heavy price. The verges of the music industry's digital highway were littered with the corpses of digital music start ups that had tried and failed to solve music industry's digital problem throughout the 2000's. Rights holder conservatism and consumer apathy proved a lethal combination for all nature of digital innovators. The victims of the industry's first digital decade numbered all manner of innovators including Rights Allies – e.g. OD2, Comes With Music; Rights Frenemies – e.g. imeem; and Rights Refusniks – e.g. Kazaa, Megaupload. Meanwhile the core of the digital market coalesced around the big three of Amazon, Apple and Google, all of whom are in the business of selling music in order to drive ulterior, non-music, business objectives. To dine at digital's top table you needed to have scale, which effectively narrowed the field down to the big three and services with multi-million dollar global businesses to fund their music venture, such as telcos and device manufacturers. Little wonder then that digital innovators and investors often saw little reason to enter the risky terrain of digital music's hinterland.

There were notable exceptions, such as the new breed of streaming music services but these services relied upon vast rounds of investment to get their seat at the table, with Spotify, Deezer, MOG and Rdio collectively raising just under half a billion dollars in investment by 2012. But not even millions of dollars of investment could guarantee success, a case made all too clearly by disruptive challenger Beyond Oblivion. Beyond Oblivion's star burned briefly but fiercely, raising $87 million before going against the wall in early 2012. Beyond's experience reinforced the views of sceptics within the investment community that the potential return from digital music did not justify the return as Larry Miller argued: "I am hard pressed to think of a digital music start up that achieved true scale via negotiated voluntary licenses with the exceptions of Spotify and Vevo. Statutory licenses have a much better route to scale, and provided Pandora with a licensing framework that enabled the company to get big, fast. However, achieving profitability as a public company is another issue entirely."

All This Has Happened Before and All This Will Happen Again[53]

The polarization of digital music innovation between slower moving, tech company megaliths on the one side and disruptive but narrowly focused start ups on the other has created a split personality marketplace. One in which disruptive innovations burn briefly and brightly before being assimilated in watered down fashion by the incumbent powerhouses. This moderating effect of the big technology companies helps to cool the rate of change to a pace that better suits that of the slower moving rights owners. That might sound like a criticism, and it is in part, but rights owners have to balance protecting their business interests and the livelihoods of their creators with identifying new opportunities. The biggest problem with disruption is often not the technology or behaviour itself, but instead being able to identify it, to differentiate it from the mass of other potential threats, and then learning how to deal with it. Trying to distinguish which disruption to harness, which to fight and which to ignore can all too easily

---

53 I am of course indebted to the Pythian Scrolls of Battle Star Galactica for this quote

beget strategic paralysis. The situation is compounded by the fact that so many digital music companies have implicitly limited life spans due to the fact they are venture funded. Any investor wants to see a return of some kind or another on his or her money. Institutional investors – who make up the majority of the larger sums invested in technology start ups – often have very templated, structured approaches to investment. These typically revolve around clearly defined rounds of investment (seed, Series A, Series B etc.), growth targets and exit windows. It is the latter that has the most significant impact on digital music innovation.

Depending on at what round an investor comes into an investment, they can typically want to have an exit – e.g. to have sold or floated the company – with 3 to 5 years of their initial investment. Some investors, such as the Orchard's, can be willing to play a much longer game, while others can pull the plug much more quickly. As we have seen, the average company lifetime of a digital music start up is just 5.8 years. This runs the risk of mutual short termism among rights owners and technology companies. Among rights owners this can present itself as large advances and equity for licenses, while among technology companies it can translate into a disregard for longer term market sustainability. These opposite ends of the spectrum create interestingly problematic tensions such as Spotify's growth ideology: Spotify, by Daniel Ek's own public admission, is focused squarely on growth. The labels want Spotify to succeed and have taken their share of equity and advances to ensure they benefit in near term, but they also want a sustainable market and to not have a Spotify-shaped hole left in the digital music market if Spotify closes or changes its approach due to a sale or flotation.

The relatively short life-span of digital music start ups also has the effect of seeing many mistakes made again, again, and again. So many music entrepreneurs come from outside of the music industry, with aspirations of helping 'save the music industry', so there is a recurring theme of these figures spending a year or two learning just how dysfunctional parts of the industry are and having to scale down their aspirations and product strategy accordingly. It is an even more prevalent problem for investors and entrepreneurs who so often think 'it can't really be that bad' only to find that it is, and some. Such was the experience of MusicQubed's founder and CEO Chris Gorman, who had previously been highly successful in the mobile phone retail sector: "The music industry hasn't embraced the market with a view to 'how can we invest, nurture and help it grow. Instead it is 'we have the assets'. I have never seen a successful model like it anywhere else in the world. They invested in the channel when it was a physical retail business, but all that has changed with digital. Everything is difficult, nothing is easy. It is not for the faint hearted, it is difficult it get in, which is a barrier to growth. I have to pay to put products on the shelf and I also have to pay to get consumers to come in and take a look."

FIGURE 25

Music Start Up Investment Surged in the Cloud Era,
Driven by A Few Big Bets and Ancillary Services
Total and Average Investment in a Selection of Key Digital Music Start Ups

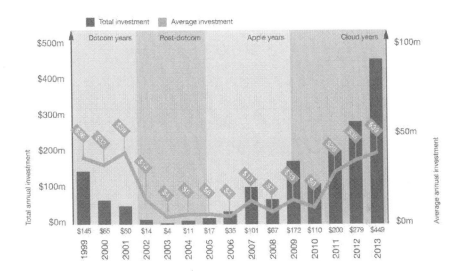

Changing Patterns of Investment

Unsurprisingly digital music investments flourished in the dotcom years and fell off a cliff when
the dotcom bubble burst (see Figure 25). It took until the latter third of the 2000's for digital
music investments to start to pick up again, with investors finally being persuaded that Apple's
success was more than a flash in the pan. It was at this stage that Adjacent Innovation
investment began to accelerate and this growth accounted for much of the increased investment
between 2007 and 2010. Once the music industry entered the cloud era investments neared
and then exceeded dotcom era levels in terms of total investment. However, as encouraging
as the headline trends are, they disguise a more nuanced picture that exists just beneath
the surface, namely the importance of a few big bets (see Figure 26). Spotify, Deezer and
Beats between them accounted for 70% of total digital music investment between 2011 and
2013 and in total have raised $743 million in finance and investment to date. If these three
streaming heavyweights are removed from the equation the total amount of digital music
investment between 2011 and 2013 falls from $918 million to $279 million (see Figure 26).

FIGURE 26

Without the Big Three Streaming Investments the Face
of Digital Music Investment Looks Very Different

Digital Music Investment Without Spotify, Deezer and Beats

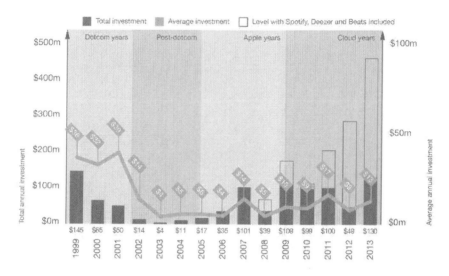

Thus digital music investment is at an all time high, with music flowing in at all levels of the business, but the actual amount of growth is distorted by two of the streaming heavyweights and one new pretender to the throne. As such their influence on the future flow of capital into digital music is both crucial and risky. If one or both get it wrong and fail to deliver a return on their investment then large scale institutional investors may well decide to put their money into lower risk, higher yield areas. Streaming music subscription service MOG provides a cautionary tale: between 2006 and 2010 MOG required investment totalling $24.9 million. In 2012 it sold to Beats for just $10 million with approximately 500,000 subscribers. If those subscribers were each paying $9.99 a month that would translate into annual revenues of nearly $60 million, the fact it sold at a negative multiple of 6 – i.e. 6 times less than annual revenue – to headphone company Beats illustrates the precarious nature of the music subscriptions business. However the resulting Beats Music service was promptly snapped up by Apple in 2014 for $500 as part of a $3 billion acquisition of parent company Beats. The industry had better hope, for the sake of future investment, that Spotify, Deezer and Apple's Beats Music do a better job of making the model work than MOG did.

CONCLUSION: Innovation and Investment in the 2010's

Since the late 2000's digital music innovation has prospered, establishing the foundations for the next stage of the music industry's story. However the transference of record label risk onto the bottom line of music services and thus their investors, via advances, has also changed the face of digital music innovation, resulting in a shift to smaller adjacent services at the periphery. Around 2010 and 2011 it was beginning to look like investment in the space was drying up all together. Investors had grown weary of protracted licensing discussions with inevitably costly outcomes and instead started to pursue easier, and often richer, pickings in other sectors such as books and mobile apps. Now though, money is returning to digital music, with hundreds of millions of dollars going into music start ups every year, and hundreds more being spent by big telco and device companies. The polarization between huge core bets and smaller adjacent gambles remains a major challenge though, and there will need to be much more attention focused on the core if digital is ever going to deliver industry-wide recovery. Much more of the core innovation needs to come from small, disruptive start ups rather than large corporate companies whose natural leanings are conservative and whose priorities are not music itself. Too much valuable innovation effort and expertise is being expended at the margins of the market, resulting in a fragmented digital consumer journey.

Chapter 8: Apple's Story

Apple's contribution to digital music is truly unique and, to date, peerless. Without Apple the digital music market would most likely be a pale imitation of its current state, which by direct implication means that the plight of the music industry would be far direr than it is. Apple transformed the digital music market because of a determination to do things differently and the ability to back up this steadfastness with ferocious negotiation skills. Before Apple there was no meaningful digital music market to speak of, nor was there any significant number of MP3 players in consumers' hands. And yet Apple was far from the first mover in either sector. Instead Apple waited for competitors to test and establish these markets. Apple was happy to let others expend time, effort, resources and brand equity experimenting on the tech savvy, hard core of consumers, while it watched, learned and waited. As soon as Apple decided that the MP3 player and music download markets were ready for primetime, Apple dived into each with products that were quantum leaps ahead of the competition. This early follower strategy has come to define Apple's 21st century renaissance but in the early 2000's it was largely a new approach for Apple whose 1980's and 1990's heritage had been built upon creating firsts. Music strategy thus set the blueprint for Apple's 21st century success, but by the close of the 2000's Apple's attentions were shifting away from music, and the music industry was going to keenly feel the consequences.

Exerting Influence

The launch of the iPod in November 2001 freed digital music from the chains of the PC and the iTunes Music Store freed the song from the CD. As the 2000's progressed music became ever more important to Apple, and in turn Apple became ever more important to the music industry, with the balance of power shifted inexorably to the former. By 2008 the digital music market was growing at a Compound Annual Growth Rate (CAGR) of 85.2% (see Figure 27) with Apple accounting for the vast majority of the revenue, including approximately three quarters of all digital sales in the US. Apple was the most important ally in the only part of the record labels' business that was growing, and it knew it.

FIGURE 27

When Apple Sneezes the Music Industry Gets a Cold: How the
Slowing iPod Sales Dragged Down Digital Music Revenue Growth
Digital Revenue of the World's Top 10 Music Markets and Global iPod Sales

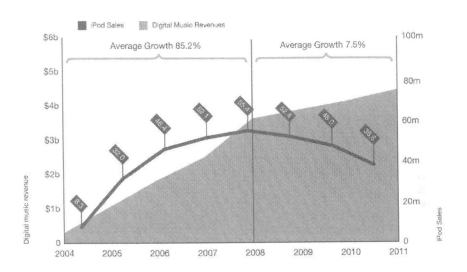

Slowly but surely Apple began to assert its new influence, advancing its own priorities such
as dropping rights protection technology and standing firm against label demands for variable
pricing, namely pricing new and more popular releases higher than older and less popular
ones. When Apple launched the iTunes Music Store it focused on the elegant simplicity of
a single, uniform price point of $0.99 per track download, a necessary and useful tool for
gently coaxing wary consumers into the new world of paid content. But it also ignored the
fact that not all music has the same monetary value. The music industry spent decades
building variable pricing into the high street retail model and consumers came to understand
that older, 'catalogue' music usually cost less than the latest releases. Apple resisted label
requests to introduce variable pricing arguing that interfering with pricing simplicity would
damage sales. Although there was sound logic in Apple's thinking it was not consistent
with its approach to pricing its own products, where it pursues a deliberate policy of pricing
older models more cheaply than the most recent ones in order to reach otherwise elusive
customer segments. Eventually in 2009 Apple did bow to label pressure, but it had managed
to delay its introduction by six years by exerting its growing authority and influence.

At the same time as fighting a rear-guard action against variable pricing Apple was also
committed to removing rights protection from downloads, the major labels however remained
firmly opposed. Eventually an exasperated Steve Jobs decided to take the debate out of the
confidential confines of the negotiating table and place it firmly in the public arena by posting
a 'Thoughts on Music' open letter in February 2007. In it Jobs argued that Digital Rights

Management was fundamentally flawed, that it hurt legal buyers of music most and that Apple only wrapped its downloads in rights technology because the record labels compelled it to do so. Jobs' letter might have seemed like a declaration of war – and it was clearly a reflection of Apple's growing confidence - but he felt compelled to get Apple's side of the story into the public arena.

The origins of Jobs' ire lay in an orchestrated push against the iTunes Store, particularly in Europe. For the first time since the start of its iPod-driven renaissance Apple was beginning to feel the brunt of consumer ill will, largely because of the presence of DRM on the iTunes Store. The media stirred up murmurings of misgivings into an apparent, if not actual, groundswell of discontent and then consumer advocacy groups picked up the baton and ran with it. The situation became pressing in Europe with consumer ombudsmen in Norway, Denmark and Sweden launching official investigations and the Norwegian ombudsman going as far as to rule that the iTunes Store terms and conditions were unlawful. All the while Apple was muted by the terms of its confidentiality agreements with the labels. Once Jobs had made his views public, the proverbial cat was out of the bag. Warner Music's CEO Edgar Bronfman Jnr. and others responded saying that rights protection was crucial to the health of the digital music sector, but the tide was now turning. Eventually, as we saw, Apple got its first major label DRM-free partner on board in the shape of EMI. That the other majors made a point of licensing DRM-free to virtually every other main digital music store before they did so to iTunes betrayed their fear that Apple was getting too strong, and in removing rights protection they saw an opportunity to help the underdogs. Their worries about Apple dominance were confirmed by the abject failure of any competitor music service to steal significant advantage from having major label DRM-free catalogue when Apple did not. Even with the odds temporarily stacked against it Apple still came out on top.

Competing Against Apple

In January 2008 Amazon had become the first download store in the US to have MP3 catalogue from all four of the majors as well as from many of the indies, beating Apple to the punch by a full year.[54] The fact that Amazon was not able to even wobble Apple's throne, let alone usurp it, was an uncomfortable wake up call for the record labels that the download model simply did not translate well outside of the iTunes ecosystem. Apple had hit upon a formula for success that no one else could replicate. The problem with Apple's vertically integrated ecosystem is that its reach is largely constrained to people who own Apple devices which is inherently a subset of the total population. Apple's device sales have been impressive – it had sold 319 million iPhones, 121 million iPads and 367 million iPods by Q3 2013. Both the iPhone and iPad – especially the iPad Mini – have helped drive Apple towards a more mainstream audience, but Apple has never been mass market in any meaningful sense of the word. Though it is adept at reaching diverse consumer segments through an increasingly diverse product portfolio, and by selling older models of devices at cheaper prices, Apple devices continue to tend compete at the higher end of each price category they occupy. Devices like the iPod Shuffle and iPhone 5C ensure they compete in lower price categories, but again at the higher end of each one. Thus Apple's installed base of addressable digital music customers has always had an inbuilt ceiling. The issue became more acute with the growth of the smartphone market with more companies selling products that compete directly with Apple and selling many more units through cheaper pricing and aggressive marketing spending.

---

54 As we saw in the previous chapter 7Digital was the first to do so in Europe.

More recently the labels put faith in Google being able to succeed where Amazon did not, by leveraging its vast installed base of 600 million plus activated Android smartphones and tablets. Google, with its Android operating system, emerged as the core challenger and beneficiary. Or rather Samsung did, becoming the de facto Android hardware vendor, with Google starting to rethink its platform strategy as it did not intend to become the software provider for one global hardware manufacturer. It was never meant to have turned out that way, instead Android was intended as a democratic platform that would ensure Google could exercise control over a fragmented marketplace of Android handset companies, exercising divide and rule to ensure no single company achieved hegemony. Unfortunately for Google, Samsung did not read the divide and rule script. But for all Google's promise of scale, Google Play – Google's main digital content thrust – struggled to make any more of a dent in iTunes than Amazon's MP3 Store. Meanwhile its well built but nonetheless me-too music subscription service Google Play Music All Access, launched in 2013 and not exactly a name that rolls off the tongue,[55] hardly had Spotify quaking in its boots.

FIGURE 28

The Fragmentation Effect: Comparison of Key iOS and Android Metrics

	iOS	Android
% devices on latest version	60%	1%
OS Market share	25%	70%
# current smartphone models	3	200+
# current tablet models	4	30+
# devices activated	700 million	1 billion
# app stores	1	50+
App catalogue	1.1 million	1 million
Apps download	45 billion	40 billion

Sources: Company reported numbers and MIDiA Research estimates

Google has been unable to replicate Apple's music strategy success because of the far looser and more fragmented nature of the Android and Google Play ecosystem compared to that of iTunes and iOS. Because Apple is the sole supplier of the hardware, software and store it exercises incredibly tight control and delivers a highly consistent and predictable user experience, with intuitive simplicity the defining characteristic. But whereas Apple had just seven current smartphone and tablet models, Android is supported on more than 230 different devices (see Figure 28). Similarly it took Apple just 5 days to get 200 million – 49% – of its 410 million activated iOS devices to upgrade to on iOS 7, the latest version of iOS, while it took one and a half years for Android to get a little over half of its users onto the latest version of its OS Jelly Bean. Even that figure masks the scale of the problem, with only 2.3% of Android users on the

---

55 The elongated name hints at an organizational quagmire: 'All Access' is the service, 'Music' is the division and 'Play' is the strategic overlay and of course 'Google' is the company. The name thus suggests that just to get to where it has, All Access has had to coalesce numerous internal Google fiefdoms.

very latest version of Android – 4.3 – by November 2013, on the eve of an even newer version of the software – KitKat – launching. One month after launch just 1.1% of Android devices were running KitKat. But the biggest reason for the underwhelming performance of Google Play compared to the iTunes Store is the intentionally looser control Google employs over its device and carrier partners. While Apple customers have one integrated content and app store, Android users have more than 50 to choose from, often with multiple stores competing on any one device. A typical Android smartphone can have, as native installs, the handset company's service, the carrier's service and one or more store and service options from Google.

The problem is compounded by the fact that many Android smartphones have been adopted by less technology savvy mainstream consumers, not because they want a smartphone, but because it is what has been sold to them when they walked into their phone store for an upgrade. Consequently we have a curious dynamic of smartphones with dumb users. Though this is also something of an issue for iPhones the problem is much less pervasive. The implications for music are clear: the consumers who need to have the simplest and most straight forward of digital music journeys have the most complex, fragmented and confusing one. All of these factors combine to result in lower conversion to purchase and subscription among Android customers compared to iOS (see Figure 29).

FIGURE 29

iOS Customers Are More Engaged Music Consumers than Android

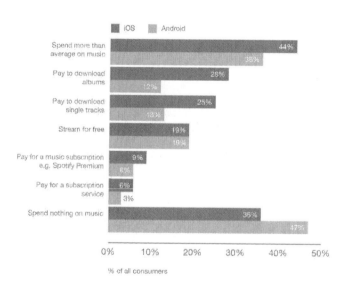

Question asks: Thinking about how you discover, consume and interact with music which of the following apply to you?
Source: MIDiA Research Consumer Survey 12/13 n = 1,000 (UK)

Consumers have not always responded kindly to Apple's tightly controlled approach, with a recurring criticism being that Apple unfairly locks consumers into iTunes / iOS with both overt and covert tactics. But for all its faults Apple has consistently delivered more consumer benefits than hurdles in the 21st century and it delivers paid music revenue in a manner no one else has yet come close to doing. Both of those factors will eventually change some day – and Spotify's revenue is certainly growing at an impressive rate – but for now Apple remains the best game in town for the music industry. Others have tried and tried again to learn from Apple's vertically integrated ecosystem master class, but none have yet pulled it off themselves, not Google, Microsoft, HTC, Nokia or Samsung. Sometimes they get one part of the equation fantastically right but another disastrously wrong. One such example was Microsoft's Zune HD MP3 player, arguably a superior device and user experience to Apple's iPod Touch. But in order to buy music for the Zune HD the consumer had to use a Zune Pass in the Zune Marketplace, a process which was clunky and buggy and which entirely devalued the device experience. Microsoft should have done better, much better, because it had control of the device, the OS and the store, just like Apple does. What Microsoft learned the hard way was the adept manner in which Apple delivers a seamless service-to-device journey. Apple does this so well that few consumers even notice it. But as with so many things in technology, making something appear so simple is often incredibly difficult.

Microsoft rolled the digital music dice again in 2012 with the launch of Xbox Music, this time relying on a much wider range of devices including Windows PCs, tablets, smartphones and of course the Xbox console. But whereas Microsoft enjoyed full control of the Zune HD ecosystem, Microsoft only provides the OS for the devices on which Xbox Music plays – the Xbox console itself the obvious exception. Thus a Windows 8 Lenovo laptop is shipped with both Xbox music and also streaming music service Rara, while a Windows Phone 8 Nokia Lumia contains Xbox Music, the Nokia Music Store and Nokia Mix Radio, as well as often a carrier service. The result for the end user is of course utter confusion. While Microsoft and Google can both boast larger installed bases of devices than Apple for their respective operating systems, neither has the control necessary to be a runaway digital music success. Apple is a compact but highly cohesive nation state while Microsoft and Google are rambling federations of competing principalities and kingdoms.

The Plight of the Retailer

Whatever challenges they may face trying to keep up with Apple, at least Google and Microsoft each have the device ecosystem card to play. The traditional music retailers never had such an asset and have in the main been swept mercilessly aside by the iTunes bandwagon. Brick and mortar retailers like Tower Records, HMV, Fnac, Saturn, Virgin and countless independents were the epicentres of music revenue in the 1980's and 1990's. Before the advent of the internet there simply was no other place to buy new music other than mail order. Retailers held all the cards and they knew it. Digital music services may find themselves having terms dictated to them by record labels, but in the analogue era the roles were reversed, the retailers called the shots. Retailers employed divide and rule tactics, playing record labels off each other, letting them duel it out for the best promotional space in return for lower per unit rates. But the retailers had it too good: a bit less comfort and a little more anxiety would have kept them on their guard. Apple understood the paradigm shift that Napster was triggering would require an entirely new set of rules and relationships. The retailers did not. As a device company, Apple was in a better position to capitalize on the emerging digital opportunity, but there was nothing preventing traditional retailers from embarking on their own device strategies, either in house or with OEM partners. Instead they failed to act quickly enough, twice. First they were too slow to recognize they needed to take online CD retailing seriously, and progressively lost that fight to Amazon and regional pure play online CD retailers. Second when they finally started to face up to the digital challenge they focused on PC centred experiences, at a time when they still had robust enough balance sheets to have pursued ambitious device strategies, even if only on a joint venture basis.

Despite the dominant retailer mindset in the early 2000's being denial at best, they still knew much more about music retailing than anyone else at this stage, Apple included. It should have been abundantly clear to them that device-less download stores were a user experience dead-end. Apple's rapid success soon put paid to any lingering doubts. At this stage the retailers should have battened down the hatches and upped their efforts against Apple, instead they played an appeasement game. Suddenly they were selling iPod accessories and iTunes gift vouchers. The enemy was now within. On the surface such a strategy appears nonsensical but it reflected the political and commercial structure of retailers. The digital divisions were small and inconsequential in terms of revenue and political influence. The executives responsible for stocking audio accessories and gift cards delivered much more sizeable income and therefore won the arguments, and they were vindicated by their short-term revenue success. Just as the Roman Empire sowed the seeds of its demise by paying subsidies to the barbarian tribes who then used the wealth to arm themselves and eventually conquer Rome, so music retailers funnelled customers and revenues to their number one enemy. The fault however lies not with the shop floor executives trying to make their numbers in an increasingly challenging marketplace, but instead with the senior executives. These business leaders allowed a short-term survivalist mentality to dictate company strategy rather than focus on building long-term vision that would have admittedly delivered weaker revenues in the near term but would have given at least a fighting chance of a long-term future. There were exceptions, such as the forward looking Virgin Mega in France, but the majority floundered as Amazon and Apple gnawed away the remaining flesh on their bones.[56] The retailers rapidly sought out ways to try to compete around, rather than against Apple, beefing up their non-music content and, in the case of HMV, getting into the live music sector. Unfortunately for the retailers the digital transition that was sweeping through music soon worked its way into movies, books and games too, and ironically Apple was once again at the fore. Wherever the retailers turned Apple seemed to be waiting. One by one the traditional retailers fell by the wayside, facing bankruptcy and administration proceedings or closing altogether: Tower, Our Price, HMV, Virgin Mega, Fame... the tombstones in the music retailer graveyard are a-plenty.

The Telco's Dilemma

Apple also scuppered the digital music plans of telcos. The ISPs failed to make any meaningful dent in the PC digital music market, unable to find any way to compete with, or around the ever present Apple. Apple was omnipotent, the telcos were impotent. Mobile carriers had a little more success, largely because the ISP's two barriers did not affect them, at least to begin with. With the exception of Japan, file sharing never really took off on mobile, beyond small scale song swapping such as Bluetoothing music tracks from one handset to another. Instead data limits, slow download speeds and limited memory all acted as natural adoption brakes for mobile piracy. Apple sat out of the mobile game for the first two thirds of the 2000's, giving mobile carriers a window of opportunity. Ring tones had been a massive success, with

56 The author recalled talking to one senior traditional retailer executive in the mid-2000's who complained that the digital division was a costly distraction from his company's core business and that he was looking forward to closing it down.

consumers often paying twice as much for 30 seconds of a synthesized imitation of a song than they would for a full download of the actual song itself online. So mobile music downloads seemed like a natural next step. There were some successes but far more money was spent building mobile music services than was earned in revenue. And then in 2007 Apple launched the iPhone and the carriers' window of mobile music opportunity was slammed shut in their faces. No mobile carrier music service made significant enough headway to withstand the Apple onslaught. Matters were complicated further by the fact that every carrier wanted to sell the iPhone to its customers but Apple cunningly restricted the iPhone to exclusive carrier partners in each country.[57] Apple held all the negotiating cards and easily ensured that it retained 100% ownership of the iTunes digital music experience. No mobile carrier was able to come even close to getting Apple to allow it to integrate its own music service. Not that they pushed that hard, after all the mobile music download business was a pitifully small excuse of a puddle in comparison to the oceans of iPhone device opportunity. Within a few years Apple's dominance of mobile music downloads was nearly as absolute as its PC download presence was. The mobile carriers had done their best, but lacking control of the device they were never able to truly compete. Apple also did something far more meaningful if less immediately obvious: it blurred the lines between mobile and PC music to a state of irrelevance. There was no iTunes PC store and iTunes mobile store, instead it was the same store optimized for different devices and platforms. In the age of responsive design this may seem like obvious common sense but in the late 2000's the mobile web world was a different country. Apple saw how the multi-screen world would look before most others did, and built a multiplatform music strategy that would not be trapped on either side of the PC or mobile fence. Apple's success in mobile music was thus also the death knell for mobile music as a discrete sector. Apple helped make everything so mobile that nothing was just mobile anymore.

New Horizons

The iPod had been a game changer for Apple as a company but the launch of the iPhone in June 2007 had even more dramatic impact. To paraphrase the iPhone ad, the iPhone changed everything for Apple. The scale of Apple's installed base of customers skyrocketed as the iPhone and then the iPad opened entire new markets. Early on Apple still traded upon its music heritage but the iPhone and then the iPad acquired a momentum all of their own, with the swift and transformational success of the App Store cutting the umbilical cord. Music was still a key activity on these devices but it was no longer what sold them. In fact even the iPod had long since evolved into a multimedia device, with the iPod Touch looking and behaving like a sans-SIM card iPhone. Though music had undoubtedly once been the iPod's killer app, the use case with which to market the device, music does a much less good job of showing off the capabilities of iPhones and iPads. Thus when Apple launches new devices, games from publishers like EA Games are used to demonstrate what the iPhone and iPad can do, leveraging to the full the capabilities of the graphics, accelerometer and multi touch controls. The announcement of Apple's Watch in late 2014 puts even more distance between music and Apple's core product momentum.

---

57 The CEOs of two mobile carriers were rumoured to have personally pushed through iPhone exclusive deals in their organizations, so keen were they to be among the first to have the phone on their networks. The iPhone was a highly sought after, scarce commodity. Everything that music used to be.

FIGURE 30

Music's Dominance of iTunes Store Revenues Long Since Passed

Apple iTunes Store Revenues by Type 2003 to 2013

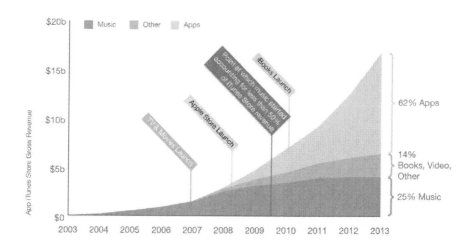

Source: Apple Reported Numbers and MIDiA Research Estimates

Despite all of Apple's assurances that it still 'loves music' – and it does – its gaze has been drawn to the allure of a much wider range of content experiences. When music was all that Apple's devices did, the Cupertino company had found itself at constant loggerheads with the record labels, continually fighting to get what it wanted. And the thanks it got for all but singlehandedly kick starting the digital music market was the record labels using MP3 licenses to do all they could to weaken Apple's position relative to its competitors. Little wonder then that when TV studios, print publishers, games houses and app developers presented themselves as eager partners that Apple opened its arms in eager embrace. Apple remains firmly committed to music because it is the key plank of their paid content business and because it remains one of the main reasons their customers use their iDevices. But with so many additional content genres to deal with, Apple's music focus has been inherently diluted, as the dropping of the word 'Music' from the iTunes Store name poignantly exemplified. Until 2003 music accounted for 100% of iTunes Store revenue because that was all that was available. Over the years Apple introduced countless new content types, each of which progressively competed for the iTunes buyer's wallet share. The step change though occurred in 2008 with the launch of the App Store. The impact was instant and by mid 2009 music already accounted for less than 50% of iTunes revenue. By the end of 2003 the transformation was complete with Apps accounting for 62% of spending and music less than a quarter (see Figure 30). Quite a fall from grace for what was once the undisputed king of the iTunes castle.

FIGURE 31

The iPhone Propelled Apple To Unprecedented Scale

Apple Device Sales by Category

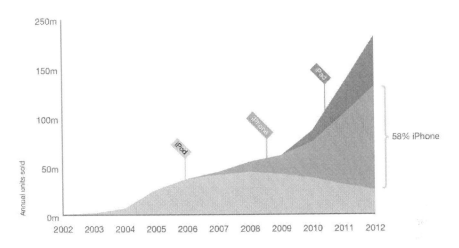

The dilution effect though, is more than a mere strategic pivot, it reflects also a sea change in consumer behaviour. Tablets, and to a lesser degree smartphones, freed the internet from the chains of the PC, enabling web experiences to be relevant to, and involved with context and location. Web sites like Yahoo!, AOL and MSN had been the internet portals of the first age of the web, tablets and smartphones are the internet portals of the current era, the windows into our digital experiences. When music was all that people could do on portable devices people bought dedicated devices such as the iPod, but now there are few reasons a consumer would choose an iPod over an iPhone.[58] By the end of the 2000's Apple's device sales started to tell the story: in 2010 for the first time ever, combined sales of iPhones and iPads outstripped sales of iPods with 62.2 million units sold compared to 47.9 million iPods. iPhones alone hit 47.5 million. From that point onwards iPod sales went into steady decline and by the end of the following year even iPad sales were exceeding those of iPods (see Figure 31). 2008 was the last year of strong iPod sales growth, it was also the last year of strong digital music sales growth: digital sales dropped off a cliff in 2009, growing by just 7% compared to 43% in 2008. This was not however the immediate effect of one bad year of iPod sales, but the cumulative impact of a slow down in the growth of the installed base of iPods. By 2008 a majority of iPod sales were to existing iPod customers and households as replacement and additional device sales. Which meant the number of new iTunes Store customers was slowing, so when iPods sales finally went into decline the music revenue slowdown was a trend already waiting to happen.

---

58 Price and being too young for a mobile phone are the two remaining key reasons.

FIGURE 32

Apple's Installed Base of Active Music Buyers Dwarfs All
Other Music Services' Paying Customer Bases

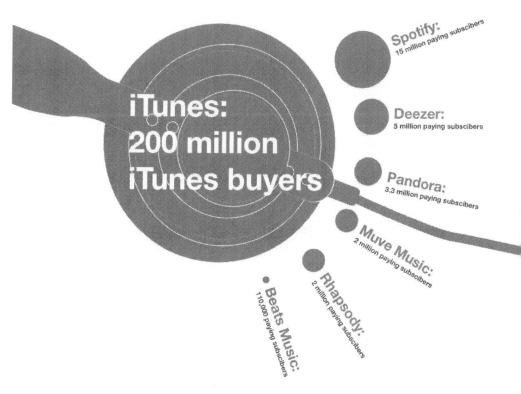

Source: Company reported numbers and MIDiA Research estimates derived from company reported numbers. : MIDiA Research 11/14

Apple's reduced music download growth meant a mirror image slowdown in the total digital
market because the competition was still unable to compete effectively. Streaming services
have been making up ground fast, comprising 28% of global digital music revenue in 2014[59]
but Apple remains the single largest generator of revenue. Apple's dominance of the
installed base of digital music buyers remains intact (see Figure 32) but things are changing.
Spotify's growth has come directly at the expense of Apple's digital music business. Before
the launch of the App Store the walls around Apple's ecosystem were impenetrable. The
App Store created a gap that third parties eagerly leapt through. Suddenly companies
like Spotify and Deezer could get straight into the hands of the most engaged digital
music consumers out there. Spotify promptly set about converting many of Apple's most
engaged music consumers into subscribers, pulling the average spending of aficionados
down from $20 or $30 a month to $9.99. The impact has been felt keenly in the broader

59 MIDiA Research

music market: 24% of music streamers stopped buying more than an album a month and download sales went into free fall in 2014 in the world's biggest music markets, such as the US, UK and Germany, in some cases declining at double digit percentage rates.

Declining music spending itself is not a major concern for Apple – it runs its music business on an at best break even basis. But what does matter is the fact that music's power as a device lock-in is weakening. Expensively amassed iTunes music collections and lovingly crafted iTunes playlists used to act as velvet handcuffs, tipping users to sticking with Apple at the next phone upgrade even if the new iPhone might not have quite as good hardware specifications as an Android alternative. But with streaming services all that goes. A Spotify playlist works just as well on a Samsung Galaxy as it does on an iPhone. Losing music revenue was an inconvenience but losing its most valuable customers to Spotify and then potentially on to Android was a business crisis. The alarm bells started to ring at Cupertino. While it would be stretching things to suggest that Apple's $3 billion purchase of Beats in 2014 was all about winning back high value music loyalists, it was most certainly an important part of the mix. The great irony is that Apple has always been in the business of selling music in order to sell hardware, but it has now been compelled to buy a hardware business in order to help sell music better.

Apple will get streaming right and when it does it will both win back a lot of its lost customers and push the subscriptions market much closer to the mainstream than it has been so far. But Apple's new streaming strategy has required a completely different approach to music innovation to that which it followed in recent years.

Although iTunes transformed the download market beyond recognition, since the late 2000's most of the innovations iTunes has undergone have been modest, iterative changes, along with a couple of misses such as Ping. Without any serious competitive pressure from music services and with its growing focus on non-music content Apple simply did not have the same need to innovate as fiercely as it did when the iPod was its focus. The resultant rate of innovation contrasts sharply with the rate of innovation seen in Apple's devices (see Figure 33). The launch of iTunes Radio in September 2013 was the first major music service innovation from Apple since the launch of the iTunes Store 10 years previously. The music industry cannot afford for Apple to progress in decade long increments. If Apple had innovated the iTunes music experience as strongly as it had its devices since the late 2000's then the digital music market would now have a dramatically different appearance. Of course Apple has had to slow its rate of innovation across its entire product portfolio as its customer base has become more mainstream with the more devices it has sold. When the iTunes Music Store was first launched Apple's customer base was defined by early adopter tech aficionados. Now an Apple customer is just as likely to be a silver surfer as he is a gadget geek. So Apple has to innovate at a pace that simultaneously entices the tech savvy aficionados but that does not alienate its new mainstream customer base. No easy balance to strike. Apple also has great responsibility: with such a large share of the global music market accounted for by the iTunes Store, if Apple gets its next music move wrong, it could have a disastrous impact on the global music market.

FIGURE 33

Apple's Device Innovation Rate Far Outpaces
Its Rate of Music Service Innovation

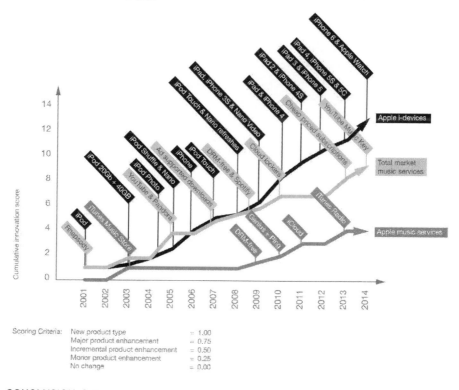

Scoring Criteria:
New product type	= 1.00
Major product enhancement	= 0.75
Incremental product enhancement	= 0.50
Minor product enhancement	= 0.25
No change	= 0.00

CONCLUSION: Still the Number One Game in Town

Apple spent more than a decade as undisputed leader in the digital music market with no service or device company able to offer anything more than token resistance. Finally in the 2010's streaming services, Spotify in particular, have risen to the challenge. Apple probably let itself drift into hubris, failing to respond to streaming until it had already started to have dramatic impact on its business. Nonetheless Apple remains digital music's most important stakeholder, with no single competitor challenging its revenue dominance, yet. Apple's devices and store transformed music consumption and business models but Apple is in the music business to sell devices. Apple is a high margin business and selling music is a low margin business, the more music Apple sells relative to its devices the less profitable its business becomes. It had started to feel like it was time to stop looking to Apple to deliver the next big thing in digital music but the realization that music has been used to loosen the very bonds Apple had used music to create has forced Apple to rediscover its music innovation mojo. Expect Apple to make streaming work in a way that no others have done yet. Apple has a vast array of assets at its disposal and an equally immense customer base. Options such as a device life time of subscription access bundled into handsets at the point of sale and blended streaming and download tiers are all on the table.

iCloud has thus far proven to be a typically smart opening gambit, easing its customers into cloud based experiences almost without them realizing. And iTunes Radio may well prove to be a strategic masterstroke, with its integration in the on-device iTunes experience so seamless that it might be exactly the simple-to-use, low effort introduction to streaming that mass market consumers need. With Beats Music layered on top Apple will have one of the most complete streaming and cloud propositions in the market. The odds are in favour of Apple getting streaming right eventually, even if it suffers some initial hiccoughs, which it most likely will. But if Apple cannot make streaming work then the consequences will be felt far beyond iPhone and iPad sales: as the iPod experience revealed, when Apple sneezes, the music industry catches a cold.

Chapter 9: Streaming's Story

The launch of Spotify in 2008 was the music industry's third digital turning point, following Napster in 1999 and the iTunes Store in 2003. Spotify's impact was to prove to be seismic but it was an early follower not a first mover. It might have fixed stream buffering but it was far from the first streaming music service nor indeed the first ever subscription service with countless predecessors including Launchcast, Napster and Rhapsody.[60] But what Spotify did was make streaming work seamlessly and effortlessly in a way no other streaming service had done before. It also had the distinct benefit of great timing: whereas Launchcast and Rhapsody had been born into in a time when home broadband was only just getting started, Spotify was a child of the age of ubiquitous super fast broadband and it would soon also be riding the crest of the wave of pervasive mobile data plans. If timing is everything then Spotify did not miss a beat, acquiring tens of millions of users and signing up an unprecedented 15 million people to monthly subscription plans.[61] Spotify has become the poster child for streaming, the on-demand successor to the iTunes Store.

But it has also become the focus of all the fear, uncertainty and doubt that streaming has wrought right across the music industry, from artists, through songwriters to small labels. In truth, neither the adulation nor the criticism are entirely accurately aimed. Streaming is not a product nor is it a business model. Instead it is simply a technological means of getting music onto people's digital devices. In fact consumers should not even have to understand the difference between a download and a stream, let alone what constitutes a cached stream.[62] Nonetheless streaming has been put centre stage, becoming the vernacular of the wider digital debate, the lens through which all of the arguments and thinking surrounding the macro issues are viewed. These issues include the shift from ownership to access, record label business practices and the plight of artists and songwriters struggling to earn a living.

Streaming services are at the innovation sharp end of digital music market change but they are a conduit rather than the paradigm itself. So although this chapter is titled 'Streaming's Story' it is more precisely 'the tale of digital music services in the consumption era'. For sake of easy identification by the reader and for a snappier chapter title, we will stick with 'Streaming's Story'.

The Case for Streaming Services

The new generation of streaming services arrived on the scene just when the record labels needed them: download growth was slowing, investment rates were dipping and digital revenue growth was still showing little sign of making up for disappearing CD revenue. Their pitch to the labels was elegantly simple as Spotify's Chief Content Officer Ken Parks described: "The promise of the streaming model is that everyone will consume more music.

---

60 Rhapsody's origins were Tune.To.com a customized radio service which was acquired by Listen.com in April 2001 and launched as Rhapsody in December 2001.
61 Spotify official numbers as of February 2015.
62 A cached stream is a temporary version of a song that is downloaded onto a device to allow offline playback and to help ensure tracks stream without buffering

This is a generation weaned on YouTube, they simply don't differentiate between access and ownership. You don't have to convince a 15 year old that the access model is good."

The new wave of streaming subscription services including Spotify, Deezer, Rdio, MOG, We7, Rara and Simfy were following the Apple approach of moving into a market that had already been established and proven by earlier entrants. In the case of streaming subscriptions Rhapsody was the granddaddy of them all. Throughout much of the 2000's Rhapsody had been the connoisseur's choice, the best featured and programmed music service in the market. It defined the music subscription category and built a niche but robust user base that remained loyal in the face of new entrants as former Rhapsody President Jon Irwin explained: "Real Networks announced the acquisition of Rhapsody the same week that Apple announced iTunes Music Store. We [were] reaping the rewards of being a first mover, we operated a sustainable business throughout those years." Irwin identified that the key catalyst for the second wave of streaming subscription services was the same as had propelled Pandora's growth: "What changed was 2009, the advent of the Apple store and the iPhone. They reinvigorated the digital music market – getting a broader range of consumers used to the idea of paying for music in a non-physical format and helping to make smartphones mainstream, putting a great music player into people's pockets. That enabled us to aggressively develop a great customer experience." Once again Apple emerges as the digital change agent, though this time with the added irony that it was also inadvertently aiding and abetting disruptive competitive threat. The labels however were more than willing to take the risk of upsetting the Apple cart this time round though because subscribers generated much higher average spend than download buyers as EMI's former CEO Roger Faxon explained: "The value of an iTunes customer is substantially less than that of a Spotify customer. A Spotify consumer is always consuming. Every action to listen creates value for the rights owner." Even the smaller labels of the independent sector grasped the opportunity as AIM's Alison Wenham stated: "The reach that streaming services offer presents an opportunity of unprecedented proportion for small companies." But as enthusiastic partners as the labels may have become it was far from plain sailing for Spotify to secure its original licenses as founder and CEO Daniel Ek recalled: "It became clear early on that this was a challenging industry to negotiate with! The rights holders value the music content they represent – and rightly so. Reaching agreement as to what is fair on both sides can be a lengthy and tricky negotiation at times, but we have worked with the labels and publishers for 7 years now, and together we have reached a situation which has allowed us to generate more than $1bn for the music industry."

One of the assets of streaming subscription services that has helped win rights holders over is their capacity to get consumers to deeply engage with music in new ways as illustrated by a story told by Jon Irwin: "One day my father in law asked me to explain what it was I did for living, so I showed him Rhapsody. He is a big Jazz fan with stacks of CDs and vinyl and everything indexed and filed on small cards. I played some Charlie Parker and while it was playing I brought up his influences, musicians he'd played with etc. My father in law was blown away and has been a Rhapsody fan ever since. That's what a music service is all about, having a meaningful impact on people with music."

FIGURE 34
Streaming Super Charged The Swedish Music Market
Comparison of 2012/13 Music Revenue Change by Type

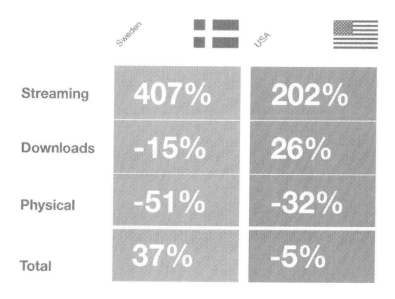

	Sweden	USA
Streaming	407%	202%
Downloads	-15%	26%
Physical	-51%	-32%
Total	37%	-5%

The Spotify Effect

Though numerous other services spent much of the 2000's establishing the streaming subscription model, it took Spotify and Deezer to propel it towards something resembling scale. Although the 9.99 streaming proposition remains inherently niche in appeal, these two services managed to unlock subscription customers in countless markets where other services did not. But while both companies have had a big impact on the number of paying subscribers, Spotify has the edge in terms of momentum and innovation, often beating Deezer to market with announcements and innovations. For better or for worse, Spotify has become the face of streaming and has had a dramatic impact on the music industry outlook in a number of smaller, more sophisticated markets, especially in its native Sweden and in the Netherlands. A comparison between the impact of streaming on the Swedish music market and that of the US provides useful context for understanding the likely long term impact and effect of streaming.

Sweden is the stand out good news story for music subscriptions, with streaming representing an impressive 95% of digital revenue in 2013 and 67% of all recorded music revenue. Downloads meanwhile accounted for a paltry four percent. Streaming growth propelled the total Swedish music market into growth for four successive years: 2011, 2012 and 2013. That growth however came at the direct expense of downloads, which declined by 15% and it accompanied a dramatic 51% collapse in CD sales. Nonetheless 2013 revenues came in at just a little below 2003 levels, no mean feat.

The contrast between Sweden and the US is stark (see Figure 34). In the US streaming grew less dynamically and only represented 23% of digital and 14% of overall spending in 2013. The strength of Apple and the download sector acted as a pronounced curb on streaming growth in the US. Neither, however are invincible, and some of Spotify's 2013 US growth came at the direct expense of download spending - little wonder Apple launched iTunes Radio in 2013 to see off the threat. In the US streaming has become an increasingly important part of the market but shows no sign of suddenly acquiring Sweden-like ubiquity. Which in part explains a five percent decline in total music revenues between 2012 and 2013. The emerging picture is one of streaming being able to quickly drive strong growth in markets where downloads never got a foothold but taking more time to impact markets with a strong download sector. Consequently it is not possible to simply extrapolate Spotify's Swedish experience onto the global market to predict future trends.

FIGURE 35

**Streaming Does Best Where Downloads Did Not Get A
Foothold (Where They Did Streaming Is Held Back)**
Digital Revenue by Type as Share of Total Revenues 2013, and Digital Growth 2012 to 2013

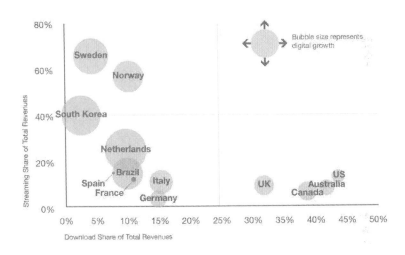

The contrast between the experiences of the US and Sweden highlight a crucial point: streaming has done best in markets where downloads never really got going. The booming Nordics are markets where streaming was effectively green field growth, where a digital market of any meaningful scale had not previously been established via download sales. Downloads were never more than 8% of Swedish music revenues compared to a high of 43% in the US. Downloads supercharged digital growth in the 2000's especially in the big English speaking music markets. The reason was simple: where Apple did well – which skewed towards English speaking markets – download sales did well which meant that digital did well. In the streaming era though downloads actually hinder digital growth. Those same markets now not only have smaller streaming and subscription revenue shares, they are also among the slowest growing digital markets. In download strongholds streaming has to chip away at ingrained download buyer behavior. Elsewhere it taps pent up digital demand (see Figure 35). The other key country level factor that has shaped the streaming market thus far is indigeneity. In the vast majority of markets where streaming has done best, there is an indigenous music company underpinning the performance. Each has also benefited from a major bundling relationship with the incumbent telco: Sweden / Spotify - Telia, Norway / Wimp - Telenor, Denmark / Play - TDC, France / Deezer – France Telecom. All these companies are European and all have eaten into Apple's global digital music market share. In music revenue terms, the stream is Europe's answer to the US's download.

FIGURE 36

Streaming Drives Stronger Digital Revenue Growth In
Sweden Than Downloads Did In The US

Comparison of Strong Growth Phases of Swedish and US Digital Music Markets

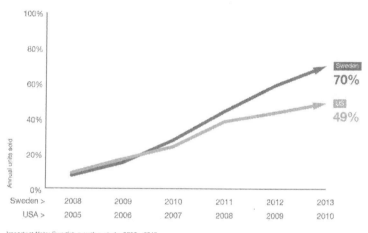

Important Note: Swedish growth period = 2008 – 2013
US growth period = 2005 - 2010

Looking at the US and Swedish experiences, particularly at streaming's impact on the total digital market and on total music sales an important divergence between the two markets emerges. In the six years up to and including 2013, streaming drove a comparable rate of overall digital growth in Sweden that downloads powered in the US in the mid 2000's. But when we plot the growth of digital as a percentage of total music sales in the US between 2005 and 2010 against the same data for Sweden between 2008 and 2013 a pronounced contrast is immediately apparent (see Figure 36). Whereas digital share growth remained strong throughout the six years in Sweden it slowed markedly in the US. Though growth returned later it didn't ever replicate those pre-2008 levels. The number one slowdown factor was the end of iPod sales growth. Interestingly digital share growth looks likely to slow moderately for both Sweden and the US after 2013. In Sweden some level of slowdown is to be expected as there is not much physical market left to transition, but there remains plenty of CD ground to be made up in the US. So streaming drove market growth in Sweden and accelerated the transition away from the CD and the download, while in the US the CD and the download both retained much greater sway, culminating in something of a worst of both worlds, with streaming apparently eating into downloads but not having enough headway to transform the market.

The Hierarchy of Exploitation

Streaming services, and subscriptions in particular, won over large swathes of music industry decision makers and are seen by many as the jewel in the crown of digital strategy. Yet they also endured the rockiest of rides, coming under sustained criticism from right across the value chain, from managers, labels, other services and most vocally, artists and songwriters. Few people disagree that a well programmed and featured streaming music service is a hugely compelling consumer proposition and that subscriptions are a fantastic means of driving high levels of spending among music fans. What has divided opinion right down the middle though are the overriding questions of whether streaming services cannibalize music sales and whether they generate enough income for all elements of the music industry, artists and songwriters in particular. The result is effectively a music industry civil war, with an often vitriolic debate that somewhat confusingly instils even deeper passions than piracy did at its peak.

Axel Dauchez, former CEO Deezer

Jon Irwin, former President Rhapsody

Ken Parks, Chief Content Officer Spotify

One of the key problems with the streaming debate is that it groups many highly distinct business models and consumer propositions into the same bucket, ranging from pure on-demand services to programmed radio services. Will Page, economist at Spotify and formerly Chief Economist at the PRS for Music, makes the case that there is a 'hierarchy of exploitation': "the more the consumer [is] able to interact with the content the higher that unit value. At one end of the spectrum [is] conventional linear consumption and at the other the exhaustion of the IP through a purchase. Most of the innovative online services that have launched since have found themselves somewhere in the middle." There is a world of difference between Slacker's personalized radio experience and the immersive on demand world of Rdio, but there are enough commonalities for them to be habitually thrown into the same conceptual bucket. Beyond the cosmetic similarities – streaming delivery, mobile consumption etc. – the crucial piece of common DNA is that personalized radio and on demand services both swap transactional ownership for metered access. Though the exact rate of rights holder compensation is determined by whether the stream is monetized via advertising or subscription fees, both result in per track payments that are far lower than those generated by downloads. And it is this continual return to the comparison with download revenue that plagues the streaming debate.

It is an entirely understandable and instinctive response, particularly for artists and songwriters who fear they are swapping download dollars for streaming cents, however the appraisal is dangerously lopsided. On demand streaming services are not the extreme of the scale, instead they sit in the midpoint of a consumption and revenue continuum, the paid download at one end and traditional radio at the other. Though they combine elements of both ends of the spectrum they are neither one nor the other, they are unique blends that do not fit the neat buckets defined in the distribution age when music was either about selling units of stuff - CDs, downloads – or programming and marketing – TV, radio. Technology and consumer behaviour have morphed to create hybrids and entirely new models that require equally novel business models. So while a free stream can generate in the region of 200 times less for an artist than a download the analysis is that it is worth a lot more than a radio listen and paid streams are worth much more than free ones (see Figure 37).

FIGURE 37

Putting Streaming into a Broader Context

Number of Plays Required in Different Music Services to Generate the Equivalent Income of One Download

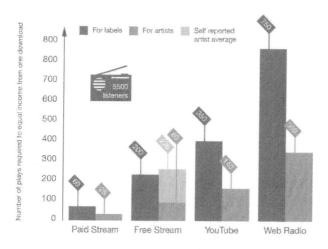

Source: record label data provided to Music Tank, & additional publicly available artist income data.
Note: data refers to fully recouped artists

Pandora, with its 76.4 million active US users[63] has had the largest impact on US consumers of all the streaming audio services and in many respects has been the most controversial. Unlike the on-demand services Pandora is a programmed radio service that only allows the user a relatively small degree of customization and is licensed through statutory licensing mechanisms provided for by the DMCA. Under these provisions a service that places limits on factors such how many songs a user can listen to by one artist in a given hour can be granted a statutory license rather than have to negotiate with record labels. Pandora was thus carefully designed to ensure that it would not be subject to expensive direct commercial licenses from labels. EMI's former President of Digital Distribution Jay Samit recalled the industry's steadfast opinion that if Pandora was going to be a free radio-like service, it had to have clear usability constraints: "If you could access a song anytime anyplace why would you buy it? That's why we put those speed bumps in Pandora. Did it hurt Pandora? Sure, but without them it would have killed a $40 billion business." On-demand services view themselves as a clearly differentiated alternative that encourages users towards immersive music discovery experiences as Deezer's CEO Axel Dauchez argued: "There is no question that streaming services liberate the usage of music but as a consequence the engagement of end users has declined. Consumers are listening but are not engaged. Smart radio services are destroying user engagement." However Pandora's Tim Westergren makes the counter argument that on-demand counterparts are strongly competitive with music sales in a way that radio services are not: "The on-demand world is a limited world. You have to be clear that it is fundamentally substitutional. Whatever commerce is worth to you, you have to factor what on-demand is worth to you against that."

Despite the more clearly defined cannibalistic threat of on-demand services, interactive radio has found itself bearing the brunt of an even fiercer degree of industry criticism in the US than the likes of Spotify and Rdio, from labels, publishers, artists and songwriters alike. At the core of this is the fact that Pandora has a much clearer precedent, in short it looks and smells too much like radio for its own good. So while on-demand streaming services can to some degree hide behind the defence that they are entirely new models that need time, Pandora had to face many of the core critiques of traditional radio, in addition to the core streaming criticisms. In the eyes of its critics Pandora is disruptive threat squared, the worst of the old and the new. Interactive radio's case is not helped by the fact that it often falls back on the self same argument that has served traditional radio so well for so long: that its value should not be measured purely in revenue terms but instead account for how it drives discovery and exposure. The promotional argument divided labels and artists at the best of times but has now lost much of its strength because:

- Radio is no longer the only serious promotional game in town[64]

- Digital discovery platforms have become destinations in themselves

- Artists and songwriters have found their collective voice

All of which adds up to the perfect storm for interactive radio. Beggars Martin Mills outlined the perspective of many record labels: "The age old promotional value argument has bedevilled us all along. It doesn't apply any more as so many discovery points are now where people listen. As Rob Dickens said 'if you play what I want when I want I'll accept it is promotion. If it is what you want when you want it is business.'" David Lowery employed a similar critique from the artist perspective: "The vast majority of the time I bring value to Pandora rather than the other way

63 Company reports as of November 2014.
64 Radio remains the most common cited means of music discovery but it now faced
fierce competition from YouTube and countless other digital alternatives.

round. Most of the time they are playing the songs of mine that are already popular and so it isn't promotion for me because those tracks have already been successfully promoted." The core critiques of radio are valid and though it is abundantly clear that radio's role needs redefining for the digital age, it will remain a vitally important part of the music landscape. Interactive radio services like Slacker and Pandora represent part of that new future for radio, where the power of digital features and functionality replace a tired reliance on 'promotional value' and 'exposure'. Tim Westergren further outlined the case for interactive radio: "All radio needs to transition from AM/FM to the web because 1) musicians get paid, 2) more musicians get played 3) you are connected to individual listeners, you know who they are, where they are and you can talk to them."

Will Page, Chief Economist Spotify

Oleg Fomenko, Former CEO
Bloom.fm

Carey Sherman, CEO RIAA

The Streaming Debate

Pandora was far from the only streaming service to have come under sustained critical fire from across the music industry value chain, with streaming services of all flavours subjected to heated criticism as the streaming debate raged. Unfortunately the debate became clouded and confused, with passions running high and the quality and interpretation of data often of mixed value at best. Artists and songwriters felt that they were not being fairly compensated for, as they saw it, essentially fuelling heavily financed music services. Something did not seem to be adding up and artists lobbied for greater transparency from the streaming services so that they could get to the heart of the matter. Countless artists posted their CD Baby royalty statements to reveal how little they received compared to iTunes and CD sales, which in turn led to many more dozens of stories, especially in the online tech press. The ensuing streaming pay-out debate was a frustrating mix of genuinely important issues confused and distorted by data misinterpretation and misapprehension. With so much 'hard data' coming directly from artists it was easy to get swept along with the ideological zeitgeist. But it soon became apparent that supposedly 'hard data' was not creating an accurate picture. The amount artists reported being paid per Spotify stream ranged from as little as $0.000088 to as 'high' as $0.01. Given that streaming services signed deals with record labels and not artists it soon became clear that there was more to the issue of streaming pay outs than the artist data at first suggested.

Some artists claimed that a stream was equivalent to 150 to 200 downloads in revenue for them, a comparison fraught with problems. Indeed, if you multiply the streaming average of $0.005 by 150 you get a value of $0.75 which is virtually the entire retail price of a download. In reality the retailer needs to take their cut from a download sale, then the label, then the publisher, then collection agencies, distributors, aggregators etc. Only a small share of artists get near that sort of rate, namely DIY singer-songwriters. A standard label artist can expect closer to $0.09 from a download – as publicised by Chuck D – which is only 18 times the streaming pay out rate. Though some artists, who are also songwriters and are on 50/50 net receipt deals and that are fully recouped, could hope to earn nearer $0.40 per download. The 'moving parts' of individual artists' commercial terms are so variable and so complex that they prevent meaningful comparisons between artists' self-reported streaming and download income. These 'moving parts' can be defined as:

a) The artist's record deal: What sort of deal the artist is on e.g. points or percentages, and if percentage rates, what level, whether they are recouped i.e. whether the label is yet paying the artist for royalties.

b) The status of the artist: Whether the artist is just a performer, or also a songwriter and therefore eligible to additional publishing royalties, or whether the artist is just a songwriter and therefore not eligible for performance royalties.

c) The status of the artists' label: Whether the label is redistributing all of its advance payments from the streaming services with artists , if the label has an equity stake in the streaming service, as many do, and therefore whether all payments it receives are eligible for redistributing to artists.[65]

d) Third party services: Whether fees for artist self-service tools like Tunecore and CD Baby are accounted for, what fees are deducted by distributors and what sort of deals these companies have managed to strike with different streaming services.

e) Streaming service's own deals: The rates that a streaming service has negotiated with rights owners – these can vary markedly between services.

f) Geographical location of service: Music services based in emerging market regions such as Latin America and the Indian Subcontinent are charged discounted rates by rights holders and often charge consumers lower fees compared to Europe and North America.

---

65 Most equity stakes will only realize any income at point of sale or flotation of a company. It is at this point that the question of whether artists receive a distribution of income arises as the income would not be directly royalty based. Additionally should a streaming service become operationally profitable then as an equity holder a label could be eligible for dividend / profit payments that may also not be subject to redistribution to artists as once again it is not directly royalty based.

For all the artist calls for greater transparency from streaming services it is clear that the more appropriate first task is for artists to get better transparency in their own dealings with labels, publishers, rights bodies, aggregators and distributors. Nonetheless the artist streaming debate raises some key issues and plays an important role for artists in a broader sense as the artist streaming debate is in fact a child of its time:

- The streaming debate is a watershed moment in artist empowerment: To have a voice as an artist in the original piracy debate you needed to be a big established artist who the press would write about. By 2012 the power of social media was well enough established to enable David Lowery's blog to rack up half a million views in two days and for him to go on to become a central voice in the streaming debate. In fact virtually all of the artists who were active in the debate and who posted data were relatively small artists. This was a democratization of digital dialogue. The artist masses had found their voices. They did not have to depend upon Lars Ulrich or organizations such as the Featured Artist Coalition (FAC) to be their voice anymore. Moreover their voices carried an air of authenticity that resonated with the media and public alike. In an instant, artists had become an integral part of the digital debate in a way that labels could only dream of. After all it is easier for a consumer to relate to a struggling artist's story than to a label exec toeing the party line. Thus in many ways the streaming pay out debate happened in the right place at the right time. Artists were finding their voice and flexing their social media muscle. Whether they knew it or not, they were waiting for an issue to coalesce around, and streaming became that issue.

- It was also a coming of age for artists as business people: Alongside gaining more influence, many artists were becoming much more informed. Not just in terms of keeping up to date with music industry issues but also by getting more data and analytics. The increased popularity of direct-to-fan platforms and self-release tools put more data into the hands of more artists. In the early stages of the streaming debate, data sprayed out onto the web like a fire hose, leaving an increasingly confused public in its wake. Over time though an average emerged, helped by sites such as SpotiDJ that took it upon themselves to aggregate reported data and eventually by Spotify publishing its royalty rates. Artists learned that they needed to use data intelligently to help them ask the right questions rather than simply rely upon data itself to provide the answers. They also learned that they should question every commercial relationship that they had, including those with aggregators, DIY sites and distributors. Finally they understood that because deals varied so dramatically according to artist and to partner there was consequently no 'artist average'. Artists get what they negotiate for, and now data is helping to level the negotiating playing field by giving some sense of the floors and ceilings of deal parameters.

While the wider artist and songwriter communities engaged in a philosophical debate about the role of streaming services, a handful of marquee artists skipped the discussion part and went straight to the action of removing or holding back some of their content from Spotify and other streaming services. Global super star artists including Adele, Coldplay, Taylor Swift and Rihanna – or at least their management - all opted to keep their latest albums off streaming services in the first months of release to mitigate against the risk of cannibalizing sales.[66] It is interesting that heavyweight artists such as these tend not to get involved in the streaming debate yet take the most direct action.

---

[66] The Black Keys were another notable streaming holdout, and indeed were one of the first to take this course of action, but they differed from Coldplay, Adele, Taylor Swift and Rihanna in that the Black Keys also actively participated in the streaming debate.

For Adele, Coldplay and Taylor Swift the decision to hold back their music for a period of time was a fairly straightforward one because their overall artist success metrics are those of traditional album artists. Each still sell large volumes of albums and only have modest YouTube and Facebook footprints in relation to their scale. By contrast, artists like Pitbull, Lady Gaga and Rihanna are very much 21st century artists who do not perform particularly strongly in album sales terms but are internet phenomena, with vast reach on YouTube and Facebook. These are consumption era artists who rely upon a diversity of income streams to make a living and thus have less at risk from streaming services.

Indeed many such artists view streaming services in the way that the likes of Chuck D and Fran Healy viewed file sharing: namely an opportunity to grow exposure in order to sell other stuff. Lady Gaga was the second highest earning artist in 2013 with $80 million[67] despite sales of her 'Artpop' album failing to set the world alight: 'Artpop' reached number 1 in the US album charts in its first week of release but did so off the back of just 258,000 sales compared to the 1.1 million first week sales her previous album 'Born This Way' had achieved in 2011.[68] Lady Gaga and her management astutely built her brand and commercial footprint across a highly diverse range of revenue streams that are helped by but not dependent upon music sales. In fact a cynic could argue that the money spent by Interscope marketing her albums essentially acts as free marketing for Lady Gaga's broader business interests.

It is not just global pop superstars represented in the ranks of the streaming holdouts. Acts like the Black Keys and Atoms for Peace both held back their content and took high profile stances against streaming services. But for all the vocal opposition to streaming audio services from holdouts, it is virtually always one rule for the likes of Spotify and an entirely different one for YouTube. In fact no rules at all apply to YouTube other than to ensure that content is on there as quickly as possible, often before it is available to purchase. This is the YouTube Dilemma at work again: artists and labels remain enthralled by YouTube's promotional potential to the extent of being in denial of its at least equally powerful cannibalistic effect on sales.

While the Black Keys and Atoms for Peace are happy to hold court with the press to argue that streaming services are damaging to the music industry they see no contradiction in populating their official YouTube channels with free streams of their music. Thus while paid subscription services drive some of the highest music consumer average spending in the marketplace and on the Hierarchy of Exploitation generate a far higher average per stream fee than YouTube, streaming hold outs continue to happily give their content away for free on one of the least effective monetization channels on the web. The allure of tens of millions of YouTube viewers blinds artists and labels alike to its detrimental effect on sales. YouTube is streaming's 'elephant in the room'. While streaming subscription services have to charge consumers a premium to let them listen on their mobile devices, YouTube is available free at point of access on virtually every smartphone and tablet on the planet. It is an egregiously uneven playing field that seriously constrains the potential scale of paid streaming services. Competing with free is one thing, competing against legal and licensed free is another entirely as Jon Irwin argued: "There are around 50 independent music services, but getting to scale is a massive challenge. There is a huge difference between users and engaged loyal users. If there is a bunch of free services out there then that impacts our ability to bring in paying customers to Rhapsody and Napster."

67 Forbes Highest Paid Musicians in 2013 http://www.forbes.com/sites/
zackomalleygreenburg/2013/11/19/the-worlds-highest-paid-musicians-2013/
68 Sales data from Nielsen Soundscan. Note that the first week sales of 'Born This Way' was
partially boosted by a temporary $0.99 promotion at Amazon's MP3 store.

There is no little irony that artists saved their communal ire not for the pirate sites, but for the legal streaming sites Pandora and Spotify.[69] Part of the reason is that artists feel that they have at least some hope of influencing legitimate business whereas they felt largely powerless in the face of piracy, but the irony of finding their collective voice for streaming remains nonetheless. Daniel Ek believes that part of the reason for this is that Spotify has become a lightning rod for artist concerns with digital in a larger sense: "This is a new business model for the music industry, and it's understandable that it will take time for everyone to understand it, and to appreciate that it's part of the solution, not part of the problem. Piracy is an intangible concept, which is of course notoriously difficult to tackle effectively. An artist can't take their music 'off' piracy, as it were, so if they want to take any action that will generate headlines, Spotify is an easier target. But I would urge ANY artist who has questions about Spotify to come to us. We sit down with tons of artists and managers, big or small, every single day and explain how they can use Spotify to further their careers, reach their fans and drive revenues."

The question that arises is whether the free tiers of streaming subscription services also contribute to the same end game of educating mainstream consumers that legal music should be free online. Streaming services such as Spotify and Deezer that include comprehensive free tiers respond that they are crucial to their being able to compete with free illegal alternatives such as peer-to-peer file sharing. Spotify's Will Page makes the case for how Spotify has helped reduce piracy rates: "The experience of Norway and Sweden shows us that streaming is converting more people from 'zeros' to 'ones' and labels are seeing their trade revenue income expand as a result. What is particularly interesting, and rarely discussed, about Sweden is that not only did their recorded music revenues display strong double digit growth in 2012, but their live music industry followed suit – expanding by 12%."

Setting the Right Context for the Artist Streaming Debate

One of the other key problems with the artist streaming debate has been getting the right lens through which to view issues. When we view the future we use the reference points of the past and the present to frame our view. So it was entirely understandable that the benchmark comparison became the download and all other income was indexed against that. But it is an outlook that is firmly rooted in the download and misses the wider context of streaming. For artists, streaming is in fact more about the way in which they can be compensated for their music every time it is listened to. A more useful way to assess the role of streaming for artists is to use a Consumption Analysis that creates a meaningful way to compare streaming and downloading income:

a) First, downloads are paid for once but played many times, so a price per listen is needed. This is arrived at by establishing the lifetime value of a purchased track and dividing the sale price by the total number of plays it will receive after purchase. This lifetime value of a song is crucial to understanding the unique attributes of consumption monetization models.

---

69 Some artists however still feel considerable antipathy towards iTunes. Who legend Pete Townshend went as far as calling iTunes 'Digital Vampires', arguing that it was sucking the lifeblood out of the music market and that Apple should be putting money back into the music industry by investing in new artists. The critique was misshapen by a fear of the digital present and a pang for an analogue past long gone. There are many problems with the digital era that are worthy of criticism, and Apple are even eligible for some of that, but there is no more basis in the argument that iTunes should fund new artists than there was for Tower Records, Virgin, HMV, Fnac or Saturn to have done the same when they were successful CD retailers. iTunes is a retailer not a record label and there is a very strong argument in favour of Apple retaining that clean distinction. If Apple got into the business of record labels it would create no end of conflict of interests with its record label partners.

b) Next the multiple moving parts that confuse the streaming debate need stripping away to enable like-for-like comparison. Streaming and download services both pay approximately 70% of income to rights owners. The amount paid per stream to rights owners can then be calculated ($0.0112) as can the average $0.005 artist pay out, as a share of that (45%).

c) The resulting net-neutral artist-to-rights owner's ratio can then be applied to downloads, and then averaged out by the total number of plays a track receives in its life time (i.e. 12 plays in 3 years).

FIGURE 38

The Consumption Analysis: Unlocking the Lifetime Value of a Song

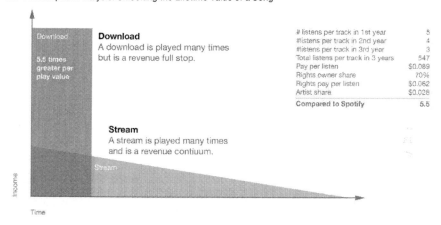

The net result is that the ratio of the income value to an artist of each play of a downloaded track compared each play of a streamed track is actually only 3-to-1, a far cry from the 200-to-1 range (see Figure 38). This Consumption Analysis methodology is not the definitive measure for comparing downloads to streams – there simply is not one, nor will there be – but it is the sort of approach that artists need in order to add context to their sales data to help them make informed decisions about streaming.

FIGURE 39

Comparisons of Average Royalty Payments for Streaming
and Downloading in Sweden and US

Sweden		USA	
Streaming		**Streaming**	
Subscribers	3	Subscribers	3
Monthly new artists per subscriber	5	Monthly new artists per subscriber	5
Annual new artists per subscriber	60	Annual new artists per subscriber	60
Streams Jul 11–Jul12	8,667	Streams Jul 11–Jul12	13,000
Streams per subscriber per year	4,333	Streams per user per year	4,333
Streams per subscriber per artist	72.22	Streams per subscriber per artist	72.22
Royalty per stream	$0.01	Royalty per stream	$0.01
Average royalty per artist per subscriber	$0.72	Average royalty per artist per subscriber	$0.72
Total average royalty per artist	$1.44	Total average royalty per artist	$2.17
Average # artists that earn per subscriber	60	Average # artists that earn per subscriber	60
Downloads		**Downloads**	
Download buyers	0.475	Download buyers	62.8
Albums per buyer per year	0.7	Albums per buyer per year	2.2
Singles per buyer per year	7.5	Singles per buyer per year	24.3
New artists per year	8.13	New artists per year	26.47
Average spend	$29.72	Average spend	$45.97
Average royalty per artist per buyer	$3.56	Average royalty per artist per buyer	$1.22
Total average royalty per artist	$1.22	Total average royalty per artist	$76.34
Average # artists that earn per downloader	8	Average # artists that earn per downloader	26

NOTES: 'Royalty payment' refers to total royalty payment i.e. inclusive of labels, publishers,
songwriters, distributors etc. Sweden listener metrics based on Spotify's 2012 reported US
usage metrics. Downloads based on actual download market in each country.

How Streaming May Impact Digital Income for Artists

Another way to consider the potential impact of streaming on artist income, particularly in
relation to download revenue, is to compare the potential impact of 'scale' on those two
contrasting streaming markets: Sweden and the US. If we first take Spotify's reported US
metrics from 2012 as a benchmark[70] and assume that the average subscriber listens to a modest
5 different artists a month then this is equal to 60 different artists per year per subscriber (see
Figure 39). Working with an average total royalty pay out of $0.01 per stream this translates
into an average royalty per artist per subscriber of $0.72 in the US. When applied to the
3 million reported US Spotify subscribers for 2013 this equals an average annual royalty
of $2.17 per artist. It is crucial to note that this refers to the total royalty payment made to
rights holders and not to whatever amount is eventually shared with the creators themselves.
Also, there is of course no such thing as an average artist, and in practice a comparatively
small number of artists would earn much more than that while most would earn much less
– there are after all more than 20 million tracks' worth of artists so the tail is super long.

70 Source http://www.hypebot.com/hypebot/2012/07/spotify-releases-us-figures-sees-more-than-13-billion-streams-.html

For downloads, the average downloader buys 2 albums and 27 single tracks.[71] If we assume each of these is for a different artist then we end up with 26 artists per downloader and an average royalty of $1.22 per artist per downloader, using a 70% royalty assumption. This rate is not in fact that much higher than streaming, but things change considerably when it is applied to the total number of US download buyers – which at 63 million far outstrips paying subscribers – and results in an average royalty per artist of $76.34 – which is again total royalty before distribution to creators.

In Sweden though, where there are more subscribers than downloaders the picture is very different. Applying the same Spotify metrics to an assumed subscriber base of 2 million in Sweden we see an average royalty per artist of $1.44 compared to $1.22 for downloads. The average royalty per buyer is higher in Sweden because a smaller number of people are buying a smaller number of downloads resulting in the revenue being split fewer ways. So we learn that streaming can generate meaningful revenue at scale but will still be lower than downloads because revenue is split more ways across a wider selection of artists. Consequently artists are effectively paying the price for the democratization of music: more artists are getting listened to more regularly and as a consequence the pie gets cut into ever smaller slices. Which raises the interesting dilemma of whether artists speaking out against streaming are also indirectly speaking out against a more equitable distribution of income among artists.

Artists Versus the Labels

Data cleanliness and interpretation will fall into place over time, but there are additional factors that have complicated matters further, specifically with regard to the role of record labels. The record label considerations can be divided into two macro issues:

- The nature of the commercial relationship between the labels and the artists

- The nature of the commercial relationship between the labels and the streaming services

The fact that the larger record labels took equity stakes in streaming services as part of the licensing process gave rise to a concern that there was a conflict of interests. That labels' commercial interests were too closely aligned with those of the streaming services and not with their artists. Off the record conversations with well-placed individuals raised questions about whether all advance payments were technically classified as advances and therefore whether some portions of them were not subject to being redistributed as license revenue. Similarly some raised the issues of how advance payments for services that did not meet their revenue commitments would be distributed to artists, if at all. While others questioned, in a similar vein, how any income realized from equity holdings might be distributed to artists, if at all. Watertight confidentiality clauses ensure that such suppositions must remain informed conjecture and hypothesis, and highlight an overriding concern with transparency.

As Marillion's Mark Kelly puts it: "The problem with NDAs is they are just another way of separating [artists] from the proceeds of our music." Whether there is any basis in the speculation surrounding record label and streaming service commercial relationships is almost less important than the obfuscation of communication between labels, artists and the streaming services themselves. The lack of clarity unsurprisingly engenders suspicious speculation. It is not just the creators who glance nervously over their shoulders, unsure of who has what deal and with what priorities, streaming services themselves worry about

71 This data is extrapolated from Nielsen mid-year 2013 digital sales data for the US http://www.nielsen.com/content/ dam/corporate/us/en/reports-downloads/2013%20Reports/Nielsen-Music-2013-Mid-Year-US-Release.pdf

the balance of the market as Deezer's CEO Axel Dauchez explained: "The point that is not yet clarified is whether the labels are building a level playing field. They need to ensure the market remains competitive." Although commercial confidentiality is an inescapable component of doing business, there is clearly a case for lessening the grip on information control in order to seed a modicum of mutual trust into the streaming debate.

Meanwhile many artists and songwriters have concerns stemming from a paucity of direct reporting data from labels. A frequent complaint from the creators is that they are unable to identify exactly how many plays they have had per title from the reports provided to them by rights owners. Over the coming years it is to be expected that streaming services will provide artists with more and more self serve data. In December 2013 Spotify announced self-serve analytics for artists, a feature that will become standard within streaming services, enabling artists to identify any discrepancies between what is played and what they earn. This will enable artists to create an accurate understanding of just how many plays they have received and to then compare this with what is reported back to them by rights owners. This should result in a wave of artist requested audits of accounts and ultimately a sea change in reporting standards.[72] Spotify was getting tired of being painted as the bad guy in the transparency debate with its hands tied by confidentiality deals with the labels. The onus is now on the labels to use this as the catalyst for striking a new generation of improved, more transparent streaming deals for artists. Ultimately it is in the labels' interests to have artists on board with streaming. It is much easier to persuade artists to become part of the solution if their earnings are not hidden behind obscure accounting.

At the bottom of artist discontent is a belief that they are being short-changed by their label paymasters, a concern that is not only rooted in accounting practices but also the share of the money they earn from streaming. Currently a majority of artists are paid for streaming on a royalty basis, the method used for music sales, with rates often translating into being paid 10% to 25% – after recouping etc. – of what the label receives from the service. This sales royalty approach sits incongruously with streaming services that of course monetize consumption rather than sales. It is an approach that seems counterintuitive at best. The fact that a standard digital license royalty would typically pay 50% of revenue to an artist gives a good indication of the rationale for using the royalty method and also for why many artists feel aggrieved. With the predominance of the 10-25% rate it is far harder for artists to feel the benefit of streaming services than it is for record labels. Some independent labels though, such as the Beggars Group of labels, have recognized that giving artists a larger share of streaming has the potential benefit of making more artists more supportive of streaming, something that will be crucial if the model is to succeed in the long term. Beggars pays its artists for streaming on a 50/50 licensing model because, as its head of strategy Simon Wheeler commented, they could not "justify [treating] it as a sale". The ramifications of the royalty payment model for artists are huge, as explained by former Talking Heads frontman David Byrne: "Right now – and I hope I'm proved wrong –- I feel [streaming] is the last nail in the coffin. Labels are distributing this income mostly on a royalty basis – which amounts to a fraction of a pittance. No one can live on this income. The income from the streaming services isn't big to begin with, but the labels skim off so much of it –- or the majors do – that the artists are left with next to nothing. Unless artists band together to represent themselves – and that is beginning to happen –- they will have close to zero income from their recordings. So then why would they bother to make recordings in the future?" The

72 Artists will be able to use any marked discrepancies as a basis for requesting sales audits from their labels. Though the traditional outcome of artist audits is for artists to sign confidentiality clauses as part of the settlement if the label is found to be at fault, labels would most likely choose to change the systems rather than expend non-scalable audit effort if there was indeed a surge in streaming-driven audit activity.

decisions for labels to pay their artists 35% more of their streaming income may represent a near term revenue hit but it is the price that needs paying to get more artists behind streaming. Without their backing the streaming subscriber count may never get into the tens of millions. 35% will prove a small amount to pay today to help safeguard much more sizeable income tomorrow.

Mark Kelly, Marillion   Jonathan Grant, Above and Beyond   David Byrne, Talking Heads

Because many of the major record labels assumed advocacy positions for streaming subscriptions it become all too easy for the dominant narrative to become one of artists and songwriters on one side and big record labels and the streaming services on the other. However over time independent record labels have begun to put their weight behind streaming too. Beggars Martin Mills takes a measured and pragmatic approach that recognizes both the threat and opportunity streaming represents, but also the unproductiveness of resisting consumer demand: "It is clear streaming services both stimulate and replace purchasing. Generally as a label we do not believe you can stop the tide coming in and streaming is one of the tides that is coming in."

The Three Sides of the Scale Argument

'Scale' is the term most frequently used in support of streaming services but it is a complex, multi-faceted concept that is not without its problems. The scale arguments for streaming services have three key vectors:

- Increased Average Revenue Per User (ARPU)

- Increased number of users

- Increased amount of music titles listened to per user

The ARPU argument is one that resonates most strongly with labels, telcos and the streaming services themselves. It is at the core of Spotify's value proposition for the music industry, as Spotify's Will Page explained: "The key economic question is, for me, repairing and restoring ARPU. Put bluntly, the majority of the adult population in most western markets pays zero for music and the minority who do spend, don't actually spend that much. I just don't think that replicating old models can address that ARPU challenge, whereas the service model can." It is a theme picked up by Oleg Fomenko, former CEO of now defunct streaming service Bloom.FM: "The focus of debate needs to shift from pence per download or pence per stream income levels to how much fans are actually spending – ARPU. When telecoms companies were able to make this shift from pence per minute to pounds per user they have generated billions and trillions in returns. This simple shift can allow us to make the whole industry a lot richer – from artists and songwriters to digital services. We need to get to the stage of thinking about how to entice consumers to spend more, not just how to divide that money up. In a shrinking market it is a tough task."

FIGURE 40
Scale Drives Streaming in Three Key Ways, But
Stakeholder Impact is Not Uniform

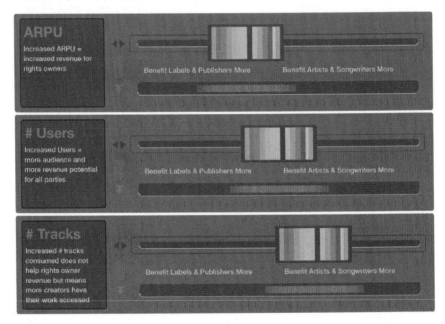

The arguments for growing the overall market are compelling, but scale does not impact creators in the same way that it does rights holders (see Figure 40). Each of these three factors drive benefits but have differing degrees of impact for each group of stakeholders. A label or a publisher will typically have thousands of works licensed to streaming services while an artist or a songwriter may only number his or her works in the tens. Thus labels and publishers will feel the benefit of streaming growth in much more substantive terms than singers or songwriters. Increased average spending and increased users will be immediately noticeable to the rights holders as the increase both across hundreds of thousands, even millions, of individual works will translate into sizeable macro revenue. Whereas the same scale of increase on a creator's catalogue of say 50 songs will be infinitesimally smaller. A publisher or a label will measure the incremental effect of a million new subscribers in terms of hundreds of thousands or millions of dollars while a songwriter or an artist or a will measure it in hundreds or thousands of dollars. Against this however, growth in total users – and even more meaningfully, total subscribers – presents creator specific opportunity too. The absence of a per-title price point encourages on-demand users to explore wider swathes of content than they ever would on a download store. So more people consuming more content represents the best opportunity for creators' smaller portfolios of content to benefit from scale.[73] The phenomenon also has a benefit for independent labels and for non-mainstream music that typically takes a little more discovering as Simon Wheeler explained: "We see streaming to be the continuing democratisation of music, it gives more people around the world more access to our music. In the downloaded era, even if someone had heard about our artists it was still an effort to go and buy it. On streaming services we're seeing approximately double the market share we're seeing on download services. A lot of the records our artists make have real longevity and thrive on streaming services."

The ability of streaming services to give exposure to non-mainstream artists is further supported by the listening metrics according to Pandora's Tim Westergren: "Of the top 10,000 artists on Pandora half didn't play on radio at all last year." Streaming services, both radio and on-demand, also have the ability to extend the half-life of a release, to ensure that a song or album retains popularity longer than the traditional life span of a chart or radio play. While album sales typically peak in the first week or two and fall off quickly thereafter, in on-demand streaming services they can retain popularity for much longer as Will Page explained: "When we talk about decay rates in product, we're assuming that what you sell in week two will be less than in week one, and so on. Broadly speaking, sales of product have been decaying steeper due to digital disruption over the past decade. In contrast, with streaming the focus is on lifetime value – either the decay rate is a lot softer or more often than not you see more streams over time as the viral coefficient kicks in. For artists, this means that if you're doing one million streams a week, you do not necessarily expect to do less the week after. That's quite a mindset change when we've been so used to discussing 'week one sales' over the years."

The overriding reason that the scale arguments carry so much importance is that they will be key to determining whether unlimited on-demand services grow the overall pie or shrink it. It is of course going to take years of data from streaming services to be able to draw definitive conclusions about just how streaming impacts sales. And in Catch 22 fashion, it is really going to require data of these services at a more significant scale than they currently are to have a clearer sense of just how the impact will be felt. There is in fact an argument to be made that we will have to wait another three to five years to truly understand the impact. This is because in the near term streaming subscription services will continue to harvest many of their customers from the existing base of digital music buyers. Which of course means that the near term effects will be biased towards transition[74] with early adopter music aficionados moving from download spending to music subscriptions. Incremental growth, if it comes, will be seen most clearly thereafter. At a macro level this will translate into higher average

73 There is however a small counter-trend, namely that streaming services typically pay rights holders by allocating a portion of their revenue for rights payments and then allocating the amount paid for each track based upon plays. This means that if one month has many more total plays per user than the previous month then the pay out per stream will be lower. The opposite is also of course true and is a reason why some labels prioritize being among the first to license to new bundled music services (where revenue is committed to the bundle partner) to increase their chances of getting a high per-stream play early on in the service's life span.
74 Transition is the more appropriate term here. This is a shift in behaviour that is going to happen regardless. Streaming services are not, in the longer-term view, competing with download services they are replacing them. Just as the horse drawn cart was not competing with motor car in a historical perspective, even if in the immediate sense it was.

spending, but in the near term it may translate into lower sales, a phenomenon identified by David Lowery: "One famous artist I know rotates his catalogue on Spotify, only leaving a small amount of it on there at any one time. Since he started doing that his album sales dramatically increased." Many artists have found that by sticking their heads above the parapet that they have found themselves subject to harsh criticism. Following Atoms for Peace's high profile Spotify withdrawal, frontman Thom Yorke tweeted that "Not enjoyed being target for facile mudslinging we've the right to discuss and opt out of #Spotify." Mark Kelly described the artist dilemma: "In complaining about how little they earn from digital services, artists run the risk of being called money grabbers. Many others don't dare stick their necks out for fear of a fan backlash."

If subscriptions are able to reach scale – i.e. tens of millions of users – then over a course of three to five years more people listening to more music should see more artists earning significantly more from streaming. Hopefully enough to make streaming income at least as meaningful an income stream as downloads, ideally more. Until then it will be important for labels and artists to understand each other's needs and priorities. Even giving the opportunity for artists to make their own informed choices does not necessarily mean that most will opt out as Simon Wheeler explained: "We've never dictated to artists; we are not going to start now. There is only one track that is not licensed to all digital services at this point in time."

The Pricing Conundrum

One factor more than any other limits the potential reach and scale of music subscription services: price. $/€/£9.99 for unlimited on-demand access to all the music in the world is undoubtedly fantastic value for money when measured against the analogue era standards of the same price or more for a single CD album. But we are no longer in the analogue era. We are in a period in which Torrents and YouTube provide all of the same unlimited on-demand access to all the music in the world for absolutely nothing. It is not however just the relative price compared to digital alternatives that encumbers subscription pricing, it is the simple fact that 9.99 is more than most music consumers spend on music. 9.99 subscriptions are stuck between a rock and a hard place, too expensive for the mainstream on the one hand and fending off the threat of free on the other. As Adam Kidron observed: "Subscriptions only work for the aficionados, ad supported doesn't work for fans and downloads are declining because they are competing with free." The very top 10% of music buyers, not consumers but music buyers, only spend that amount a month across all music products.[75] 9.99 is not a mass market price point, it is the average spend of the crème de la crème of music buyers. Consequently 9.99 music subscriptions are always going to have an inherently low ceiling of opportunity in the single digit per cent range of any country's total population. The leap from the free music of YouTube and ad-supported audio streaming to 9.99 is an exceptionally large one, which according to Jon Irwin makes it difficult for subscription services to bring new customers on board: "There is a gap right now between people wanting free and 9.99. That's a big leap. If you break it down logically 9.99 for unlimited access to 20m tracks is incredible value, why would I ever pay 1.99 for 1 track ever again? But it is an emotional disconnect, the leap from a small one-off payment to a substantial monthly fee."

The 9.99 price point, and some of the criticism of it, reflects a tendency for rights owners to overvalue music – in actual market value terms, not emotionally or culturally – and a tendency of consumers, and many technology partners, to undervalue it. Re-educating consumers of the long-term monetary value of music might be a worthy long term goal, but it is not going

75 MIDiA Research estimates based upon data from BPI / Kantar Wordpanel.

to solve today's problems. In addition, the ubiquitous availability of free music means that any 're-educated' perceived monetary value is going to be far lower than it was in the analogue era. There is a world of difference between taking away people's free alternatives and persuading them that the paid for alternative is valuable. So the near term challenge is how to establish a workable middle ground between 9.99 and zero. Some innovative subscription services have persuaded record labels to start experimenting with radically different price points.

One such service is UK based MusicQubed that powers telco music services such as Telefonica's O2 Tracks. Unlike a standard subscription service O2 Tracks allows consumers to pay just one week at a time for £1 ($1.60) or £5 ($8) a month, giving them in return a curated, programmed music experience. Unsurprisingly MusicQubed did not exactly find it easy securing the licenses for a £5 a month mobile subscription service but over time the labels have become more supportive of the concept of mass marketing subscriptions as MusciQubed's founder and CEO Chris Gorman explained: "The music industry is finally coming around to embracing new markets with a view to 'how can we invest, nurture and help them grow'. Instead of the historical 'we have the assets' mindset, they recognise the need to invest in digital as they did when music was a purely physical retail business." Gorman also argues that the business case for affordable, mass market subscriptions does not just lie in the restricted reach of premium subscriptions but also in the fact that digital as a whole still does not reach most consumers: "Apple famously are known for nailing the relationship between economy and creating a great user experience, but even Apple's impact on the majority of music fans is limited. We have not simply built a platform and an application. We have spent two years and over £20 million to get to a strong go to market position. The fact that over 60% of all subscribers are female proves that we attracting a very lucrative and previously unreached customer."

Jack Horner, founder Frukt   Benji Rodgers, founder and   Chris Gorman, founder & CEO
                              President Pledge Music   MusicQubed

Another low price point service was Russian TNT Media Investments backed Bloom.FM which allowed users to 'borrow' specific numbers of tracks by selecting from a range of cheaply priced subscription tiers, starting as low as £1 ($1.60). Bloom.FM was born out of the ashes of mFlow, a previous more traditional take on the subscription model, and according to CEO Oleg Bloom that experience effectively built Bloom.FM's pricing strategy: "Our experience with Mflow taught us that the £10 price point as an entry level for mobile would have to be broken down. £1 is the price point where you move the barriers to spending, where people are willing to take a punt. Some labels took months to get over the idea of the £1 price point." Unfortunately for Bloom.FM most of the labels never really bought into the £1 a month concept and Bloom. FM allegedly ended up having to pay more in license fees than they charged consumers. Bloom.FM eventually succumbed to the inevitable and went out of business in 2014.

Meanwhile UK supermarket chain Tesco bought ad supported streaming service We7 to create Blinkbox music which, in addition to a Pandora-like free tier, launched a £1 a week curated subscription. Spotify's Daniel Ek remains committed to a highly robust – perhaps too robust – free offering as the best way of bringing new consumers into the subscription marketplace: "I think we will watch closely how the mobile free product works before we consider any other changes to the pricing. We think the free product for mobile that we recently launched has the potential to be a complete game changer for Spotify and for the music industry. We know that more than half of our new users come to us through the mobile platform, and the new free product gives us a chance to engage those music fans and get them engaged where they are increasingly actually using the product – on the mobile. And we know that the more music people play, the more likely they are to pay." Unfortunately for subscription services the free tiers tend to be major cash drains on the business, paying out to rights holders at around $0.05 a play but most often not making enough ad revenue to cover costs.

In the cases of both Blinkbox music and MusicQubed there are encouraging signs of label willingness to experiment with pricing, but an even more adventurous approach is required from the record labels. Label conservatism is rooted in a fear that too much experimentation with low prices will cannibalize the core 9.99 business, and that many of those top tier customers will realise that they are paying for an all you can eat buffet when all they really want is a light lunch. It is a point made by Fomenko: "Regular subscription services are the equivalent of having an unlimited supply of Coke piped to your house when all you want is a single can." But if a portion of premium customers are indeed paying more than they need, they will eventually churn out of those services whether there are cheaper alternatives or not. In fact if there are no cheaper alternatives then the only place to go thereafter is free. What labels and services need to establish is a mix of clearly differentiated service propositions and price points that target diverse consumer segments, building on the overarching lesson of the music industry's first digital decade: one size does not fit all. Additionally this strategy will need to embed clear consumer transition paths to ensure that consumers migrate up or down to the right service and / or tier for them at the right time.

Though this may fill some label executives with dread, it is better for a subscriber who is beginning to lessen music interest to be migrated from 9.99 to 4.99 than it is for him to simply churn out to zero. Similarly any lower tier subscriber who starts to exhibit the characteristics of a higher tier subscriber needs to be exposed to the benefits of higher tiers and to be encouraged up the ladder. All of this will require a detailed mapping of subscribers against consumer life cycle models, which in turn will require a far greater degree of collaboration between music services themselves than currently exists. In effect subscription services will need to be able to do customer 'hand overs' to others, no small ask for competitors. For this to work labels need to exert persuasive pressure and incentives to make it worth the while of the services and to help them realize that the beneficial impact brought to the market will benefit all services. Of course direct competitors that operate at the same price tier will have little reason to encourage customers to jump ship to each other, as Jon Irwin argued: "If we are investing in sensibly building our business by giving people great music experiences and encouraging them to build some music collections, why should we want them to take that elsewhere?" A commercially incentivized migration path from a $3 tier service to a $9.99 tier service however has clear benefits for all parties.

A further missing part of the puzzle is top-up/Pay As You Go (PAYG) payment. The mobile phone industry learnt long ago the crucial value of enabling customers to choose between monthly recurring billing and individual one-off payments. If PAYG proved to be an invaluable pricing option for a need-to-have utility like a mobile phone, then its necessity for a nice-to-have service like music is beyond compare. The case is further supported by the challenge of getting consumers over the hump of the ownership to access to transition: a one off top-up payment that gives the user access to a full music subscription service, but for a limited period of time makes a subscription feel like an a la carte purchase. As such it is a hugely useful tool for getting consumers familiar with the access model by dressing it in the clothes of a download. The model is already well proven in the mobile app arena with more than three quarters of the revenue from the 250 top grossing iPhone apps coming from in-app purchases.[76]

Currently games account for the majority of these in-app purchases but music is a natural fit as long as the right game-like dynamics can be utilized, such as unlocking exclusive playlists and content. Although the 30% fee that Apple charges app companies within its App Store is a far from insignificant hurdle, the opportunity is just too big to ignore. It is likely that over the coming years Apple, rights holders and music services will collectively find some form of compromise that either reduces the 30% fee or spreads it across multiple parties. Also, though Apple's App Store remains by far the best monetization platform, Android in-app purchasing is accelerating strongly, growing by 200% quarter on quarter in the first half of 2013.[77] The business case is simple to the extent of being blunt: without in-app purchases money is being left on the table.

Telco Bundles: The Monetization Third Way

Another means of addressing the pricing strategy is the third way of bundling subscriptions within a telco subscription so that the service feels free or close to free to the end user. Whereas there had been plenty of telco own branded services in the 2000's few had been run away successes. An inability to break into the iTunes ecosystem was one key hurdle, another was the fact that telcos expended their marketing efforts educating consumers about what their services actually did. Meanwhile all Apple had to do was put up billboards of dancing silhouettes with white earphones. For as long as Apple was the only truly strong digital music brand in the game, the telcos' opportunities were heavily restricted. Two things changed everything:

- The rise of new, strong, pure play music service brands like Spotify, Deezer and Rdio

- The App Store opening up a chink in Apple's armour

New brands: Spotify and Deezer were both quick to understand the value of telco partnerships as a means of supercharging subscriber growth and, perhaps most importantly, sitting on the shoulders of vast telco advertising budgets. France Telecom with Deezer, and Telia with Spotify, provided mutually beneficial strategic marketing partnerships. The

76 Distimo
77 Google

telcos got clear association with cool new brands and the music services got otherwise unattainable marketing support. In both instances the music services were hard bundled into telco subscriptions, effectively giving the consumer unlimited, on demand, mobile streaming for free. Many other telcos were quick to follow suit and by mid 2013 there were nearly 50 telco music partnerships live across six different regions across the globe[78].

The App Store Opportunity: A key reason that streaming subscription services were suddenly so interesting to telcos was that Apple's App Store suddenly provided a direct route into the iTunes ecosystem. Now telcos could partner with leading music brands and be on iOS devices. The missing piece of the telco music equation was now filled and the floodgates opened with Apple's approval of Spotify's iPhone app in September 2009. At the time it looked like Apple was making a rash move, essentially inviting a direct competitor into its front room but it was in fact a calculated and well-reasoned decision. Streaming subscriptions were not ready for prime time, so Apple was happy for other companies to burn through their investors' cash while they established a market that, if it later looked inviting enough, Apple could jump into. Apple was also highly conscious of the need not to appear to behave in too closed a manner for fear of regulatory intervention. Besides, if or when Apple decides to launch a feature that competes with apps within its App Store it has the distinct advantage of being able to tightly integrate it within its devices at a native level. Such was the case with iTunes Radio which competes directly with the Pandora iOS app but sits as a native extension of the iTunes device experience and thus far deeper in the user experience than Pandora could ever be. Apple might have revealed a chink in its armour, but only large enough for the smallest of flesh wounds to be inflicted.

Hard bundled telco music services are a crucially important means of bringing subscriptions to consumers who would otherwise not pay. They are effectively a third way of monetizing music audiences, combining the best of reach and average spend. Currently too much of digital music strategy is polarized between the low scale / high average spend premium services at one end of the monetization pyramid and large scale / low average spend free services at the other. More needs to be done to reach the squeezed middle. Adam Kidron explained the strategic importance of the approach: "Labels have a romantic concept of what music's value is across the world. My bet is that the value of a year's worth of digital music is somewhere between $10 and $50 depending on where you are. The cost of subscriptions has to be almost invisible to consumers. The question is what is that cost and how can you persuade the labels to take the risk. Unless we solve that there will be no market." Building them directly into smartphones and tablets is an even more effective iteration of the strategy, so long as the right commercial model can be established and that there is enough cooperation between carrier and handset company to ensure Comes With Music mistakes are not repeated. Muve Music, the hard bundled music service of US carrier Cricket Wireless, used the approach to great effect reaching more than two million subscribers by October 2013 with a bundled smartphone music download offering, representing approximately a fifth of all Cricket's subscribers. No mean feat when it is considered that a) Cricket's subscribers tend towards lower income and b) the service is only available on mid-range smartphones. If there is any exemplar of the huge potential of bundled music services it is Muve Music.

Muve, however, was a success because Cricket desperately needed something to help turn around its fortunes and it bet its future on music. Few telcos though see music partnerships as anything other than strategic marketing investments, short term initiatives

---

78 Building the New Business Case for Bundled Music Services

aimed at driving sales and aiding market positioning. If telcos are going to be a long term, sustainable part of the digital music marketplace they need to learn how to transform their relationships with music services from one night flings into long term relationships.

The Tyranny of Choice

Alongside pricing the greatest issue that streaming services must successfully address if they are to ever reach meaningful scale is discovery. The problem with providing unlimited access to all the music in the world is knowing where to start looking. In 2008 the average digital music service catalogue size was 4.3 million, by 2013 that number had exceeded 18 million.[79] Many leading services boast in excess of 20 million tracks with some as high as 30 million and others adding 100,000 new tracks every month. But the catalogue boasts ring hollow unless users have meaningful ways of finding the music they want. There is so much choice that there is in effect no choice at all. This is the Tyranny of Choice. All of the streaming services talk a good fight around discovery and have gone some distance towards building richer discovery features, but most of the road is yet to be travelled. Until streaming services master how to surface the best content to the right people, the sheer enormity of their catalogues will make on-demand access an insurmountably daunting prospect for mainstream consumers.

Implementing discovery features that work for the early adopters who make up most of the current user base of subscription services is only half an achievement: these are engaged music aficionados who have an appetite and an aptitude for hunting out music. Mainstream consumers need leading with highly relevant programming and curation. It is this second term in particular that streaming services embraced with the zeal of the converted. To the average person in the street curation has the unfortunate effect of conjuring up images of fusty bespectacled librarians, but to streaming services curation has become the holy grail, the passport to success. Each streaming service has thus far taken a distinct approach to curation, relying upon both human and algorithmic approaches and Jon Irwin believes the variety of approach will come to define the competitive landscape: "The differentiation of streaming services will increasingly be in editorial and programming."

Curation though cannot simply be a series of blunt recommendation instruments like 'here are three songs you might like' but instead should be an integral and seamless part of the DNA of the service experience itself, bringing rich context to the music. Artist manager Keith Harris makes the case that this deeper approach to curation should help build a story around the music: "One of the things we need to get better at is helping people find music. We haven't been good at recommending through narrative. Narrative lines are what would bring people back into music." The difficulty most incumbent streaming services faced, Rhapsody notably excepted, is that they were not built from the ground up with discovery at their core and thus had to layer discovery features on top of their core music offering once they were in the market. By contrast new entrant Beats Music was designed from the outset with discovery at the centre of its proposition according to its CEO Ian Rogers: "The thinking with Beats Music was that the service has to be really good and it has to be cool, a product that is truly differentiated because it is curated,

---

79 Based on a random selection of 10 top tier artists on iTunes on average just 10% of the tracks listed for an artist is actually music by that artist, not even accounting for the large numbers of authentic duplicates from original albums, re-mastered albums, EPs, greatest hits, compilations etc. (Each track is listed as a separate song in the catalogue even if it is the exact same song. The vast majority of the remainder of tracks listed for each artist is filler drivel, endless cover versions, tribute acts and karaoke tracks. Many of these cover versions sound all but identical to the original, while others have full intent on being identikit copies but poor musicianship and production leaves them sounding pitifully poor. In among them are the occasional examples of leftfield creativity, such as 'Bass Parodies of Coldplay' by Joe Bob's Upright Bass Trio. But artistic expression is hardly being tested with the likes of 'Yoga to Coldplay', 'Led Zepellin Lullabys' or 'Dance Tribute to Lady Gaga vs Black Eyed Peas'.

personalized and close to the artist." The first generation of streaming services had focused on giving seamless access to all the music in the world and were thus centred around streaming technology capabilities. Beats Music had the benefit of being able to sit on the shoulders of giants, to simply co-opt this innovation and instead place their core focus on building a service that attempted to solve the problem of making sense of all that music. While Spotify et al spent their millions on designing new technology, Beats Music focused much of its on building out teams of human editors and music experts, while also touring the globe to establish a network of leading, trusted music brands to help programme music. People are accustomed to channels, whether that be on TV, radio or websites. This is how streaming services will evolve over the next few years. All of which is an unintentional nod back to how MySpace first approached music. The additional challenge for streaming services though is that because they are adding up to 100,000 new tracks to their catalogues every single month however good their curation tools are, they have to be 100,000 songs better at what they do each month just to be as good as they were last month.[80] It is a break neck pace arms race that bodes well for few other than the creators of the sound alikes and karaoke that fill music service catalogues with low quality dross.

Despite all the talk of the value of curation it is not clear that streaming services always place a monetary value on it as was highlighted by a spat between Ministry of Sound and Spotify in the second half of 2013. Ministry of Sound sued Spotify for breach of copyright of its compilations due to the presence of user generated playlists that replicated its own compilation track listings. The action was the culmination of frustrated licensing efforts as Ministry of Sound CEO Lohan Presencer explained: "Spotify say 'we only value content, we won't pay you for your curation' yet they allow people to upload MOS playlists even with the artwork images. This illustrates the importance of curation even in the age of the playlist." The case divided opinion and raised important questions about whether the copyright of a selection of songs holds legal water in the digital arena in the way that sound copyright does. Although that question was the pivotal one from a legal perspective, the far more important strategic one was whether curation is important enough to have a monetary value for streaming services.[81] Critics argued that this is simply the reaction of a traditional business model being disrupted by new technology. But the core question here is just how much do streaming services actually value curation? Do they value it in terms of 'yes it is a nice little extra to have' or do they view it as 'it is a crucial part of our users' experience and therefore of our future success and we thus value it at x'? If it is the latter it is time for them to put the money where their proverbial mouth is. If it is not then it is time for streaming services to stop talking about the value of curation. In the end Spotify and Ministry of Sound reached a behind-closed-doors settlement which effectively deferred industry level resolution of this crucial issue.

---

80 As stated by 7Digital CEO Ben Drury.
81 Kieron Donoghue, founder and CEO of UCG playlist site Playlists.net, blogged on the Ministry of Sound case to make the case for user curation, and cited a popular UCG playlist on his site as evidence. Intriguingly the creator of the playlist, in a comment on the blog post, explained that he was in fact "mimicking already established compilations."

Figure 41

The Post-Subscription Consumer: Distribution of the
Music Subscriber Audience The Churn Effect

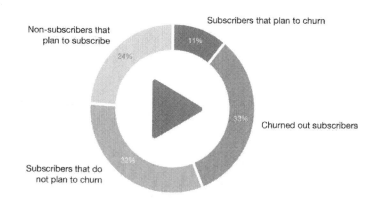

NOTE: Data shown as % of all four segments

A final, but crucially important element of the streaming story is the role of churn. Every subscription business is about managing churn and music subscriptions are no exception to the rule. In fact they face an even harder task of retaining their customers than many other subscription offerings because their core product is not a scarce commodity. If a consumer opts to stop paying for a TV subscription he will lose access to specific programming such as live sports; if a consumer cancels her mobile phone contract she will no longer be able to easily communicate with her friends on the go. But cancel a music subscription and all the music in the world is still immediately available – for free - on YouTube and on Torrents, as well as countless radio stations, TV channels, music TV shows, without even considering the ex-subscriber's own music collection. Cancelling a music subscription simply turns off the tap on convenience, not on the content itself, and the share of people who are willing to pay 9.99 a month for convenience is not exactly vast. Consequently churn is a major issue for subscription services: looking at the entire base of consumers who have either previously been subscribers, currently are, or plan to become subscribers, 44% have either already churned or plan to do so. Just 32% are current subscribers who intend to remain so (see Figure 41).

This base of churned music subscribers poses a key challenge for the digital marketplace: these consumers have tasted unlimited on-demand music without ads, on their phones, but are now going cold turkey. The question is where they will get their next fix? If it is not from subscribing to another service then the illegal sector beckons. This is the challenge that the music industry must meet over the next couple of years. It must ensure that these consumers either reengage with full fat music services or instead are nudged towards lower price point alternatives. On a positive note, the fact that 56% of the entire base are either current subscribers or plan to become so suggests modest growth. But even this 'glass half full' spin cannot distract from the fact that there is scant evidence of dynamic growth ahead. Subscriptions have reached an initial saturation point and require that something extra to kick them onto the next level.

The Cannibalization Effect

Another key challenge posed by subscriptions is the way in which they have eaten directly into download sales: during 2013 while subscriptions and ad supported grew by 32% download revenue actually shrank by 4% with much of that decline coming in the US, the home of the paid download. The net effect was a slow down in overall digital growth to just 2% globally in 2013. In 2014 across the UK, US and Germany download sales declined by an average of 10%. Ultimately as consumers move more and more towards on-demand based experiences all digital revenue will transition to access models. So revenue transition is a natural part of the process. The reason it is proving so painful is that because 9.99 subscriptions skew so strongly towards aficionado enthusiasts the customers who are adopting are the consumers who were the most engaged and highest spending download buyers. So what happens is that a consumer who once spent $20 to $30 a month downloading albums and singles goes to spending 9.99 a month on a subscription. Overall revenue takes a hit and downloads are left with a gaping revenue hole.

No one has felt the pain more than Apple who by opening up its ecosystem to third parties with its app store started losing its most valuable download buyers to streaming. As we have seen, this is part of why Apple bought Beats Music, recognizing it needs a quick answer to streaming services in order to start winning back its core digital music customers. In doing so, Spotify et al are put in a fragile position: until now they have won their customers directly from Apple's user base. If Apple tightly integrates, even bundles for free, a subscription offering in its devices, the streaming competitors will find it far harder to fish in Apple's waters. Apple has always loss led on music, it might just be ready to take that investment to a whole new level.

Through The Streaming Window

The concerns over streaming hurting sales have led to a host of reactions from artists and labels, some of them well thought out and others less so. One tactic some larger artists have used is windowing, the tactic of holding back their latest releases from streaming services. It is a strategy that works well for the movie and TV industry but is controversial in the music arena. Artists such as Coldplay and Adele have resisted allowing their latest albums onto Spotify et al until they have felt confident the albums have sold as well as they are likely to. The most high profile example was Taylor Swift who both held back her '1989' album from Spotify and pulled much of her back catalogue. The album went on to become the only million selling album in the US in 2014. While it is impossible to prove the exact degree of causality, it would be fatuous to claim that windowing had done anything less than not hurt those sales. Windowing is an issue that refuses to go away but is a natural effect of the transition the music industry finds itself in. Some artists and labels were just as fearful of iTunes in the 2000's as they are now of Spotify. It took the Beatles seven whole years to finally license their catalogue to iTunes. Right now there is still a very sizeable music sales marketplace. 79% of all recorded music revenue in 2013 came from sales. So it is understandable that some labels want to protect that Golden Goose as long as they can. And it is little compensation for labels that declining music sales are made up by increased live revenues.[82]

However the shift to consumption models is an inevitable process. The long view shows us that licensed streaming music will be ubiquitous five years from now, music sales will not. Even if Taylor Swift is still at the top of her game in 2019 she won't be selling any 1 million albums anymore. The pragmatic solution is to treat free and paid streaming tiers as

---

82 In even the most label friendly 360 deals music sales are still the core revenue stream.

different windows. Paid tiers are where the music industry's most valuable customers are and they should be treated as such, getting the best new music first, before anyone else. Spotify's position is that the free tier is so crucial to acquiring new subscribers that they do not want to mess with the model. But if tier based windowing is not introduced and enough high profile artists pull their latest releases then the model will have messed itself up.

The biggest irony in all this is that the free streaming services face no such blocks. All of Swift's videos were still on YouTube and her music was all over Soundcloud. Yet while Spotify was windowed YouTube remained because the music industry still views it as a marketing channel rather than a consumption channel and as such it is measured by different standards. Thus 10 million YouTube views is a promotional success, whereas 10 million Spotify streams is x thousand lost sales. This hypocritical inconsistency has to end. Spotify premium customers are some of the most valuable music fans there are, most YouTube users are not. In the streaming era, streaming to drive discovery is an oxymoron. In the streaming era consumption is the end point. There are no end sales. The advert has become the product.

CONCLUSION: The Future, Now

Streaming services have encapsulated so much of what is core to the music industry's digital experience in its second digital decade. They represent a completely different usage paradigm from downloads and will ultimately result in a dramatically different music consumption marketplace. But until we get there – and the transition will be truly measured in generational terms, not years – much of the brave new world will look daunting in the extreme. It is a cheap and lazy cliché to say that 'change is difficult' but it is, and often because people view the new world through the same eyes they viewed the old one. When the iTunes Music Store first launched many artists were sceptical. Established top tier artists including the Beatles, Led Zeppelin, AC/DC, Bob Segar, Kid Rock and even digital innovators Radiohead held back their catalogue for years – eight years in the case of the Beatles and 10 years for AC/DC.[83] These acts stayed off iTunes because they feared that it would result in lower sales and in albums being picked apart by fans in search of just the singles. The irony is that now that the debate has moved onto streaming services, artists hold up iTunes downloads as the gold standard for artist income against which all other income sources are benchmarked. The change that had felt scary at the outset has become the epitome of safety and security.

As of 2014 streaming music services are still in their relative infancy but the long term opportunity is clear for both interactive radio and on demand services. Pandora's Tim Westergren highlighted the scale of the transformative change that interactive radio could bring: "We are currently 7% of US radio listening. If we were 70% we would be literally talking about re-writing the entire radio economy." In a similar vein Omniphone's Phil Sant made the case that: "Subscriptions are only getting started: there are 7 billion people in the world. 7 billion minus 20 million is still 7 billion." Streaming subscriptions have the potential to have transformative impact but pricing, discovery and the product itself all require major innovation before the proposition is ready for primetime. And when it is do not count against Apple flicking the switch on a game changing offering, deeply integrated into its iOS ecosystem. In the more immediate term subscription services need to learn how to break out of the aficionado beachhead as Kidron argued: "Most music services today appeal to those who are already willing to pay. All these guys are fighting over the same customers and this is why the digital music market is $3.6 billion and has grown so slowly."

83 The Beatles were licensed to iTunes in 2010 while AC/DC arrived in 2012.

It will take time, years, for non-superstar artists to really feel the benefit of streaming as subscriptions hit scale. In the meantime the challenge all artists must rise to is understanding how to make it support the wider mix of artist revenue streams. Streaming, at least the subscription part of it, will become the major revenue generating platform, but for now it must also be viewed as a marketing channel. This is where artists can find some of their most engaged fans, many of whom will be core targets for all the other things that artists do, such as live, special editions and merchandise. If streaming is eating into sales then the obvious next step is to drive other spending from streaming music consumers. This is the time for artists and labels to find their popcorn. What do I mean by this? Well when the cinema industry started out it was a loss making business. To try to fix this cinemas started by experimenting with the product, putting on double bills but that wasn't enough. Then came innovation in the format by adding sound. Then the experience itself by co-opting the new technology of air conditioning from the meat packing industry. Still no profit. Finally cinemas found the solution: popcorn. With a 97% operating margin, popcorn along with soda and sweets quickly became how cinemas become profitable entities. Artists need to find their popcorn.[84]

Unfortunately it is not entirely straight forward: simply because some one is listening to a song does not mean they are necessarily going to want to buy anything from that artist. Instead streaming services, artists and labels need to think more subtly, looking at how to nurture an artist-fan relationship rather than simply trying to sell someone a t-shirt because they happen to be streaming a track. Artists and fans are closer than ever but this journey is only getting going. And now that artists are building deeper relationships with their fans while sales revenues decline, they need to get smarter about how to monetize them. The key question though is whether this can be enough to offset the impact of declining music sales revenue. Meanwhile non-performing songwriters (i.e. those who write for others) need to plan ahead and establish new commercial agreements that swap out some of their royalty shares for overall revenue shares so that they too can participate in this new music economy.

---

84 I am indebted to my former JupiterResearch colleague Nick Thomas who is the originator of this concept.

Chapter 10: The Artist's Story

To properly understand how digital impacted artists we need to take a brief look at what came before, long before. A well rehearsed argument from file sharing supporters is that the recorded music industry and its supporting copyright regimes are historical anomalies, that piracy is in fact heralding a return to how things used to be, to purer days for artists not contaminated by the blight of commercialization. Confusingly though these piracy advocates have conflicting opinions of how things have changed. The two premises are:

- Things are better now than they used to be: Copyright enabled artists and songwriters to earn unreasonably large amounts of money that were not tied to the true value of their creativity, or

- Things used to be better than they used to be: Artists and songwriters used to earn entirely comfortable livings before copyright and will do so again when it is gone.

There is some truth in the first argument, that there is a tier of artists who have never had it so good, but there is little basis in the second assertion.

Things are better now: Peter Jenner argued that it took until the 1970's, and the birth of the album, for artists and songwriters to really start making money as he explained: "Back in the days of the single very few artists got rich, but with album sales artists suddenly had the opportunity to earn much more." The album era also saw the rise of a small number of artists become fabulously rich superstars. This though is as much an effect of the age of mass media as it is a consequence of copyright, as we can see in other areas of entertainment where copyright either does not exist or plays a lesser role yet superstars still emerge. Examples are sports personalities, reality show stars, TV show presenters and celebrities whose celebrity is based purely on celebrity itself. The poverty/wealth divide in music is accentuated by the fact that more artists than ever are now trying to make a career out of music, just when fewer people are paying for it. Inevitably the majority of artists rather than enjoying commercial success instead struggle to make ends meet. Yet despite continually swimming against the tide most continue to hold true to the dream. Indeed the dream is the magic dust upon which the music industry is built as Paul Vidich explained: "The dream remains the most important currency for young artists and that is never going to change." It is a point also made by David Byrne: "The musicians I know make me optimistic. They are flexible, open and smart – as well as being innovative and creative. They want to be survivors. But look at those recent articles about the finances of Grizzly Bear and others – it's really tough out there – OK for an emerging band sometimes, but for keeping with it and keeping it vital for your whole life? That's tough! That said, it's one of the best "jobs" one could ever hope for, so one can't complain too much really."

Things were better then: What has most certainly changed is that copyright, rather than being some tool of moral extortion, has enabled creators to monetize music across the vast geographic distances mass media allows music to travel. Only a cursory glance back in history is required to reveal that copyright for the first time helped artists emerge as a professional workforce entity.

Many cite the middle ages as some sort of culturally pure heyday for musicians, but in truth there was more of a superstar economy than there is now, with musicians grouped into three sets:

- Troubadors: The elite of musicians, but also the elite of society, typically nobility and royalty, including King Richard Lionheart of England. They didn't make or even ask for money, it was an elitist pastime.

- Minstrels: Artisans who travelled around, relying on the patronage of the wealthy and aristocracy, such as the great patron of the arts Eleanor of Aquitaine. A small number become fixtures at a court, most were forced to travel around most of their lives in search of the next fee.

- Jongleurs: These were the majority of musicians. Typically itinerant, and paid infrequently and poorly. A poor existence that was only marginally more lucrative than being a field-tilling serf.

After the middle ages royal and noble courts developed the practice of supporting retained musicians who were commissioned to compose. These musicians were pitifully few in number and were vulnerable to the whims of their often volatile paymasters. Many musicians considered great now, struggled financially in their life times. Thus before effective monetization of copyright most musicians and composers struggled for money. The arrival of copyright and entities for monetizing and protecting it created the foundations of a professional musician and songwriter class. An historical incident that helped create the modern era of copyright illustrates the transformative impact it would soon have on artists and songwriters: In 1847 a then popular French composer by the name of Ernest Bourget was drinking sugared water – the chic drink of the moment – in a Parisian café and heard the house orchestra play some of his music. When the waiter arrived with the bill Bourget refused to pay, arguing that he had already paid by having his music played by the orchestra without their having paid him anything. The dispute led to a court case that found in favour of Bourget who went onto form the collective rights organization SACEM (Société des Auteurs, Compositeurs et éditeurs de Musique).[85]

This brief glance over our shoulders at the music industry's ghost of Christmas past serves to remind us that there is no historical safety net that artists can fall back on. So when some artists saw the arrival of the internet as an opportunity to do away with the music industry, they did not fully comprehend what had gone before, and just how difficult it would prove to be to try to go it alone.

In digital music's early days many artists viewed the internet as a paragon of opportunity. Artists, feeling constrained by their record label contracts and mistrustful of their business practices viewed the internet as a great leveller, heralding a new age of music distribution in which labels would not have a role. Large portions of the media also started falling under the sway of the seductive vision of a great democratization of music industry relationships and roles. After all, so the thinking went, who would need a record label anymore when the whole world was accessible to anyone who had a website? Build it and they would come. Prince, never one exactly known for his love of major labels, believed he was pioneering the post-label age when he launched an ahead-of-its-time artist subscription service in 2000.[86] NPGOnlineLtd.com gave Prince fans the choice of two monthly subscription fees in return for which they got exclusive music monthly and additional content including concert ticket offers, pre-concert sound checks,

85 Collective Management of Copyright and Related Rights. Daniel J. Gervais □Kluwer Law International□, 2010, Page 171 □□□□
86 Prince had famously written 'slave' on the side of his face during fractious negotiations with his record label Warner Music in 1993.

listening sessions, member only parties and interviews. Although NPGOnlineLtd.com enjoyed some early success the popularity of the site soon tailed off and by 2004 Prince had gone back to a major – Sony Music's Columbia Records. Prince had learned the hard way one of the core values a record label brings to an artist: marketing. When Prince went it alone he was a global brand, but what he had not realized was how much work his record label had been putting in to keep that brand alive and relevant. Once he had cut his ties with the label's marketing resources Prince watched his audience dwindle away steadily, month by month. The first great direct-to-fan experiment by a major label artist had, despite having a great product, illustrated not just that record labels still performed an important role but that the internet was a channel not a business model. The myth of the internet disintermediating the record labels might not have been entirely debunked but it had certainly had a major reality check. It was a lesson that David Lowery also learned: "My deal with Virgin was ending and I thought with my first solo album let's see if free actually works. I put the first three songs up as videos on YouTube and basically nothing happened. Without the label's resources (promotion, publicist, out and out bribery etc.) you are only selling music to your same core group of fans and you are probably only reaching 10% of them. My digital utopianism started to sour, my thoughts of disintermediation started to fail."

Coming to Terms With Piracy

Even before Prince had embarked on his post-label direct-to-fan adventure, the artist community was neck deep in a digital identity crisis. While the record labels were largely united in their view of file sharing as a disruptive threat – and those who were not, in the main changed their opinion during the 2000's – the artists were much more divided in their outlook. With his action against individual file sharers Metallica's Lars Ulrich had become the focus of anti-file sharing artist sentiment[87] and in 2000 argued that "if the record labels are not making the money, then the internet companies will be, and if they are not paying the artists, they are profiting illegally". Ulrich however found himself at the opposite side of the argument to other established artists such as Limp Bizkit and Public Enemy's Chuck D. Chuck D went as far as to say that he thought file sharing would help drive a period of unprecedented prosperity for the music industry and stated "I think there's going to be more music sold than ever." The artists who came out in favour of file sharing typically did so because they saw P2P networks as an opportunity to get their music in front of an even larger number of potential fans than selling albums could do, because there was no price tag attached. Travis's vocalist Fran Healy was quoted in 2003 as saying: "Kazaa and Napster and all that stuff is a brilliant way for kids to taste the album" while earlier the same year Robbie Williams, fresh from having signed a record breaking deal with EMI, called file sharing "great".[88] The then British Minister for Culture Kim Howells somewhat credulously responded by claiming that Williams was supporting "gangs and prostitution".[89] In 2005 Madonna, angered by leaks of her forthcoming 'American Life' album appearing on Kazaa took the unusual step of uploading repeated loops of the words "What the fuck do you think you're doing?" to Kazaa disguised to appear like MP3 files of her album. The tactic backfired

---

87 See chapter 1 for more detail.

88 The Guardian 30th September 2003.

89 Howells' comment toed the line being pushed by the music industry trade bodies at that time that online piracy was a front for organized crime. Though that argument held some water for industrial-scale physical piracy, most P2P networks were VC-backed, technologist driven companies and on the whole did not have explicit ties with organized crime. The attempt to associate online piracy with organized crime may have won some political support but it met with an often sceptical public response. The IFPI recognized the importance of the organized crime association in political lobbying efforts and were not averse to exaggeration to build their case. For example in 2007 the IFPI reported raids on a Sicilian 'illicit distribution network' resulting in the seizure of 2,000 CDs and DVDs and also a 'significant seizure of arms and bombs....as well as several stolen archaeological treasures, such as ancient Roman and Greek pottery" as well as suspected Mafia links. Guns and bombs were hardly necessary for selling a few dodgy CDs. The weaponry and items were the trappings of a criminal gang who happened to be dealing in some small scale CD and DVD piracy in addition to their core criminal activities. This sort of 'over egging the pudding' only served to weaken the credibility of the industry's position on piracy, making them appear to be lacking crucial perspective.

though when her site was hacked by disgruntled file sharers and free versions of tracks from the album were posted along with the words "This is what the fuck I think I'm doing."

Artist attitudes to file sharing continued to be strongly divided throughout the first half of the 2000's until 2007 Radiohead changed the dialogue entirely. Following their departure from EMI Radiohead decided to self-release their next album 'In Rainbows' on their own site as a download, with fans told to "pay what you want", as little as nothing if they so wished. The initiative was hugely innovative and broke important new ground for artists online, and indeed music product strategy more broadly, but playing online piracy at its own 'free' game was far from a definitive victory. Although the 'In Rainbows' project was very successful, with 1.2 million downloads on the first day alone, vast numbers of consumers still went to download 'In Rainbows' for free from file sharing networks, with BitTorrent downloads alone reaching 2.3 million in the four weeks after the album's release.[90] Artists could not even beat free with free. However 'In Rainbows' did have a long term legacy as the band's manager Brian Message explained: "With 'In Rainbows' Radiohead had the belief and the courage of their convictions to shape their business the way they wanted, in the process inspiring a whole generation of artists to take control themselves and paving the ways for companies like Kobalt to set up artist friendly label services models."

By the latter part of the 2000's many artists were waking up to the fact that online piracy had at least some form of causal relationship with the continuing annual decimation of sales of their music. But by this stage the debate among the artist community had become more nuanced, with the pro-file sharing artists focusing much of their comment on opposition to music industry enforcement strategy and supporting legislation, particularly the move towards three strikes policies. In 2008 U2's then manager Paul McGuiness started to lobby in favour of enforcement while the Featured Artists Coalition (FAC) – a British musicians' advocacy group set up in 2008 – argued against. Fresh from his success with 'In Rainbows' FAC Director and Radiohead guitarist Ed O'Brien wrote in September 2009 in the London Times that: "File sharing is like a sampler, like taping your mate's music." O'Brien's comments marked the start of a brief but intense British artist debate on piracy. Lily Allen felt compelled to respond with a blog post on her MySpace page, suggesting that the FAC had the luxury of being able to adopt their stance because they were already successful, established artists but that emerging artists were not in such a fortunate position. Allen described file sharing as a "disaster" for emerging artists because it was "making it harder and harder for new acts to emerge". She got significant artist support for her position, including backing from James Blunt, Take That's Gary Barlow, Spandau Ballet's Gary Kemp and Bat For Lashes' Natasha Khan. Muse's Matt Bellamy went a step further and in response to Allen's lament, proposed that a levy should be placed on ISPs to compensate content owners and creators for the illegal file sharing that occurs on their infrastructure. Bellamy argued for "a taxed, monitored ISP [model] based on usage which will ensure both the freedom of the consumer and the rights of the artists."[91] O'Brien maintained his position against punitive measures against file sharers but agreed on Allen's position on emerging artists, responding "I completely agree with Lily Allen. We're certainly not going to suffer. A lot of people have downloaded our music for free, but ultimately we don't suffer as much as a small band."[92]

The most significant legacy of Lily Allen's highly public stance against piracy though was the response from file sharers themselves, resulting in her quickly closing down an anti-piracy blog

90 'In Rainbows, On Torrents' Will Page and Eric Garland.
91 http://www.hypebot.com/hypebot/2009/09/lily-allen.html
92 http://pitchfork.com/news/36594-lily-allen-quits-piracy-debate-possibly-quits-music-business-as-well/

because "the abuse was getting too much." The file sharing community and its supporters did not take kindly to Allen's position and the internet swiftly filled with often vitriolic responses from tech journalists and bloggers. Their readers promptly picked up the baton, posting even more rancorous thoughts on message boards, comments fields and Twitter. Extra spice was added to the mix by the fact that many of Allen's detractors considered themselves to be fans because they had downloaded her music from file sharing networks but had not actually bought any of her music nor gone to any of her concerts. This could have been, and should have been the start of an important process of raising awareness about how file sharing impacts artist income, not just record label balance sheets. Instead Allen was, understandably, scared out of the debate by the bullyboy tactics of internet trolls and ideologically charged tirades from technology thought leaders. The free-economy bias of the web had won out again.

The FAC was sufficiently concerned by the strong divergence of opinion among their membership and the wider artist community to call a closed extraordinary session in September 2009 to hammer out its position, particularly with regards to proposed UK government legislation that would cut the broadband connections of file sharers. Jeremy Silver was acting CEO of the FAC and chaired the meeting: "I chaired the meeting of 80 artists in Air Studios to discuss the impending Digital Economy Act legislation. There were conflicting views on whether fans should be cut off from the internet. We had the likes of Nick Mason [Pink Floyd], Billy Bragg, Lily Allen, Dave Rowntree [Blur] and Ed O'Brien [Radiohead]. George Michael was upstairs in a mastering suite and had a runner popping in and out to keep him to date, Annie Lennox had a woman there on the phone. It was a very heated debate but we managed to arrive at consensus that file sharers should have their broadband speed squeezed rather than disconnected." The FAC meeting highlighted tensions between the artist community and the labels around attitudes to piracy and how to deal with it as Silver explained: "Artists were in a very squeezed position. They felt the label lobbying efforts didn't make sense when it came to their fans but a lot of artists soon began to back down. They began to feel that their careers might be at risk by taking such strong stances against the labels. They had to take a very clear look at which side their bread was buttered. Yet at the same time their recording income was declining and live was increasing so their fan relationships were becoming more important than ever. Ed O'Brien said to me 'it became increasingly difficult to sustain in your head both the creativity and the business thinking.'" With the FAC gaining mindshare, and most importantly getting in the way of the labels' carefully orchestrated lobbying efforts, it was inevitable that it would soon find itself in open conflict with the labels as Silver recalled: "When I was at the FAC Lucian Grainge [now Universal CEO and then Chairman of Universal Music International] called me the Taliban. There was a very clear, solid and robust music industry line on piracy and Lucian was at the heart of that. But artists were much more ambivalent about the issue. They were pissed off their music was being ripped off but they recognized the promotional value. They understood the value of the fan relationship in a way the labels did not.

The tide of opinion surrounding file sharing took a significant turn in 2012, thanks to a blog post by a young US National Public Radio (NPR) intern by the name of Emily White. White wrote an NPR blog post explaining that she had only ever bought 15 CDs yet had an iTunes library with more than 11,000 songs. White went onto explain that only a small portion of those tracks were from file sharing sites and that most were from swapping CDs and hard drives with friends and family and posited her utopian music service vision: "one massive Spotify-like catalog of music that will sync to my phone and various home entertainment devices."[93]

93 http://www.npr.org/blogs/allsongs/2012/06/16/154863819/i-never-owned-any-music-to-begin-with

Normally an NPR intern blog post would pass quietly under the radar, but this one became an instant ideological battleground for the piracy debate. David Lowery posted a lengthy 'Letter to Emily White' that set about explaining how artists are impacted by piracy and debunking a number of preconceptions he believed file sharers had. These included the beliefs that file sharing is ok because a) labels screw artists b) artists make money touring and selling t-shirts c) artists are rich. Lowery made an impassioned case for how piracy hurts artists the most, explaining how difficult it is for the average artist to make a living out of music in the piracy age.

Lowery's blog post became a lightning rod for debate and comment. His site – the Trichordist – received half million visits in two days and spawned a whole series of responses from all sides of the debate. The free-economy contingent still found its usual voice, but this time theirs was no longer the loudest. The artist community had finally found its voice and was beginning to hold its own in the piracy debate. The ripple effects of the argument were quickly felt, with comment and discussion arising among many young file sharers who began to confront the realization that their activity could be hurting their favourite artists. Of course the free-economy advocates still posted actively in comments fields and discussion boards but whereas in the past they had the assumed the role of representing the people and even the artists against the fat cat labels, now they appeared to be supporting no one other than file sharing advocates. Newly empowered artists and fans began to question "Who gives you the right to speak on my behalf?" Whatever evidence may be presented on either side of the piracy argument it was finally clear to fans and artists alike that artist income from music sales deteriorated at break neck pace at the exact same time that piracy had flourished.

Live: Picking Up the Album Slack

Piracy advocates argue that the decline in recorded music revenues is simply a transition of music industry revenues from recorded products to other incomes such as live and merchandise. While there has clearly been a marked revenue shift separate to piracy, the argument does not address the way in which piracy has also played a causal role, helping create the situation in which artists have to rely upon other incomes. Piracy's obliteration of content scarcity helped accentuate the value of live as an entirely scarce commodity and fans' music spending shifted accordingly. Because consumers no longer have to spend money on albums and singles they can spend their money elsewhere, including on live. More often than not though, consumers simply opt to spend their 'saved' money on something not related to music at all.

For those who do go to live events though, the experience is an inherently unique one. Even though it is possible to watch a concert live online or on TV, or watch a recorded version later, the experience of actually being there is unique and cannot be pirated. In just the same way that a cinema experience, with all of the associated social elements, big screens, soda, and popcorn cannot be replicated by watching a pirated movie downloaded from a Torrent. Fans inherently value this uniqueness of experience and are willing to pay handsomely for it. In fact music fans explicitly indicate that they value live performances of their favourite artists many times over the value of the recorded music from the same artists. For example the cost of a ticket to see Adele play at the Royal Albert Hall in 2011 cost between $100 and $455 a ticket for approximately 120 minutes worth of entertainment, representing between $0.83 and $3.75 a minute and an average of $2.29 (see Figure 42). To buy her back catalogue of albums would cost $21.88 for 91 minutes of music, representing $0.24 a minute. Thus the cost of a minute's worth of live Adele music is worth, monetarily, 9.6 times more than a minute's worth of recorded Adele music. The ratio is broadly similar for artists with extensive back catalogues too, with the ratio for the Killers at 8.8.

FIGURE 42

The Average Cost Per Minute of Live Music Far

Outstrips That of Recorded Music

Cost of entire back catalogue of selected artists compared to cost of selected concerts of the artists

	Cost	Time	Cost per minute
Adele			
	21	$11.88	$0.25
	19	$10.00	$0.23
Total Recorded		$21.88	$0.24
Live at the Royal Albert Hall 2011		$100.00	$0.53
		$450.00	$3.75
		$275.00	$2.29
Ratio of cost per minute live to cost per minute recorded			9.6
Killers			
Direct Hits	$15.32	75.31	$0.20
Battle Born	$9.15	51.16	$0.18
Day and Age	$10.25	40.49	$0.25
Sawdust	$10.00	70.12	$0.14
Sam's Town	$10.49	44.14	$0.24
Hot Fuss	$9.00	45.39	$0.20
Total Recorded	$64.15	326.63	$0.20
Live at Wembley 2013			
Maximum	$56.45	$120.00	$0.47
Minimum	$358.06	$120.00	$2.98
Average	$207.26	$120.00	$1.73
Ratio of cost per minute live to cost per minute recorded			8.8
One Direction			
Midnight Memories	$15.00	48.22	$0.31
Take Me Home	$10.00	42.16	$0.24
Up All Night	$10.00	45.12	$0.22
Total Recorded	$35.00	135.52	$0.26
Live at Manchester 2014			
Maximum	$385.16	120.00	$3.21
Minimum	$75.40	120.00	$0.63
Average	$230.28	120.00	$1.92
Ratio of cost per minute live to cost per minute recorded			7.4

For touring artists this changing role of live has been hugely important, but in a far from uniform way with some artists prospering and others struggling. While recorded music sales plummeted the global live music ticket and sponsorship music revenue tripled between 1990 and 2013 from $6.9 billion to $27.5 billion,[94] with growth driven both by increased demand and by steady

94 Sources: MIDiA Research, Informa Media and Telecoms, Pollstar, PRS, GfK/BDV and PRS

increases in ticket prices. In 2011 U2 set a live music industry record with their 360 Tour which sold in excess of seven million tickets over 100 shows, in turn becoming the highest-grossing tour in history at $750 million. The growth in live revenue was also spurred by a concerted change in live product strategy, shifting the focus from hard-core fans crowd surfing and jumping around in mosh pits to highly polished, theatre-like experiences for mainstream music fans of all ages.   It is a process that still has some distance to go though, according to Songkick's Ian Hogarth: "Live music wasn't designed as a product for a mass market demographic in the way that the CD was. Now though, live needs to change if the mainstream fan is going to go to more (than the current average) of one concert per year. The biggest problem is accessibility." Indeed live remains a significantly less mass market product than recorded music, with the percentage of consumers who regularly go to live concerts, gigs or to watch DJs play sitting at just 16%, compared to 36% for buying music and 38% watching music videos on YouTube. [95] Nonetheless its contribution to total music revenues is sizeable, growing from 45% in 2008 to 54% in 2013, gaining share in line with recorded music revenue falls (see Figure 43).

FIGURE 43

While Recorded Music Revenues Have Stumbled
Live Has Grown Both Share and Scale
Global Live Ticket and Sponsorship Revenues and Share of Total Music Revenues

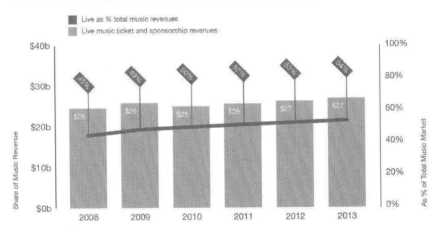

Source: Informa Media and Telecoms

The contribution of live, and associated sponsorship and merchandise revenues for artists has been crucial throughout the uncertain years of the digital era. Whereas music sales accounted for 31% of total artist income in 2000, by 2013 its contribution had fallen to 20%, while live grew from 39% to 45%, merchandise from 4% to 9% and publishing from 26% to 28% (see Figure 44). In fact all three of these additional artist revenue streams grew between 2000 and 2013 while music sales declined. To be clear that increase was not just in the total market value for each, but in terms of how much of that income made it back to artists.

95 MIDIA Research Consumer Survey 12/13 UK only

FIGURE 44

At A Macro Level Artist Income Experienced Steady
Growth Despite Declining Music Sales

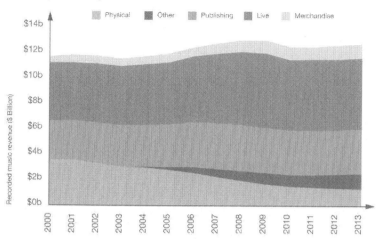

Source: MIDiA Research
Note: Revenue refers to share of revenue that is earned by the creator, not the total market value

As much as live music may have boomed at the expense of music sales it has not been entirely
plain sailing. The live sector keenly felt the impact of the global recession with rows of empty
seats in arena tours by frontline artists such as Spice Girls and the cancellation of many music
festivals. In 2010 global live ticket and sponsorship revenues declined by 3% and although
income started to recover again the following year it took until 2012 for revenues to recover
to the pre-drop high. Many concert promoters and ticket agencies began to realize that the
hikes in ticket prices left them exposed in times of weak consumer spending, particularly when
reseller mark-ups were factored in. StubHub, a ticket trading marketplace reported that ticket
prices dropped by nearly a fifth between 2008 and 2010.[96] Even without the consideration of
economic cycles, the revenue from live does not flow back to artists in an evenly distributed
way. The live ecosystem has become more crowded with a greater number of entities taking a
share of revenue, leaving less for the artists themselves even though fans were paying more than
ever. The price of a ticket covers the costs of multiple stakeholders including, but not limited to:

- The venue (typically an upfront fee charged to the promoter or the artist)

- The promoter

- Tour costs (lights, sound, roadies, hotels, travel etc.)

- Artist management

- Taxes

- Booking fees

- The artist

96 http://www.economist.com/node/17963345

On a ticket that sells for $60 (including taxes and booking fees) an artist can expect to get in the region of $30 to $35.[97] Depending on the profile of the artist and the costs of the tour this can be higher or lower. But the ratios go out of the window when ticket reselling comes into the equation. If a tout sells a $60 ticket for $100, $40 extra revenue has been created but $0.00 of that value has gone back into the live music industry or to the artist. Some estimations of the live industry actually count the $60 ticket sale and the $100 cumulatively as separate ticketing events, so that the total revenue is recorded as $160 even though the net spend was only $100 and the total live industry revenue was only $60. Ticket touts [scalpers] have always been a component of the live music business, but whereas in the analogue era their remit was largely restricted to standing outside concert venues with fists full of tickets, eCommerce fuelled a golden era for ticket reselling. eBay has become established as a key destination for resold tickets, but rather than just real fans getting rid of unwanted tickets, ticket touts buy up whole swathes of tickets in bulk and then sell them at inflated prices. Consequently smaller quantities of tickets are available for genuine fans thus creating extra demand for the resold tickets. Rather than let the thriving ticket reselling business remain the exclusive domains of scalpers the live industry decided to get in on the act, relabeling the practice with the more respectable term 'secondary ticketing'. A number of secondary ticket sites arose to capitalize on the opportunity, including Seatwave, Viagogo, Get Me IN! and Ticket Hub, the last of which is unsurprisingly owned by eBay. Matters are complicated further by the fact that ticket retailers often use dynamic pricing systems that result in prices rising as fewer tickets are left.

The price inflation double whammy may have helped ticket prices recover from their global recession-led lull period, but it hits fans hardest and often sees little or no extra money going to the artist. And to make things even worse, the traditional ticketing agencies decided to get into the secondary ticketing business too, using the cynically defeatist logic that 'if you can't beat them, join them'. This strategy manifests itself in a number of ways, ranging from pre-allocating portions of tickets for secondary platforms and sharing the additional revenue with exclusive partners, through to actually owning a secondary platform. Such is the case with Get Me IN! which is owned by primary ticketing company Ticketmaster, who in turn advertises Get Me IN! tickets on its own site when it has sold out, which happens more quickly than it used to do because it allocates blocks of tickets to, yes you guessed it, Get Me IN!. The conflict of interests is blatantly obvious: it is in Ticketmaster's commercial interests to have as large a share as possible of its customers buying higher priced tickets from Get Me IN! and therefore to ensure availability on Ticketmaster.com is limited. With all of these complex additional moving parts in the live business model, headline live revenue growth numbers are far from a clear indication of the vitality of the market from an artist's perspective.

Some artists do fantastically well out of live, others struggle to make a living, but the common denominator for all artists is that they never even get to glimpse vast chunks of the live revenue pie. In just the same way that many artists struggle to feel positive about rocketing streaming income because they are on 15% royalty deals, it is hard for many of them to feel good about growing live revenue when they see so little of the growth trickle down to them.

It is the growing seepage of live revenue to third parties that is most responsible for driving down the share of total music revenue that makes it back to artists. Indeed between 2000 and 2013 although total artist income grew from $11.6 billion to $12.6 billion, the share of the total that revenue represented declined from 23% to 20% (see Figure 45). In fact, on average only

---

97 Superstar artists often do direct deals with promoters, getting paid a flat fee for a set number of dates.

80% of the total $27.4 billion of global live revenues made it back to artists in 2013, compared to 39% for merchandise and 62% for publishing – for songwriters. Only recorded music revenue fared worse, with just 15% of income making it back to artists. Though while the artist's share of live revenue is declining, for recorded music it is growing thanks to factors such as many independent labels giving their artists 50/50 deals on streaming revenue. Consequently the artist's share of recorded music revenue grew two percentage points from 13% in 2000.

FIGURE 45

The Growing Influence Of The Secondary Ticket Sector
Helped Drive Down Music Creator Income Share

Evolution of Music Creators' Music Revenue and as Share of Total Revenue, 2000-2013

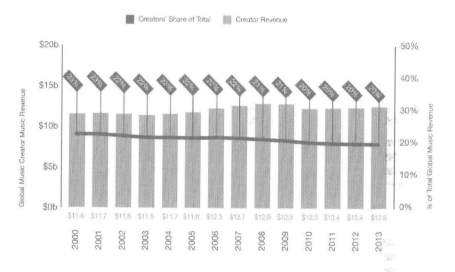

While the recorded music business has been turned upside down by new technology the live business is clearly one with great inefficiencies and inequalities and it is ripe for disruption. It is an opportunity that sites like Brazil's Queremos! and Songkick's Detour are trying to meet, by bringing crowd funding dynamics to live music, enabling artists to go straight to fans, cutting out all the middle men. Ian Hogarth explained the thinking behind Detour: "Many fans hate the secondary market, and lack of transparency around booking fees. With Songkick and Detour we are trying to make booking fees transparent and upfront. Detour is reimagining the entire system redefining what a ticket is in the digital realm. The system that enables bands to play live is the same as it was in the analogue era. We are trying to create a network era version of a ticket, centred around the connection between artists and fans."

Artists being left short changed in the live equation is however no new thing as Mark Kelly of Marillion recalled: "In the 1980s we'd be selling out arenas and at the end of a 12 month tour the manager would come to us and say 'here's your money lads' and I'd get £20,000. At the time it seemed like a fantastic amount of money, now I realize just how little of the money from the tour actually made it back to the band." Because of improvements in technology and because Marillion has taken direct control of their operations Kelly argues that: "Touring is more profitable for us now than it has ever been. You don't need a fleet of articulated lorries to tour anymore." The onus on making tours profitable income-generating ventures intensified as music sales fell. In the heyday of the CD touring was, along with promo videos, often seen as a vehicle for helping sell albums. In the digital era that relationship, if not quite reversed, has most certainly recalibrated according to Hogarth: "For many artists recorded music can be a loss leader for live." For established artists, live has become a much bigger part of their revenue mix, but the role of recorded music remains paramount as Cooking Vinyl's Martin Goldschmidt observed: "Music sales account for between 5% and 25% of total artist income for established artists. But there always comes a time when the tour agent says 'you need a new album if you want us to book that tour again next year'. Labels provide marketing and promotion and the trickle down effect of that drives all income streams."

David Byrne has watched music sales become a progressively smaller part of his revenue but also identified that he is still benefiting from the effect of historical music sales: "I probably make a little on record sales still, but I suspect most of my income is from live shows and licensing now. Some part of my connection with part of my audience was established before the record business convulsed and fell over. I had marketing money spent by Warners and others to help myself and Talking Heads get a leg up when things were different in the music business. I can't deny that I benefit now from having had some success in that long ago time. The knock on effect/benefit is considerable, I suspect some of the film licensing I get offered is due to that. Movie editors and directors know my work or grew up with it, so it comes to mind more often than not."

The shifting sands of the music consumption landscape have also created a new tier of artists who are big enough to sell out mid sized venues but are unlikely to have broken through into the mainstream consciousness. These are artists who have built strong online fan communities and dedicated, organic live followings, selling tens of thousands of albums but not gate crashing the charts. It is a trend that Brian Message highlighted: "It is becoming harder to book theatre-sized venue tours unless done so many months up front; there are a lot of bands capable of filling these mid-range sized venues." But for every success there are examples of artists who instead of seeing a net increase in income do not see live picking up the slack for declining music sales. Jesper Bay of the Danish Arts Board – an organization that is in the unique position of providing grants both to leading live venues and to artists – has seen a rise in artists failing to make ends meet: "Some of the more established bands that would not normally apply for grants have started to because they have started to find it too difficult to make money. The rich are getting richer and the poor are getting poorer, while the middle class is getting marginalized. Since the financial crisis venues have been cutting costs too, including cutting fees. The big stars still command the same fees though which means less left for the rest. Some of the fees paid out today are totally the same as I was paying out 30 years ago when I was running a venue. People talk about how revenues have moved into live but it is the big artists who are making most of the money while smaller and mid sized artists are struggling. It is a superstar economy."

With more people making more music than ever before and fewer people buying it more artists are chasing fewer dollars. This is what is at the heart of the apparent contradiction of there being a larger middle class of artists than before but at the same time more of them struggling. On the surface this can appear to be the death of the middle class of artists but in fact it is simply the effect of them being squeezed because there are so many of them. As Bay puts it: "There are many more bands coming up which is great culturally but it also means there is less money to go around. Lots more bands are competing for the same money and gigs." With such fierce competition the artists who sit between the superstars and those starting out become the squeezed middle, unlikely to suddenly have an upsurge in fortune but too committed to give it all up, however little they might be earning. With income from music sales down, live becomes inherently more important but the vagaries of unpredictable audience sizes and the sizeable costs of touring mean that for the squeezed middle, trying to eke out a living on the live circuit can be a futile effort as David Lowery observed: "The decline in royalties from recorded music has absolutely not been offset by touring and merchandize sales. We always toured to sell albums. With touring then and now you make all of your money at the weekend at the bigger shows and usually lose money during the week at smaller shows. If you're getting five to six hundred people every night then you can aspire to earning a living comparable to that of a high school teacher. Camper van Beethoven did a European tour in the summer of 2013, we did four shows in the UK and then two weeks in Germany, Austria and Switzerland. We came away from that tour with €200 profit each. It's a good job we all have other income sources."

The live venues sector has also not yet caught up with many of the implications of the digital era, particularly with regards to the multiple new tiers of artist success. In the analogue era an up and coming artist was defined by the size of venues they played, with the step up from bars and clubs to a few hundred capacity venues being the first major ascendency milestone. Typically at this stage a record label contract would see marketing support, and radio play that would, if successful, drive album sales and propel artists to venues of the 1,500 to 3,000 capacity range. But these neatly segmented career stages have become less meaningful in the digital era, with many artists establishing themselves at multiple intermediary levels of success that pose no difficulties in the entirely flexible environs of the web, but that simply do not translate into the live sector. It is a point made by Sumit Bothra, manager of acts such as the Boxer Rebellion and PJ Harvey: "There is a distinct lack of 500 to 1,000 capacity venues, there are many bands who simply aren't ready to jump from club venues to the 1,500 capacity stage but would be able to comfortably do a tour of 500 to 1,000 capacity venues. There are many more grades of success now, because of the volume of artists there is so much diversity and variety of career paths now."

Smaller artists who are at an earlier stage of their career usually have not built up enough of a following to generate a steady income from live and thus rely more heavily on music sales. But piracy and now the growing shift to streaming services has made it increasingly difficult for early stage artists to carve out a living. An observation from Barcelona based artist IreneB is typical: "Streaming revenue for artists is very small compared to sales and these services are lowering the sales of music." Lowery has also felt the effect of streaming and piracy first hand: "We don't sell anywhere near as many albums off touring as we used to, even though the gigs are of a similar size. When younger kids get turned onto us they either consume via YouTube – where we get paid a pittance, or via Spotify – where we get paid a pittance, or they download it for free from file sharing networks."[98] Also the increased ease with which artists can release music online has the potential to create a skills gap on the live side of the equation as David Byrne observed: "Luckily, I began my life in music as a live act, so that isn't an area I have to figure out as do a lot of acts now. I sense that I know how to perform, make a show and budget a tour (with help). A lot of emerging acts find it (relatively) easy to write and record a record but then supporting a band, and rehearsing, and what does one

---

98 Though Lowery's experience is impacted by the fact that his career is at a later stage than younger artists the shift of consumption from paid to streaming and to piracy plays a key role.

do on stage? That doesn't always come naturally to a songwriter. And it's time consuming and expensive – I don't envy acts trying to figure that out having just made a great record."

A divide is emerging between the big success stories of live and an increasingly populous but struggling lower tier of artists. For many successful artists live revenue can be as much as ten times greater than income from recorded music while others can easily find that mounting costs and poorly attended gigs can leave them losing money from playing live. Jonathan Grant of dance act Above and Beyond highlighted the situation: "There is a bigger gap than ever between the rich guys and the poor guys. Live is hugely lucrative if you are the top of your game but very different if you are not established. It only really works if you have a big profile and there is also a much longer gestation period now before acts start to cut through." Erik Nielsen, who has worked with more than two dozen artists including managing Marillion, concurs: "The rich-poor divide is getting bigger and it is getting harder for new artists to break through. Live is where you make your money if you are an established artist. As a new artist you need to have publicity and profile, you can't just book a tour. Live revenue is also hugely predictable for smaller artists: if you are playing arenas then you sell out in advance and revenue is predictable. But if you are doing clubs you still rely on a significant share of sales from walk ups. On a recent tour of one of the acts I work with – the Hoosiers – the city that all the data suggested would be the best selling gig – Glasgow – was in fact the worst selling because it happened to be on the day of a particularly bad storm. This is the sort of unpredictability small artists have to deal with in live."

Superstar Artists

At the other end of the spectrum top tier artists have been able to make live an incredibly lucrative revenue stream, and in some instances inflate ticket prices so high that after all other costs have been deducted they can still take home between 70% and 90% or so of the ticket's face value. The Rolling Stones are a stand out example, charging up to $650 per ticket in 2013 while tickets for Justin Timberlake and Jay-Z's 2013 "Legends of Summer" tour were priced at more than $200. By contrast some big name artists have put their fans ahead of their fans' wallets and insisted on low ticket prices. Examples include Kid Rock who fixed the maximum price of tickets for his 2013 joint headline tour with ZZ Top at $20, and Garth Brooks who regularly sets a $25 cap on tickets to his concerts. But these are the exceptions not the norm. Instead, while middle class gigging artists often struggle to make live pay, superstar artists rake in millions by charging fans exorbitant prices. It is an imbalanced bubble market that risks implosion.

Also, the superstar live acts are getting older, with so called heritage acts such as the Rolling Stones, Bon Jovi, Bruce Springsteen and Madonna dominating. Global accountancy firm Deloitte estimated that 60% of the 20 top-grossing US live acts were aged 60 or older.[99] Meanwhile Madonna was the top grossing music artist in 2013, with the revenue from the tail end of her MDNA tour being a key contributory factor.[100] The big question is whether the same trend will play out for digital era artists. The heritage acts that sell out stadium tours now built their fan bases with multi million selling CD albums. With album sales plummeting and streaming services encouraging music fans to listen to a wider selection of music – and therefore inherently spend less time concentrated in a smaller number of artists – it may be that this current phenomenon of superstar granddads – and grandmas – may never be repeated. This concentration of revenue around yesteryear's stars creates a top-heavy age pyramid that will soon topple under its own weight. The question the live

99 http://www.deloitte.com/view/en_GX/global/industries/technology-media-telecommunications/tmt-predictions-2011/media-2011/d97f8f036907d210VgnVCM200000 1b56f00aRCRD.htm#.Uj2KQWRAQZi
100 Forbes.

industry should be asking itself is if the recorded music industry continues to struggle, who will be selling out stadiums in 15 or 20 years from now? The live industry could quite easily follow the same trajectory as the recorded business, simply with a 15 or 20 year delay.

Beggars' Martin Mills argued that the older artist bias in the higher echelons of live acts reflects an underlying change in the music business: "There has been a fundamental change in the relationship between live and the recording career. They used to go hand in hand but that has changed. The really big bands can make records that not many people are interested in but people still buy the tickets to see them play live. I first started seeing this in the 1980's. Acts like Gene Loves Jezebel were outselling Queen but Queen were still filling stadiums. Artists can go beyond the peak of their recording career but not peak in live until much later. There is a point when an artist reaches their breaking point, they have reached the point where they have sold more than they ever will again. Yet live can continue to flourish." The Rolling Stones is a stand out example of this phenomenon: a band that peaked creatively in the 1970's, saw their music sales peak in the 1980's and have a live career that continues to find new peaks even in the 2010's.

This creates a conundrum for labels: they help build the careers of artists who will prosper across different income streams long after label returns dwindle. Little wonder that many labels, independents and majors alike, simply choose to cut artists loose at this stage of their career by opting not to renew contracts. Or if they do renew they increasingly ensure artists sign 360 contracts that give labels the ability to benefit from those other income streams. The stand out precedent for this approach was Robbie Williams and EMI in 2002. Tony Wadsworth, now Chairman of the BPI, was Chairman and CEO EMI Music UK & Ireland at that time: "When a successful artist is up for renewal it is highly competitive. You might end up paying for your own success and sometimes it might even be better to walk away. We ended up in this situation with Robbie Williams in 2002 and at that time it proved to be the right thing to do a mega deal. He was coming to the end of a four album deal and he was one of the biggest artists in the world. We knew all the other labels would pay whatever it took to sign him but if we lost him it would look bad. The solution we hit upon was the right one, to move goal posts and sign a 360 deal, to move the relationship further on." EMI signed a record breaking £80 million ($130 million) deal with Williams and in doing so set some of the benchmarks for future deals with superstar artists that enable labels to ensure they participate in strong revenue even if an artist's recording career has peaked.

The Superstar Artist Economy

The older artist bias of live is also part of a broader trend, namely the concentration of music revenue around a very small number of artists. The music industry is a superstar economy, that is to say a very small share of the total artists and works account for a disproportionately large share of all revenues. This is not a Pareto's Law type 80/20 distribution but something much more dramatic. In 2013 the top 1% of repertoire accounted for 72% of all artist music income (see Figure 46). The concept of superstar economies has been around for some years and was also recently developed further in Alan Krueger's paper 'Rockonomics: The Economics of Popular Music'. Intuitively the democratization of access to music – both on the supply and demand sides – coupled with vastness of digital music catalogues should translate into a dilution of the superstar economy effect. Indeed the long tail theory posits that consumers will increasingly engage with the niche content across digital services because of ease of access and discovery tools. However the opposite has proven to be true, across all of artists' revenue streams.

FIGURE 46

The Music Economy Has Become Progressively
More Concentrated Around the Superstars
Evolution of Music Income by Category of Artist

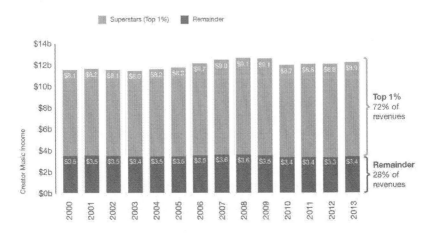

Definitions: Revenue refers to digital and physical music sales
All revenues refer only to artist's share of revenue.
'Superstar Artist' refers to the Top 1% of artists per revenue category
Source: MIDiA Research

The concentration of revenues among the Top 1% Superstar artists is more pronounced in some income streams than others. For publishing it is 77% because of factors such as the bias of synchronisation revenues to superstars – big brands and big TV shows tend to like big artists too. The mechanical royalty element of publishing generated from radio also skews towards the top of the pile: a typical radio station will play just 0.05% of the catalogue of a streaming service in any given year.[101] The Top 1% revenue concentration for live is 68%. Although live industry tracker Pollstar reports that the top 1% of live acts accounted for 56% of all live revenue in 2012, up from 26% in 1982, big acts typically make far greater profits than smaller acts. Thus the share of artist income from live accounted for by the Superstars is markedly higher. The Top 1% only account for 56% of merchandise revenue however, due to the fact that mid size artists tend to have a higher per capita merchandise spend among their fan bases and also tend to sell more of their product directly to fans at shows while big acts tend to rely on more costly retail channels.

The division between the Superstar artists and the rest is crucial in understanding the impact of the digital era on artist income. It is truly a tale of two cities. While Superstar artist income grew by 10% between 2000 and 2013, revenue for the remainder of artists fell by 2% over the same period. It is undoubtedly true that the internet has opened up countless new opportunities for artists connecting directly with fans, but it has also brought more artists into the market, competing with a smaller amount of revenue for the bulk of artists. This is why the marketplace

101 Calculation assumes that a radio station will play approximately 1,250 unique tracks per month,
or 15,000 per year, which translates into 0.05% of a 30 million song catalogue.

is full of apparent contradictions, of artists extolling the freedoms of the digital age, of prospering on the road while others struggle to make ends meet. It is because both are true. Many artists are doing better than they have ever done before, but most are faring worse. The paradox of the democratization of the music industry is that it has consolidated the power of the elite.

FIGURE 47

Artist Metrics for Success Are Transformed in the Digital Era

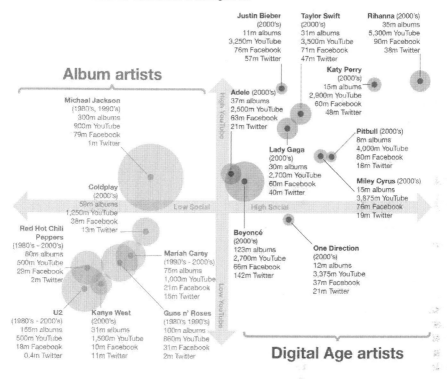

Measuring Success

The growing importance of multiple revenue streams for artists also means that what constitutes success for an artist is changing. In the analogue era success was easily measured in terms of units sold and chart positions, even though both could be easily gamed: for example labels would often pay retailers to over stock on albums which would be tracked as sales for the charts, and once the albums hit the charts more people would buy them. In the digital era though there are many artists who, when measured in terms of album sales look underwhelming at best, but when they are measured against social metrics transform into hyper-successes (see Figure 47). Success stories of the 1980's and 1990's, and not just the stand out ones, would sell north of 50 million albums during their peak years. Contemporary top tier frontline artists though cannot rely upon anything like as strong sales. Kanye West for example has sold 30 million albums and is considered a global success with a robust back catalogue spanning a decade. Compare that to big acts of the 1980's and 1990's such as Guns n' Roses, Michael Jackson and U2, all of whom sold north of 100 million albums each. Jackson sold a staggering 300 million albums though his career stretches over a much longer period, both when he was alive and posthumously. The biggest pop stars of the 2010's will never get anywhere close to selling 300 million albums in their entire life time nor after, despite arguably having even more pervasive media reach and profile than Jackson did at his peak. This additional reach exists because social platforms and digital media connect audiences with more content, more often than was true in the analogue era. The contrast between the opposite ends of the spectrum is clear: at the top right Rihanna is peerless in terms of YouTube views – 3.7 billion – and social reach with 35 million albums sold: scant return for such dramatic social metrics. At the opposite end sits 1980's alternative rock titans U2 with 150 million albums sold but just 400 million YouTube views, again a scant return for a band with such an important back catalogue. The contrast is partly explained by the relative stages of the artists' respective careers, but largely due to the fact that YouTube's music audience is relatively young and is much more focused on consuming contemporary releases than it is diving into the history of music. Adele sits stranded between the camps of album artists and digital era artists. The core demographic of Adele's audience is older and more likely to buy albums, especially CDs, and in many respects Adele is a 1990's artist stuck in the 2010's. But the sheer strength of the quality of the album '21' transcended boundaries and borders, meaning that as a contemporary frontline artist she has also racked up impressive social metrics. Adele is in fact the artist with the best balanced sales and social numbers, but she is the stand out exception not the norm.

Acts like Taylor Swift, Miley Cyrus and Justin Bieber are poster children of the YouTube era and collectively account for more than 6 billion YouTube views. They similarly each have many tens of millions of Facebook users and Twitter followers. These are measures of success in the digital age, and just as with the analogue era success metrics these too can be easily gamed with tactics such as auto generated YouTube plays, and fake Facebook likes. Nonetheless they remain crucially important currency for artists: as part of the mix they are validation of an act's worth. Some labels will not even start attempting to plug their acts to radio until they have reached certain thresholds of Facebook likes and YouTube views. Neither metric is a guarantee of success nor of quality, but an act that performs weakly on either will certainly give label A&R execs and radio DJs pause for thought. Strong social metrics are quite simply most often necessary for an artist to become part of the conversation. Artist manager Bothra described the situation: "In this day and age it is how many YouTube views and Facebook likes you've got that are the measures of success of a band. Now when pluggers go into radio and TV to pitch for broadcast media opportunities for bands, which are getting fewer and fewer, they absolutely have to use those metrics. If we're starting a conversation with a label or a brand they want to know what the social reach is."

Thus for all digital era artists, though especially so for the frontline pop acts, social metrics are much more than just performance measures, they are the tools with which other revenue opportunities can be had. With recorded music income often less than a third of total income for artists, the extent to which a few hundred million YouTube views will directly cannibalize sales of the single is a measured cost with much greater potential benefit to other revenue streams the artist has more direct control over and does not have to share with the label. For some artists the disconnect between album sales and social metrics is particularly pronounced. As a global superstar, in terms of album sales Pitbull is a relative nobody with just 9 million to his name, but with 2.7 billion YouTube views he is on a par with Lady Gaga and Justin Bieber. In part this is because Pitbull is much more of a singles artist than he is an album artist, but he also benefits from the self fulfilling prophecy of momentum: he is successful on YouTube so he becomes more successful on YouTube. Top tier artists ranging from Jenifer Lopez, through Shakira to Marc Anthony fall over themselves to record collaborations with Pitbull because he is seen as a guaranteed way of driving YouTube views which in turn ensure radio, TV and retail pick up a release. And by collaborating with such prominent artists Pitbull's fame grows further and on and on.

The pendulum has swung too far though, with many label marketing executives and other support staff who are part of an artist's team often having social metrics as measures of success in themselves, in effect making the case that a successful marketing campaign is a successful release. In truth one does not inherently lead to another. Just as an analogue-era label would not have congratulated itself for having paid Tower Records to overstock on an album until, or if, it drove a greater amount of organic sales, the same caution should be applied to social numbers. They are a strategy, not the outcome.

The importance of social metrics also varies markedly depending upon the size of the artist. For superstar artists, adding up the social millions is a core part of the equation because it is the platform from which they can launch their other revenue streams as Jack Horner, co-founder of music focussed marketing agency FRUKT argued: "As investment in artist development decreases, and the 'risk' profile labels look at for new signings becomes ever more conservative alternative revenue streams become even more of an integral part of an artist's commercial world. In fact, none of this is new. Commercially-focused artists, that is those who put fame, celebrity status and wealth over artistic intentions, have always taken money from whoever will pay their premium rate. Pop stars playing at wealthy oil magnates' kids birthday parties, syncing their tracks to completely mainstream TV ads, opening shopping centres, featuring in fashion ads and attending product launches... and more. Much more." But for smaller artists who are more squarely focused on eking out sustainable careers the adage that 'you can't buy a beer with a Facebook Like rings true'. Artist manager Nielsen believes that the meaningful success metrics for artists further down the food chain are far more tangible: "If you want a measure of how successful an artist is you need to look at their bottom line. Can they pay the mortgage? It is not as sexy but it is what counts."

Making Your Way as An Artist

Seeing the shift of artist revenue away from music sales, labels attempted to capitalize with the introduction of so call 360 Degree Deals that required artists to sign over percentages of their additional income to the labels. To artists these deals often appeared to be the acts of overreaching greed, particularly as for many artists these are the exact revenue streams they now depend upon to make ends meet. The labels' view however was that it was the albums, singles and associated marketing campaigns that created the audiences for these artists to perform to so they should also benefit from the income streams that effort helps drive. In doing so labels have had to be wary of giving the impression of being desperate, something they have not always done successfully. If labels can convince artists that with a 360 degree deal that they are bringing more to the table, that they will help the artist get more out of live and branding, then the pitch is more compelling. But if they give the impression of 360 terms effectively being a tax on extra income streams then artists rightly feel aggrieved. In a sample of emerging artists interviewed as background for this book, live and merchandize accounted for between 35% and 90% of their revenue. Signing away a share of this revenue to a record label is going to impact any artist and the pain of doing so is usually only softened by an advance from the label. With plummeting music sales it is no easy task getting to the stage where an artist has earned enough money to pay off the advance and to start earning royalty payments from the label as Lewis Silkin's Cliff Fluet argued: "Before 2001 it was simply a matter of time of getting signed if you were good enough. Now, not getting signed to a major label has nothing to do with artistic quality and/or talent. I think that most artists now recognise that the first label cheque they get might be the last."

Mark Kelly argued that this has contributed to imbalanced interactions between artists and labels: "Artists have reconciled themselves to an uneven relationship with the labels. Artists expect to get screwed in the beginning with the hope that they can renegotiate at the 2nd contract. What has changed is that you can be a YouTube sensation and not be able to earn anything." In the analogue era bands started off hyper local but progressed more quickly to label deals and then onto national scale and beyond. Now artists often establish themselves with international footprints through social tools and other online platforms before they get to the point of signing a record deal. Labels now have to be more cautious about how they invest their money and want to see that artists are able to build their own fan bases and, to some degree, for that to be demonstrated through highly measurable metrics such as YouTube Views, Facebook Likes and Twitter followers. Although no sensible label would sign an artist on social metrics alone – in no small part due to the fact that all of those metrics can be gamed – they nonetheless provide strong supporting evidence to validate a band with good music, image and presence. Labels have thus progressed to signing artists later in their careers but often working with them from an earlier stage as Martin Mills explained: "An artist has to do a lot more to build their own profile nowadays and we are signing artists later on in their career. However from an early stage we will give them tools to get started and help them build relationships." AIM's Wenham agreed that "We find a lot of labels working with artists before being signed" but Kelly believes that the approach can have a detrimental impact on artists: "The only musicians who have a chance of making it these days are those who can afford to work for nothing for years before being discovered. The live scene whilst bigger in overall size is actually supporting a smaller number of artists." All of these factors combine to make it much harder for artists to be able to make a living out of music before they break through to commercial success, which in turn runs the risk of skewing the artist landscape towards middle class kids whose parents can afford to support them. Keith Harris, former GM of Motown and manager of artists such as Stevie Wonder observed: "It is much harder for people who do not have financial means to forge a career in music, due in large part to there being so much background noise. So the opposite of what everyone thought was going to happen has taken place."

With so much extra career responsibility on the shoulders of artists in their earlier years Harris believes that "most young artists are bewildered about what they should be doing." Analogue era artists were able to focus most of their efforts on writing, practicing and performing, with putting together an occasional photocopied newsletter representing the extent of most bands' foray into 'engagement'. Now though emerging artists must develop a sophisticated range of social media, marketing and business skills to ensure they are able to both survive financially and to build a demonstrably solid following, all the while improving as an artist. On the one hand this multidisciplinary approach helps ensure artists are much more business savvy by the time they come to signing a deal, but on the other it takes time away from the music. The importance of business savvy should not be underestimated though, and as Peter Jenner explained, artists used to learn these lessons the hard way after having signed a deal with a label: "Those early records are crucial for an artist, they will give you the hits and the opportunity to learn the game. Before you have hits you don't know the game, you make mistakes, you have too many roadies, pay people too much etc. There are so many initiation costs but such a big delay in receiving revenue. You're not given money to invest, you're allowed to spend." Though it might on the surface appear much preferable to making the mistakes on someone else's tab, labels of course recoup all of the costs, so it is the artist who pays in the end. One artist recounted living the high life with a steady stream of drugs and prostitutes when he was at the top of the US charts only to find out that these items were deducted from his final royalties. When he complained that they had been provided without his request the reply from the label was 'yes, but you didn't refuse them did you?'

Some artists learn their lessons early though, including David Byrne who pursued a sensible approach that paid dividends throughout his career: "I've always been fairly hands on – and been careful about not living beyond my means. I sense that a lot of the younger artists I come in contact with are like that too now. This wasn't always the case – irresponsible and reckless behaviour was considered a career prerogative back in the day – to often deadly effect. Most musicians now know better, not all, but most. It's refreshing."

Surviving longer before getting signed by a label is not the only new challenge that artists face: more artists are getting dropped by labels earlier than in previous decades. Labels have less financial ability to be as patient with struggling artists as they once did as Peter Jenner argued: "When I started you never dropped artists until after their third album, unless they went completely off the rails. Now you can be dropped if your first single isn't picked up by radio." Getting dropped early not only has near term consequences, according to Jenner it also curtails an artist's ability to establish a long term income from royalties: "The bands that collapse before the fourth album never have the opportunity to make real money. By the time of the fourth album every time a band releases a new album they sell more back catalogue. But the moment you don't do anything you become a pure catalogue artist and at that stage no one has any incentive to repackage and sell your music unless you are huge."

The Burgeoning Importance of Managers

The growth of non-sales revenue in artist income and the trend of labels getting involved with artists later in their careers have both contributed to managers playing more important roles. Managers have always been important in securing record deals and in other commercial arrangements, but more recently they have additionally become the difference between an artist making it through the pre-label years and falling by the wayside. Managers have had to acquire as equally diverse a set of additional skills as the artists they represent and one of the most important of these, according to Beats Music's Ian Rogers is understanding their target audience: "The notion of fan segmentation has become a serious part of a manager's arsenal." Keith Harris believes the artist manager is a more crucial role than ever but it is an insecure one: "Managers always used to be on top of everything but now they are also central to everything happening. They are responsible for creating the assets for the artists, for partnerships, engaging the fan base. But their position is as precarious as it has ever been. It is increasingly difficult for any artist to cut through the background noise so it is increasingly difficult for artist managers to sustain themselves through the development stage of an artist's career."

According to Brian Message the manager's remit once an artist is signed to a label has also transformed: "In the late 1990's and early 2000's I was very much the representative of the artist at the record label table. It is a very different world now. That function still exists of course on certain occasions but the role has expanded dramatically, often incorporating record label services. I have never looked at recorded music in isolation, it is part of a bigger mix of income streams for all the artists we work with." Erik Nielsen summarised his perspective on how the artist manager works: "I think of the fans in the front row as the ones we can rely on to buy everything, those in the rows behind as ones we can help increase their attention and engagement while those at the back who leave early are probably the ones who stream the band for free and will not buy much. My role as a manager is to identify what to target each of those groups with and how." However, according to Jeremy Silver, the combination of the pivotal role of managers securing label deals and the reduced likelihood of royalty income can create a conflict of interests: "9 out of 10 bands fail, and if as a manager you can get £25,000 as your cut of the advance then that might be all the money you ever see from that deal. Which could make you motivated to start managing an additional artist to get them signed for another advance, and so on. At this point the label effectively becomes the client rather than the artist. This creates real tension and conflicts of interest."

Although there is a growing professional class of managers, and a number of positive efforts to formally improve their capabilities, many managers in their early days are just as bewildered as the artists themselves by the complex range of choices and possibilities. It is a situation highlighted by Silver: "We're seeing a gradual improvement in the quality of the manager community. It is still less well trained and still suffers from the fifth member of the band / the drummer's brother syndrome. Yet managers need business skills more than anyone else in the value chain." Harris countered that any lack of formal skills are compensated by the dedication of a manager: "Most managers start out as the key fan of something they have discovered and they do everything they can to make them heard. If you take that cog out of the wheel you have a lot of undiscovered talent."

Direct-to-Fan Beginnings

Though Prince discovered to his cost that record labels still play a crucial role even in the digital age, a growing number of artists have since found ways to go it alone and be successful. Sites and services such as PledgeMusic, Topspin, Bandpage, Mobile Roadie and Kickstarter have given artists the tools to go directly to their fans without the support of a record label. They have enabled a tier of artists to either change the way they work with labels or to go it alone entirely. Erik Nielsen argued that the turning point was the very first online platforms that enabled artists to start interacting directly with their fans: "The balance of power began to shift when bands realised that they had fans outside of the concert halls by talking with them online. It used to be that you would spend thousands on direct marketing, mailing catalogues to people in your fan base list. But those tactics only do a good job of reaching your existing fans not finding you new ones. The rise of online changed all of that." Though a majority of the artists who have gone it alone are either up-and-coming or post-record label established artists, this artist trend – usually referred to as this direct-to-fan (D2F), or do-it-yourself (DIY) – is the single most disruptive change to have ever occurred to the artist-label-fan relationship. For emerging artists en-route to a label deal, D2F tools enable them to build strongly engaged fan bases and to generate crucial income from these fans. For artists who have come to the end of their label deal and want to do something different these tools enable them to sell directly to the core of their already established fan bases. Erik Nielsen argues that one of the reasons alternatives to traditional relationships have evolved is because as music sales have declined, the priorities of labels and artists have become increasingly misaligned: "Labels are focused on selling units, whether that be physical units or streams, not on selling t-shirts or concert tickets which is where artists make their money. They have a narrow remit which is of course why they started acquiring merchandize companies and doing 360 deals. Yet underneath it all their core commercial priorities are very different from those of artists."

The rulebook for the D2F revolution was not however written by a digital success story, but instead has its origins in the analogue era, right at the start of the emergence of the internet as a music platform. The original D2F success story was that of a once chart topping global rock band stuffing envelopes in the back of their studio. British progressive rockers Marillion enjoyed a highly successful career in the 1980's but were dropped by their major record label in 1995. Though they found another label, by 2000 Marillion decided to leave the traditional label route and went directly to their fans to fund the next album 'Anoraknophobia'. As big a gamble as it was, it was not entirely a jump into the unknown as they had already turned to their fans once before and to great effect as keyboardist Mark Kelly recounted: "In 1997 our US label went bust so I told our fans through our mailing list that we wouldn't be able to do a US tour. When asked, I explained that we would need $60,000 to cover our touring shortfall. In response, a bunch of fans clubbed together and raised the money themselves. One guy from the UK donated £800." The experience left a lasting impression on the band and came to the fore of Marillion's thinking in 2000 when they came to the end of a three album deal with Castle Communications that they did not want to re-sign. Kelly picks up the story: "Inspired by the '97 tour fund I suggested we ask the fans to pay for the album in advance. This would give us the money we needed to survive whilst writing and recording the album without having to sign another recording contract. We emailed our database of 6,000 fans and asked if they would consider paying for the album in advance if we sent it to them when it was ready. In return for their trust and loyalty we would reward them with a special version of the album 'Anoraknophobia'. Eventually we took over 12,000 orders which added up to more than a typical label advance." The scale of the success was unprecedented and got the keen attention of music industry executives and journalists alike. 'Anoraknophobia' was a DIY project in the truest sense of the term with every member of the band pitching in on far from glamorous tasks: "We all had laptops and did data entry from hand written mail-back cards sent to us by fans in exchange for a free CD. We used to do two hours of data entry followed by five hours of music each day." Buoyed by the success of 'Anoraknophobia' Marillion took the same approach in 2004 for their next album 'Marbles', this time reinvesting the more than £300,000 of the profit from the pre-order into marketing the album and in turn securing the band's first UK top 10 single since 1987 with 'You're Gone'.

Marillion's experience straddled the music industry's early transition from the analogue era into the digital age. It tested the boundaries of fan relationships, showed what could be achieved without a record label and demonstrated the early capabilities of the internet as a marketing and distribution platform. It also happened as dwindling music sales were transforming what constituted success with artists and labels alike learning that more could be achieved with less as Kelly explained: "Everything we have done has been out of necessity. The internet came just at the right time for us. When we were dropped by

EMI in 1995 we were selling over 250,000 copies per album which nowadays is a healthy enough return for a major label artist." Marillion set a crucial precedent that established the business case for many of the digital D2F services that we have today. It also revealed that artists could extend their recording careers, that getting dropped by a record label no longer needed to mean the end of the road. Artists who had loyal fan bases could now continue to forge careers for themselves, even if record labels were no longer interested in them.

Reinventing the Artist-Fan Relationship

It took another half decade for the first wave of digital crowd funding platforms like Sellaband to emerge, and a decade before the likes of Kickstarter and PledgeMusic managed to make the model truly work for artists. Before that though a number of sites picked up the artist-fan baton and ran with it, most notably MySpace. Founded in 2003 by Chris DeWolfe and Tom Anderson, MySpace became the first global social networking success story, creating the blueprint that Facebook would build its runaway success upon. Although Facebook went onto establish itself as crucial platform for artists, music was a far more central component of MySpace, so much so that in its peak years in the mid-2000's MySpace was the crucible of artist-fan relationships online. On MySpace artists and fans could communicate in real-time, at scale, for the first time. In the analogue era the closest most fans got to their favourite artists outside of gigs was an occasional photocopied newsletter. MySpace transformed the artist-fan relationship forever. Artists were able to develop much more intimate connections with their fans and as a direct result create more engaged and loyal fan bases. Engaged MySpace communities helped acts like the Arctic Monkeys and Lily Allen find early chart success, with the former shooting from near-obscurity to number one in the UK singles charts with their debut release. Neither the Arctic Monkeys nor Lily Allen however, were DIY successes. Lily Allen's MySpace strategy was orchestrated by her record label Regal, an imprint of major label EMI. The Arctic Monkeys distanced themselves from their MySpace page, explaining that their fans had created the page not them[102] but they still owed their success as much to the stellar marketing efforts of their record label Domino as to their fan base.

MySpace created a new type of bond between artists and fans, one that persists at the core of D2F services today. The launch of digital distributor TuneCore in 2005 transformed that potential into hard cash by allowing artists to get their music directly onto key digital stores like iTunes without a record label. In 2006 Sellaband became the first big consumer facing D2F service, enabling artists to run fundraising campaigns, normally with a view to releasing an album. However the service came undone due to a combination of overly ambitious funding targets – sometimes in the tens of thousands of dollars – and the fact that a project could not commence until 100% of the funds had been invested by fans. Thus many projects were unsuccessful, leaving artists and fans out of pocket. Artists did not always take their responsibilities seriously either, including Public Enemy, whose fans went more than a year without any communication from the band despite the fact that some of them had each invested over $1,000. Sellaband eventually went bankrupt in 2010 but it had already primed the market for a new wave of D2F services including the French MyMajorCompany in 2007, and more significantly the launches of ReverbNation (2006) and TopSpin.

TopSpin and ReverbNation took the artist-fan engagement dynamic in a very different direction. Instead of forcing artists and fans into the often undignified 'church roof fund' fundraising

---

102 Arctic Monkey's interview with Prefix Magazine. http://www.prefixmag.com/
features/arctic-monkeys/arent-fooling-around-part-1-of-2/12565/

dynamic, they used the relationship as the basis of a more practical commerce and marketing platform. By allowing artists to quickly build their own digital destinations and market and sell directly to their fans online, TopSpin put artists in the driving seat, letting them go direct to their fans without the need of a record label. Artists could be their own independent, self-sufficient business. This was DIY. DIY was not the death of the record labels, but was instead allowing smaller scale artists to forge viable careers as cottage industries, and to sometimes move onto bigger things. It also allowed artists to apply their creativity to the broader tapestry of their career as former TopSpin CEO Ian Rogers identified: "I saw that at the artist end of the spectrum there was always appetite for experimentation." D2F was an alternative avenue for smaller artists who were either on the way up, down or who had simply found their level and were not quite ready for record labels at that stage in their career. They also gave a new option to artists who simply did not want to be signed to a record label. A new strata of semi-pro artists had been established, resulting in more people creating more music for more people to listen to, with obvious positive and negative connotations. Paul Vidich, now a ReverbNation board member, believes this artist groundswell has profound implications across the industry: "The gap between celebrity and obscurity is changing. The majors will move downwards and the likes of ReverbNation will move upwards. ReverbNation has three million bands and 20 million visitors."

The debt of gratitude owed by TopSpin and ReverbNation to MySpace for the emergence of the semi-pro artist market is clear. MySpace was the first service with true scale to allow artists to build global niches, to add zeros onto their fan base numbers. MySpace enabled the global niche to become a very real and attainable concept and tried to monetize this opportunity by partnering with Napster founder Shawn Fanning's SNOCAP service to enable unsigned artists to sell their music direct on MySpace. Unfortunately for Fanning lightning did not strike twice for him and although 100,000 artists signed up to SNOCAP it was far from a Napster-like success. After a disappointing performance Fanning was compelled to lay off 60% of SNOCAP's staff and sell the outfit to streaming music service imeem, which in an ironic twist of fate was later sold to MySpace.[103]

By the end of the 2000's the D2F movement was gaining pace. Artist eCommerce and marketing platform Bandcamp launched in 2008, giving artists the ability to sell and promote their music on Bandcamp microsites. The following year saw the launch of two key services: Mobile Roadie and PledgeMusic. Mobile Roadie – a creator of mobile apps for artists, and others – gave artists the power to embrace the potential of the smartphone boom. PledgeMusic meanwhile picked up the Sellaband baton but executed the concept in a far more authentic manner, utilizing a set of features that made it stand apart from the pack. PledgeMusic not only understood that scarcity had been ransacked, but has built a business upon reinventing it. Instead of asking fans to pour money into a fundraising target – artists are in fact prohibited from publishing targets – PledgeMusic artists raise their funds by getting their fans to pre-order music products and experiences. Products range from limited-run albums through to highly personalized items, such as signed handwritten lyric sheets and personal gigs in a fan's living room. It is a recipe that has bred success with fans spending an average of $55 and 85% of artist campaigns proving successful. Founder and CEO Benji Rogers expounded the founding principles: "For the idea to work everyone had to win: fans, artists, everyone across the value chain. Removing financial targets from campaigns and distancing ourselves from the term 'crowd funding' were both really important, they changed the dynamics of the relationship between the artist and the pledgers." Not all artists were initially comfortable though with the increased level of intimacy with their fans

103 http://news.cnet.com/8301-10784_3-9796327-7.html

that PledgeMusic campaigns required: "A lot of artists were very uncomfortable about opening up the process. One artist said 'I don't talk to my fans', but when she ran the campaign and realized that it was a private dialogue she said 'wow, I have found the way I want to communicate with my fans'. A lot of artists are [also] surprised by how real time feedback actually works and how exciting it can be. With a traditional release you never saw results immediately. Many are also surprised that it does take work to build a genuine conversation with your fans." Intriguingly 82% of Pledgers buy a physical product. It is a statistic that has far greater significance than at first might appear: Pledgers opt to buy tangible demonstrations of their support for their artists. For them it is about much more than just buying music, it is about getting close to their favourite artists, engaging with them, supporting them and having a unique badge of honour for having done so. The music file itself is not scarce and that is not where the value sits, but instead it lies in the unique link between the fan and the band. Rogers' vision is that "every album can be released in this way. There is no downside with giving consumers what they want. People have been given very many ways to buy music but very few reasons." The D2F approach does not work well for all artists however and has inherent limits on how far it scales while being done authentically as Mark Kelly argued: "Allowing fans personal access probably isn't scalable for super big artists, they simply have too many fans to do it. For mid-sized bands like Marillion it works well, plus it's quite rewarding for us and fans get to see we're real people."

D2F has become one of the more pervasive digital trends with, somewhat paradoxically, record labels getting into the act too, launching and acquiring their own D2F platforms – such as EMI's acquisition of Recordstore. Selling directly to fans has quickly become part of the fabric of the online music landscape, particularly for more unique product experiences and higher end products such as deluxe vinyl boxsets. Although the labels had been burned by their forays into direct to consumer distribution with MusicNet and Pressplay, building artist sites with robust eCommerce and social functionality has enabled them to get more out of the fan end of the artist equation. Which of course infers that money is being taken out of the value chain before it gets to the stage of the main online stores and services. At present the scale of this disruptive threat is small but it will get bigger. The decisive question is whether the diverted income from the relatively small number of high spending core fans will significantly dent spending with stores and services. It is most likely to hit download sales far harder than subscriptions.

One of the highest profile successes of the DIY movement was former Dresden Dolls member Amanda Palmer. In 2012 having left her major label deal a few years before, Palmer turned to Kickstarter to raise money to record and promote her 'Theatre is Evil' album. The fundraising was a runaway success with nearly 25,000 people backing the project to the grand total of $1.2 million, in turn making the project a Kickstarter record for a musical project and translating into an average pledge of $47.94. Palmer started the campaign with the bold statement that it was 'the future of music' and had set out for the more modest fund raising target of $100,000. With such dramatic success it was inevitable that Palmer would soon find herself the subject of a backlash. The turning point was when she advertised for fans to play at her shows across different US cities, but instead of offering a fee she offered to "feed you beer, hug/high-five you up and down (pick your poison), give you merch, and thank you mightily."[104] Before the Kickstarter campaign the move would probably have passed unnoticed and without criticism, but now Palmer was not just a millionaire, she was a millionaire funded by the same fans she now wanted to play at her gigs, for free. The move caused an online furore and Palmer eventually backtracked and agreed to pay participants a performance fee.

104 http://www.amandapalmer.net/blog/20120821/

independent label arena. Amanda Palmer recognized the crucial role that distribution would play in making her crowd funded 'Theatre is Evil' a success beyond the echo chamber of the original Kickstarter pledgers and so hired Cooking Vinyl to provide distribution in Europe. It was not D2F instead of a label, but in addition to, on terms that suited the artist and, crucially, it involved the artist retaining the copyright. Thus the most commercially successful D2F campaign to date still fell back upon record label infrastructure to take the release to the next level of distribution.

Cooking Vinyl has a long history of label services, having agreed the first ever label services deal, for UK protest folk singer-songwriter Billy Bragg in 1993. The deal was the brainchild of Bragg's manager Peter Jenner: "I became convinced that an artist should never sign a deal with a label that involved assigning copyright, that there is no money in that for the artist. So I helped devise a label services contract for Billy Bragg with Cooking Vinyl." According to Martin Goldschmidt the deal has been renewed six times "virtually unchanged because both parties are very happy 20 years later." In recent years the label services sector has turned into a growth industry with advent of companies like Kobalt's AWAL and even the major labels doubling down on their label services efforts and poaching staff from the specialists.

All of this has happened because artists have more choice and more autonomy than ever before. The labels may have retained their near monopoly over the demand side of their business – i.e. licensing – but they now face fierce competition on the supply side i.e. artists. Though the role of the label remains pivotal for all the reasons previously discussed artists have much more choice about who they want to perform that role and how they work with that partner. Traditional labels, big and small, have had to start being more flexible in order to win and retain the business of the artists they want to work with. The balance of power is shifting and a new artist career path is emerging whereby an artist starts off DIY until they have proven their worth to a label (see Figure 48). Once they have established themselves as a successful unsigned act in the Pre-Label Phase a band will then work with a label for a number of years, establishing a fan base and enjoying some or all of their peak years in the Label Phase of their career. It is at this stage that in the old model an artist would either sign a new deal with a record label or disappear into obscurity with no label being willing to offer them a new contract. Now though artists have the power of choice and many are opting at the Post-Label juncture in their career to either go DIY or D2F with a label services arrangement. We are currently in at the beginning of the first large scale phase of artists going this route, but it is probable that it will lead to another, third phase, of an artist's career whereby an artist either fades away or returns to a more traditional label relationship in order to rebuild their fan base.

FIGURE 48

Labels Must Offer the Right Services at the Right
Stages of the Digital-Era Artist Career Path

Typical Career Cycle of an Artist

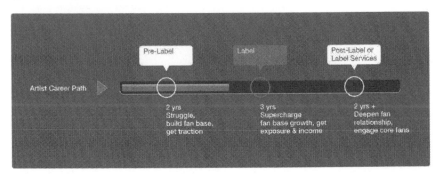

Other artists though, once they have tasted the freedom of DIY simply cannot countenance signing with a record label, and some of these have started to think more deeply about what else the new model might offer. One such example is avant-garde cellist Zoë Keating, another DIY success story, who addressed the concern of low royalty payments from streaming services by suggesting that if royalty payments could not be higher then she would be happy to be paid in user data also: "The law only demands I be paid in money, which at this point in my career is not as valuable as information. I'd rather be paid in data".[108] Keating, the exemplar of DIY artists, is beginning to realize that DIY is not just about getting by without a record label, it is an entirely different way of pursuing a career in music that will increasingly present unique business opportunities not always open to artists signed on record labels. As such DIY as a sector will place ever growing pressure on labels to innovate but will also remain essentially a record label counter culture. An ideological alternative for artists who want to do things differently but still want to make money from recorded music.

The record label role that the D2F sector has yet to seriously threaten is risk taking. Record labels, particularly bigger ones, are structured around taking risk, on investing money and resources into artists who are as yet unproven quantities. A label's appetite for risk will often manifest itself in an expensive marketing campaign to break an artist. But the appetite for risk of DIY artists and artists on label services deals is usually much more modest as Tony Wadsworth explained: "When a label is paying an artist will naturally want the best possible marketing campaign, but when the artist is paying the focus will be on the most cost effective instead. It can sometimes be difficult for an artist when they see that more than half of their income is being kept by a record label to market and promote their music but there are investment decisions that only labels can take because of the fact that they manage a portfolio of artists." Labels have the benefit of taking the long view and as a consequence can make decisions and investments that a DIY artist simply cannot. Consequently the risk of the rise of DIY as an option for the earlier stage of artists' careers is that more artists slip through the net, never getting that first break that would propel them onto success. Also the ability to reach global fan bases at scale remains an area in which labels continue to consistently perform far more strongly than D2F platforms.

108 http://gigaom.com/data/data-isnt-just-the-new-oil-its-the-new-money-ask-zoe-keating/

Sony's Edgar Berger argued that labels are now beginning to combine their strength of influence with greater flexibility for artists: "We as a label need to provide as complete a service to the artist as possible, to customize the services to the needs of the artist. The key thing is to put your muscle behind the artist, to try to break the artist on a global scale, aligning the vision of the artist with that of the label." For artists who want to be global stars major labels and big independents continue to be the safest bet, but expectations will be high and patience often a precious commodity as Wadsworth explained: "If you sign to a major don't be surprised if they want to sell lots of records and if somewhere down the line that they say it isn't working. You are entering into a pact that they are investing large quantities of resources into your music. You are buying into muscle, brain and heart. You are not making a deal with a major label to tread water." The well oiled machinery of a big label's marketing organization is not however for everyone and critics of the model argue that size does not always equate to quality. FRUKT's Jack Horner claimed that big labels often fall short of many artists' expectations: "Far too many artists are pushed to become 'the next Take That', with a ton of investment into duplicating the previous success stories and no real drive to create the NEXT new brand in music. Videos, websites, Facebook campaigns and promotional schedules which adhere to some sort of universal template. It's quite simply, lazy marketing. I've heard hundreds of stories from artists who, having signed their deal with a label, had assumed that a sharp, effective team would be deployed to help take them and make them successful... all too often it ends in friction and disagreement – with product managers being young and poorly paid, often entire marketing departments with no real marketing training or experience." He added that the other end of the spectrum can often be equally challenging for artists, if for other reasons: "It's the hard path for sure, as you'll probably end up with a minuscule marketing budget from an independent label to help you sell the one thing you have conceded to sell, which is the music."

When Brands and Bands Collide

Brands have been touted as an alternative revenue source for artists ever since music sales began to tumble. The brand-as-label concept got an early case study par excellence when UK dance act Groove Armada left Sony Music for Bacardi but it was a false dawn for the model. Instead brands have usually played a more opportunistic role, teaming up with artists to directly promote their wares rather than pursuing creative partnerships. Most often these emerge as opportunities for established artists with proven 'brand equity' and audience pull that the brand can benefit from. A few branded showcases aside, the brand opportunities for emerging artists are much less clear, with few brands having any interest in investing valuable resources and capital into nurturing unknown artists so that they can become ready for primetime. A highly notable exception is energy drink brand Red Bull, investing extensively in creative initiatives such as the Red Bull Academy that helps educate and empower young musicians. The Red Bull Academy has been running for enough years now that it has a growing number of successful graduates and these alumni return to teach at Academy sessions. It is a genuine virtuous circle of creativity that illustrates the possibilities of brand partnerships when they are imaginative and creative, rather than vapid and poorly thought through. When done in a non-intrusive manner, such as a telco sponsoring a tour or UK mobile carrier O2 renaming leading music venues, brand involvement can feel like an authentic partnership. Another noteworthy success story was when Converse's marketing agency Cornerstone commissioned Santogold, the Strokes' Julian Cassablancas and Pharrell Williams to create the collaboration 'My Drive Thru' in 2008. This little, funk infused gem was only available as a free download on Converse's site but was a critical success and garnered acclaim for the artists and brand alike. Too often though the result is awkward, transparently commercial and risks alienating fans. Such an example was a Rihanna gig sponsored by clothing company River Island: when the singer called to her audience: "Let me hear you say River Island" she was greeted by embarrassing silence.

Horner has worked on artist and brand partnerships for more than a decade and believes that working with brands is no less overtly commercial than signing with a major label: "The old argument about artists selling out is in my view, simply redundant. The notion that working with a brand is any worse than lining the record label chairman's already gold-plated pockets doesn't make sense. Of course you still need a smart management team to ensure your commercial affairs are being managed in a smart way – but if this is in place, there's no reason to think that working with a consumer brand is any worse than taking an onerous restrictive advance from a label, and then have a bunch of execs telling you who to write with and how to market yourself. Artists who get on their high horse about not selling out are often unaware of the irony that they have already sold themselves to labels, agents and managers who are all incentivised with commission, whose livelihood is dependent on getting 20% of something."

Changing Creativity

The advances in digital music distribution technology and artist tools have been mirrored by transformative innovations in music production technology. In the mid 1990's professional studios were in the main the only option artists had for recording release quality music. Artists would save money to buy studio time, record demos on an analogue studio set up, and then send the demos to record labels. By the turn of the 2000's the recording world was changing dramatically. Digital recording technology was becoming both sufficiently powerful and affordable to start an inexorable colonization of recording studios large and small. Digital production suite Pro Tools was en-route to becoming the industry standard in professional studio, and analogue mixing desks and outboard equipment were becoming superseded by digital alternatives. But the real revolution was happening at the lower end of the market with computer based production software such as eMagic's Logic – later acquired by Apple – Steinberg's Cubase and Cakewalk giving bedroom producers the ability to create high quality, sometimes even release quality, music. As the 2000's progressed with computer processor power and software improving further, more and more of what traditionally constituted a studio disappeared inside the computer in the shape of software equivalents. By the late 2000's reverbs that had previously only been attainable with standalone units that cost thousands of dollars could now be recreated with software that cost hundreds of dollars. The sounds of rare vintage analogue synthesisers are now available in software synthesisers. Apple's Logic Studio enables an artist to create an entire track within the programme with synthesisers, effects processors, drums, guitars all embedded natively. Music production has been democratized and the barriers to entry lowered. When this is coupled with D2F tools and self-publishing services like TuneCore a whole strata of artists can make music and push it out into the world without having to encounter a single part of the machinery of the traditional music industry. From bedroom to iTunes in just a few clicks.

The increased ease of access to music production technology has not however come without its own risks and challenges. Justin Morey, senior lecturer in music business and music production at Leeds Beckett University and previously a studio owner described some of the permutations: "Since the late 1980's music production has increasingly become a browsing and choosing process for many people working at an amateur or semi-professional level. It started with multi-timbral synthesizers with banks of 100s of preset sounds, and samplers with even larger libraries of pre-recorded instruments, beats and effects. Now, with software like Logic Pro, there are presets for pretty much every aspect of the production process, so even if you're recording guitar or vocals, there are ready-made channel strips you can use for compression, EQ and effects. So there are lots of presets that can make your production sound alright, and while that may feel like it offers more choice, it actually becomes quite restrictive, because it encourages aspiring producers to apply someone else's ideas of production sound to their music, rather than looking to find their own sound." Above and Beyond's Grant concurred: "When I started out making music, samplers had limited memory capacity and samples were a relatively scarce resource. Now you have kids who are going on to Torrents and downloading massive sample banks and construction kits." By relying so heavily on masses of pre-programmed sounds and samples budding producers risk missing out on the important learning process of creating sounds themselves. Nowhere more has this automation of production been seen than in dance music, where the core reliance on synthesised and sampled sounds was always tailor made for computer based production techniques. Bedroom producers can now produce high quality dance tracks using the exact same technology that big name DJs and producers use. Music production technology has also evolved into the performance space with software such as Ableton Live and hardware such as Native Instruments' control surface Maschine enabling real-time interactivity and creativity, in turn creating an entirely new form of live performance. Meanwhile DJs can slot working demos straight into their mixes and hone the sound based upon dance floor reaction, a far cry from when they used to have to queue up on a Friday to have their latest tracks pressed onto acetate in order to play on the turntables. Grant recalled: "We'd wait in a queue full of jungle and drum n' bass producers to get a 10 inch dub plate cut that would probably only play properly a few times, to take it to a DJ to play that night."

The effects of the democratization of production also rippled throughout the music industry, bringing down the costs of making records. It is a trend observed by Grammy award winning music producer and songwriter Keith Thomas who has worked with artists such as Amy Grant and Vanessa Williams: "The cost of making records has decreased dramatically. You can buy Logic X for $200, which comes with all the sounds and tools you need to make a record and does everything and more that my old Sony 3348 did for a whopping $185,000, while at the same time, my competition has undoubtedly increased: I used to spend a full day just getting the drums set up properly for a session. Now you can buy great drum samples for less than $100. Kids are making great records in their basements for under $5,000. There are drummers here in Nashville who have rigs set up at home with Pro Tools and will overdub drums for $100 per track, studio cost included. Some record as many as 8 or more songs per day." One of the downsides of the lowered barrier to entry is that the quality filter has diminished. In the analogue era producers would typically expand their kit piece by piece as they progressed, which in most cases translated into their production skills improving too. So by the time they had enough equipment to be release-quality-ready they would typically have acquired a robust and rounded set of production skills and capabilities. Now that it is possible to get to that technology point immediately more people can make sounds that sound plausible, more quickly, and without the rounded set of skills. According to Thomas: "the democratization of production means lots of people aren't the full package, so they produce bits, which encourage labels to pick and mix, to piece together a full song from fragments of others."

Morey voiced similar concerns: "The influence of the democratization of music production on music has been over stated. In terms of very talented people making great music, that has not changed much, because talented and driven people will find a way to get their music recorded and released. Talent transcends the medium in which it operates. I'm not convinced that the ease with which people can produce their own music on a laptop or a home computer now means that there is a lot more great music out there. Rather, I think it means that plenty of modestly talented writers and musicians are able to create competent-sounding but mediocre music more readily than was previously possible." The ability to create solid sounding productions quickly using affordable music production software has begun in some music genres to lead to an under appreciation of the skilled music producer but as Tony Wadsworth observed: "The value of producers is subtle yet it can be the difference between thousands and millions of sales. With a producer like Rick Rubin sometimes it is hard to put a finger on exactly what he has done, yet he will most often have transformed the record."

The increased reliance on production technology has also led to a growing trend of artists becoming less concerned with perfecting a recording performance, knowing that they will be able easily edit together the best parts of various takes in order to create a composite take. This tendency to cut back on rehearsing and preparation time by artists is according to Morey a case of artists "effectively reneging on their responsibility to deliver a great performance. With digital recording, there has almost become an assumption that the producer will construct a performance from multiple takes, rather than the artist deliver a definitive performance that might need a couple of minor repairs or drop-ins."

The increased ease of music production access also coincided with the rise of celebrity culture to create a potent and often toxic blend of incomplete ability and improbable expectations. The rise of talent shows such as the X Factor and America's Got Talent sell everyday music fans the dream that they too can be superstars. But with the emphasis on appearance and performance at the direct expense of creativity and song writing, the dream bypasses nurturing creative skills and cuts straight to performing in front of millions. This not only has the effect of engendering a preoccupation with celebrity over authenticity but it also leaves many of the artists who take the shortcut to success shorn of the skills they need to build sustainable careers. Thomas believes that: "Compared to a decade ago, for a lot more of younger artists it is all about being famous rather than the music itself. They need to learn how to connect with their fans in a meaningful way, how to tell their story, but they just want to shortcut to fame and success. With social media everyone has the ability to be seen by and connect with many people, which gives them the sense that they are every bit as good as a superstar." But whatever the motivations for making music might be, the underlying truth is that the music itself ultimately needs to have worth as Jonathan Grant concluded: "If you strongly believe in something musically then the odds are that someone else will too. But if you are constantly trying to second guess your audience, delivering them what you think they want rather than what you feel is the right thing to do, then the odds are that eventually you will come unstuck."

FIGURE 49

The Anatomy of a Digital Single

Distribution of income from a $0.99 single and associated costs for each stakeholder

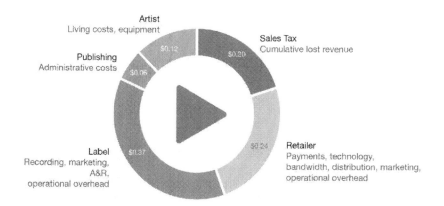

Note: Artist is recouped major label artist. Sales Tax set at EU average.

CONCLUSION: What It Means To Be A Digital Era Artist

Only a cursory glance at where the revenue goes from a typical 99 cents single track download (see Figure 49) is necessary to understand why many artists have at one time or another struggled to demonstrate much more than ambivalence to the state of the digital music market. A fully recouped artist can aspire to earn just 12 cents for each download while most will never see even this because they remain perpetually indebted to their record labels. Despite this, few artists any longer argue that piracy has a net positive impact though a number still see it playing an important role in exposing consumers to their music. None though would dispute that the internet – across PCs and connected devices – is rapidly becoming the best way of reaching their most engaged fans. But for the majority of people embarking on a career as a professional artist in the digital era the career proposition they face is a much more complex and unpredictable one than the one that they would have faced in the analogue era. The days of selling music being synonymous with success and income are quite simply gone. But there remains a disconnect between social metrics success and revenue success for artists. The gap will narrow only once artists, labels and managers better learn how to monetize social audiences and the outcome will redefine relationships across the triumvirate. The boom years of the 1980's and 1990's provide a stark contrast with the leaner digital era that is not always helpful, especially for artists who had experienced the plentiful bounty of the CD years. Though the superstar artists continue to strike it big, more artists are understanding that a realistic aspiration of success as a professional musician is to earn a decent wage rather than get rich. The paradox is that recorded music remains the main way the majority of people interact with artists as Erik Nielsen observed: "The thing that is most important is the music, which ironically now has least commercial value. Instead it has become the gateway drug for getting fans hooked enough to sell them other stuff." Jonathan Grant made the case that the growing importance of live income over music sales skews the marketplace to artists who perform: "There is not much room anymore for anyone who just makes records. It is important that we as an industry invest in people for whom making recorded music is their art." Labels meanwhile are getting smarter about how they can monetize an artist even after the recording career peak. They are doing so with a three pronged approach of 360 deals, label services and simply dropping artists when they have peaked.

The emergence of the semi-pro artist has created an entirely new tier of artist but the experience has not been entirely net-positive though, with many artists finding that D2F tools merely enable them to downsize from full time careers to part-time ones. Statistics about the income of artists, including DIY artists, are beginning to paint a picture of decreasing income and opportunity for professional artists.[109] This is partly because more artists are making more music so it is becoming increasingly competitive, with the squeezed middle feeling the pinch most. As Marillion's Mark Kelly put it: "The promise of the internet making it a level playing field has turned sour. Artists are free, sure, but free to do what? To not earn a living?" There are also creative implications of the rise of DIY artists. As Justin Morey explained: "There was a reason for the feedback loops in the traditional model: A&R, the studio engineer, the producer, the manager. Many of these checks and balances are gone for smaller acts, and that has an effect on the quality of their output because there's no one pushing them to make their record as good as it possibly can be. Artists are not always the best critics or editors of their own work."

The democratization of artist income is beginning to look like it is as much about bringing established artists down to the lowest common denominator as it is about elevating enthusiasts. However there is no denying that the internet also creates unprecedented opportunity for artists with niche appeal to build niche audiences on a global scale and thus establish a career where before there would have been none. However, what is becoming clear is that the bulk of artists are feeling the digital pinch more than labels are, a point made by Roger Faxon: "The artists and the musicians feel the economic loss most acutely. Senior executives at record labels are still paid pretty much what they were a decade ago." The ascendency of the Superstar artist in the digital era is one of the greatest paradoxes of the democratization of the music business, thrusting more revenue share into the hands of an elite just as it should have been making income distribution more equitable. Outside of the Top 1% digital era artists are, just in order to survive, having to become as good at business and marketing as they are at song writing and performing. Jay-Z's 2005 lyric from the 2005 Kanye West track "Diamonds from Sierra Leone" reads like an artist's motto for survival in the digital era: "I'm not a businessman. I'm a business, man!"

---

109 The US Bureau of Labor Statistics reported that jobs in "musical groups and artists" dropped by 45.3 per cent between August 2002 and August 2011. Though the numbers need very careful secondary analysis for use in music industry terms (the trend is in fact much less severe) the underlying trend that fewer people are able to make full time careers out of music none the less holds true. Similarly the Digital Music News website reported that the average Tunecore artist earns less than the US annual wage (http://www.digitalmusicnews.com/permalink/2011/111123tunecore). The calculation was based upon the fact that only top 749 Tunecore artists in 2011 earned more than $1,280, roughly equivalent to the average wage. The statistics, like the US Labor Bureau statistics need significant additional analysis – e.g. Tunecore revenue typically makes up just one part of a DIY artist's income, sometimes less than 10% - but the underlying trend is nonetheless broadly correct i.e. that semi-pro income is exactly that, less than a full salary.

Chapter 11: The Songwriter's Story

The emergence of digital music happened back to front. First the audience got their needs addressed with disruptive services like MP3.com and Napster. Then the labels got involved and started to bring law and order to digital's wild west. Next the artists became part of the dialogue and also started benefiting from ways of connecting with fans. Then, as the 2010's got going, the songwriters finally started to make their voices heard. Ironically any song happens in the exact reverse order: first it is written, then it is performed, then it is recorded and finally the fan gets to hear it. Yet only once the digital music market had become a global entity, only once the likes of Apple and Pandora had accumulated hundreds of millions of digital music customers, did the songwriters become part of the digital discourse. It happened this way because this is how the digital music landscape is structured: pirate sites can accumulate millions of users before being taken down; labels lead the commercial negotiations with music services; artists are the recognized faces of music. But the songwriter, when not also the artist, is a typically faceless entity known only by song-writing credits on liner notes and all but invisible in online services where there is no space for such credits. Matters are not helped by the songwriter's side of the rights equation being the most complex and fragmented part of the digital music value chain, with both publishers and Performance Rights Organizations (PROs) responsible for rights licensing.[110] (While publishers typically sign deals only with songwriters they expect to make a significant amount of money from, any songwriter can join a PRO).

Whereas the recording side of the business is relatively visible to fans and industry professionals alike, the publishing side is by comparison obscure and confusing. With significant quantities of popular music, especially pop music, being written by professional songwriters, these composers are responsible for many of music's most memorable lyrics and melodies but are usually largely invisible, with the performer getting the limelight. This is of course only a natural consequence of the chosen career path of professional songwriters, but it also means that they were for too long a largely absent voice from the digital debate. The implications of this are twofold:

- Songwriters do not have as much influence as performing and recording artists

- The digital debate is framed by concepts and metrics which make sense for performing and recording artists but not songwriters

The second point is particularly important. Many of the music industry's critics support their case for the demise of record labels and other traditional industry practices with an argument that in the digital age artists must rely upon their new emerging income streams in place of sales of recorded music sales. But while a performing artist can look to touring, merchandize sales and even brand partnerships for future revenue, a songwriter has no such options. A songwriter relies on the recorded work for their income.[111] As award winning songwriter

110 While a label normally owns an artist's master recordings, a songwriter usually retains ownership of the original composition, assigning a music publishing company to exploit their works in return for a share, or all, of ownership. Songwriters will also most often become a member of a PRO, such as BMI and ASCAP in the US, PRS for Music in the UK, JASRAC in Japan and GEMA in Germany.
111 A songwriter can also look to synchronization revenue from their songs being licensed to adverts, movies, TV shows, computer games and other such channels. However the sync market is becoming saturated as illustrated by the comments of PJ Bloom,

Helienne Lindvall put it: "There is money in the internet but it is just not going to songwriters. Songwriters feel like the stepchild at a family reunion. People say 'do gigs, sell t-shirts' but all that songwriters have is the music. There is a real sense of helplessness and frustration. They feel that they are getting left behind. It is the behind the scenes people who are most affected by what is going on because they have the least heard voice with which to resist."

Thus songwriters felt the digital pinch more keenly than the higher profile performing and recording artists, both in terms of piracy helping drive down music sales and the growing impact of streaming services. While a performing artist can soften the blow of streaming pennies replacing download pounds with an understanding of how the increased exposure drives other revenue streams, a songwriter only sees the small payouts. In 2012 US songwriters took centre stage, lobbying in Washington against the Pandora-backed, proposed Internet Radio Fairness Act that aimed to reduce online radio royalty payments. The debate was a complex one with strong arguments on both sides of the divide but it did have the effect of shining a rare light on the plight of songwriters. One such songwriter, Ellen Shipley, presented her royalty payments from streaming services to illustrate their impact. Ellen claimed that for 3.1 million streams on Pandora of the Belinda Carlisle song 'Heaven Is A Place on Earth' – which she co-wrote – she received $39.61, and for around 100,000 streams on Spotify she received $9.22.[112] There are a host of extenuating variables that need to be considered when interpreting these numbers – such as what share of the writing credits she has, any additional income she should receive from other rights bodies, and whether those rights bodies are paying her the appropriate amount – but the broader issue is key. Namely that streaming revenue must stand up in its own right in the long term for songwriters to continue to earn adequate income for their work. While the digital music market narrative and economics have centred on the recorded work copyright of the label and the artist, the compositional copyright of the songwriter, publisher and PRO has remained in the shadows.

Fragmentation and Complexity

One of the long term tensions in the digital music market is the contrast between the overtly commercial remit of record labels and the quasi-commercial approach of the collection society PROs that act both as commercial entities and as egalitarian societies for their members, where the smallest songwriter's interests should, in theory, be represented alongside that of the superstar. Whereas the key driving forces of digital music – record labels and digital innovators – usually function on a fully commercial basis, collection societies do not and this has two key implications:

- A collection society should, in theory, represent the needs of a minor artist just as much as it does a top tier artist

- PROs are not-for-profit, quasi-commercial organizations

---

music supervisor for TV shows such as Glee and CSI. Bloom, in an interview with MusicWeek. He stated that he was surprised TV shows even still paid for music as in his view it was such good exposure for the music. He also explained that in his view the ability to charge a premium for sync that was prevalent in the mid 2000's has gone. Of course Bloom's comments must be considered in the context of a licensee establishing his negotiating position, but it is nonetheless illustrative of a broad trend and attitude. https://www.musicweek.com/news/read/pj-bloom-on-changing-sync-revenues-and-opportunities-for-rights-holders/054069
112 These figures were quoted directly by Ellen Shipley in the comments section of this post on the author's blog: http://musicindustryblog.wordpress.com/2012/12/06/spotifys-bold-new-transition-from-streaming-music-service-to-music-platform/

The story of digital music is defined by record labels playing catch-up with rapidly changing technology. The dynamic of fast innovator and sluggish rights holder is amplified many times over with collection societies. While commercial imperatives drive record label and digital innovator business decisions, PROs have a different priority: to represent the needs of their members. While this brings an important balance to the digital market dialogue it has the inadvertent effect of acting as a braking mechanism on already slow processes.

The PRO approach has thus proved to have both positive and negative implications. On the one hand they tend to represent, in most markets, the majority of the rights – in stark contrast to a record label – but on the other they can be less willing to take an entrepreneurial approach to licensing and also tend to move much more slowly. Whereas labels operate in quarterly cycles, collection societies do so in annual cycles. One music service executive commented that in his experience a 12 to 14 month negotiation period with a PRO would be considered 'relatively quick' while others have taken 2 to 3 years. The longer time cycles of PROs also manifested more publically in the streaming debate, with songwriters contrasting their low payouts with the success of streaming services. The comparisons were most often wrong however because the statement represented the state of streaming one year previously due the 12 month delay in accounting and payments with many PROs. The January 2014 announcement from SoundExchange that the US PRO would start paying monthly royalties set a welcome standard for other PROs around the globe to strive towards.

Publishing rights are the most complex piece of the licensing puzzle to fix and although fragmentation plays a key role, the difference in commercial approach is just as important. Whereas record labels learned the importance of flexibility and agility, publishers and collection societies lean towards a more rigid outlook, born not so much out of obduracy but instead of a very different set of experiences and remit. While record label revenues tumbled throughout the 2000's publishing revenues grew by six per cent between 2005 and 2013.[113] The increase was driven by growth in performance royalties – digital radio, online radio etc. - and by a booming music synchronization market – the licensing of music to channels such movies, adverts, games. The implication of this synchronization strategy is that although consumers are spending less on music, music is being licensed to more of the non-music products that consumers are spending their money on instead. Thus when publishers and collection societies approach digital deals they can afford to be more risk averse, to be willing to slow down a market if need be, as they have less need of the digital gamble to pay off than their record label counterparts. This engenders a stronger negotiating position and many publishers have come to acquire a reputation for sticking firmly to points of principle even when it can make a proposition commercially unviable. As a consequence record labels often find themselves unable to pursue some of their more adventurous digital experiments because they cannot make the numbers add up without publishers being willing to take the risk of making income concessions. Record labels need to give every digital experiment serious consideration, publishers do not.

---

113 Enders Analysis

Seeking Out a Fair Share

One of the unintended consequences of the record labels having driven so much of the commercial structure of digital music is that label royalties far outweigh publishing royalties across most digital music services, sometimes to the extent that labels are paid 7 or 8 times more than publishers. Publishers have consequently been locked in a battle to increase their share of the royalty pie from digital music services or as David Israelite, the President of the US music publishers' trade body the NMPA put it, to get a fair share: "Songwriters are bound by a bad rate standard while record labels negotiate in an open competitive market. We believe we deserve a rate that gives us a fair share. There is no justifiable reason why our royalty rate is governed by regulations and the labels' is not." Robert Ashcroft put the issue in a broader context: "There are two big aspects to the issues of rates: 1, the total amount going back to rights holders as a share of the total product value proposition and 2, how that income is divided between labels and publishers." Publisher discontent stems from the disparity between how much record labels are paid for digital services versus how much they earn. For a typical $0.99 single a record label can earn between 60% and 70% of the net total – depending on the territory, and then minus any distributor payments for smaller labels – while a publisher will earn something in the region of 10% – again depending on the territory. Thus songwriter royalties are priced at approximately one sixth of the recording royalties. One music publisher executive argued that matters are compounded by the fact that publishers and collection societies are usually among last to the licensing table, so that when the likes of Google and Apple allocate a rights budget they first negotiate away the lion's share of it with the big labels.

On the surface it looks like a highly inequitable state of affairs but the situation is not clear-cut. Labels argue that the higher share paid to them is reflective of their role in the broader music industry ecosystem. Record labels are the ones who take the larger degree of risk investing in artists, most of whom will lose them money. Thus, the argument goes, a higher share of royalty payments is the labels' means of reclaiming some of that lost investment. Although publishers also pay advances to songwriters the model is intrinsically less risk heavy as the sorts of songwriters who most often get advances are those who are either already signed or on the way to being signed by a label, or instead are professional songwriters who usually have a proven portfolio of label and artist clients. Nonetheless whether a six-to-one ratio is a fair reflection of this difference remains a compelling question, as is where the extra publisher digital income share would come from: the labels or the services? Or both? Tom Frederikse, partner at law firm Clintons fears that some music services may end up as collateral damage, caught in the cross fire between labels and publishers: "For publishers there is now a new agenda: rebalancing revenue share between themselves and record labels. This is an internal industry issue that is being played out behind the curtain but that will likely result in killing off one or more digital music services before it is resolved – and goes some way toward showing how tricky the relationship between labels and publishers is." Lewis Silkin's Cliff Fluet believes that the implications may be even further reaching: "In my view, by fragmenting rights publishers may have ossified the market. Services now have a 'lowest common denominator' offering as opposed to be consumer-focused and/or innovative. Some will take massive up-fronts and minimum guarantees on the assumption the deal will fail but that they will make their numbers."

Adam Kidron, former founder and
CEO Beyond Oblivion

Peter Jenner, manager Pink Floyd
(former), Billy Bragg

David Israelite, President and CEO
NMPA

The Challenge of Unattributed Revenue

One of the contradictions of the digital music business is that it can deliver a degree of data accuracy and accountability never dreamed of in the analogue era and yet also continue to be dogged by concerns about quality of reporting from music services and rights owners alike. In principle digital music service analytics present an unprecedented opportunity to assess exactly who is listening to what, when and just how much. But where the system breaks down is with the processes that underpin digital music, with multiple databases and cataloguing schemes employed across different territories, music services and rights holders. Robert Ashcroft argued that the situation is complicated further by the withdrawal of rights by publishers: "The impact of publishers withdrawing rights has been massive and whatever the pros and cons from a licensing perspective, it has created real challenges in the back office. When you license on an international basis, but all of the data is held nationally, even small discrepancies in works registration data cause problems, particularly when you are processing the usage data for hundreds of billions of streams." Complications with cataloguing and reporting of data contributes to significant quantities of unattributed revenue, income delivered from music services that cannot be allocated to specific songwriters or artists. Jim Griffin believes there are incentives for this income to remain unattributed: "Publishers and PROs like unattributed income more than they like attributed income because they don't have to share it and distribute it." Questions of unattributed income lingered throughout the short history of digital music and though reporting quality is improving the issue refuses to go away as Ross explained: "I have heard that up to 20% of songwriters' digital revenue is lost due to mis-administered and wrongly associated rights claims. If I was an artist or songwriter I would be asking 'if my royalties are so low because 10-20% is going missing due to bad data, why can't the industry can't get data into shape?' Of course everyone blames everyone else, but there is so much data messiness right across the industry." Data quality issues though are far from the exclusive domain of publishers, with similar issues translating directly into the label side of the equation as Ashcroft suggested: "Data quality across all portions of the digital music value chain is a key issue. There is no doubt that users of copyright works have less of an incentive to convey accurate usage data than publishers and PROs have in receiving it, but for the system to work efficiently their data is critical." AIM's Alison Wenham believes that unattributed income affects songwriters and artists on independent record labels much more keenly than those on major labels due to their scarcer resources available for concentrating on data cleanliness: "Metadata is incredibly important, you need to manage the rights wherever they are used. Unattributed digital income accounts about 20% of all revenue and it skews much more heavily towards independent labels. For under resourced independents there is a very real risk that revenue is being misdirected."

Concerted efforts are however been made on the publishing side of the equation to bring improved accuracy and efficiency to reporting, particularly in the shape of the Global Repertoire Database (GRD). The GRD is an effort aimed at creating 'a single, comprehensive and authoritative representation of the global ownership and control of musical works' and is backed by numerous major PROs, publishers and commercial players such as Google, Apple and Omniphone. The GRD aspires to deliver accuracy and costs savings to rights data but was still in the requirements and design phase in 2013 despite the project being commenced in 2009. Though the task ahead of the GRD is clearly vast and crucially important it is also limited by dint of being restricted to Europe and only addressing the publishing side of the digital music business. So although it is ambitious it is far from being the single, central digital database that the digital market so desperately needs. Nonetheless, even with those caveats the GRD is an important step as Ashcroft explained: "The GRD is crucial, because if we are doing pan-European licensing than we need to have a pan-European view of rights. The GRD will become an increasingly authoritative record of rights." Frederikse also believes the GRD will help address the issue of unattributed revenue: "The [GRD] will be a vitally important leap forward in licensing, not least because it will be enormously helpful in clearing up the 'black box' of unmatched works and unallocated payments."

Conclusion: A Road Still Chock Full of Challenges

Copyright is an inherently defensive mechanism – it is designed to protect the rights of creators – and is thus always going to lean towards reactive rather than proactive strategies. Copyright simply cannot move as quickly as technology innovation, both because of its intrinsic nature but also because of the processes and practices built around it. The nature of PROs means that the much needed change that is beginning to take place will take time to take effect and then longer still for many of the benefits to be felt. Now that publishers and songwriters have started to find their voice, this side of the rights equation will become a much more central part of the digital dialogue throughout the remainder of the 2010's. That publishers started to pay such close attention to digital was a natural consequence of the contracting music market. Throughout the 2000's publishers had seen their revenue grow strongly thanks to growing synchronization of revenues from licensing more music to more places, such as games, movies and adverts. The plight of the record labels felt an unfortunate but entirely distant predicament. But it was inevitable that sooner or later the publishers would start to feel the pinch, with declining music sales translating into shrinking publisher revenue for the underlying compositional works in CDs as David Israelite explained: "Mechanical revenue has declined to one third of the revenue mix for songwriters from two thirds a decade ago because fewer people buy and in the new business models we are currently split 9 to 1 compared to what the record labels get."

There will be many key tests over the remainder of the 2010's that will determine the new balance of power between labels, publishers and PROs in the digital music market. It is hoped that all three constituencies will recognize the importance of not killing off crucial digital music services in the process. Though there may be a perception in some quarters that one defunct service will swiftly be replaced with another that will be willing to pay even higher royalty rates, the reality is that investors are watching this space carefully. And if they choose to put their money elsewhere, the music industry will need to find some other means to inject capital into the digital arena. No small task.

Underpinning it all is the plight of the songwriter. If publishers are getting better deals from music services then it is crucial that this upside is passed onto songwriters. Helienne Lindvall summed up the outlook for songwriters: "There are many older songwriters who have seen their income drop and there are many younger songwriters who feel that they can never aspire to get to those levels." While artists can offset the transition to access based models by turning to alternative sources of income, songwriters have no such option as Grammy award winning producer and songwriter Keith Thomas explained: "If you're just a songwriter the outlook is tough. You live and die on royalties but it is harder than ever to make a living with sales declining, royalties are getting smaller. And there is no 'back-end' for songwriters, they don't tour or sell t-shirts." The shift to streaming might be worrying for artists, it is simply terrifying for songwriters.

Chapter 12: The Pirate's Story

Today piracy is a term laden with politicized meaning referring to a plethora of technologies, but up until the mid 2000's it was synonymous with P2P file sharing. From the advent of Napster file sharing became the single largest force in digital music: it was in the right place at the right time and for the right people. Because the consumer internet itself was in relative infancy in the mid 1990's, the technology aficionados who constituted Napster's first wave of adopters were a disproportionately large share of the internet population. The fact that they were eager early adopters, ever willing to experiment and test boundaries ensured that their impact was doubly strong. Coupled with the demand vacuum created by the absence of major label licensed services this ensured that P2P effectively got a free run until the labels finally hit upon a coordinated response. Napster did not invent file sharing but it was the first app to have genuine appeal outside of the narrow confines of the super tech savvy hardcore. Though Napster's user base was still skewed towards early adopters, it was far closer to the mainstream than those who had previously turned to Usenet, File Transfer Protocol (FTP) servers and Internet Relay Chat (IRC) to find music online.

The rapid growth of Napster's user base, rising from 1 million users in 1999 to 60 million in February 2001, demonstrated just how much wider its appeal was. And it was not just the labels who were quickly understanding the potential of P2P, investors were too. EMI's then President of Digital Distribution Jay Samit saw the dangerous implications of for the labels: "I knew there was too much money being pumped into pirate businesses and that we couldn't compete with Silicon Valley dollars. The main point of the court cases was to convince investors not to put money into piracy." The labels' legal action thus had a clear business strategy but it also had strategic legal objectives as the RIAA's Cary Sherman explained: "We embarked on strategic litigation efforts to establish key principles of law, targeting practices that risked setting adverse precedents."

FIGURE 50

The Evolution of Music Piracy

Timeline of Key Music Piracy Networks, Applications and Legal Rulings

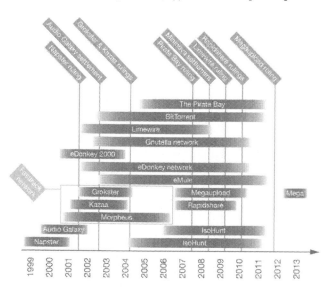

In the early days of Napster and MP3.com enforcement was the major labels' digital strategy. Throughout the first half of the 2000's the RIAA was the key focus of the music industry's enforcement efforts, suing a succession of file sharing networks including the likes of Music City Morpheus, Kazaa and Grokster. All of the cases, though eventually usually successful for the labels, were lengthy and costly and music piracy continued to grow regardless. Not only that, the creators of the file sharing networks reacted swiftly directly to the legal process, altering their technology to circumvent the labels' latest legal victory. Fragmentation became the watchword, with an increasingly bewildering array of new P2P alternatives (see Figure 50).

The agility of the pirate entrepreneurs' response effectively rendered the labels' enforcement strategy impotent. However many pirate sites the labels succeed in taking down, multiples more filled the breach with even more sophisticated alternatives that were designed to negate the legal tactics that had won the labels their last case. Thus the music industry found itself locked in an innovation arms race, frantically trying to respond to technology innovation with new legal tricks and by lobbying for more favourable legislation. But try as they might, the labels and their industry bodies simply could not match the pace of their adversaries. The simple fact is that online technological change can be measured in days, even hours, while judicial and legislative processes are measured in months and years. It was a case of a heavily armoured and superbly equipped but slow moving army being picked off mercilessly by quick-moving guerrilla units that no sooner had they attacked, melted away into the darkness. The labels' legal approach had been conceived as a decapitation strategy, severing the business head from the file sharing operations to stop it dead in its tracks. But in fact file sharing proved itself to be a many headed hydra, unhindered by the removal of any single business head.

By 2007 there were close to two dozen main P2P networks with many more P2P applications running on top of them, with the total number of P2P sites in excess of 500 (see Figure 51). The first generation of P2P networks had been closed down because they had centralized networks, the second generation went decentralized, but once the music industry learned how to track people within these networks a new wave of anonymous networks and clients emerged. The technology was in a perpetual state of flux. Industry leaders hoped that this fragmentation of supply would inevitably lead to the fragmentation and diminishment of the audience too. Unfortunately that hope remained ever elusive. Fragmentation did not appear to have any discernible negative impact on the growth of piracy. It quickly became apparent that P2P users were improving their technological sophistication in incremental steps to keep up with the new demands of the ever-evolving P2P technology. The extra steps file sharers had to take seemed to do more to improve their web sophistication than it did to deter them from using P2P networks. Thus an unexpected, and entirely unintended by-product of the 'war on piracy' was to improve the collective technology IQ of the pirates themselves, both the developers of the services and the end users too. The more the music industry fought the pirates, the smarter the pirates got.

FIGURE 51

The State of P2P in 2007

P-to-P Networks	Network Type	Main Application	Generation	Notes	Network Active?	Encrypted?	Notes
Napster	Centralised	Napster	1st Generation	P2P	No	No	Closed 2001
Audio Galaxy	Centralised	Audio Galaxy	1st Generation	P2P	No	No	Closed Sept. 2001
Scour	Centralised	Scour	1st Generation	P2P	No	No	Closed 2000
Soulseek	Centralised	Soulseek	1st Generation	P2P	No		
FastTrack	DeCentralised	Kazaa, Kazaa Lite	2nd Generation	P2P	No	No	
Gnutella	DeCentralised	Limewire, pre-V6 Bearshare, Grockster	2nd Generation	P2P	No	No (yes with 12Phex)	
iMesh	DeCentralised	iMesh, V6 Bearshare	2nd Generation	P2P	No		Settled with RIAA, developed legitimate DRM paid offering and layered in social networking
Shareeza	DeCentralised	Gnutella, Gnutella2, EDonkey Network, BitTorrent, FTP and HTTP	2nd Generation	P2P	No	Yes	
Morpheus	DeCentralised	Gnutella, Morpheus	2nd Generation	P2P	No	No	Subsequent releases restricted following legal action
MLDonkey	DeCentralised	eDonkey network, Overnet, BitTorrent, Gnutella, Gnitella2, FastTrack, Kad Network, OpenNap, SoulSeek, DirectConnect	2nd Generation	P2P	No	Yes	
Hydranode	DeCentralised	DirectConnect, BitTorrent, Ares, etc.	2nd Generation	P2P	No		
AppleJuice	DeCentralised		2nd Generation	P2P	No	Yes	
eDonkey2000	Centralised	MLDonkey, Shareeza	2nd Generation	P2P	Yes	No	Closed down by RIAA
Overnet	DeCentralised		2nd Generation	P2P	No	No	Closed down by RIAA 2006
eDonkey (ED2K)	DeCentralised	MLDonkey, eMule, Shareeza, aMule, Imule, Hydranode etc.	2nd Generation	P2P	No	Yes	Settled with RIAA ($30m) & agreed to cease distribution & prevent use of previous downloads. Network usage not impacted, eMule now accounts for 90% of all traffic
Kad Network	DeCentralised	eMule, aMule, MLDonkey	2nd Generation	P2P	No	Yes	
BitTorrent	Hybrid	Numerous BitTorrent clients	2nd Generation	P2P	No	Yes	Closed 2001
GnuNet	DeCentralised		3rd Generation	P2P	Yes	Yes	Anonymous network
Rshare	DeCentralised	Rshare, Stealthnet	3rd Generation	P2P	Yes	Yes	Anonymous network
FreeNet	DeCentralised		3rd Generation	P2P	Yes	No	Anonymous network
ANts P2P	DeCentralised	StealthNet, Includes eDonkey support	3rd Generation	P2P	Yes	Yes	Anonymous network
Mute-net	DeCentralised		3rd Generation	P2P	Yes	Yes	Anonymous network
I2P	DeCentralised	Multi-app support in. BitTorrent, Gnutella I2Phex	3rd Generation	P2P	Yes	Yes	Anonymous network
Entropy	DeCentralised		3rd Generation	P2P	Yes	No	Anonymous network
Tor	DeCentralised		3rd Generation	P2P/F2F	Yes	Yes	Strongly enforced usage etiquette
WASTE	DeCentralised		3rd Generation	F2F/ Darknet	Yes	Yes	Anonymous – designed to work on small friend networks
Turtle F2F	DeCentralised		3rd Generation	F2F/ Darknet	Yes	Yes	Anonymous – designed to work on small friend networks
Galet	DeCentralised		3rd Generation	F2F/ Darknet	Yes	Yes	Anonymous – designed to work on small friend networks

The practical limitations of what a decentralized network operator could do were largely restricted to ceasing distribution of the client software. At a push, a network could issue an update to its software that effectively deactivated the local peer that downloaded it but the effectiveness of any such measure would dissipate with users quickly notifying others not to download it. Also if a P2P network did anything with a software update that angered its user base a 'rogue' version of the app would soon arrive, thus nullifying the impact of any update that was designed to kill off a network. In a move laden with irony Sherman Networks, the operator of file sharing network Kazaa, issued DMCA takedown notices against the makers of an app called Kazaa Lite++ that allowed users to bypass the ads served up by the formal version of the app.

The consequences for rights holders were profound: you could annihilate a decentralized file sharing network in the courtroom, win every single facet of your case and still the network would function undimmed because it existed as an organic entity out of the control of its creators. File sharing had transformed into Frankenstein's monster (see fifty one). Piracy went from strength to strength, getting bigger with each passing year, growing from 11% in 2002 to 15% in 2007, reaching more than two thirds in Spain. As piracy rose recorded music revenues declined (see Figure 52). Piracy was now a permanent part of the music landscape, a property developer throwing up a glut of new buildings without any concern for planning permission or the existing communities.

FIGURE 52

The Rise of Music Piracy Correlates Strongly
With the Decline in Recorded Music Revenue
Global Recorded Music Revenue (Trade Values) and Active P2P Penetration

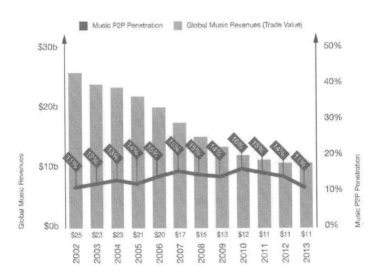

File sharing technology metamorphosed in response to legal rulings just like a medical virus mutates resistance to antibiotics. The emergence of decentralized file sharing networks established a modus operandi that continues to define the music industry/file sharing relationship even today: whatever action the labels may take file sharing responds with haste and great effectiveness. Due legal process is hardly renowned for its speed and agility while legislative process is an even slower moving beast. Yet these were the key weapons with which the music industry tried to fight piracy in the late 1990's and early 2000's. It was like lining up a marathon runner in a sprint against a 100 metre specialist. They were the wrong tools for the job. Legal and legislative processes were invaluable for helping define the business environment by creating clear legal precedent but they were too slow to act as a brake on file sharing innovation. While legal milestones were measured in months P2P software propagated in hours and days.

Going After the Consumer

In September 2003, realizing it could not get the results it wanted by solely by suing the piracy businesses, the RIAA changed tack and decided to go after the file sharing consumers themselves. The RIAA's Sherman explained the reasoning: "A whole new wave of P2P sites emerged that were simply an evolution of the Napster model, architected to avoid the Napster ruling. So we were shocked that the district court and then the 9th Circuit Court of Appeals said these new P2P services were okay. It was clear that it would take a long time to overcome these legal rulings so we had to go after the file sharers themselves." If the first wave of legal action had attempted to sever the head then this drive aimed to drain the blood running through its veins. Suing your own customers is not a decision that any company or industry takes lightly and the labels did so because they felt that they had no other choice. However the deterrent theory component of the strategy, though based upon some sound logical reasoning, was quickly to prove a painful and prolonged public relations disaster for the music industry. The economics and practicalities of suing individual file shares meant that the RIAA was only ever able to target an infinitesimally small share of the entire P2P user base. Therefore the remit of the cases against individual file sharers was not to directly reduce the level of music piracy but instead to set an example that would send shock waves across the file sharing community and thus, so the thinking went, indirectly push piracy down. This was the labels' shock and awe strategy, however as events would transpire there was to be plenty of shock, but little in the way of awe.

The shock component of the strategy was to set high profile examples that would supposedly terrify consumers away from file sharing. Thus the size of the fines which were meted out were often highly punitive, rising up to $62,500 per uploaded track in the case of Jammie Thomas-Rasset, resulting in a total fine of $1.5 million. Thomas-Rasset was in fact the first defendant to take the RIAA action through to court, but she was an exception, with the majority settling out of court at much more modest rates – typically just a few thousand dollars – and thus accepting legal culpability.

The music industry's decision to sue individual file sharers, though rooted in robust legal argument, was a PR disaster waiting to happen and had far from universal support within the labels' own ranks as Jim Griffin recalled: "I felt a looming sense of horror of what was coming. I was going to RIAA meetings and I realized they were going to go after the fans, and I knew the fan would come back at them and win." Suing one's own customers is never a recipe for success, however much of a last resort. The RIAA's legal offensive swiftly fomented a groundswell of public antipathy towards the music industry, with a backlash spreading like wildfire from online forums and tech press into mainstream media. The labels were losing the public at just the time they could no longer take their customers for granted and needed their support more than they had at any previous time. The RIAA did not help itself, with an often heavy handed and inflexible approach, resulting in eminently avoidable PR disasters such as the case of trying to sue a dead alleged file sharer.[114] Yet despite all the negativity, legal action against individuals was, and is, a necessary part of label enforcement strategy. It is important that a benchmark of legal culpability is established that clearly demarcates legal from illegal, and that clearly apportions consequence to the latter, in just the manner as for other laws of the land.[115] Also, European counterparts to the RIAA, such as the British Phonographic Industry (BPI) and the national bodies of International Federation of the Phonographic Industry (IFPI) have proven over the years that the strategy can be implemented with more subtlety and flexibility. This necessary demarcation however should not be mistaken for attempting to reverse a sea change in consumer behaviour. Piracy was the technology vehicle with which digital era consumers learned on-demand, access based consumption behaviour. The media industries as a whole have in turn had to embark on a journey of learning how to embrace this new paradigm of consumer behaviour with their own technology solutions. It is an inherently endless journey and while the parameters will always be stretched by new technologies, there will always be a dividing line between legal and illegal. Whether that bar will forever be set too high because of the slower moving nature of rights owners is another question entirely, but the principle of using enforcement to establish the rule of law applies as much to copyright as it does any other aspect of law enforcement.

In April 2008 the RIAA finally succumbed to public pressure and ceased its programme of suing file sharers, having racked up more than 30,000 suits in five years of operations. It was not however a definitive end to the strategy, with outstanding court cases continuing to drag on for years after and European bodies still suing individuals to this day. But the focus of industry enforcement strategy had shifted, recognizing that suing neither file sharers nor the piracy businesses was creating a substantial, incontrovertible decline in digital piracy. Judicial process had proven to be far too slow moving a beast to tackle piracy and also much too unpredictable, with landmark cases such as the Thomas-Rasset case going to countless retrials and judges frequently siding against the labels. The record labels and their industry bodies shifted their focus to a two-pronged approach of political lobbying and technical measures.

Getting Off the Back Foot

One of the problems with industry legal action and lobbying is that it addresses business level concerns, not consumer needs, the focus is on turning off the tap of illegal content not filling the sink with comparable legal alternatives. The term comparable is crucial. For all that record label executives in the early days of digital music pointed to the likes of MusicNet, Pressplay and early OD2 services as reasons why consumers did not need to pirate anymore, anyone who had been within sniffing distance of those services immediately knew that they were anything but comparable. Limited catalogue, a la carte stores with restrictive rights technology and no device portability were hardly reasons to stop using P2P sites. Only now, more than a decade on with services like Spotify and Deezer do consumers have genuine comparable alternatives to piracy. In the earlier days of P2P, with no comparable services, the effect of prolonged court

114 In 2005 the RIAA named 83-year-old Gertrude Walton as a defendant, accusing her of having uploaded more than 700 songs onto file sharing networks. Walton had died in December 2004. The case inevitably resulted in surge of scathing press stories revelling in headlines such as "I Sue Dead People".
115 Some might dispute the validity of copyright as a legal concept, and therefore the right of labels to sue file sharers, but currently copyright is enshrined in legislation and judicial precedent, and as such legal process remains a valid, if controversial, course of action.

cases was simply to raise consumer awareness of file sharing at just the time consumer demand was beginning to accelerate. It was clear that attempting to throttle piracy at the commercial source was doing little more than raising the profile of target companies as Wayne Rosso, President of file sharing network Grokster from 2002 to 2003, explained: "When the music industry sued Grokster it was the greatest thing, it had taken them from obscurity to mainstream media." The legal actions also had the unintended consequence of priming successor P2P networks and clients with a tick list of needed features to evade future legal action. All the while, more and more consumers were turning to file sharing networks. What had started off as a comparatively niche activity quickly seeped into the mainstream. In the late 1990's and early 2000's many consumers genuinely did not know what was legal and what was not.

Consumers were not interested in esoteric issues of copyright being contested in court cases that often looked like they could go either way. Instead they wanted to know how they could get lots of cool new music online. The internet had an exhilarating wild west air about it in the 1990's and there was a genuine sense that rules were being rewritten for a new way of the world. Napster had played delaying tactics with the labels because it genuinely believed it could compel the labels to license on the terms it wanted if it managed to build up a large enough user base. Napster was swept along with dot com hype and hubris, where business models mattered less than eyeballs, where old world economics did not apply, as if the internet did away with the need for balance sheets and profit margins. To be fair to Napster and its dot com peers, it is a mindset that pervades no small number of music services even today.

The dot com crash of the early 2000's brought most internet business minds back to reality, but the transformation in attitude and outlook among consumers remained. The proverbial genie was out of the bottle. Consumers had grown accustomed to file sharing and no amount of enforcement or counter measures were going to change their digital expectations any more than a child could be expected to unlearn the desire to play by simply taking away his toys. With the supreme benefit of hindsight, there is a well rehearsed argument that the record labels could have had a much smoother entry into the 21st century had they opted to embrace file sharing rather than embark on a Don Quixote-esque conflict, or if they had engineered some form of commercially licensed agreement with the dominant player or even created a blanket licensing framework.[116] Doing so could indeed have nipped much of the commercial challenge in the bud and even more importantly would have been able to address the critically important shift in consumer attitudes to paying for music that was getting underway in the late 1990's. But the problem with this argument is that file sharing was not a single entity. If Napster had been the age of empire, post-Napster file sharing was the chaotic age of competing principalities and rival successor kingdoms. There was no single entity to work with. Though there were successive dominant players, such as MusicCity Morpheus, Kazaa and Limewire, each quickly petered into insignificance once the labels got too close. There would never have been a unilateral commercial deal with all file sharing networks, whatever had been agreed with the leading networks would have been taken by the rest as a challenge to circumnavigate and compete around.

The P2P blanket license argument also does not account for the ideological chasm that divided the file sharing community and the rights owners. The majority of file sharing network developers built their networks and applications as a direct challenge to the music industry establishment. They considered the music industry to be archaic, inflexible and ripe for replacement and themselves as technology revolutionaries, bringing the walls of the ruling

116 A blanket license in this context refers to a standard licensing framework which any service could use to acquire content rather than negotiating directly with each label and publisher. Napster had hoped for a catch-all license on its terms.

elite tumbling down, usurping the tired old guard. Money still talked though, and the venture capital-backed Napster eventually accepted the music industry's money, with Napster's VC paymasters having a firm eye on an exit rather than waging an indefinite ideological war.

One of those P2P companies with a strong commercial vision was Grokster. Wayne Rosso had been brought in as President by Grokster's founders to architect a viable business model: "Behind the scenes they wanted me to find a way to partner with the record companies. We knew that copyright theft wouldn't continue, that it had to stop." Rosso lived a life of split personalities, in public appearing on countless media outlets to push the case for P2P while working closely with labels around the negotiating table. Rosso saw the media's growing obsession with the music industry's fight against piracy as a priceless marketing opportunity: "Other file sharing networks were hiding in the foxholes and I knew mainstream media were looking for people to talk to. I would wake up at night dreaming up the most crazy stuff I could say. We could track media hits to downloads. [But] we knew the ride would eventually come to an end so we were putting pressure on ourselves to try to cut deals with the labels." Perhaps unsurprisingly, given his widely quoted controversial opinions, Rosso found his initial engagements with labels far from plain sailing: "I went to everyone I could and they all said one of two things: 1) 'we didn't reward pirates' 2) 'shut it down and then we can talk'. They always thought it was a system we could turn off and it would all stop, that we could simply turn off the network. They also didn't understand that when customers go they don't come back."

The turning point for Grokster came in October 2003 when Sony Music's veteran CEO Tommy Mottola was replaced by former NBC COO Andrew Lack. Mottola had transformed Sony Music from an $800 million business in 1990 to a $6 billion business in 2000 but did not have as progressive a technology outlook as his successor. Rosso saw an opportunity: "I called Andy up and we met in his New York office, Phil Wiser [Sony Music CTO and formerly co-founder of Liquid Audio] who was there too was terrific and I got on beautifully with Andy. The discussions led to trying to get all of the P2P guys together to go legit. But most P2P networks were scared to death, Morpheus took 6 months to sign an NDA. Others point blank refused to cooperate as they were on a crusade against the media companies." Trying to pull together the other P2P networks proved to be an impossible task, in part because some of them had absolutely no interest in working with the labels because it went against the very essence of why they were doing what they were doing: "Morpheus didn't want to give up the fight, it was strictly ideology of freedom of information for them, their investors were whack balls, they were like a digital Tea Party".

Realizing that his attempts to coalesce the file sharing network companies around a legitimate, licensed strategy were only ever going to come to naught, Rosso decided upon a different tack. So in 2005 Rosso founded a legal, licensed P2P network called Mashboxx because "those other P2P operators were either too terrified or too stupid to do anything." After securing $200,000 in seed investment Rosso partnered with Shawn Fanning's Snocap to filter out unlicensed content from the network, a key requirement for labels. He then started reaching out to labels for what would be a fruitful but frustratingly slow burning licensing process: "I told Andy [Lack] I was going to build a legal P2P network and he was right behind me. I called Zach Horowitz [President and Chief Operating Officer of UMG] who said he'd do a deal and added 'I'm not going to let Andy Lack be savior of the music industry.'" Despite the initial enthusiasm it took Rosso two years to secure major label licenses, but secure them he did: "All the licenses had to be created from whole cloth, we had to create entirely new licenses, it wasn't easy work. The Universal license was about four inches thick when it was signed." The label Rosso had real difficulty with was Warner Music: "I was getting along with all the label heads except [Edgar] Bronfman." Even though negotiations with Warners were not proving fruitful when Rosso contemplated launching Mashboxx without the major on board he got a call from an WMG executive stating "'If you launch without us we'll sue you.'" An understanding was eventually reached with Warners and by July 2006 Mashboxx had signed term sheets for a $12 million investment from Richard Branson's Virgin Investments. Unfortunately for Rosso, the investment fell through at the last minute and ultimately Mashboxx folded without ever getting to market. Rosso "lost everything [he] had." Rosso had flitted between the roles of label pariah and would be industry saviour but ultimately ended up empty handed in a very real and tangible sense.

In the UK Paul Hitchman and Paul Sanders were also trying to establish a licensed P2P service in the form of Playlouder. Backed by Beggars, Playlouder had emerged out of a number of early digital music ventures including a digital store, a digital marketing agency and white label services. These initial forays gave the Playlouder team early experience of what to expect from working with labels on digital projects. This included an abortive attempt in 2002 to launch a music subscription service in partnership with UK TV broadcaster Channel 4 that would have combined music downloads with video and additional programming. Hitchman recalled that: "We couldn't get the majors on board with the store. They were always insisting we launch with each of their own proprietary technology, such as Universal's Bluematter." Eventually Sanders and Hitchman turned their attention to the rising challenge posed by piracy and to exploring whether there were any commercial solutions that could monetize the increasingly prevalent activity: "We started to think about how we could leapfrog the chaos to create a commercial solution. Digital music wasn't free, because people had to pay money for the internet access with which they got that music. Lots of people were thus paying lots of money for music, but the revenues just weren't flowing back to the rights holders." The solution they hit upon was a niche ISP hard bundled with a music subscription. Using the backbone of ISP Bulldog, and later Tiscali, Playlouder combined a central music subscription hub where consumers could download rights protected files with, most controversially, a framework that enabled subscribers to continue to share files via P2P with other subscribers. Using a combination of Audible Magic to identify tracks and Deep Packet Inspection (DPI) technology to stop music leaving the network, Playlouder would monitor and then monetize P2P activity for rights holders. It was a brave move and would be a step too far for major labels even today let alone in 2003, when it was launched as a proof of concept trial with content from Beggars and some other independent labels. By 2004 Sony BMG had at least licensed to the centrally served rights protected component of the service thanks to the SVP of the label's Futures Division Clive Rich "having the vision to understand the potential of the offering." EMI also eventually followed but Hitchman realised that: "We couldn't launch because we couldn't get all the labels on board and the ones we did have on board were just too nervous. I thought the content owners would welcome us in and discuss how to get to a solution, not look at us as the enemy." So Playlouder switched strategy and started to pitch the concept as a white label offering to telcos and quickly got interest from UK cable company Virgin Media. However once Virgin Media showed serious intent Universal Music inserted themselves in the equation as: "They saw Virgin as a great potential partner but Universal's view was that P2P was the enemy." Virgin would go on to almost but not quite launch an unlimited MP3 service with Universal and Playlouder would go on to become a licensed telco music provider under the guise of MSP (Music Service Provider) for the likes of Eircom, but their brave attempt to monetize piracy was over.

The Pirate Bay

The advent of Napster in June 1999 may have marked the birth of file sharing but the arrival of a new technology just two years later marked its coming of age. In July 2001 a University of Buffalo computer science graduate Bram Cohen released his new creation BitTorrent into an unsuspecting world. Napster's dependency on central servers had proven to make it highly vulnerable to closer and censure. BitTorrent was by far the most significant and also most effective of the emerging decentralized networks that turned the computers of its users into an entirely decentralized network. While contemporary decentralized file sharing networks used multiple alternative 'mirror' sources the BitTorrent protocol instead groups users' requests into 'swarms' with multiple users simultaneously downloading and uploading from each other. This distributed approach resulted in highly effective bandwidth management, so effective in fact that many legitimate content providers have since licensed BitTorrent's technology to distribute their content. With BitTorrent, users' computers replaced large central servers to distribute large volumes of digital content highly efficiently on an unprecedented global scale.

Some argue that BitTorrent was the most important digital music invention of the 2000's but its transformational impact was not immediately felt. Instead the music industry was squarely focused on the efforts of 2nd generation networks such as Kazaa and MusicCity Morpheus. But just two years after Cohen had unleashed BitTorrent a site launched that would have such dramatic impact that rights owners would look back at the early 2000's with fond longing in comparison to the decimation of its revenues that the newcomer would facilitate. The site was the Pirate Bay. The Pirate Bay had started out in 2003 as a distinctly Scandinavian affair, a Swedish language alternative to the then popular Direct Connect. Unlike many of its influential file sharing predecessors the Pirate Bay was not a file sharing network itself but was instead a Torrent Tracker, an index of Torrents on the BitTorrent network. This was the new distributed face of piracy writ large, a site that was to become public enemy number one for the music industry was not a network itself but instead a piracy search engine that mapped the BitTorrent network. The music industry was no longer simply engaged in combating the underlying networks themselves but now also had to combat an entire supporting ecosystem that was more far reaching in practice and ambition than Napster had ever been. BitTorrent was the future of digital content distribution and the Pirate Bay was the anti-establishment interface that sat upon it. As idealistic as the founders and investors of 2nd generation file sharing networks might have been, few were prepared for the ideological crusade that this new rising star of piracy was about to wage. Whereas Napster, Kazaa and others defended themselves with the argument that their networks had legitimate, non-infringing uses, the Pirate Bay had no intention of hiding behind that flimsy barricade. The name itself was a clear statement of intent and the site had been set up in 2001 by a Swedish anti-copyright group Piratbyrån (The Piracy Bureau).

The Pirate Bay truly began to prosper once BitTorrent had got onto the labels' radar. Not however because of raised exposure resulting from industry enforcement but instead because the Pirate Bay was if not the last then at least one of the few main tracker sites left standing once the labels had started distributing cease and desist notices. Popular torrent sites such as Slovenian tracker site Supernova succumbed to rights owner pressure and closed down which in turn created a window of opportunity for the Pirate Bay as its co-founder Peter Sunde recalled: "These sites were closed down not because of legal rulings but because of legal threats. Because most of the sites were run by teenagers they were scared into closing by the threats of big business. We got a threatening letter and decided that we were going to ignore it. The site was legal in Sweden so we weren't going to close it down, we knew we had the law on our side. Either we were stupid or brave."

Soon after its launch 60% of the Torrents uploaded to the Pirate Bay were Spanish even though the site was entirely in Swedish. For a while the most torrented file was a Swedish-to-Spanish language course because Spanish Pirate Bay users were trying to teach themselves enough Swedish to work their way around the site. Sunde realized: "we needed to make a website in English and then as the other Torrent sites closed down usage took off". The Pirate Bay swiftly became one of the most pervasive entry points to file sharing and helped the BitTorrent network account for 35% of global internet traffic in November 2004.[117] The Pirate Bay swiftly found itself in the cross hairs of the music industry's legal big guns but the site's founders held firm, confident of their legal position in Sweden. What the Pirate Bay's Founders had not counted upon was quite how seriously their media industry adversaries were taking the conflict. Sunde picks up the story: "There was a letter from the Swedish prosecutor from six months earlier stating that the Pirate Bay was legal. Then the record labels and Hollywood got the White House to pull the Swedish Minister for Justice over to America and told him they would impose trade sanctions unless he took action against the Pirate Bay. So the Justice Minster came back to Sweden and did just that. 50 police officers came to multiple locations [in May 2006] not really understanding what they were looking for. They took computers, keyboards, mice, anything with electricity in it. They took 250 machines and had to hire trucks to take it all. I was at home sleeping while it all took place as they didn't seem to know about me at the time and they also completely missed two actual Pirate Bay locations."

It took a few years for the music and movie industries to feel ready to put the Pirate Bay in the dock but when they did so the weight of their evidence and legal argument won the day. Swedish prosecutors filed charges at the end of January 2009 against three Pirate Bay founders – Frederik Neij, Gottfrid Svartholm and Peter Sunde – and an associated business man Carl Lundström. The trial started in February and finished in April with all four defendants found guilty and sentenced to one year each in prison and a fine of $3.5 million. Their sentences were reduced on appeal but the fine was increased. Sunde however does not believe that he and his co-defendants got a fair trial: "We got really screwed by a corrupt court and a judge employed by the music industry." Indeed following a Swedish radio investigation it emerged that the presiding Judge Tomas Norström and other members of the prosecution team had worked with and were associated with various bodies and organizations linked with copyright advocacy including the Swedish Association for the Protection of Industrial Property. Eventually, following lengthy legal process, other members of the Swedish judiciary ruled that these affiliations did not represent bias or a conflict of interest but instead enabled the individuals to improve their knowledge of the copyright sphere. Not surprisingly the Pirate Bay's supporters felt aggrieved in the extreme and viewed the ruling as the act of a corrupt establishment attempting to snuff out the flame of revolution. Piracy had become politicised so it was entirely logical that a political party emerged as a mouthpiece for the ideological ambitions of the file sharing community. Headed by the eye patch wearing Rickard Falkvinge the Pirate Party has gone to become a significant political pressure group in a number of European countries, particular within the Nordic region. In the 10 days after the trial more than 25,000 people joined the Swedish Pirate Party, rising its total membership to over 40,000 and in turn making it the fourth largest political party in Sweden at the time in terms of membership.

---

117 Cachelogic

In the midst of the court proceedings a curious chapter in the history of the Pirate Bay took place. In June 2009, with the combined might of the global music and movie industries attempting to crush the Pirate Bay a Swedish entrepreneur called Hans Pandeya attempted to buy the site for $8.5 million through his company Global Gaming. Sunde recalled the incident: "When I first met [Pandeya] I thought he was crazy and that he wanted to do fun things. He seemed like a great fit for the Pirate Bay. We were getting bored by then as most of what we were doing was tedious admin, moderating, tech maintenance etc. He was going to put the Pirate Bay on the stock exchange with only one share allowed per shareholder which would have been real distributed ownership. It was going to be a real 'fuck you' to the business world, right in their own back yard. Running a site that is always fighting legal action against media companies is a real cost drain, so we saw selling the Pirate Bay as a great opportunity to start a well funded organization to fight SOPA and other legislation that was beginning to arise at that time. We thought, 'if it messes up the Pirate Bay, it doesn't matter, we can start over." Pandeya approached Wayne Rosso to help him pull together the acquisition: "I brought in financiers from London – David Glick's Edge Investments – and we started to make the deal move ahead. Pandeya though only had an option to buy for 60 days and we needed an extension as it wasn't possible to get the rights licensing done in time." As the process progressed it dawned on Rosso that the deal was not going to reach a successful conclusion: "In the end $3 million was the price we settled on for buying the Pirate Bay but it fell apart when the Pirate Bay kids turned around and told us to stuff it. It was a mixture of greed and idealism." Fault also lay with Pandeya who Rosso insists is "one of the biggest frauds on earth. He had got an option to buy the company but he didn't have the cash." Pandeya had insisted his Global Gaming company had the funds to pay for the acquisition and that he also had sufficient personal wealth to guarantee it. In reality the company was broke and Pandeya had his car and boat towed away by the Swedish tax authorities. In 2010 Pandeya faced bankruptcy proceedings in which Rosso, who had never been paid by him for his Pirate Bay work, testified against him. Sunde however argued that though Pandeya himself might not have had the finance he had backers who did but they faded away: "He had the money through the backers he had with him at the start but they started to back out when they saw how the headlines were going."

Even with the added 'benefit' of the aborted acquisition the effect of the Pirate Bay court ruling and of it being upheld at appeal did not prove to be the silver bullet rights owners had hoped for. Instead of disappearing from the face of the web the Pirate Bay instead even now remains a focal point of the piracy landscape. Countless country level domain blocks have been implemented and numerous servers closed down but the site has always, through one means or another, re-emerged, a perpetual phoenix.[118] More than a dozen countries have blocked access to the Pirate Bay yet a host of workarounds such as proxy servers and VPNs ensure that users still find their way to the site. Most frustratingly for the music industry the Pirate Bay has remained determinedly antagonistic throughout, launching new products such as a browser specifically designed to circumvent domain blocking. Sunde argued that: "The Pirate Bay was always about fun. [It] has a reputation for being crazy and for doing crazy things so exploring options such as placing servers on zeppelins and in micro nations fits in with that. It shows people there is a way to play around with your opponents, to do things they cannot easily do anything about."

Although the Pirate Bay continues to function and maintain a high profile Sunde believes that it is doing more harm than good to the file sharing movement: "I really feel that more

---

118 This included the Pirate Bay being hosted in the Cyberbunker until a 2010 German court ruling forbade hosting and imposed fines and prison sentences for copyright infringement.

people should have done a Che Guevara and moved on after the revolution was won. The Pirate Bay is blocked in so many countries now. When a site is blocked so much you need a new brand, to start over. It would be good if the Pirate Bay could be closed down as it would force people to look elsewhere for something new. The Pirate Bay has become a huge monument that gets in the way. We need a spring clean." The Pirate Bay and BitTorrent are arguably the most potent technology challenges the music industry has yet faced, in terms of both commercial and cultural impact. Though both still exist much of the political lifeblood of the piracy movement has seeped away and to some degree the consumer interest has been neutered by the industry's embracing of free as a legal business model. Sunde however remains unimpressed: "If you crushed Spotify with a free alternative – free as in 'freedom' – then it would be so much better for the community and for culture. So much these days is being controlled by American companies and money forcing their culture and values on us. Where is Spotify's success? Users? Subscribers? Financially it is a disaster."

Nonetheless the Pirate Bay's transformation of file sharing into an ideological crusade has politicized the whole file sharing debate, not only creating a backdrop for the lobbying efforts of tech superpowers but also seeing the emergence of an overtly political movement. The language of the Pirate Party's Falkvinge shows a willingness to use the same strength of language against the labels as they themselves have used against P2P networks: "More and more people realize, against the tenacious deceptive talking points of the copyright industry, that the copyright monopoly is not related to property rights at all but is a governmentally-sanctioned private monopoly that limits property rights and free trade."[119]

The Rise of Cyber Lockers

Pirate Party grandstanding aside the music industry started to score successive big legal victories including the closure of Limewire and Megaupload as Cary Sherman explained: "When Limewire was closed down, more than half its users did not go back to file sharing or to other illegal sources. 7 out of the top 8 locker services responsible for music piracy have changed the way they do business since Megaupload was indicted. Strategic enforcement can really make a difference." The Megaupload case proved to be one of the most intriguing in the history of music piracy. Megaupload was a cloud locker service run by the larger than life character Kim Dot Com, a self-styled digital vigilante taking on the traditional media industries in a one man crusade. At its peak Megaupload had 50 million active users and accounted for 4% of the globe's entire web traffic, having become a 'safe' alternative to peer-to-peer file sharing. In the figure of Dot Com piracy advocates relished having a fearless advocate fighting their corner but they soon discovered that he was a very different figure than Peter Sunde. For all his Robin Hood routine and internet freedom rhetoric Kim Dot Com was simply a man on the make. When his home was raided pictures emerged of his sprawling New Zealand mansion, helicopter and fleet of luxury sports cars. Megaupload's raison d'être had been Kim Dot Com's personal enrichment.[120]

The Lobbying Effect

With piracy evolving and maturing almost despite industry counter-measures, the record labels through their trade bodies such as the RIAA and IFPI, intensified their lobbying efforts, seeking to influence politicians directly and also to impact them less directly by becoming active voices in the political dialogue. The initial thrust of the lobbying efforts was to place a

119 http://torrentfreak.com/copyright-monopoly-trends-and-predictions-for-2013-121230/
120 Jurisdictional controversy resulted in the case against Kim Dot Com crumbling, with questions raised over the legality of America's FBI spearheading New Zealand police activity.

burden of culpability and responsibility upon telcos. The culpability issue was in many respects the most controversial. Telcos, and big technology companies such as Google relied on the same net neutrality argument that Napster had tried to use in its legal defence. The position of telcos and search engines was that they were no more responsible for what passed through them anymore than a postal service is responsible for the written content of a letter. It is an argument that has solid enough legal basis, sound precedent and remains centre stage in any consideration of the role of telcos in digital content.[121] The music industry has thus had to fall back on convincing legislators that telcos should assume a degree of moral responsibility for the financial, societal and cultural consequences of the content that is distributed via their networks. In essence responsibility for disputed culpability. The approach began to bear fruit, with the music industry finding it relatively straightforward to convince the politicians that the rise of piracy and the decline in music sales were far too closely co related for there not to be a causal relationship. Of course there were, and are, many other contributory factors but politicians across Europe and the US were sold on the basic premise of the arguments. With the first lobbying objective achieved the next thrust was to persuade those politicians to take the logical next step of accepting that the telco attributed responsibility should translate into responsibility for taking action to remedy affairs. This was the genesis of the graduated response strategy in which telcos would be obliged to take progressively strong actions against their customers for illegal file sharing – a policy most commonly referred to as three strikes. It was a genius move, now the music industry would not have to go after its own customers because it was going to get the telcos to go after their own customers instead. PR nightmare diverted, or at least that was the theory, unfortunately for the music industry it did not quite pan out that way.

Unsurprisingly telcos across the globe fought keenly against the pervading legislative zeitgeist and stepped up their own lobbying efforts. Though the PR battle was proving to be gruelling the labels nonetheless won a succession of notable legislative victories, including the Digital Economy Act in the UK, HADOPI in France and the Copyright Act in the US.[122] HADOPI established the legal framework for a three strikes policy by which repeat file sharers could have their internet connection cut off following three warnings, while the Copyright Act enshrined the ability of labels to demand damages ranging from $750 to $150,000 for copyright infringement by file sharers. HADOPI was watched keenly across the globe by labels, telcos and politicians alike. It was the purest and firmest interpretation of the three strikes policy, establishing the authority to enforce the implementation of a three step email, letter, cessation of internet connection process. The bill nearly did not make it through parliamentary and senatorial passage despite explicit support from then French President Nicolas Sarkozy. HADOPI did eventually make it into law, despite further legal challenges, and was heralded by rights owners as a model of excellence for legislative strategy. The results however fell well short of expectations and despite some initially promising music industry supported research, HADOPI had no discernible impact on music sales. An industry supported study suggested that French consumers were buying more digital music as a result of HADOPI but once the end of year music sales data was reported there was no such uplift visible in the numbers, illustrating the danger of reading too much into consumer research. Unsurprisingly the wind dropped out of the labels' sales instantaneously and politicians started paying ever closer attention to the arguments and evidence being put forward by the big technology companies. The consequences of which potentially present rights owners with even wider reaching implications

121 The only significant chink in the telcos', and Google's, cases is that they willingly drop their neutrality
position in respect to specific content types such as indecent images of children.
122 HADOPI is an abbreviation for Haute Autorité pour la Diffusion des Œuvres et la Protection des Droits sur Internet.

than piracy did, namely an overhaul of the entire approach to copyright in the digital arena.

The labels had bet big with HADOPI, it was meant to be their proof point for piracy strategy, showing that enforcement would reduce activity and in turn drive sales. The true picture though is far more complex than that. Behaviours are so deeply rooted that enforcement will always have minimal short term effect, just as the millions that are spent on illegal drug enforcement have not been able to prevent the continued rise of the drug trade. Would music piracy and illegal drug trafficking be more widespread without enforcement? Most probably, but neither will disappear because of it. To build the case that enforcement would deliver a near immediate upturn in sales was as naïve as it was misplaced. Deezer's Axel Dauchez correctly argued that piracy is the "dividend of convenience" but if copyright is overhauled through legislation then that will be the dividend of anti-piracy lobbying.

In 2011 the major US ISPs bowed to record label – and movie studio – pressure and agreed to a six strikes enforcement scheme, though implementation did not start until late 2012. Meanwhile in the UK the British music industry successfully got a Digital Economy Act pushed through Parliament in the last days of a dying Labour party government. The Act stopped short of three strikes but did put significant responsibilities on ISPs such as monitoring offenders and facilitating letter sending to repeat offenders. The newly elected Conservative and Liberal Democrat coalition government in 2010 quickly distanced themselves from the Act, with the Deputy Prime Minister Nick Clegg even proposing repealing the legislation.[123]

The legislative tide was changing and this was seen nowhere more clearly than when the labels over-reached in 2012 with the Stop Online Piracy Act (SOPA) SOPA and PROTECT IP Act (PIPA) bills in the US. The acts stipulated greater powers for combating organized copyright infringement, including commercial and legal sanctions against companies enabling infringement. The labels were over zealous with the SOPA legislation, particularly with regard to attempting to accrue domain blocking authority, and in doing so once again cast themselves in the role of pantomime villains. Opposition groups voiced concern that, among other things, the proposed legislation made it too easy for rights owners to have overseas sites blocked without sufficient checks and balances and due process. A highly coordinated response followed from a loose coalition of privacy advocates, freedom of information campaigners and big technology companies including Google, Mozilla and Flickr. SOPA was a step outside the comfort zone of politicians and consumers, and with the help of effective counter-lobbying from the technology sector – including Wikipedia going 'dark' in protest on January 18 2012– the bill fell at the final legislative hurdle. Comparisons to the Great Fire Wall of China simply proved too much for American legislators.[124] By January 20 both bills had been removed from further voting and were indefinitely postponed. It was a decisive victory for the amalgamation of advocacy groups and the piracy lobby, and a resounding defeat for the media companies. By once again trying to achieve too much, though this time with the concerted support and cooperation of other media industries, the record labels sunk the most important legislative tools they have yet had. It may yet prove to be their legislative high water mark.

The winds of change were blowing over in France too. In August 2012 the new French Minister for culture Aurélie Filippetti hinted that HADOPI may be closed down because it had not delivered definitive results, saying: "I do not know what will become of [HADOPI], but one thing is clear:

---

123 Nick Clegg, the leader of the UK Liberal Democrats, and his party voted against the Digital Economy Act while in opposition, before becoming part of the coalition government.
124 The author himself came up against the impact of IP filtering when he unsuccessfully tried to access the Pirate Bay blog when researching another chapter of this book.

HADOPI has not fulfilled its mission of developing legal content offerings".[125] Once again the music industry was discovering that slow moving tools such as legislation and judicial process are ill equipped to combat the every changing, and fast moving opponent piracy had become. It was also further evidence that lobbying was a high stakes game that could easily backfire.

Rights owners learned the valuable lesson that they risked losing everything if they overstepped the mark in their increasingly rare windows of legislative opportunity. The lobbying tide was beginning to tip decisively away from the media companies and towards the technology sector. Technology lobbyists saw this as an opportunity to push their digital agenda, to capitalize on the backlash against piracy enforcement as a vehicle for pushing for copyright reform. Thus the legacy of over weaning piracy enforcement ambition may be much wider ranging changes to copyright. Enforcement hubris may just have begotten a strategic copyright setback of spectacular proportions of which we have not yet started to feel the full effects. The appropriate role for legislation is to ensure legitimate activity can be appropriately rewarded so that innovation can occur, but this balance has rarely been well struck. The labels' lobbying efforts undoubtedly helped bring a meaningful amount of digital IQ into copyright legislation but the reactionary tendencies of some of the lobbyists have engendered a sense digital-era protectionism being imposed to sustain analogue-era practises. Up until the dramatic failings of SOPA and PIPA it appeared that the labels had managed to establish a legislative digital buffer zone, but now that too looks vulnerable. Even without the digital agenda threat of conflating piracy enforcement with copyright reform, creating a degree of legislative protection from piracy risks breeding innovation complacency because it means there is less need to rely upon technology and business model innovation to solve the piracy problem. But now with the copyright reform strategy of Google et al there is the distinct possibility that adequate legislative foundations for digital copyright may be disrupted distinctly in favour of the technology sector. If that scenario does indeed transpire then it will simply be a reaffirmation of the learning that a legislation dependency is a habit that can suck energies away from innovation and manifest decidedly unfortunate side effects.

The net result of the all out lobbying world war is that politicians have become increasingly skeptical of both sides' intentions and evidence sets. Also resulting legislation has inevitably ended up either a watered down fudge that leaves neither side content – e.g. the Digital Economy Act in the UK – or has ended up lobbied out of existence – e.g. the SOPA and PIPA bills in the US. The record labels' enforcement strategy has gone through many iterations and deserves credit for adapting to the changing realities of the market, albeit at something of a pedestrian pace. A single mindedness in combating piracy has not always been conducive to winning the hearts and minds of the public, but it has kept the labels' agenda firmly at the centre of the debate and it won some important legislative concessions. Courtroom action against piracy entrepreneurs also successfully closed down many piracy businesses while suing file sharers has given consumers little excuse for not knowing that downloading music from file sharing networks is illegal.[126] But what all of the labels' enforcement strategy has patently failed to do is irrefutably reduce piracy and stem the decline in sales.

Labels and rights bodies have an ever-growing body of data to support arguments, but no definitive 'smoking gun' evidence, and all the while music sales continue to tumble. Though the labels' enforcement strategy has evolved over time, it has remained on the back foot, responding to the changing piracy landscape rather than setting the agenda.

125 http://arstechnica.com/tech-policy/2012/08/french-anti-p2p-agency-hadopi-likely-to-get-shut-down/
126 In fact one could argue that the pendulum has swung too far in the other direction with a growing number of consumers unsure of the legality of licensed services such as Spotify.

Of course this dynamic is inherent in any enforcement strategy but it unambiguously reveals the paramount importance of the labels doing all they can to get the licensing strategy right. Unless the licensed digital music marketplace provides genuine and compelling alternatives to piracy, then no amount of enforcement will stimulate dynamic market growth. For as long as a demand vacuum exists – which currently continues to be the case – piracy will find a way of filling the gap. Put another way, it simply does not matter how big the record labels' stick is if the carrot is small and unappetizing.

Fighting Technology With Technology

With lobbying and legal action yielding modest results labels – and particularly their trade bodies – began to develop extensive technology capabilities to open up a new additional front in the war against piracy. This included creating their own versions of file sharing clients so that they could invisibly navigate through the networks harvesting data on the people using the networks. This approach gave the labels the twin benefit of being able to identify file sharers for legal process as well as acquiring a deep insight into how file sharers were behaving.[127] The labels did not just use technology as a defensive weapon, often devising ways to use it offensively such as seeding P2P networks with spoof files. These files were tagged to appear like genuine music files but instead contained silence, a super short loop of the track or anti-piracy messages. The one controversial course of action that was discussed behind closed doors but never implemented at scale was seeding P2P networks with viruses. The tactic would have undoubtedly been highly successful in deterring users away from P2P networks but would have created a huge risk of legal culpability on behalf of the labels with respect to damage to file sharers' computers. The experience of Japan shows us just what impact could have been had: the popular Japanese file sharing network Winny became infested with worm viruses called 'Antinny' in 2003. The spread became so endemic that the popularity of the network collapsed and Japanese consumers never regained their trust of PC file sharing networks.

In the early 2010's the labels began to step up their pursuit of another 'offensive' technology tactic: IP Filtering – also known as domain blocking, a tactic which may yet prove to be the music industry's most effective enforcement tool, despite the SOPA legislative setback. IP filtering stops consumers being able to access specific sites and domains, normally by domain level blocks put in place by the user's ISP. IP filtering has worked effectively in many markets, such as the UK where key sites like the Pirate Bay have been blocked by ISPs at the labels' behest. Although IP filtering is a far from watertight enforcement methodology it arguably has much clearer immediate effect than judicial and legislative efforts, and most importantly is less toxic from a PR perspective. Targeting piracy entrepreneurs and individual file sharers had created very real and tangible victims around which popular sentiment readily coalesced, domain blocking though has no such tangible victim. What it does have however is the more ephemeral but vastly important and emotive debate around freedom of speech and internet freedoms more broadly. Critics argue that IP filtering strikes at the very heart of the freedom and impartiality of the internet, that blocking domains is nothing more than censorship. From a pure libertarian perspective the critique holds water but in the context of a young medium establishing its identity the argument is some distance from incontrovertible truth. Over the coming decades legislation, regulation and business and cultural practices for the internet will become more defined in just the same way that they did for the previous global platforms of telephony, radio and TV. In these still early days it is easy to be caught in the excitement of the

---

127 As the saying from Sun Tzu's 'Art of War' goes: "Know your enemy."

moment and to think that fundamental rules of society and business do not apply to the web. To some degree this worldview is a product of the culture of free – free in terms of no cost and in terms of no restrictions – that raced through the veins of the internet's pioneers. The internet is not a different world, it is part of wider societies, political systems and business environments across the globe. As such it will ultimately have to conform to the demands of these if it is to remain a mainstream component of each of them. Granted the internet is utterly unprecedented in terms of its ability to create a sense of global uniformity and of challenging traditional out dated practices. But for better or for worse – and sometimes both – the established orders in business, finance, politics and society will have their voices heard and heeded. We are only in the earliest stages of this process, with events in 2013 such as Google agreeing to block results for a large number of child pornography search terms and the FBI closing the online black market the Silk Road both illustrative of the first signs of law and order being imposed on the web's wild west. IP filtering fits part of this narrative, what is not resolved is whether the appropriate reference point is combating shoplifting in the high street or information censorship in totalitarian regimes.

A Cautionary Enforcement Tale

Attempts to use technology to combat piracy have not been entirely constrained to the macro level. UK independent label Ministry of Sound decided to try using technology to address the impact piracy was having on its business. The label's experience however has a dark twist and acts as a cautionary tale for record labels and artists. Ministry of Sound's CEO Lohan Presencer has long assumed the view that piracy "is not something we can have an impact on. It is a fact of life, you cannot stop the rain from falling. But we have always been open to ways of trying to lessen the commercial impact on our business." Presencer was approached by a company that claimed it would be able to identify the people downloading Ministry of Sound albums illegally and would be able to obtain their postal addresses from IPSs using a UK legal procedure called a Norwich Pharamacol Order.

Up until this point all of the legislative three strikes efforts adhered to the telcos' position that customer addresses were confidential and should not be handed over to the labels. Hence the establishment of the HADOPI body in France and the reliance upon the telcos to send warning letters in the UK and US. Being able to get ISPs to hand over postal addresses so easily seemed to be too good to be true, but it did indeed work. The company showed Presencer that "40,000 people in the UK alone were downloading our compilations every week. We were horrified. So we started working with the company via a small ISP, getting infringers' addresses and then sending them warning letters in the post, they could avoid legal action by deleting the files and making a small contribution to our legal costs. Speeding fines disincentivize speeding, why shouldn't that work for music piracy?" The initiative worked surprisingly well and Presencer decided to step it up a notch by going next to the largest UK ISP British Telecom (BT). It was at this point though that things took a decidedly downward turn. BT resisted delivering the names, driving up their legal costs and then sent Ministry of Sound a legal bill for £150,000. Ministry's website then received a denial of service attack from Anonymous and their lawyers received a bomb threat – the firm eventually had to change its name. Ministry of Sound was made to feel the wrath of the piracy community for daring to try to protect its intellectual property as Lohan recalled: "All this for trying to stop piracy and seek some sort of compensation for illegal use of our content. We just had to back down. The world is stacked against the small guy."

Ultimately piracy enforcement strategy is only ever going to be partially effective, technology will always be one step ahead of the music industry's counter measures. Nonetheless the industry remains committed to the fight and to expanding its enforcement arsenal though industry bodies are now more cautious with their PR strategies so as not to distract from labels' innovation efforts. Therein lies one of the perennial problems with piracy enforcement: it diverts crucial efforts and expertise away from developing and supporting compelling legal alternatives. It also runs the risk of rights holders relying too heavily on anti-piracy strategy as an alternative to innovation as Cooking Vinyl's Martin Goldschmidt argued: "The industry has used piracy as a rationale for protecting a completely failed business model. They failed to recognize behaviour had shifted. What it should be about is understanding where consumers want to go, and embracing and monetizing that. If you fight your consumer you're dead. You cannot fight piracy without an alternative business model to back it up. The carrot must be significantly bigger than the stick."

The Statistics War

Another key strand of the piracy debate has been the confusing morass of conflicting data from all vested interests. Rights owners had originally seen data as an opportunity to level the playing field in an online environment where the dialogue was so heavily skewed towards the anti-label and anti-copyright advocates. Bodies such as the RIAA and IFPI had their PR work cut out for them and it became clear that the labels' opinions alone were not going to sway the debate. So they resolved to seeding the marketplace with data and data-evidenced argument. This ranged from straightforward consumer survey data indicating that file sharers spent less money on music through to sophisticated models that attempted to quantify the revenue impact of piracy on the music industry.[128] Much of this data was also submitted to politicians as quantitative evidence in support of their direct lobbying efforts. If the labels had been hoping for their data to bring a definitive close to the impact of piracy debate they were to be soon disappointed. The problem with statistics in the internet age is that data, just like music, is no longer a scarce commodity. Not only is virtually every data point ever published now available online, any organization, company or other vested interested can easily commission a consumer survey and publish the results online as 'definitive evidence' to support their argument. Anyone with even a passing familiarity with consumer surveys will understand how easily the results of a survey can be determined by the phrasing of the questionnaire and the presentation of the data. Indeed, as the famous phrase goes, there are "lies, damned lies and statistics."[129] Unfortunately the record labels, and in particular their industry bodies, were not always immune from massaging the data themselves and sometimes tried to push their estimates too far. So the labels found themselves hit with a data-double-whammy of a growing distrust of their data evidence and a surge of counter-evidence. The net result, rather than bringing definitive clarity, was to make observers and the general public increasingly sceptical of both sides of the argument. Politicians too began to question whether the data being presented to them as evidence was actually that, or instead political spin.[130] The net result is a debate that is as cloudy as it has ever been.

---

128 For sake of full disclosure, the author was the lead analyst on industry loss model projects for the BPI and the NVPI. These models – conducted by JupiterResearch and by Forrester Research respectively – estimated the total amount of recorded music revenue in the UK and in Holland that had been lost, and would be lost in the subsequent five years as a direct result of online piracy. It is important to note that piracy was modelled as just one factor among many, including wallet share competition.
129 This quote was originally attributed to the 19th century British Prime Minister Benjamin Disraeli but has subsequently been attributed to American author Mark Twain.
130 The author experienced this process directly, being summoned by a government minister to explain the methodology employed in a research project.

Piracy's Heavy Impact on Artists

Although significant questions remain about enforcement strategy, there is little remaining ambiguity in the debate around piracy's impact on the music industry. Throughout much of the first decade of digital music numerous commentators, lobbyists and academics built arguments that piracy was a positive force for the music industry. But now, with more than a decade of global recorded music revenue decline and an increasingly bleak music sales outlook for the middle tier of musicians there are few who would argue with the assertion that there is at the absolute least a correlation between piracy's rise and industry decline. That is not to say that there are not still concerted efforts to build a case for piracy's positive impact, but most fall back on overused yet unsupported arguments from yesteryear. Two prevailing lines of thinking are 1) that artists should be happy with their lot and not prostitute their art and 2) that artists can earn their living from live, merchandize and brand sponsorships. As we saw in the Artist's Story most of the assumptions about the contribution of live to artist income are flawed and mistake ticket seller, and ticket reseller, prosperity for artist prosperity.[131] Many academics and observers also get confused by the fact that some of the most engaged music buyers also download illegally, not understanding that piracy is just one of multiple digital activities that many tech savvy music fans conduct.

In truth, outside of the superstar category, artist income has declined markedly as piracy has risen, and most likely largely because of it. The BPI's Geoff Taylor believes that fewer artists now have long-term careers now: "This may reflect the greater choice of music that consumers now have, but also the long-term impact of piracy. Piracy reduces sales, which means that fewer albums make a positive return on investment – so options for later albums are often not taken up, given disappointing sales. I would like to hope that if we can do more to push piracy to the margins online, it will help sustain longer artist careers." Some artist have felt the impact more keenly than others though as Taylor also noted: "Illegal downloading has been very prevalent among young males. Ironically, this means that new rock music – a genre that is very popular in that demographic – has been particularly hard hit, making it more difficult for talented rock bands to get signed and break through. Pop has weathered the storm better."

Streaming: the Cure for Piracy?

When Daniel Ek launched Spotify into the world, the ability of the service to reduce piracy took centre stage in his pitch to labels and to media. The thinking was that if people could access al the music in the world legally without having to pay for it one song at a time then piracy would wane. Though the reasoning was sound enough it has thus far proved difficult to demonstrate definitive causal effect. The reason lies in the fact that the free tiers of streaming music services – the parts most likely to compete directly with piracy – are not a like-for-like replacement. Whereas a file sharer can do anything that he wants with the files he downloads, put them on any device, share with others, a free streaming user cannot do any of those things, cannot listen on demand on his mobile device and has to tolerate adverts and usually listening restrictions. Streaming's most likely impact on piracy is to make file sharers download less, becoming a sampling tool for them to decide what to download from Torrents in order to listen to on their phones and tablets, and to simply keep. All of which is an ironic echo of how many music buyers learned to use P2P networks as a tool for deciding which songs to buy. Thus streaming has had less of an impact in the absolute numbers of file sharers than it has helped reduce

---

131 There are few robust, evidence based arguments for piracy's supposed positive impact on music revenue, but there are many flawed ones such as the LSE's 2013 paper Copyright and Creation: A Case for Promoting Inclusive Online Sharing.

the amount of music that people pirate. Early indications from Nordic markets suggest that streaming can help drive music sales, but the impact on piracy is harder to quantify definitively.

This however should not detract from the ability of streaming to dent overall file sharing volumes as Spotify's Director of Economics Will Page argued: "You can see that streaming takes the heat out of piracy. This is especially visible in the case of Rihanna's single Diamonds, as you can see the sales-to-piracy ratio improving once the track was on the Spotify service. An intuitive question to ask is this: would the Torrents have taken off had she been on the service from day one?" It is also clear that streaming services are among the best tools for helping piracy addled countries start on the road to recovery. In markets such as Spain, Italy, Portugal and Greece, where piracy has been pervasive for so long, attempting to convince consumers to pay €0.99 for a song is simply not a viable option. In these markets where years of ubiquitous piracy educated consumers that music should be free, the best way to fight free is of course with free itself. In these markets piracy has often evolved as a digital extension of existing behaviour, so the education process is going to be a long term challenge. In Spain physical music piracy had become so prevalent and had damaged the domestic repertoire sector so much that Spanish music aficionados would turn to 'La Manta' chart to identify the hottest new Spanish music. 'La manta' is Spanish for 'the blanket' which counterfeit CD sellers would display their merchandise upon on street corners. Spotify's Page sees Spain as a key opportunity for streaming to undo some of the damage of piracy: "If there is an example of a large music market that needs fixing, then it has to be Spain. I was shocked to learn that from January to October 2012, the lowest sales of a number "1" album was 1,057, and for singles/tracks it was 2,673. I would like to think we can offer this troubled market some light at the end of the tunnel".

The Experience Innovation Threat

Perhaps the biggest surprise of piracy is that it has restricted its innovation to the mechanics of file sharing, rather than innovating the user experience. On this count due credit must be paid to the music industry's anti-piracy strategy in that the piracy innovators have been too preoccupied with outsmarting the labels' counter measures to focus on anything else. So although piracy is more fragmented and harder to police than ever before, it continues to deliver aesthetically dull user experiences just when legal music services are undergoing a user experience renaissance. The nightmare scenario for media companies is that the piracy innovators turn their attentions to developing great user experiences rather than just secure means of acquiring content. What if, for example, a series of open source APIs were built on top of some of the more popular file sharing protocols so that developers can create highly interactive, massively social, rich media apps which transform the purely utilitarian practice of file sharing into something fun and engaging? Such an outcome would utterly cripple the digital music market. Piracy sites and networks emerged in the years when digital was predominately about infrastructure but we are now in the experience era and for now the legitimate market has an advantage as Peter Sunde observed: "The file sharing community has gone stagnant, the user experience sucks on file sharing, it is all about infrastructure. Apple is rising up not because of technology but because of user experience." The nightmare scenario for the music industry would be for the piracy sector to turn its attentions to developing high quality, interactive user experiences to wrap around free, unlicensed music. So far the only real effort in this direction has been on the video side of things with the Netflix look alike Popcorn Time that delivers movie and TV show streams from P2P torrents. No one has yet applied that sort of approach to music P2P. While piracy innovation efforts are focused on privacy and anonymity the legitimate digital music market has the advantage, whether it can capitalize upon it is another issue entirely.

Next Generation Piracy

In many respects the focus on P2P misses the point about piracy in the 2010's. In the late 1990's and 2000's P2P networks were the only serious piracy game in town. But by the mid 2000's some consumers had started reacting to music industry piracy enforcement by leaving P2P networks for non-network alternatives such as hard drive swapping, Bluetooth swapping and even dark nets. Although each one of these tactics was small scale on its own, together they began to add up to scale. By the late 2000's in some markets, including Germany, where P2P had declined in the face of law suits, the net audience for non-network piracy was higher than it was for P2P. Now that trend continues apace but with mobile as the catalyst. Free music download apps are now used by 11% of consumers, rising to 22% for 18-24 year olds, meanwhile just 7% of consumers use P2P to download any type of content, not just music (see Figure 53). These apps have a veneer of legitimacy because they are readily downloaded from Apple's and Google's official app stores, most often topping the music app charts in each store. While they position around downloading legal free music from legitimate destinations, this cover story holds as much water as did Napster's and Kazaa's claims they were predominately for legitimate purposes. An equally important additional strand to non-network piracy today is that of YouTube rippers, accounting for a further 5% of consumers. Again these apps give the impression of being legitimate because Apple and Google approve them for their app stores despite the fact they are clear breach of the terms and conditions of YouTube, allowing users to turn all music videos into downloads on their phones. Often this is done with a neat playlisting interface that rivals the iTunes mobile experience. This is where cutting edge mobile user experience meets piracy. Once these apps have hit the top end of the music charts record labels take notice and work with Apple and Google to ensure the downloading functionality is disabled resulting in a torrent of bad reviews, clearing the way for the next near-identical app to take its place. If P2P enforcement felt like whack-a-mole, this is like trying to fight a highly infectious virus. One might question why Apple and Google are happy to let these apps rise to prominence in the first place, especially as Google's very own YouTube is the core target for them. The answer is quite simply that delivering a high quality mobile experience for their users is a far higher priority than music rights enforcement for both companies. One senior record label executive, when presented with this data, argued that this mobile era non-network piracy did not give cause for concern in the way that P2P did because it is typically used to pirate smallish quantities of music such as albums and playlists rather than an entire artist's discography. Unfortunately that viewpoint is grounded in an out dated worldview. Consumers do not need to hoard music anymore. In the early 2000's there was a genuine sense of needing to fill up with vast quantities of music before the tap was turned off. But that was the psychology of a generation of consumers conditioned to the ownership model. Today's digital natives have no need to hoard files. Every single song is available at the swipe of a finger on YouTube. Instead all they need from piracy is snack sized chunks of music to have with them on the go. And because these consumers engage less in albums, instead more frequently flitting across a broad selection of artists a few tracks at a time, mobile apps such as these are the perfect fit for their needs. As such, this new generation of piracy technologies are every bit as much of a threat as their P2P predecessors. More so in fact because of their pseudo legitimacy and highly user friendly interfaces.

FIGURE 53

The New Face Of Music Piracy

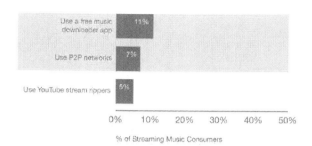

% of Streaming Music Consumers

MIDiA Research Consumer Survey 06/14 (UK and US) n = 2,000

Conclusion: An End in Sight?

P2P file sharing kick started the digital music revolution and Napster and BitTorrent will rightly go down in history as two of the great consumer technology innovations. Their legacy, for better and for worse, is more profound and farther reaching than that of iTunes. File sharing changed consumers' relationship with music for ever and by doing away with scarcity shook the music industry to its very core, shattering business models and revenues streams, and transforming power relationships across the value chain.

Piracy is a much less central issue than it was up to the late 2000's but it remains particularly prevalent in many emerging digital music markets such as China, India, Russia and Brazil. Although this presents its unique set of challenges for the nascent legitimate digital sector in these markets there can be immediate opportunity to convert piracy to paid as Cooking Vinyl's Goldschmidt observed: "I learned in China that putting things out legally will immediately take 10% of the pirate market share, reducing piracy from 100% of the market to 90%."

From the launch of Napster and throughout much of the 2000's the war on piracy was asymmetrical: although the labels had the heavy artillery when it came to the legal equation, the legitimate music services were drastically under gunned and simply could not compete on a level footing with P2P. Now music services have immense catalogues and robust free tiers, resulting in a much more level playing field. YouTube and Soundcloud have seized the free music mantle. They also have high quality user experiences to tip the scales in their favour. Piracy has not gone away and continues to dent music sales and next generation mobile piracy apps are very real concerns. But P2P file sharing may well be nearing its twilight years, in part because of the rise of non-network piracy but also because the user need that piracy met is fading in the age of the cloud as Roger Faxon observed: "[P2P] Piracy is an expression of hoarding, we have grown up to perceive music as a scarce good. The whole psychology of music consumption has changed." Though illegal streaming and other technologies are on the rise, P2P file sharing was the killer app of the post-analogue transition phase, but in the cloud based consumption era it is becoming as out dated as the horse and trap was when the first Model T rolled off the production line.

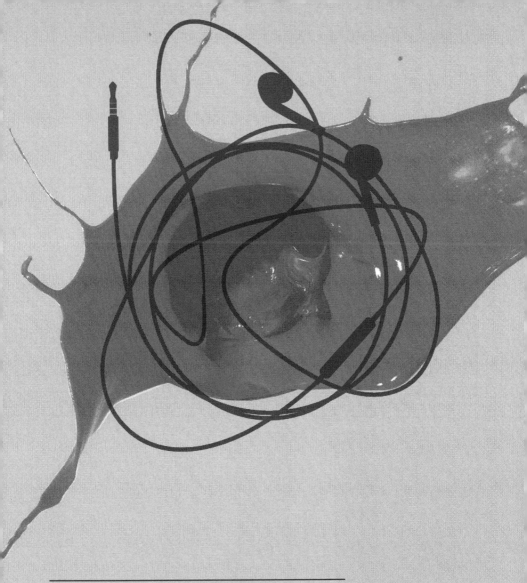

Part 3:
Vision for the Future

Awakening by Mark Mulligan

Chapter 13: Hurdles

Immense progress has clearly been made since digital music first started bubbling its way up into the music market and it is clear that a corner is being turned. But the route to success is not an inevitable path, with a host of hurdles and disruptive threats that need navigating first. We are now in the fourth five year window of digital music (see Figure 54). Each of those phases has heralded transformative change, with each building on the former and leveraging contemporary technology to the full. Though it is still too early to make the definitive call on which crop of services will define the latest phase, it is most likely to be the lean back Listen Services such as MusicQubed, Songza and Mix Radio that deliver highly curated music experiences. The experimentation with cheap subscription pricing by some of these will also prove pivotal to this next phase of digital music.

FIGURE 54

We Are Entering the Fourth Five Year Phase of Digital Music

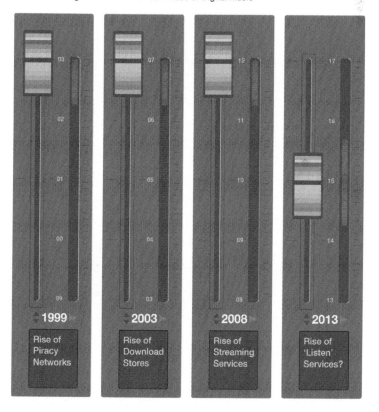

But for all the progress, the CD was still the largest single music product category in 2014, accounting for nearly half of global revenues. Apple got the digital market through the first lap, and streaming services are now supercharging the spending of those same customers. But there are a host of industry issues that need to be fixed before the digital music market can start to move towards the mainstream. Music services and artists alike struggle for commercial sustainability while a lack of transparency plagues the industry. The decisions that will be made over the next two years will determine whether history looks back at these as simply the growing pains of a new market or irreconcilable structural failings. Some of these are long term underlying components of the space, others the result of more recent change. All however need fixing:

- Rights fragmentation and complexity: Copyright itself is fundamentally sound but its mechanics are not. The relative simplicity of the analogue copyright landscape has been replaced with an excessively complex intertwined mess. Just to secure the publishing rights for a single song, but with multiple writers, for one country can easily require permission from 3 or 4 different rights owners, while most music services have catalogues comfortably in excess of 20 million tracks. Multiply that over multiple territories and millions of songs and the scale of the problem is immediately apparent.[1] The other consequence of this situation is that different fees can be charged for each right by each rights owner. Which means that songwriter x may get paid less for writing more of a song than songwriter y because songwriter y's publisher had negotiated directly with music services while songwriter x still relies upon a collection society. Matters are complicated one step further by the fact many of the PROs – though most certainly not all – are slow moving by technology market standards. Securing licenses can typically take a year, sometimes 3 or 4. In a year an entire digital market can come and go – just ask Turntable.FM. For companies of the scale of Apple or Google securing licenses is an operational inconvenience. For small start ups with limited resources and licensing expertise but that are the lifeblood of innovation, it a strategic dead end. Unable to get the operational certainty that they have legally acquired all of the rights across all of the territories small start ups are forced to either push ahead regardless – and risk legal action – or simply launch in a small handful of markets. The net result is that the market is skewed towards the big players, most of whom do not sell music for music's sake but rather to help them sell their core products.[2] Deezer's former CEO Axel Dauchez went as far as calling rights fragmentation the 'cancer of music licensing'.[3] Matters are complicated further by publishers now seeking a higher share of rights payments from music services. In truth too much of digital copyright is rooted in analogue era practices. Licensing discussions get bogged down in issues such as distinguishing whether a digital file counts as a performance or a so-called mechanical right, differences that made sense in physical analogue products but have little relevance in the digital era. It is the licensing equivalent of trying to work out where the gear stick is on a horse drawn carriage.

  SOLUTIONS: Sadly the structure that exists around copyright is too large, too rigid and too entrenched for change to occur at both the pace and scale required. Legislators have tried to intervene, sometimes with success – e.g. Sound Exchange in the US – but usually they have only succeeded in making things worse, such as in Europe.[4] Such a comprehensive

---

1   Even a catalogue of say 4 million songs with just 1 songwriter for each translates into 800 million works to be identified and licensed for a service that launches in 100 territories.
2   Apple sells music to sell iDevices, Google to propagate Android and Amazon uses music as the bait to hook customers in so that it can sell them much higher margin products such as PCs and fridge freezers.
3   Quoted from a panel discussion moderated by the author at the World Creators Summit 2013 in Washington DC.
4   The European Commission's half baked attempts to liberalize the European rights landscape while simultaneously not wanting to upset key stakeholders has resulted in a fudge that has worsened the status quo. It is this very action that has

programme of reform is needed that it would take a whole extra book to explain in sufficient detail. A boiled down headline summary list of actions reads as: establish rights portals where licensees can identify who owns what rights and where they can be licensed; deploy beta licenses that evolve with the financial growth and of start ups; improve reporting systems and data technology; consolidate and / or pool rights; establish one stop licensing solutions and maybe even collective licensing.[5] None of these solutions are easy but the change they will herald is crucial for the long-term viability and sustainability of the digital music market.

- Relationships: Since the mid 2000's increasingly large expanses of clear blue water have emerged between the positions of rights holders and technology companies, especially among Google and many of the telcos. Music was crucial to the early growth of broadband and is one of the most widely conducted activities on smartphones and tablets. It is also a huge source of traffic – and therefore advertising – for Google. But of course all of these behaviours can be, and usually are, conducted without any revenue being generated for rights labels, publishers or artists e.g. listening to already owned music on a phone, downloading music from a Torrent on a PC. Thus any licensed alternative is going to by definition be far less profitable for technology companies. This is why Amazon and Google, rather than licensing point-and-match locker services initially opted for the much less convenient-for-user but license-fee-free, DMCA-compliant upload locker services.[6] It was a natural progression for many big tech companies to start to try to change copyright law as an adjunct to licensing. Sometimes this activity is overt and transparent, such as lobbying legislators. But on other occasions it is more covert, such as Google sponsoring research and apparently independent blog posts on copyright reform and the impact of piracy, or supposed lack thereof, on music sales. This makes for an incredibly schizophrenic value chain. Companies like Google on the one hand license services such as Play Music All Access, but on the other lobby against the rights holders and post take down notices to chillingeffects.org. This rights frenemy posture creates unnecessary tension and conflict between rights holders and technology companies, breeding a mistrust that pollutes everything, everywhere.

SOLUTIONS: More dialogue is needed between rights holders and technology companies. Virtually all dialogue between the two constituencies occurs either in commercial negotiations or in court rooms, both of which engender adversarial relationships. Technology companies and rights holders have more common ground than either imagines, but need to discover it by engaging in regular informal and formal dialogue that occurs strictly outside of the confines of commercial constraints. The more that each side can better understand the other and identify common strategic objectives, the more likely that the digital music market can evolve

---

enabled many publishers to withdraw their rights from collection societies, thus increasing fragmentation, not reducing it.

5   Collective licensing for recorded works would allow music services to secure the licenses from a centralized body at statutory agreed rates. This is the model that is currently used in the US for DMCA compliant services such as Pandora, with statutory body Sound Exchange administering rights collections and payments. It is highly unlikely that record labels, major labels in particular, would opt to give up their right to negotiate directly with music services. This is not just because they would lose their ability to negotiate commercially favourable terms, but also because they would face the possibility of losing control of what music services get licensed to. Although this would clearly have some innovation positives for the digital music marketplace it would also bring significant risk of disruption. Label licensing strategy is not just geared around getting the best possible deal for the label – though of course that plays a big role – but it also focuses on ensuring a balanced marketplace evolves, one with clearly distinct segments, pricing tiers and positioning. Thus for collective licensing of recorded rights to even stand more than a fleeting chance of implementation, labels would need up front assurances of watertight checks and balances, which would most likely include the right to say 'no' to any single service. Though this may seem like a fundamentally unworkable compromise for a compulsory licensing framework, the benefits of licensing standardization would still be great. Cliff Fluet made the case for collective licensing: "The CD operates under a collective license. Radio works under collective license. We need a rights framework that ensures integrity of rights and that people are fairly remunerated."

6   With upload locker services users manually upload copies of their music to the cloud, creating new cloud copies of their music. With a point-and-match service users simply match their music against a preexisting complete catalogue in the cloud and then access the songs they own from that cloud catalogue. The former requires no licenses under the terms of the DMCA. The latter requires licenses from rights holders.

in ways that brings greater benefit to all parties. This approach requires far more trust than currently exists and that trust will take time to earn. Rights holders and technology companies alike worry that the other party would in such circumstances be waiting to jump on a passing casual remark as a legally binding precedent for negotiations. So this process needs to start small and informal, building trust one small piece at a time before progressing onto something far more ambitious. Years of mutual mistrust cannot be wiped out in an instant.

- Commercial sustainability: The VC driven, five-year start up life cycle has created a perpetual state of impermanence in the digital music market. The pervasiveness of laser-focused product strategy and grow-to-exit business strategy skew the market away from holistic, robust and sustainable business models. Start ups typically expend their investment acquiring customers in the quickest possible manner rather than pursuing sustainable growth. When this is done by market leading start ups, the rest often have to play by the same rules or fail, even when it means sacrificing their commercial sustainability. Consumers feel the pinch when start ups are acquired by bigger companies that seek commercial return and start to turn off features such as free access. And of course start ups do not have any exclusive on unviable business models. Big technology companies continue to show insatiable appetite for running digital music services as loss leading, or at best break even, businesses to help sell their core products. Which in turns sets the tone for licensing standards, with rights holders working on the principle of 'if that's what Apple pays, then that is what the market pays'. Consequently digital music has become a low margin business that is much easier to be in if you have big pockets and can rely on other revenue streams to pay the bills. The sustainability problem is less obvious to record labels because so many digital services pay advances and agree to minimum revenue guarantees so that the labels get a steady flow of digital income that is effectively divorced from the viability of the services. Because the law of averages dictates that only a small share of services will be successful, the majority of services do not achieve sustainability while paradoxically label digital revenue does. The already difficult situation is compounded by publishers looking to increase their share of royalty payments. Although they expect the majority of the extra income to come from labels, digital music service margins will most likely also be further squeezed.

SOLUTIONS: Rights holders need to do more to help smaller, early stage start ups succeed and in return start ups need to give more back to rights holders. But the reciprocal payment needs to be in kind, rather than cash. Start ups need to reach out to key rights holders much earlier in their business journey than they do now – which is almost always not until the licensing stage. This way start ups and rights holders can get on the same page, align strategic objectives and ensure that the licensing process, when it comes, is far smoother. It also means that rights holders – labels in particular – need to be more flexible with deal structures. Labels have already done much praiseworthy work in this direction but more needs to be done. For example advances should not automatically be pegged against the size of investment a start up has acquired but should be mapped against the degree of effort the label needs to put into managing the relationship. The scale of license fee should ideally start off small and grow in scale with the business. In return start ups will need to give labels much greater visibility of their user numbers. Start ups also need to acquire a greater degree of responsibility, developing sustainable business models that are not predicated on simply reaching enough scale to achieve an exit.

- The good enough method: Because the biggest technology companies use music as a tool for selling their core products their focus inherently leans towards building services that are good enough for the task. If a locker service and a download store are going to be good enough to help sell a smartphone, why waste extra investment building a cutting edge music service that will win plaudits but may deliver little additional sales lift? Margin reduction is a hard enough sell when it is a business necessity let alone when it is simply for strategic largesse. The good enough method has served the big technology companies well, it has served Apple exceptionally well. The music industry however has fared less favourably. Instead of seeing digital music innovation rush ahead at the same pace as smartphones and tablets, the music industry has had to content itself with longer lulls between innovations. For example Google Play Music All Access was a fantastic version 1.0 product build but it did nothing to move the innovation needle. The world needed a Spotify successor not a Spotify imitator.

SOLUTIONS: It is time for the big players to move beyond me too strategies and work with rights holders to create truly ground breaking digital music products and experiences. For this to happen rights holders need to give them much more incentive to innovate more bravely. The big record labels all crave the scale of opportunity that the big technology companies offer but that all too often evaporates in the smoking ruins of another half-baked good enough service. The incentive will likely involve cold hard cash somewhere along the line but there are also many other assets of value that rights owners – and especially labels – have to offer, such as data and access to artists. Consumer technology companies love having famous pop and rock stars associated with their products. Technology companies could effectively become the music product R&D arms of record labels, with the two sets of parties working together to create music products that thrust the market forward in quantum leaps rather than in shuffling steps.

- Catalogue bloat: In the early days of digital music services were locked in a music catalogue size arms race. At the time there was some relevancy in the respective boasts as significant portions of the world's music were missing. Once the market matured and most labels had licensed, the obsession with catalogue size died away. After all what is the difference between five million songs and six million songs to the average consumer? But once the all you can eat subscription services started their land grab, the catalogue arms race recommenced, the logic being that if you were selling the value proposition of all the music in the world then you had to dazzle consumers with a truly bewildering quantity of music. The problem is that too much choice is in fact no choice at all, consumers become paralyzed by the Tyranny Of Choice. The supposed benefit of more choice has become a barrier to adoption, making digital music services too daunting a proposition to mass market consumers. And with 100,000 tracks being added every single month, the problem is worsening at an alarming rate. The issue is compounded by the contagion of catalogue spam. The majority of the new tracks appearing on digital music services are sound alikes, karaoke versions and shoddy covers. These cynically produced tracks are churned out in their thousands every single week with the sole intent of filling up the search results of digital music stores and services, distracting consumers away from the original tracks. Often the sound alikes are so similar to the original that most would not notice the difference. No one wins other than the contemptuous producers churning out this drivel.

SOLUTIONS: 30 million tracks is a meaningless number: it would take more than two centuries to listen to that much music. It is time to focus on delivering to consumers the relatively small number of tracks that matter to them, not 30 million that don't. Music services talk a good talk about discovery and curation but far too little progress has been made. Some services are beginning to understand that the best way to solve the problem is not to start with 40 million tracks and attempt to sign post a journey, but instead to start with a far smaller number of tracks and work up from there. Whichever end of the spectrum a music service occupies, discovery and curation cannot be optional appendages, instead they need to be as central to their core product DNA as playing an audio file itself. Also, concerted action needs taking against catalogue spam, with haste. While there may be some market for karaoke tracks – many consumers do love them – their place is not in the main catalogue of music services. They need filing away in separate karaoke sub-sections of music services. Sound alikes on the other hand have no place in digital music services, they need excising from digital music catalogues. Once the music services and digital distributors have weaned themselves from their catalogue size obsessions they will find turfing out the catalogue drivel a truly empowering experience. And if these sound alike producers really feel that their music has cultural value then they should feel absolutely free to launch their own music services populated solely with sound alike songs. I'm sure the public will come flocking...

- The static audio file quandary: Perhaps the most fundamental digital challenge that the music industry must address is that of creating truly digital era products. The digital music market has long been too preoccupied with retail and business models, with user experience being dragged along at a distance when of course it is user experience that should be driving the conversation. Despite all the innovation in content delivery – e.g. progressive downloads, cached streams, mobile streaming – the underlying product remains the same, namely a static audio file, streamed or downloaded. This has to change if digital music products are to have long-term relevance and viability. However good a business model might be, it matters naught if the product is a dud.

    SOLUTIONS: The music industry desperately needs extensive innovation from right across the value chains, that brings together experimentation and creativity from labels, artists, managers, songwriters, publishers, technology companies, device manufacturers, even live venues. The future of music products must be built upon a collective vision with shared principles and objectives, to build something that can truly be called digitally native. This is the topic of the next chapter.

The piracy UX innovation wildcard: If there is one indisputable success story for the music industry's war on piracy, it is that innovation in the piracy sector has been largely limited to anonymity and convenience. The presence of a permanent frontal attack has forced piracy innovators onto the back foot, inherently responding to industry counter measures and legal action. The emergence of BitTorrent in 2001 was arguably the last great piracy innovation. The nightmare scenario for the music industry would be if the piracy sector started to focus their efforts on creating high quality user experiences around unlicensed content. As we have seen, Popcorn Time is thus far the only serious move in this direction, other than mobile piracy apps. Should someone double down on creating a piracy sector next generation streaming service they would have none of the rights restrictions that currently prevent the legitimate sector building such products. If this did happen the music industry would have to dramatically overhaul its entire licensing and product strategies to play catch up, else be relegated to an also ran in a race it is just beginning to win.

Chapter 14: Business Models

The future evolution of digital music will be defined by the same three key factors that shaped its history, namely choice, scarcity and convenience:

- Choice: If there is one universal truth that the rise of digital music has taught us thus far it is that one size does not fit all. Digital consumers are faced with an abundance of choice of user experience, portability, size and type of catalogue, usage permissions and payment models. However it is clear that the balance needs to be struck, that an overabundance of product choice risks begetting confusion and fragmentation.

- Scarcity: There is also a more basic choice that digital consumers face: whether to pay or not to pay. Spending money on music has become the equivalent of an honesty box because music is no longer a scarce commodity.[7] Consumers choose to buy music because of one or more of four reasons:

  1. It is convenient e.g. buying downloads in iTunes

  2. It is a habit / they do not know any other way

  3. They are scared of the consequences of downloading illegally

  4. They really care about a particular artist

  Quite simply consumers need more reasons to pay for music. The solution lies in a mix of business models – which will be discussed in more detail in the next chapter – and product strategy. Scarcity needs reinventing for the digital era, and because content scarcity is gone for good, digital age scarcity must be built around scarcity of experience. It is a lesson that the big technology platforms learned fast and upon which the success stories of paid content are built. Xbox, Playstation, Kindle, iTunes: all of these platforms deliver scarce user experiences that cannot be replicated outside of these ecosystems. Sure you can download an episode of Madmen from a Torrent, but it will not seamlessly play on your iPad unless you download it from the iTunes Store. Similarly you can download cracked versions of Xbox games, but if you do so you risk losing access to Xbox Live, which can only exist within the Xbox ecosystem. In fact when Microsoft turned off access to Xbox Live functionality for gamers who had illegal copies of Xbox games on their devices there was uproar in the gaming community. It was a highly effective measure, illustrating the priceless value that Xbox Live represented to Xbox gamers. When it was launched it was little more than a gimmick but over the years it became established as integral to the value proposition of the Xbox, even though it is an entirely intangible service. This is how scarcity can be created in the digital era.

---

7   See chapter three for a detailed assessment of the role of scarcity.

- Convenience: The third key defining characteristic of the digital market – both in its licensed and illegitimate guises – is convenience. Ever improving connectivity and processing power raise consumers' expectations of frictionless content experiences. Analogue music experiences were inherently inconvenient, and although some traditionalists argue that there was a certain magic in the inconvenience of the physical experience, the fact remains that digital consumers expect something far smoother, quicker and more elegant. When convenience is done right it is enough to persuade consumers to pay for music despite boundless supplies of free music elsewhere on the web.

FIGURE 55

The Digital Music Strategy Consumer Targeting Pyramid

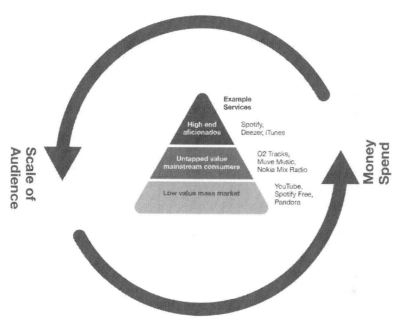

The future of the digital music market requires a coherent and consistent product and business strategy framework that harnesses choice, scarcity and convenience. Addressing all three requires a unity of vision that is currently lacking, with too many services inadvertently competing with each other for the same small selection of music consumers. The music industry needs a joined-up product and business strategy based upon a macro segmentation of the music consumer population. This translates into the Digital Strategy Pyramid, a structured hierarchy of business and product strategy in which all services and objectives have a clear place and direction of travel (see Figure 55). The Digital Strategy Pyramid works on the core assumption that there are three macro groups of music consumers, each with broad sets of common characteristics. Although more detailed segmentation and targeting are appropriate within each of three groups, the overlying framework provides clear parameters and boundaries to reduce unnecessary competitive overlap. The Digital Strategy Pyramid is mapped from low scale / high average revenue at the top through to large scale / low average revenue at the bottom:

- Top Tier: These are the core music fans and aficionados. Although relatively small in number they are the beating heart of music spending. These are the consumers who go to concerts regularly, engage with artists online and account for the majority of music spending. The products and business models built around these consumers should be focused on premium. That does not necessarily mean super deluxe digital box sets – although it can – but instead the majority of paid music products: albums, subscriptions etc. This was once the core of music product customers but is now consolidating around the rump of super engaged music fans, the vanguard of digital music adoption. These are the same consumers who drove the rise of iTunes and are now driving the – albeit smaller – rise of subscriptions. The temptation that must be avoided is to slow innovation down to the rate of the more mainstream early followers that are finally beginning, slowly, to go digital. This is same dilemma Apple faced following the runaway success of the iPhones: it had to slow down innovation to a rate that suited the less adventurous appetites of the tens of millions of new mass-market customers. This though is exactly why the innovation bar needs to be set high for the top tier of consumers: if they disappear, the recorded music industry follows. They cannot be taken for granted.

- Low Tier: At the opposite end of the consumer sophistication scale are the mass market consumers for whom music plays a far less prominent role. Many of these consumers either never bought music at all or have fallen out of the habit of doing so. The small share of them who do still buy have mostly not gone digital yet and rely on outlets like Best Buy, Carrefour and Tesco for their CD purchases. The low average value of these customers is offset to some degree by the fact that they are a huge addressable audience, representing in fact close to two thirds of all consumers. Such a large group simply cannot be ignored but at the same time they must not be chased at the expense of diverting attention from the upper tiers. These consumers either spend very little or nothing at all on music and are thus targets for free music business models such as ad supported streaming. Most of these consumers are unlikely to migrate their way up the value chain. This is why it is so important that streaming services that run ad supported tiers as a loss leading customer acquisition tool are able to identify and sunset out these customers rather than carry the commercial burden in perpetuity. But for services for whom advertising is the main business model this segment is the core audience. Spotify's January 2014 announcement to drop listening limits for free tier users risks bleeding Top Tier consumers long term into what should be the exclusive domain of the Low Tier, except of course for 'showing a bit of leg' to tempt Top Tier users into paid tiers. A cynic might argue that the move is more about killing off Spotify's competition than it is a structured approach to customer segmentation.

- Mid Tier: The growing dependence upon the ever-smaller Top Tier creates a clear strategic vulnerability for recorded music revenue. As valuable as the digital aficionados are, a music market that is built entirely around them will be a considerably smaller one than we have now. Little wonder then that record labels began in the late 2000's to prioritize working with services that had the potential of 'scale'. It is a smart strategy but must follow, rather than lead Top Tier product innovation efforts. The Mid Tier is clearly a route to scalable growth but this is set against the fact they are modest spenders. Full priced premium products such as 9.99 subscriptions will simply not gain meaningful traction among the Mid Tier even though the product proposition is a good fit. Monetization will thus centre around working with partners – such as telcos and device companies – who can subsidize some or all of the cost of premium products. Examples are two years of in-car music subscription included in the cost of the car, 12 months of a music subscription included the cost of a mobile subscription, a half priced music subscription bundled with a home broadband tariff. However the danger of this strategy of making premium music products feel like free, or close to free, is that it engenders a perception that they should always be free.

The Digital Strategy Pyramid also helps put each target consumer within a customer lifecycle path, identifying where they are on their music consumption journey and on which of three paths they should be set: stay the same, migrate up, migrate down. But it is only a macro framework within which specific business and pricing strategies need to be built that accounts for a complex interplay of factors including:

- The innovator hegemony: Arguably the biggest single barrier to the music industry pursuing transformational business strategy is not its own rate of travel but instead the intransigence of its three most important partners, Apple, Amazon and Google. In different ways each of these three are critical to the music business and they know it. The balance of power in the digital landscape lies firmly with these channel partners, forcing labels into choosing between doing something resource intensive with all major partners, or nothing at all.

- Pricing: The labels eventually succeeded in bringing variable pricing to downloads yet they have become enamoured with invariable pricing across most other music products. With the exception of a limited number of pricing experiments from small vendors such as MusicQubed, Bloom.fm and British Telecom, $/€/£9.99 has become the universal price point for portable subscriptions.[8] For digital music products to reach as wide a range of consumer segments as possible it is crucial that far more is done to experiment with pricing. This can range from elasticity experiments within the largest music services, through to testing a greater range of new price points with a larger number of smaller services. Labels fear lower priced tiers may steal customers from the top table but long term sustainability depends upon ensuring that as large a number of consumers are on the right product tier not that a small number have been inadvertently locked into the wrong one.

- Positioning: As Apple, Amazon and Google tighten their collective grip on digital music, labels will become increasingly tempted to protect big partner revenue, yet their ascendency is exactly the reason for experimenting more voraciously. With so much of the digital market concentrated in so few players the most disruptive impact any one licensed start up will have will be to compel those incumbents to respond with new products and features. They are not going to be instantly disrupted by any single licensed service.[9] Labels and publishers need to think strategically about how they license and to whom in order to create a sophisticated map of services that are positioned at distinct target audiences with distinct pricing and features.

---

8   $9.99 when converted at standard international currency exchange rates, is equivalent to €7.67 and £6.49 even though subscriptions are price uniformly at 9.99 across Europe and North America. Given that the costs of labels and publishers doing business in the UK are not the 35% higher than in the US that effective prices are, suggests that there is sufficient flexibility in the rights owners' operating margins to be more ambitious in pricing experimentation.
9   The emphasis on 'licensed' is crucial. As a measure of last resort, rights owners can turn off the tap to licensed services. However the opportunity remains for an unlicensed service to utterly disrupt the market in just the same way Napster did in the late 1990's.

- Service coexistence: There are more than 500 licensed music services across the world with many times that number of associated products such as discovery tools, games and social music apps. The result is a highly fragmented and confusing picture for anyone other than the most sophisticated of music consumers. There is no doubt that the digital dots need joining. In the near term rights owners will have to perform a delicate balancing act that allows for increased consumer targeting while simultaneously simplifying the user journey. In the long run however the situation could be far simple. Assuming that subscriptions overcome current sustainability, pricing and transparency issues, and if streaming service app and developer platforms flourish, then it is feasible that they will contribute to a far more cohesive digital music landscape. In this scenario music services merely become the fuel that powers a rich ecosystem of music experiences. Instead of having to go to multiple – and often incompatible – destinations music consumers could access them all within one single music subscription.[10] This would facilitate far easier customer targeting, segmentation and migration between price points.

Managing the interplay of these four interdependent factors is a phenomenally difficult task but must be done nonetheless and two specific priorities stand out:

1. Telco partners

2. Apps

Telco Partners

The transition of telcos from prospective perfect business partner to conduit for piracy caused considerable friction in the first decade of digital music as the BPI's Geoff Taylor explained: "We all felt that ISPs would be the perfect business partners. After all without content networks are a commoditized business. But the opportunity didn't translate because broadband providers made so much more money from data than they would have with music services." Not that telcos did not dabble in digital music but those that did exactly that, dabble, unsurprisingly found themselves at the helm of abject failures, while those that tried harder still couldn't crack Apple's iTunes walls. The emergence of app stores though opens up a new era of opportunity for telco music services, giving them a priceless window into the iTunes ecosystem and sophisticated Android users. Streaming is now centre stage of the new wave of app-enabled third party music service strategy and represents unprecedented telco opportunity. This is not only because it gives a route into iPhones and iPads, but because the subscription model fits more neatly with telcos' business models than download stores. There are a number of success stories in this new era of telco music:

- Telia / Spotify: Telia hard bundled Spotify into its mobile data tariffs in Sweden making the service available for no extra cost.[11] Telia heavily promoted the partnership and acquired a large number of customers. The partnership was a success for Telia in terms of branding and customer acquisition, and of course for Spotify who got invaluable exposure, marketing support and customer acquisition.

---

10 Ideally subscription services will also implement inter-service roaming, enabling users to move their cloud collections, playlists and apps between services. This remains a distant objective though, as subscription services view these assets as the very tools with which they can enforce customer loyalty. Much in the same way Android and Apple do with mobile apps and content. A similar problem existed in the early mobile industry when carriers each had their own proprietary SMS systems. Eventually the International Telecommunications Union (ITU) corralled the carriers into implementing interoperability to enable the cross-carrier SMS system we all take for granted today.
11 The term 'hard bundle' means that the service was automatically bundled in regardless of whether the consumer specifically requested it and does not therefore necessarily mean that the service was ever used by the customer.

- France Telecom / Deezer: This partnership was similar to Telia's but was hard bundled with home broadband packages instead of mobile. Both parties got clear benefit, with France Telecom including subscriber retention rates and Deezer getting the platform for global success.

- Cricket Wireless / Muve Music: Unlike the other two examples Muve is an in-house service developed by Cricket. Cricket, was a small regional US mobile carrier[12] that was experiencing poor core operational metrics and developed Muve to reverse the trend. Hard bundled into $50/$60/$70 monthly price plans on mid-range phones and targeted at Cricket's lower income user base Muve had the odds stacked against it. Despite this it proved a huge success, with Muve breaking the 2 million subscribers mark in 2013 representing more than a quarter of Cricket's entire mobile subscriber base. Muve also helped drive Cricket's core business metrics and position it for sale. Given the mass market, lower value profile of the audience Muve is one of the standout success stories of digital music. Muve did so well for a number of reasons including: understanding its predominately Mexican origin customer base incredibly well; getting really good (cheap) deals from labels because they convinced them they were targeting an otherwise unreachable segment for music services. It was strongly supported right across the Cricket business including, crucially, strong sales support such as incentives for sales staff and in-store out of the box instructions for users.

The common denominator of these case studies is that senior management bought into the vision and ensured it was sold in and supported across their organizations. They were all also measured across a comprehensive range of success metrics incorporating branding objectives and differentiation as well as harder measures such as churn reduction, net subscriber growth and ARPU.[13] Success stories such as these illustrate the potential benefits of digital music but there is still much distance to go. With the notable exception of Muve Music each of those examples are fixed term strategic marketing initiatives. The music industry's challenge for telco music strategy is how to move from a fling to a long-term relationship. To move from the foothold of telcos valuing music as a branding tool towards a Muve-like model where it becomes an integral part of the telco's business model. The reason that this all matters so much to the music business is that telcos are the best opportunity for delivering subsidized music products to consumers that are either heavily discounted or are free at point of consumption. Telcos present the best means of squaring the circle of generating premium revenues from lower spending consumers and as such are the best route to the Middle Tier. Even if they are not always the most likely to be success stories, many telcos – mobile carriers especially – will continue to demonstrate strong interest in digital music. Indeed as Omnifone's Phil Sant said of working with telco clients: "we've never needed to convince anyone they needed to be in the music game".

It is crucial though that the music industry does not mistake this latent interest for an opportunity for a quick buck nor for being a sure thing. There is huge competition for telco attention from other content and services, many of which are both better fits for telco business models and are also often much more straightforward industries to do business with. As one telco executive succinctly put it "music simply isn't that important to us and certainly not worth the hassle that launching a music service inevitably generates." Telcos are a potentially pivotal partner for the music industry but if that potential is

---

12 Cricket was acquired by AT&T in 2013.
13 Because of the vast complexities of calculating factors such as customer life time value and of appropriately allocating costs and revenue recognition across the various parts of large telco organizations, it is incredibly difficult to prove definitively the impact of a music service on core business metrics.

ever going to be realized they need to be given every ounce of support available.

After the App Bubble

In-app purchasing has quickly become established as the most effective method of monetizing digital content, with close to three quarters of app revenue coming from in app purchases.[14] The problem for the music industry is that the vast majority of this revenue comes from games. Although in-app games purchases are clearly a unique case, there are nonetheless many important lessons for the music business. While Spotify and Deezer have stirred up a hornets' nest of debate about the validity of the freemium model, the games sector has built a vibrant business around freemium that is not dogged by the concerns of the music sector. The difference is that the mobile games freemium model operates within mobile device-content ecosystem. In iOS the first payment is frictionless, with the billing relationship already established with Apple which contrasts sharply with establishing a new billing relationship with a new music service, navigating the hurdles of inconvenience and mistrust. In-app purchases are then equally effortless – perhaps too much so! – and a wide choice of cheap price points mean that the purchase consideration is minimal. It is this nearly imperceptible transition from free to paid that lies at the heart of the success of mobile gaming. One other factor plays a central role too: scarcity. Consumers pay for mobile games and the in-app purchases within them because they are consuming something not available elsewhere, a stark contrast to music. A Spotify customer still has his entire music collection and free access to all the music in the world with YouTube if he decides to stop paying his monthly subscription fee. But there is no other way to throw fuming feathered creatures at greedy pigs other than by playing Angry Birds. This is why the freemium debate is moot in mobile gaming.

Even without the asset of content scarcity at its disposal, music is well positioned to benefit from in-app streaming, whether that be topping up individual tracks in an album app or paying for a subscription. One hurdle that rights owners will need to help music services clear in the iTunes ecosystem is Apple's 30% fee on transactions. Adding nearly a third onto the cost of a song or subscription makes little sense to consumers and immediately negates the frictionless benefits of in-app purchasing. If labels and publishers want to harness the power of in-app purchasing they need think about sustainable ways of reducing their license fee rates for in-app purchases.

Despite all of the clear potential of apps, caution is needed. We are in a boomtown economy and it is a matter of when, not if, the app bubble will burst. The market is hurtling along so fast that sustainability and viability are disappearing out of sight for most sectors of the app economy. Currently the app economy is predominately two things:

1. A games economy

2. A marketing platform

With 60% of apps having 2,500 or fewer downloads, 67% of developers below the app poverty line and app discovery becoming quasi-impossible, a perfect storm is brewing.[15] A market realignment will occur, resulting in a major shakeout. This will not destroy the app market, instead it will strengthen it just in the way that the dot.com crash and the failure of WAP 1.0 (the over hyped first generation of mobile internet) helped create much more robust internet and mobile economies. There will undoubtedly be casualties, but

---

14 App analytics company Distimo reported that 71% of the revenue of the top grossing 250 iPhone apps in the US in February 2012 came from in-app purchases from free apps and a further 5% from in-app purchases in paid apps. Paid apps made up the remainder.
15 Developer Economics. Vision Mobile. Vision Mobile define the app poverty line as earning $500 or less per app per month.

if the music industry gets its timing right it will be in the right place to pick up the pieces and reap the rewards of being at the vanguard of the next phase of the app market.

Chapter 15: Product Strategy

Business models, back end systems and distribution channels all underwent dramatic change to enable the digital music market to exist. Music products however changed much more modestly, a failing that must be fixed if the digital market is to fulfil its potential. The sky rocketing adoption of smartphones and tablets has transformed consumer behaviour but at the same time also accentuates the innovation gap between these devices and digital music product strategy. These devices are designed for audio-visual, interactive experiences, not for listening to static audio files. Though music was the killer app of the monochrome screen iPod, in the era of retina display, touch screen, location aware tablets and smartphones music competes with literally millions of other apps.[16] Critically the majority of these digital era products such as Angry Birds and EA Games Real Racing utilize the full capabilities of the devices they are consumed on, from accelerometer, through graphics accelerator to multi-touch in ways that the static audio file simply does not. Of course listening to music is still one of the most popular activities on these devices, but it is something that is done in the back ground, in lean back mode while digital era content products require audiences to lean forward and interact.[17]

It is not just touch screen devices that make the case for an overhaul of digital music product experience. Since the mid 2000's consumers' broader digital experiences have transformed almost beyond recognition:

- Dynamic content: Facebook's Timeline feature has brought the concept of dynamically updated content to the mainstream.

- Video: YouTube, Hulu and iPlayer have put video at the centre of online entertainment.

- Social discovery: Services like Zeebox and GetGlue have extended communities around entertainment programming.

Many forms of traditional media have done more to reinvent themselves for the digital era than music has. TV was also once entirely a lean back medium, but has now acquired a strong lean forward focus thanks to innovations such as time shifting, the Electronic Programming Guide (EPG), on demand streaming, and real time chat via Smart TV apps and services. What makes a content type successful in the digital age is not whether it comes from old world media or from new world technology, but how it harnesses the capabilities of the digital environment. There are usually one or more of three key factors that contribute to the success of digital content products:

- Content: They utilize new forms of content created for digital era products that were not widely utilized in the analogue products.

- Features: They have new user features that consumers interact with on digital products.

---

16 By June 2013 Apple's App Store contained 900,000 apps, Google's Play store catalogue numbered 740,000 and Microsoft and Blackberry collectively numbered about 50,000. By the end of 2014 Google Play had 1.4 million and Apple's App Sore had 1.2 million.
17 A UK Music study attempted to attribute a monetary value to the value of music functionality as part of smartphones and tablets, using a conjoint survey analysis methodology. The report concluded that up to 4.35% of the price of a smartphone and 6.7% of the price of a tablet were attributable to music functionality in consumers' minds. The report can be found here: http://www.ukmusic.org/assets/media/UK%20Music%20-%20OO%20Copyright%20Research%20Presentation.pdf

- Functionality: Their underlying technology innovations that power, and are unique to, digital products.

This framework reveals that even that most traditional and analogue of products, the book, has multiple new mainstream content types such as Amazon Shorts – a digital interpretation of the novella – and episodic delivery of chapters.[18] These are new content innovations that appeal right across book audiences. By contrast the key music content innovations – stems for remixes, mash ups and unreleased tracks – tend to appeal more to the engaged Top Tier of music fans rather than the mainstream. With TV, non-traditional broadcasters such as Netflix and Amazon have brought content innovation to mainstream audiences by commissioning series such as Arrested Development and House of Cards that traditional broadcasters were unwilling to re-commission. Netflix's release of the entire series of House of Cards all at once turned the history of TV programming on its head. This is exactly the sort of brave and disruptive innovation the music industry can learn from. And it is not just new entrants that are innovating in the TV space, for example traditional broadcasters have created web only episodes – webisodes – such as the SyFy Battlestar Galactica webisode series 'The Resistance' distributed via YouTube and the BBC's pre-series iPlayer-only Sherlock mini-episode.

Digital music services such as Spotify and Deezer have done much to enhance the core user experience with innovations in discovery and free tiers. But these changes are dwarfed by the transformational change that gaming had to undergo in order to embrace the connected device opportunity. People tend to think of the games sector as native to connected devices but games' success on those platforms was built upon radical and disruptive innovation. Touch controlled games may now be the norm for portable gaming but it was not always so. In fact the touch screen is far from an ideal choice for a control mechanism because the gamer's fingers inevitably have to obscure some of the gaming display. And yet the gaming sector found ways to incorporate touch and all other major aspects of smartphone and tablet functionality. Games companies – both incumbents like EA Games and younger companies such as King. com, Rovi and Mojang – realized that games needed to be defined by the devices on which they would be consumed. This approach contrasts sharply with the dominant traditional media strategy of trying to squeeze analogue era products into digital formats. Games publishers reinvented gaming for connected devices and also for social platforms. The expansive remit of this reimagining encompassed everything from the very nature of the games themselves, through pricing to core usability. The smartphone and tablet revolution threatened the gaming sector to its core, posing major risk of cannibalization of established gaming platforms and devices, especially portable gaming devices such as the Play Station Portable and Nintendo DS.

Instead of running, the games industry stood its ground, embraced the disruption and raced forward at breakneck pace. Of course the process has seen the rise of new players, and a shift of balance of power among platform providers, but the net effect for the games industry has been growth and prosperity. The industry delivered an entirely new generation of gaming products and in doing so opened up a vast new seam of mass market gamers that had previously proved elusive.[19] Gaming companies also quickly learned to embrace in-app purchasing to drive unprecedented monetization of casual and core gamers alike. The result is utter domination of mobile app revenues by gaming companies. Games accounted

18 Episodic release of chapters is actually a return to a 19th century practice when authors such as Charles Dickens and Thomas Hardy released their books one chapter at a time in monthly magazines.
19 The casual gaming sector first rose to prominence in the mid 2000's with internet portals quickly learning that bored housewives were just as viable a target for games as teens and 20 something men. But it was the combination of the emergence of Facebook and the iTunes App store that really propelled casual gaming to the fore.

for every single app except one of the top 50 grossing on the US Play Store and all but three on the US Apple App Store in January 2014. These are the rewards that transformational innovation can bring and they set the standards to which music products must aspire.

The failure to date of music product strategy to truly seize the digital innovation mantle is not a reflection of intent per se, but instead the result of a combination of complex industry issues:

- Rights ownership: Record labels – currently the driving force in digital product licensing and business model innovation – only own a fraction of the rights necessary to power the next generation of music products. In fact they cannot even create digital albums with as much content as CD equivalents because they do not own the rights to the lyrics or many of the artist photos. Too many separate parties control the diverse mix of rights an interactive multimedia product requires. Even when all of the rights owners can be brought to the table, publishers most often do not have the same appetite for risk or commercial flexibility that a label often has. Unless something changes next-generation products will not get into the market place.

- Innovation vacuum: All of the big music industry innovations have come from technology companies, not the music industry.[20] But now technology companies have shifted focus and an innovation vacuum has arisen. For all of the record labels' valiant innovation efforts, they simply do not have the heritage, expertise or resources necessary to drive technology innovation of the nature and scale required. Small technology start ups are an ideal option for filling the breach, but their MVP feature focus and the quagmire that is music licensing stack the odds against the sector creating a true next generation music product that can scale.

- Mistaken identity: While the above two issues are governed by factors largely outside of the music industry's control, there is one for which blame can be laid squarely at its feet: a misunderstanding of what digital consumers value. The audio file that was the product is now just one component of an interactive, multimedia web. YouTube, the world's most popular music service, sets even the most mass market of expectations far above a static audio file. Fans, especially younger ones, expect much more than just the music. Indeed MTV's 2013 consumer research revealed that 53% of Millennials say the more an artist shares online about themselves, the closer they feel to them.[21] Labels routinely create vast quantities of this added value content but they do not consider it product; instead it is viewed as marketing content because music is the product. Of course this is culturally and creatively true, but from a product strategy perspective it is out dated. In the digital era the experience built around the music is what makes the product.

Scarcity, or rather the lack of it, binds these three factors together and it is the music industry's ability to address this issue that will define the next stage of the evolution of the digital music market.

The Music Product Bill of Rights

The opportunity for the next generation of music products is of the highest order but to fulfil that potential, the lessons of the 2000's must be heeded. This means that the relics of the analogue age that encumber digital decisions must be either removed or navigated around so that digital music experiences are not corroded down to the lowest common denominator. It

---

20 Although the CD was co-developed with Sony Electronics, Sony Music did not come into being until in 1987 with Sony's acquisition of CBS Records, five years after the release of the first CD album: Billy Joel's '52nd Street' in 1982.
21 "Music to the M Power" MTV 2013

also means that strategy needs to be dictated by the objective of meeting consumer needs and not by technology company good enough thinking nor by rights owner commercial affairs teams' T&Cs. The next generation of music products must be commercially viable for all parties but they must be defined by consumer experiences not by business models. Done right, this next generation of music products will in fact both increase rights owner revenue – at an unprecedented rate in the digital arena – and will fuel profitable businesses. But to do so effectively, 'the cart' of commercial terms, rights complexities and stakeholder concerns must follow the 'horse' of user experience, not lead it. In fact, to ensure bad history does not repeat itself, the next generation of music products needs to be grounded in fundamental and inalienable user experience principles. These coalesce into the four key principles of what we will term the Music Product Bill of Rights (see Figure 56):

- Dynamic: In the physical era music formats had to be static but now that consumers are perpetually online across a plethora of connected devices there is no such excuse for the current music product stasis. The next generation of music products must leverage connectivity to the full, to ensure that relevant new content is dynamically pushed to the consumer, to make the product a living, breathing entity rather than the music experience dead-end that the download and stream currently represent.

- Interactive: Similarly the uni-directional nature of physical music formats and radio was an unavoidable by-product of the broadcast and physical retail paradigms. Consumers consumed. In the digital age they participate too. Not only that, they make content experiences richer because of that participation, whether that be by helping drive recommendations and discovery or by creating cool mash-ups. Music products must place interactivity at their core, empowering the user to fully customize their experience. Unless digital music products embrace the lean forward paradigm they will soon find that no one embraces them.

- Social: Music has always been social, from the Neolithic campfire, through the mixtape to the social playlist. In the digital context music becomes massively social. Spotify and Facebook's partnering builds on the important foundations laid by the likes of Last.FM and MySpace. Music services are learning to integrate social functionality, music products must have it in their core DNA.

- Curated: Consumers need guiding through the bewildering array of content, services and features, they are paralysed by the 30 million song Tyranny Of Choice. High quality, Convenient, Curated and Context aware experiences will be the secret sauce of the next generation of music products – these are the Three C's of music product strategy. These quasi-ethereal elements provide the unique value that will differentiate paid from free, premium from ad supported, legal from illegal. Digital piracy means that all content is available somewhere for free. That fight is lost, we are inarguably in the post-content scarcity age. But a music product that creates a uniquely programmed sequence of content, in a uniquely constructed framework of events and contexts will create a uniquely valuable experience that cannot be replicated simply by putting together the free pieces from illegal sources. The sum will be much greater than its parts.

The sharp eyed reader will have noted that the initials of these four sets of rights spell the word D.I.S.C. The irony of the acronym of a physical format for a digital product is entirely intentional – digital music product strategy needs to go back to the rich visual experience of the physical album and build from there.

FIGURE 56

The Music Format Bill Of Rights

A	B
Music format Bill of Rights	They must be:
Music is born free and everywhere it is in chains. We hereby call for certain inalienable rights for all future music formats.	**Dynamic** Always change and update with new content **Interactive** Empower user interactivity and customisation **Social** Place social functionality and connectivity at the core **Curated** Curate discovery programming and editorial
DATE / TIME NOISE REDUCTION ☐ON ☐OFF	DATE / TIME NOISE REDUCTION ☐ON ☐OFF

MM90

DYNAMIC SUPER LOW NOISE HIGH OUTPUT

AD·15 MM90 BILL RIGHTS

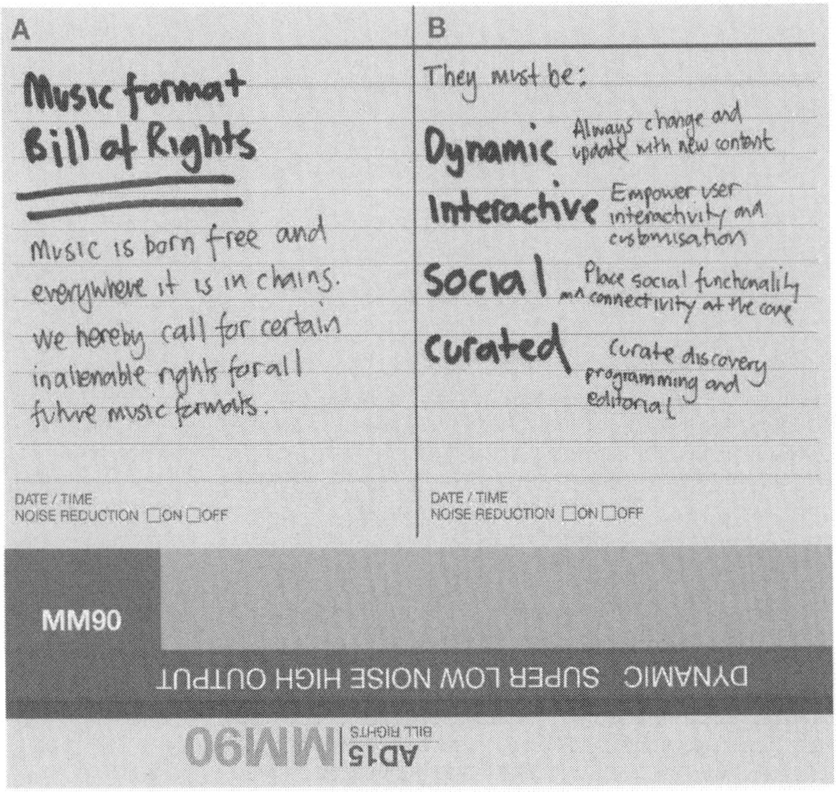

A Blueprint for the Next Generation of Music Products

Applying the D.I.S.C. principles to the dominant product strategy of the key media industries, it becomes apparent that music is outperformed by most other media types across most criteria (see Figure 57). This is rooted in music products lagging behind other digital media products in terms of new content types, dynamic updates, interactivity and in-app purchasing. The next generation of music products – which we will refer to as D.I.S.C. products from hereon – will need to plug the gaps in current usability and functionality.   Most crucially, and learning from the lesson of the games sector, they must be defied by the devices on which they will be consumed.   This means that D.I.S.C. products will be app-like experiences that leverage the interactive and multimedia capabilities of connected devices consumers own, and the software context of the app to create self-contained mini-content-ecosystems.   The emphasis however is on app-like experiences rather than apps specifically.   It does not matter whether

D.I.S.C. products are delivered via native apps onto smartphones or with HTML5 to laptops via secure browser windows. What matters is that they deliver engaging, immersive music experiences, and to do this requires innovating across content, features and functionality:

* Content

* Features

* Functionality

FIGURE 57

How Media Industries Have Leveraged the D.I.S.C.
Principles in Content Product Strategy

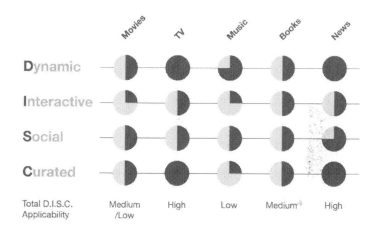

Content: The music industry must innovate with the music itself just as the games and TV industries have. Too little has been done, at scale, with music content itself other than user generated mash ups and audio stems for remix apps and contests. Both of these are perfectly valid and will be a good fit for many artist D.I.S.C. products. But both require active participation and creation from the audience, which inherently limits the scope and appeal. Now is the time for structured and concerted experimentation with music content. The watchword is experimentation: it is still too early to know what will resonate most with consumers so it will be a case of throwing everything at the wall and seeing what sticks. The burden of this experimentation will fall as much on artists as it will on labels and technology partners. Lady Gaga's 'Artpop' album app may have taken user creativity and participation too far for some of her fans but it nonetheless was a gloriously innovative experiment that the market and fans alike benefited from. Bjork's 'Biophilia' is another fine example of using technology to do something truly different with the music itself. But these are isolated exceptions, early settlers in the new world of interactive music product strategy.

Although there remain clear economies of scale of marketing a collection of songs, there is no longer any compelling business model reason for creating albums. Most artists will still aspire to create albums but they will need to think harder about whether an album is always what their fans want. Freed from the album straight jacket artists and labels should test out formats that do not originate from the physical constraints of analogue media, such as: shorter songs; longer songs; multimedia EPs; living-albums that are continually revised and added to; audio video and image bundles; multi-track audio etc. It might just be that the 3 to 4 minute song is the best creative construct for popular music but we have it largely because of the legacy format restrictions of squeezing a song onto a 45 rpm 7 inch vinyl single. By contrast dance music, which had 12 inches of 33rpm 12 inch vinyl to play with, evolved into 7 to 8 minute track lengths.[22] Analogue music format legacy track-lengths certainly warrant being stress tested in the unconstrained digital context.

Music will always be the raison d'être of any music product but D.I.S.C. products will additionally need to complement and enrich the music with other content types. These will include 'marketing content' such as artist interviews, acoustic session and back stage footage rightly claiming their role as actual product. On its own, such added value content will not convince many consumers to pay, but as part of an immersive multimedia experience this content can create the free-to-paid tipping point. Collectively the content in D.I.S.C. products should be anything and everything that helps tell the story of that specific body of work, from artwork sketches, through working demo recordings through to post-release interviews. Nor is this just for aficionados: an X Factor viewer seeking out the life story of a contestant requires just as much additional multimedia content as a Muse fan wanting to learn about the making of the latest album.

Features: D.I.S.C. products will need to tread a careful balance between providing rich interactivity and not getting in the way of the core music listening experience. Thus the core feature set will be focused on listening, but with a rich mix of additional features that sit alongside, acting as calls to action to encourage the listener to dive deeper in. Discovery and programming will be core, but not with the artificial yet pervasive 'here are three songs we think you'll like' approach. Instead discovery and recommendations will be integral parts of the experience, so deeply and seamlessly integrated that they will often be invisible. User behaviour and preferences will be fully leveraged to ensure that the entire experience is customized and tailored not just to the individual user, but to exactly what he is doing at that precise moment in time. Programming and featuresets will evolve in response to behaviour and preferences, with each user getting a dynamically tailored experience.

Social and location will also be baked into the DNA of D.I.S.C. products, often with one cross-referencing the other. Social music experiences are not simply about pushing out playlists to Facebook timelines. Instead they should empower users to share in collective discovery and experience, enabling them to make authentic and meaningful connections with likeminded music fans. Layering in location extends these social possibilities, whether that be the set of a DJ playing in a nearby club, the set list of a band that has just been onstage at a festival, or sharing tracks with people around you.

Functionality: These features are probably enough to make a developer quake in his or her boots. Indeed, a foundation of highly robust and sophisticated technology architecture will be crucial to the success of D.I.S.C. products. They cannot afford to be all form and no function. D.I.S.C. products must catch up with contemporary leading edge app standards, and then surpass them to set a whole new raft of standards. Some functionality will require more effort from rights holders than developers, most notably multiple device support. Rights

---

22 There are other factors at play, especially the need to create long undulating soundscapes in DJ sets but the capacity of 12 inch vinyl was pivotal.

holders need to understand they are in the age of multiple device ownership, that limiting the number of devices consumers can access music services on is a throwback to the early days of the MP3 player. Music services must be licensed on a per person basis not a per device basis, otherwise the music industry will simply continue to slice the proverbial baloney.

One major contemporary innovation that D.I.S.C. products must embrace is in-app purchasing. Music products lend themselves perfectly to the in-app purchase dynamic, whether that be adding extra tracks into an album, unlocking exclusive content or paying for access to a special in-app event such as a live concert stream or an artist chat session.

FIGURE 58

Future Music Formats Must Be: Dynamic Interactive Social Curated

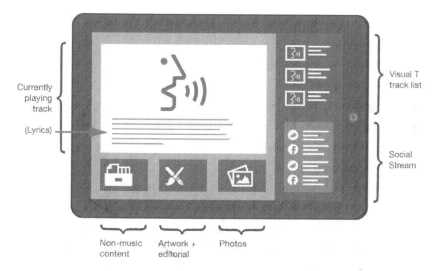

Put into practice, the D.I.S.C principles will manifest like this (see Figure 58):

- Dynamic: When a consumer buys a D.I.S.C. product it will already contain a core of content, but as soon as the product is activated it will automatically update with all new content that has created since the app was shipped and will then update automatically, continually throughout the lifespan of the product, which will range between 12 and 24 months.

- Interactive: D.I.S.C. users will be able to fully customize their experiences and to copy preferences across from one artist to another - this is the next generation of music products, not an excuse for a disconnected mass of siloed artist apps. Users will be able to create playlists, remix, create mash ups, play games etc. But they will also be able opt to simply lean back and enjoy the music. This point is crucial because interactivity must be relevant and organic, not imposed. Some consumers prefer more of a lean back experience, as illustrated by the success of Pandora. Others prefer to interact more, but even the most engaged of fans sometimes also just want to lean back. Thus D.I.S.C. products need to be built around use case scenarios not just target consumer segments, because any single consumer can exhibit entirely diverse behaviours on any given day based upon factors such as location, time of day and device.

- Social: D.I.S.C. users will be able to connect with other D.I.S.C. users within the app, again, across all artists. They will also be able to import their Twitter and Facebook friends lists to extend their social graph into their music experiences. Social functionality will also extend to artists, who should invest time participating in their D.I.S.C. communities, whether that be inviting feedback on demos they have seeded into D.I.S.C. environments or actually chatting in the forums.

- Curated: D.I.S.C. content will by the very nature of being content be pirateable, but D.I.S.C. experiences will not. The curation of content in D.I.S.C. products will create a unique context. Someone could choose to hunt down all of the photos, sketches, videos, narrative and music of a stream of D.I.S.C. content but without the programming and curation of the D.I.S.C. channel it will be a meaningless collection of unrelated artefacts. The unique value lies in the context and curation not the content itself. Thus D.I.S.C. products will create scarce experiences that will have an intrinsic value, in turn reintroducing scarcity into the digital realm. Content scarcity is dead, long live experience scarcity.

So we have seen the technical parameters of a D.I.S.C. product, but to work as a premium product that music fans will pay for, appropriate pricing, positioning and programming are crucial. D.I.S.C. products are intended primarily for the engaged music fan. Although winning over fading passive music fans is a strategic priority it cannot be done at the expense of neglecting the core customers. These are the consumers who choose to pay even though there is no reason for them to do so and thus far they have been reasonably content with relatively conservative products. But their tolerance is a finite resource and above all else the music industry must ensure it does enough to keep these fans engaged. Chasing the bright lights of the mass market mainstream consumer will matter naught if the 20% of buyers that account 80% of spending disappear. These music fans simply cannot be taking for granted but with their experience expectations elevated elsewhere that is exactly what is at risk of happening.

All that said, D.I.S.C. product pricing is designed to create a frictionless entry point that can easily additionally tease in mainstream consumers. There should be two key pricing options:

- Entry level tier: A free app with a cross section of content highlights such as an audio track or two, some video interviews, some photos and some editorial. The app will be structured to clearly communicate that there is extensive additional content 'missing' from the free tier. Consumers will have the option to select specific packages – see below – or instead to add small amounts of extra content through in app-purchasing. This will be best achieved by utilizing a points or credits system where blocks of credits are purchased and then can be redeemed against different content types. For example £/$/€0.99 will buy 10 credits, with a full song equalling 50 credits and a photo shoot equalling 20 credits. This approach enables passive fans to get a real taste of the music experience in a frictionless manner. What will be lacking from the a la carte in-app purchases though will be the full context of regular content updates and curation. That is where the next price tier comes in to play.

- Main tier: A one-off upfront price in line with a deluxe album price. A fine balance needs to be struck between baking in enough margin to make the product commercially viable but not so expensive as to scare off most consumers. So something in the region of a 30% price premium on the standard digital album price is a decent compromise. For this the consumer gets 12 months of rolling content, that includes *everything* that the artist creates over that period and mostly before it goes anywhere else. In fact D.I.S.C. products should have their own release window that trumps all others. Keeping a steady flow of content from the artist has stifled some previous efforts at artist subscription models, but the simple fact is that this is where the future of artist products needs to be and it is the job of labels to ensure artists deliver. To lessen the fulfilment load a little it makes sense to tie D.I.S.C. products into the pre-release cycle, taking it to market a couple of months before the main release's street date and populating the app with 'build up' content, such as interviews and advance singles – which incidentally should hit D.I.S.C. products at the exact same time as radio play (see Figure 59).

FIGURE 59

Mock Up Of Staggered Content Release Cycle For a D.I.S.C. Product

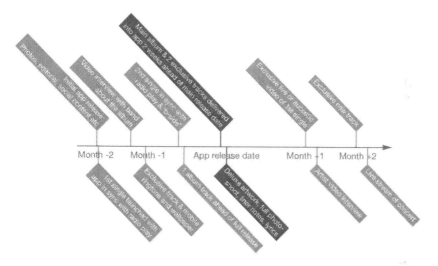

D.I.S.C. Implications

D.I.S.C. products are a perfect fit for reimagining the album both as a creative construct and a product. In the early years the album will be the crown jewel of the product, but freed from the straight jacket of the current album format, expect the 14-linearly programmed songs model to fade. Think of the story an artist could tell using photos, video, interviews, dialogue, animations, games, sketches to wrap around the music. The structure also lends itself well to formats that sit somewhere between the album and a single. Welcome to the EP renaissance. There is a more than even chance that in the longer term the album will diminish as a consumer proposition, and if it does D.I.S.C. products have the flexibility to respond accordingly far more readily than traditional albums. Currently the choice is a binary one between album and single.

The curation and programming that will set D.I.S.C. products apart from the rest will certainly require significant work and effort. The reward up for grabs though is no less than saving premium music products. It is unreasonable to expect that prize to be won simply by signing a few licensing deals. Music fans love music because it is the fruit of artist creativity. The additional multimedia content that will differentiate D.I.S.C. products is also the fruit of creativity and must be programmed and curated creatively. Anything less would be short-changing music fans and will ultimately fail. The curation itself will be part of the creative process. Labels, publishers, artists, managers and fans will need to come together to create high quality curated content experiences that blend the best of editorial and crowd sourcing to create truly unique experiences that are defined by their context. New music formats need to leverage all of the rich additional content that artists create to build a rich, premium experience that would make a mere stream or download pale in comparison. This is why rights owners need to bang heads, ruffle feathers, bruise egos, upset legal, anger artist relations, whatever it takes to make this happen.

Perhaps one of the most intriguing implications of D.I.S.C. products is that they will be a death knell for the access versus ownership debate. They will put clear blue water between ownership based products and access based services. Music fans will pay for unique curated experiences from the artists they really love and will use streaming services for the rest. The CD / Radio equilibrium will be reinvented for the digital marketplace. Money spent on a standard all AYCE subscription will be an entirely distinct and complementary expenditure from the money spent on a D.I.S.C. product. D.I.S.C. products will marry the best of access and ownership in one combined entity: consumers will pay to own access to a unique content experience. Finally the debate will be able move on to more meaningful topics. Because in the end, what matters is whether music fans are enjoying music and whether artists, rights owners and commercial partners are getting fairly compensated. The rest is bunk.

Streaming Artist Subscriptions

D.I.S.C. products target engaged music aficionados of all kinds, whether they prefer to own, download, watch, listen or stream. Because those engaged aficionados are also the core demographic of streaming subscriptions a D.I.S.C. streaming strategy is required. For all of the positive impact that streaming services have on the digital music market one of the many challenges they pose is the subjugation of the artist brand to that of the music service. With download services and CD stores the customer buys artist specific products, but with a streaming service the transaction is for all of the music in the world. The brand of any individual artist is inherently diluted. Artist D.I.S.C. apps are thus an artist-level subscription for the most engaged music fans, an opportunity to develop artist brand experiences across digital platforms. However as more of consumers' music experiences occur within access based environments, more needs to be done to build artist specific experiences within them. Doing so not only makes good business sense, it makes for better user experiences too: 30 million tracks is a meaningless consumer proposition without an effective means of getting to the miniscule fraction of that content that any one consumer is interested in.

The solution is the introduction of artist subscriptions within existing streaming services, with users paying a small monthly fee – say $/€1 – for a month's worth of artist content. With the cost added directly to a monthly music subscription, users get access to a curated channel of artist content including:

- Core catalogue: The entire standard catalogue of the artist programmed with editorial such as story of the making of each album and features such as musical influences.

- Exclusive and rare catalogue: Music that is not available elsewhere on the streaming service, such as unreleased rarities from each album, remixes, specially made tracks for the artist subscription etc. This might require some rarer content being withdrawn from the main service to be held back for the artist subscriptions.

- Exclusive programming: Non-standard music content such as acoustic sessions, simulcasts of concerts, music video etc.

- Non-music content: Audio visual content that helps tell the artist story, such as editorial, photo shoots, artwork and video storyboards, artist interviews, back stage footage, live chat sessions with artists etc.

It is crucial that artists' streaming subscriptions are not simply a collection of playlists but instead adhere to D.I.S.C. principles. Potential overlap with stand alone D.I.S.C. products should not be a concern: the core fans who are going to want an entire year's worth of an artists' output are either going to buy the core product or subscribe for a year to the streaming version. Either way, the same scale of revenue is created. No cannibalization exists. Co-existence strategy is key though, so any consumer who has paid for a standalone D.I.S.C. product must be given a key to unlock the streaming version of the subscription. In the long term, if streaming services become most consumers' point of digital music consumption it will make sense to fully fold D.I.S.C. products into them, but that time is a long way off, except of course for the uber streaming markets of Sweden, Denmark, Norway and the Netherlands.

Delivering such a diverse suite of content types into subscription services will clearly require a user experience above and beyond that of the standard streaming offering. It does not however require a fundamental reworking of streaming technology architecture. The success of artist subscriptions depends upon them being immersive, programmed, content experiences that tell the artist's story to new fans and enrich it for existing fans rather than relying upon technical functionality to stand out. The programming effort will again be significant and the burden will need to fall as much on the labels as it will the services. One major hurdle exists for artist subscriptions: monetization. Currently the deals streaming services have with the labels prevent them from being able to charge for the apps within their services which prevents the emergence of a vibrant app ecosystem. The labels and streaming services need to find common ground on this issue post haste.[23]

To mitigate resourcing concerns, a template-orientated approach will ensure scalability as well as a consistent user experience. It will also be possible to rotate a majority of the content over periods of 4 to 6 months. This is because just as music buyers buy an album and listen to it for a time before moving onto a new one, artist subscriptions will be swapped around and changed on a constant basis by users. Most fans will have a few artists they will always want to keep connected to, but will also want to have ability to dive deep into a new selection of artists every month or two.

Artist streaming subscriptions not only create a rich user experience, they also solve multiple streaming business challenges by:

- Creating artist specific revenue: Artist subscriptions also help mitigate the income threat of

---

23 The closure of lyrics app TuneWiki in June 2013 illustrates the problem created by 3rd parties not being able to charge for streaming apps. In late 2012 TuneWiki was one of the top 10 most popular apps on Spotify. But the inability to charge for the app due to the nature of Spotify's deals with the labels, prevented TuneWiki from being able to charge and ultimately led to its closure after having burnt its way through $10 million of funding.

streaming services turning download dollars into streaming cents. They do so by giving consumers the ability to commit spending to the artists they like, and by enabling artists to build rich, immersive channels of content and editorial around their music. The revenue opportunity for artists can be extended further by tight integration of ancillary revenue retailing, such as exclusive live-streamed sessions, merchandize and concert tickets.

- Ease free users into paid subscriptions: If artist subscriptions are additionally made available to free tier streaming users they present these users with the opportunity to ease themselves into subscriptions. Thus a free user could pay just a couple of €/$ to have their favourite artist channels alongside the free tier content. Zero to €/$/£9.99 is a big leap, but zero to a few dollars or euros is a far more palatable shift. To deliver clear value artist subscriptions will need to provide mobile and ad free listening even when paid for by free tier subscribers. This will additionally help drive free-to-paid conversion by accentuating the usability contrast with the rest of the streaming experience for free tier users. Once they have started enjoying the benefits of ad free mobile listening for a small selection of artists, the chances of migrating them to full subscriptions are much increased. A careful balance will however need to be struck to ensure that consumers do not swap $/€/£9.99 subscriptions for 3 or 4 artist subscriptions.

- Giving music fans the music they want: Artist subscriptions give users an alternative and more intuitive way to navigate streaming services than currently exists. At the most basic level they can be thought of like smartphone and tablet apps, supercharged bookmarks, gateways to immersive and interactive artist experiences. At a more sophisticated level they can become the foundations of the programming architecture of streaming subscription services. Artist channels can be grouped into collections such as genres, decades (80's 90's etc.) to curate music channels, which then can be sold as bundles in the same way a pay TV provider sells bundles of programmes. Instead of paying for movies, sports and documentary packages, streaming users could opt for bundles such as 'alternative rock', 'EDM' and 'Urban'. The bundle approach is not without its complexities, such as how much of an artist's standalone subscription content would get into a genre bundle, and which artists would make it in. But the clear advantage of the approach is that artist subscriptions, and bundles of them, turn the amorphous mass of streaming services into richly programmed music content networks. Just like a TV customer will chose which bundles of channels to pay for as part of their TV package. In fact, artist subscriptions are the pay TV model translated to music.

AYCE subscriptions still have a long way to go before most doubts will be eased, but streaming artist subscriptions represents an opportunity to accelerate the process by simultaneously addressing concerns of sustainability, user experience and artist pay outs. Streaming artist subscriptions is not the entire answer, but it can be a big part of the puzzle.

Three Product Proposals For Underserved Consumer Segments

The D.I.S.C. framework provides a macro approach for interactive product strategy and the blueprint for core music fans who are at risk of being taken for granted. The music industry cannot however afford to rely solely upon its super-fans, to do so would create the strategic vulnerability of over dependence on the whims of too small a customer base. As we have seen, the rise of digital music has thus far left behind too many mainstream consumers and music fans for whom digital technology plays little or no role in their music consumption. The digital music market has in the main been so laser focused on the needs of the transition generation early adopters that it risks being unprepared for the needs of the next generation of digital natives. This is the demographic pincer movement that music product strategy must outflank and to do so three further columns of product strategy are required:

I. The PlayBox

II. Tangible product strategy

III. CD migration strategy

I) The Play Box

Once the music industry has future proofed product strategy for its most loyal customers it can then start worrying more about how to try win back fleeing mainstream buyers. But that has to be the order of preference: secure the home borders before embarking on expansion. Although D.I.S.C. products will serve as a useful entry point into premium products, the majority of mainstream music fans will remain just that: mainstream, and unlikely to start buying premium products. The mainstream want easy, convenient products that fit seamlessly into their lives and that just make sense. To do that digital music needs to get into the place where mainstream music consumers are most used to having music: in the living room. But because of the relentless advance of TV technology, music is no longer guaranteed to have a footing in the room that it once called its own. Apart from the emerging multi-room streaming audio segment and the ultra-high end, the Hi-Fi market is now a sad little backwater of consumer electronics. Where once a shiny new Hi-Fi once sat as the pride of the living room, there now sits either a dusty old midi system, a docking station or worse still an empty space because the stereo has gone into the bin or into storage. If music disappears out of the mainstream living room for good it will take a huge chunk of the music market with it. The size of the task, and of the risk, are sizeable with the narrow window of opportunity poised to slam shut. This is the last big chance to migrate mainstream CD buyers to digital else risk losing them as music buyers entirely. When the CD player is gone, music's foothold in the living room is gone too.   The solution is as ambitious as it is simple: to create a PlayBox for the living room. A Wi-Fi connected piece of hardware with integrated speakers that comes preinstalled with a year or more of unlimited, ad free, streaming music. The PlayBox will be a new living room beachhead for the music industry, a starting point for digital strategy throughout the mainstream consumer's household. But to work, execution must be elegantly simple in the extreme and highly affordable. This means that it must be:

- Easy to use: Simply unbox, plug and play. Issues such as registration should be taken care of at point-of-sale, though of course Wi-Fi configuration will still need to happen at home. Customer phone support for this stage will be key.

- Affordable and value for money: The mass market does not spend large amounts of money on music so the price has to be sub-$200. Working on a retailer margin of 50%, a manufacturer margin of 25% and a rights owner discount of 30% on standard wholesale streaming rates the PlayBox can retail at $195 with a year's worth of music.

- Cool and aspirational: Even the mass markets want cool tech and although a $195 piece of hardware is not going to be built from cutting edge technology there is no reason it cannot have aspirational design ethics. Also because this is a piece of living room hardware, size and weight are not at a premium, so previous generation components that are heavier, bigger and slower – but much cheaper – can do a great job of delivering a contemporary higher end technology experience at an affordable price. And this almost certainly means a touch screen of some kind.

The core of the PlayBox proposition is a tangible manifestation of an intangible product for the mass market, a physical 'play' button for streaming music. It will help transform the esoteric challenge of nudging people from ownership to access into a readily understandable concept with clear, real-world benefits: all the music in the world, no monthly fee, no fuss, no dusty CD racks cluttering up the living room.

Of course, this fight for the living room can continue to be easily sidestepped, but the long-term damage will be irreparable. There are a few attempts to solve the problem, such as Sonos, Pure and Apple's Airport Express but those are solutions for the reasonably well heeled and the tech-savvy. This opportunity is for the mass-market consumer and it is one that any of the current streaming music services could seize. But perhaps the most exciting opportunity is for a consumer electronics company like Samsung or Sony who could use the PlayBox strategy to open up new music hardware and content markets around Apple, instead of continuing to try – and failing – to compete head on for the same customer base.

Rights-holders will need to support the PlayBox with both intent and cash, in the shape of the 30% discount on music subscription wholesale rates. Also they will have to accept the starting point of treating the license for the PlayBox in the same context as a PC i.e. at the $4.99 price point, not the mobile $9.99 price point – and applying the 30% discount to that rate. The benefits will far outweigh the costs though as the PlayBox is the only way of realistically opening up the mainstream living room to music subscriptions, thus turning the addressable market for subscriptions from 10's of millions to 100's of millions. But give up the fight for the living room now, or get there too late, and it will be the TV, movie and gaming companies alone who will be at the party, not the music industry.

II) Tangible Product **Strategy**

Whenever any major change takes place many of those at the vanguard of adoption become absolute converts, throwing away every vestige of the previous behaviours, products or technology. There is no more ardent faith than the zeal of the converted. The emergence of digital content is no different. The vast majority of consumers and business decision makers who together shaped the digital content marketplaces in the 2000's were digital immigrants, consumers who had grown up in the analogue era and who had a heritage of understanding content as existing in a purely physical context. But these digital immigrants enthusiastically shunned CDs, books and magazines for iPods, Kindles and iPads. Through the eyes of these early adopters the future was incontrovertibly going to be one without the trappings of physical media, living rooms transformed to minimalist caverns devoid of bookshelves, CD shelves and magazine and newspaper racks. A version of this future will most likely come to pass but it will not be one entirely devoid of physicality because, ironically, the natives of the digital world will demand the exact tangible extensions of their digital content experiences that digital immigrants spurned.

The process of any change is akin to the swing of a pendulum, traveling all the way to the limit of the range of the swing. But a pendulum must always swing back towards the centre and that is exactly what will happen next to digital music product strategy and it will be a phenomenon shaped not by the digital immigrants but by the digital natives. Whereas digital immigrants viewed the casting off of physical media as a badge of digital honour, digital natives have only known a world of unlimited on-demand content. They do not have to over compensate to prove their digital credentials. For them there is no acclaim in being digital, it is simply how the world is. Free of the suffocating digital ideology that shapes digital immigrant behaviour these consumers have no qualms in appreciating the benefits of tangible physical experiences. There is no contradiction in these consumers having an insatiable appetite for YouTube and Torrents while also being fervent purchasers of 7 inch vinyl. The fact that so many of the digital natives who buy vinyl do not have turntables to play it on misses the point. They are not buying vinyl because they want to listen to the music – they can already get the music for free online – instead what they want is a physical manifestation of their digital experiences.[24] Many artists see similar behaviour within their fan bases, with fans buying CDs and vinyl as a hybrid of merchandize and music product. It is an observation made by Above and Beyond's Jonathan Grant: "2013 was the first time digital sales will overtake physical sales for us because CDs and vinyl really matter to our fans. Many of them bring them along with them to our shows to get them signed. For them it is more than just the music."

The winners in the next stage of digital music innovation will have to learn to understand how and when to add physical experiences to their digital products. This is Tangible Product Strategy and can be defined as follows:

• A natural extension of the digital experience: Most digital music experiences offer less than their physical counterparts. So simply creating a new way to deliver liner notes, lyrics or large-scale album art will be a natural physical extension of many digital products. But this approach is too narrow in scope and misses much of the objective. Creating a physical manifestation of a digital product does not mean simply resuscitating physical products as digital appendages. Instead it is an opportunity to be highly creative without the constraints of having to be a music format per se. The digital file – whether a stream, a download or a video – does the job of delivering the music, a physical companion piece should not try to just be a physical playback format, in fact it may often be better off by not trying to be.

• A genuine complement to digital: Because Tangible Music Products do not need to be occupied with delivering music files, the range of creative possibilities for them is limitless. For example a series of collectible pieces of art, a set of artist postcards, an artist wristband, a high quality artist print, a mobile phone cover with the artist image. But whereas these are the sort of items that one might expect included in a deluxe CD box set or on a PledgeMusic campaign, Tangible Music Products will differ in that they will be physical extensions of digital experiences. Thus each of the aforementioned examples should also enable unique music experiences. The four different art pieces located around a room would affect the playback of a song as the listener walks between them, adding an extra vocal part near one and a new guitar riff near another, opening up the resonance on a filter near another. Similarly the postcards would be augmented reality cards that turn into animations with the viewfinder of a smartphone when a particular track is played. An NFC chip in the wristband would redeem against a playlist of exclusive tracks in a streaming music service.[25] The artist photo would have a 2D barcode to deliver a song directly to the

---

24 Also many young music fans see 7 inch singles as a way of 'giving back' to their favourite artists. Vinyl has become a way of opting back into music spending but in a highly tactical and targeted manner.
25 There are countless potential implementations of the NFC enabled wrist band, such as: taking home the set list of a band from the concert (far easier to deliver than a USB file of the performance); taking home the set of DJ from a club; a showcase of an indie label's roster made available in a local boutique coffee shop. Nokia set the wheels in

user's phone.[26] Meanwhile the mobile phone case would be part of an artist multimedia phone bundle including the physical case, screen saver, ringtone, video and songs. Thus the phone becomes a material adjunct of the music experience, allowing fans to both immerse themselves in the artist's creative output and to portray their musical identity to others.[27]

- Portray musical identity and taste. Music matters to us because of how it makes us feel and also because of what it says about us. A song can be shorthand for how we feel, the artist whom we aspire to be, a genre for how we see ourselves in the world. We all use music to say something about who we are, sometimes we do this subtly, other times less so. The history of recorded music is littered with examples of music as self-expression: rock 'n' roll quiffs and leather jackets in the 1950's; long hair in the 1960's and 1970's; boom boxes / ghetto blasters in the 1980's; ring tones in the 2000's; and the timeless loud music playing out of the open window. Perhaps the most common expression of all though is racks of vinyl or CDs in the living room or bedroom, giving the visitor an instant eye into one's musical world. Projecting identity is at the centre of what makes music matter to us all. But with music collections increasingly residing on hard drives and more listening occurring via headphones, the avenues for self-expression through music lessen. Tangible Music Products enable music fans to project their musical identity in novel and unique ways, reinventing the use of music as a badge of identity.

- Occupy experiential white space: Freed of the shackles of being a music format, Tangible Music Products should try to be something that neither a digital nor traditional product can be. This will often mean occupying the senses that music does not, or engaging the aural senses in new ways. The creative possibilities are limitless: video montages that project on walls from a smartphone; a collection of small battery powered speakers positioned around a room that play individual additional elements to a song; 3D song videos that are watched through artist branded 3D glasses that incorporate headphones and 360 degree audio to create immersive audio visual experiences; 3D printing templates of 7 inch singles.

Innovations such as the Anki robotic toy cars that are controlled via iOS devices and Nokia's NFC enabled Nokia Mix Radio playlist stickers are early hints of the fusion between the physical and digital world that will accelerate in the coming years.[28] What is crucial is that Tangible Music Products are retailed as part of the digital music experience. Not as giveaways or promotional gimmicks but as product bundles that offer the fullest and richest experience. It will not always be appropriate to have physical extensions to digital music products, and in the earlier days the opportunities will often be tactical and opportunistic. But failing to provide them when the opportunity presents itself will leave digital native opportunity on the table. As with D.I.S.C. strategy the objective is to create extra, scarce value that cannot be easily pirated and for which people will pay a premium. Unlike D.I.S.C. products the extra value is wholly tangible and clearly demonstrable.

In Japan the importance of Tangible Product Strategy is already well understood, with

motion with its NFC playlist stickers for Nokia Mix Radio, the momentum will eventually become irresistible

26 For as long as NFC functionality is not available on all popular smartphones – that means you iPhone - 2D barcodes are the best way of reaching as many mobile consumers as possible. Before too long though 2D barcodes will become obsolete and will be superseded by other technologies such as NFC.

27 The mobile phone package is also a useful entry point for artist subscriptions. A selection of top tier frontline artist subscriptions would be retailed in phone shops with display shelves containing artist branded phone cases. The retail price of each case would include multimedia phone content in addition to three months access to the artist's subscription. Consumers would also be able to purchase artist subscription pre-paid cards with credit that can be used on any mobile artist subscription.

28 Tangible Music Product Strategy is in many respects a strand of the Internet of Things, the concept of a growing number of 'dumb' devices having smart functionality, of internet enabled features being built into an increasingly diverse array of products. These include products such as ambient umbrellas that can tell the owner whether it will be needed that day and home climate control systems controlled from a tablet.

J-Pop artists often releasing multiple editions of an album with the same songs and artwork but with different 'free gifts'. Similarly fans of reality TV Japanese girl band AKB-48 have to buy the album to get the voting slip to decide which 48 girls will comprise the next line up. On the day of release bins in the streets are overflowing with discarded CDs that were bought simply for the voting slip. Similarly some Japanese artists have 'handshake' sessions where fans get to shake their hand after handing over a voucher from a CD album. Sometimes five vouchers will get the fan a hug and a kiss, while rumours abound that some artists might go even further for even more vouchers. Japan is of course culturally unique and we should be careful not to try to apply learnings too literally from other markets. But the underlying importance of physical extensions beyond the music product is clear. The opportunity for Tangible Product Strategy is to take this dynamic and imbue it with smart functionality and awareness. To take digital into the physical realm.

III) CD Migration Strategy

The CD has been declining in revenue terms every year for well over a decade yet continues to account for the majority of global sales because of the comparatively slow rate of adoption of digital products. In two of the world's biggest music markets – Japan and Germany – the CD still reigns supreme, accounting for 80% and 70% of revenues respectively. The situation is exacerbated by the fact that the CD as a playback technology has retained even more traction across most music markets – even in strong streaming markets the average household still has at least one CD player somewhere. Thus the success of digital music as a whole is inextricably tied to the migration of CD consumers away from the incumbent technology. The equation is as inherent as it is simple: the poorer a job the music industry does of convincing CD buyers to go digital the smaller the digital market will be.

CD migration strategy though is a far from straightforward task and will be shaped by three key dynamics:

- The CD market will polarize between extremes: The majority of the digital transition opportunity exists within the middle of the CD market, among the engaged solid spenders. Consequently this is the part of the CD market that will diminish most quickly, leaving the sector to consolidate around the value-driven low end and the high-value premium end. While standard priced front line CD albums lose ground to digital the super-deluxe box set edition segment will prosper, growing both organically and at the expense of vinyl. [29] Similarly heavy discounting, cheap catalogue re-releases, cut price compilations and 'bargain bins' at supermarkets and motorway services will drive a high volume, low margin business from the physical holdouts. There are however important channel implications: the polarization of the market between two core niches will be something of a death knell for what is left of offline retail, though with some notable exceptions. While it is hard to see a future for mainstream music retailers, new opportunities will emerge for high-end specialist retailers, for music bargain stores and for enthusiast experiential music stores e.g. a vinyl store with a restaurant and in-store live entertainment. [30] For record labels this will mean developing networks of new retail partners. As the market polarization takes effect, the case for tiered pricing in new releases will grow with every passing day. Record

29 Just as the CD enters its death throes the super-high-end audiophiles have started to embrace the format, with many increasingly shifting vinyl purchases to CD.

30 New partnership opportunities will transpire also. For example stores within stores: specialist box set retailers using space in high end audio equipment retailers and alongside audio equipment departments in multi-product retailers. Some novel music retail stores have also emerged, including in a Pie and Vinyl store in the south of England.

labels have already experimented with multiple priced editions of frontline releases but backed away from full scale deployment because in trials too many consumers simply skipped the middle, main tier. In the context of the middle falling out of CD sales, cheap and premium priced editions change from interesting possibilities to market necessity.

- Many CD buyers will simply fall out of the market: Many passive music buyers who only buy the occasional CD will simply disappear from the market. Though stand-out music events such as Adele's '21' will continue to sporadically pull fading buyers out of the proverbial woodwork, these are exceptions that push against an inevitable tide. Instead, those music buyers who only buy a CD or two a year will either simply retire out as they age – much like newspaper readers – or they will sate their appetites on free alternatives such as satellite radio, music TV and YouTube. The likelihood of any meaningful share of these consumers being converted to digital spending is negligible. Given the low average spend of these consumers there is a case for actually accelerating the retirement of this segment, a managed cull. These consumers are typically reached via traditional mainstream media such as TV and so have a high acquisition cost but low customer value. Gently nudging these fading buyers out of the market by turning off the supply to their outlets of choice may sound like a counter intuitive move and will undoubtedly result in some revenue decline, but it will leave a more profitable, higher value customer base. The remaining rump can be served with cut-price products in non-specialist outlets, without expensive marketing support.

- The CD is still the most complete music product: The elephant in the room for CD-migration strategy is that the CD – and for sake of balance, the vinyl LP – is a more complete product proposition than most digital alternatives. In terms of audio quality and extras such as lyrics, liner notes, photos and most importantly simplicity, CDs still outpace most digital products. They also outperform in technology and channel contexts too because of their superior interoperability; installed base of compatible devices; and international reach. Convincing a techno-phile to go digital is an effortless task, but persuading a technology-sceptic to give up a trusted format for what can be perceived as a confusing and inferior product is a hard sell.

Set against the backdrop of these three dynamics CD migration strategy must do the following:

- Demonstrate the benefits of digital to analogue holdouts: Back in the early-to-mid 2000's record labels experimented with enhanced CD album formats that played music videos and also prompted the entire music content to be played in a proprietary player. Though there were obvious faults with the approach, most notably forcing consumers to use the inbuilt player and grapple with Digital Rights Management technology like the Sony rootkit debacle, the concept of delivering digital music-like experiences in the CD product remains a useful approach for migrating physical holdouts.[31] These consumers need to be convinced of the additional benefits of digital products before they can be convinced to pay for them. The behaviour transition will be the precursor to purchase transition. But digitally enhanced CDs must also be clear calls to action, such as making extra content available when unlocked online, in order to capture user details and kick start digital behaviour. Once consumers have engaged with online content the next step is to get them to interact with digital experiences that are related

31 SonyBMG deployed a DRM scheme called Extended Copy Protection (XCP) between 2005 and 2007 on more than 20 million CDs. The software interfered with basic computer processes to prevent CD copying – even though of course in America fair use copying is permitted by legislation. Upon installing itself the software hid itself which made it highly difficult to remove, behaving to all intents and purposes as a virus. The fact that the software hid from the user any file beginning with "sys" created a vulnerability that was quickly exploited by malicious programmers. When SonyBMG finally distributed an uninstall patch to users it inadvertently created a more serious vulnerability. SonyBMG ultimately faced a class action suit in the US and a deluge of bad press.

to, but separate from the CD, such as locker services like Amazon's AutoRip CD.

- Play the long game: Converting analogue holdouts is a long term play, at both the micro and macro levels. For individual consumers it will be a steady, often slow journey, moving from tentative steps, through experimental CD/digital co-existence through to final transition. Not all physical holdouts will make the entire journey and the PlayBox will be a crucial additional tool in the box. As hard going as progress may prove to be, it is nonetheless crucial work: failure to pull over the rump of mainstream CD buyers will leave the digital market with too few customers to deliver the value artists, labels and music services need from it. The super fan 10% segment will be engaged but not the remainder.

Putting Product Strategy into Action

It may be a truism to state that product strategy and business strategy should be symbiotic extensions of one another. However this is not the natural state of affairs for the digital music market, largely because there are three key types of business strategy (see Figure 60):

- Rights owners want to grow the overall digital business and to transition over physical revenue. Priorities: Scale and Revenue

- Large technology companies want to use music in a cost effective manner to help sell ancillary products. Priorities: Cost and Scale

- Start ups want to gain market traction in order to sell the company or to go public. Priorities: Innovation and Scale

FIGURE 60
Scale Sits At The Heart Of All Three Key Types
Of Digital Music Business Strategy

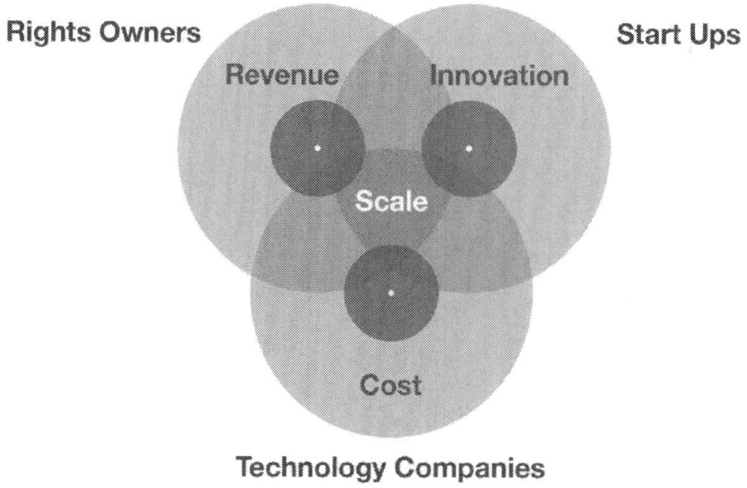

Rights Owners   **Start Ups**

Revenue   Innovation

Scale

Cost

Technology Companies

Although scale, revenue, cost effectiveness and innovation are each to some degree objectives for all three parties, priorities differ, resulting in highly fragmented digital product strategies. Crucially revenue and scale are only priorities for one party each: rights owners are alone in prioritizing total revenue while the same applies for start ups' preferences for innovation. Matters are complicated by the fact that there is a varying degree of negative interdependence between cost effectiveness and each of the other three objectives. Increased innovation typically comes at the expense of cost effectiveness, as does an aggressive push for scale in which a music service tries to extend its user base as quickly as possible even if that means making a large loss to do so. Thus revenue can easily compete with cost effectiveness. By way of illustration, Daniel Ek when questioned about Spotify's profitability is fond of explaining that his company's three priorities are "growth, growth and growth." In the context of a music service, a start up might have ambitious revenue targets set by its investors that can only be met quickly by increasing the cost of sale so far that profitability is obliterated. While a record label's digital revenue is the largest part of the cost base of a music service.

Consequently the innovation burden falls most heavily on the start ups but their focus on short term goals and Minimum Variable Products means that digital music innovation becomes a morass of disconnected features that burn brightly and quickly. A burden of responsibility falls upon rights holders to leverage their effective monopoly on supply of content to help drive all four strategic objectives. This means being less dazzled by the bright lights of the hundreds of millions of users of each of the big technology players and instead placing innovation responsibilities on their shoulders. It is time for the rights owners to stand their ground. Sure each of the big technology companies may try to bully them down, threatening to pull their content or focus elsewhere, but ultimately the products that Amazon, Apple and Google make their profits from depend strongly on music. The power in the relationship really does lie with the rights owners, even if it is not yet manifest. Rights owners must also do much more to empower the smaller start up end of the equation, empowering these companies with much greater flexibility and commercial maneuverability with tactics such as experimental licenses. This will encourage a greater flow of investment into the space that in turn will accelerate innovation.

All of this needs to be set against the macro framework of the Digital Strategy Pyramid, ensuring that each partner:

- Is incentivized appropriately to achieve their objectives

- Has an appropriate balance of objectives

- Is targeting distinct market segments

- Has a business model that co-exists with rather than cannibalizes others

Done right, this approach will result in a neat segmentation of business models and product offerings that combine the best of precise targeting and market simplicity. With each partner having a clear understanding of their position in the landscape and their role in the broader market, product strategy and business strategy will become far more closely aligned, helping to bring some much needed solidity of direction to digital music.

Chapter 16: Labels

The labels confounded many of their critics by not only surviving the digital onslaught but reinventing themselves as commercial entities. But for all the perennial doubts about whether labels will survive, it is artists and songwriters who are genuinely worried about whether they can make ends meet, not labels. Though the major record labels have undoubtedly consolidated their positions the independent sector has done an equally, if not better, job of getting onto a sound footing. A large number of independent labels started life after both Napster and the launch of the iTunes Store and learned how to build viable digital era businesses. The improved operating margins of digital music have enabled labels to operate more effectively even at lower volumes. And yet despite all this success something is missing, a final crucial part of the puzzle, a vision for what a label should be in the 21st century. Labels have been so busy fighting to survive, grappling with an endless barrage of multiple disruptions that they simply have not had the luxury of time to reflect on whether the fundamental question of 'what is it all for?' has a different answer now than it did in the 1990's. As Roger Faxon succinctly put it: "Simply put the music business lacks a vision of the future."

In the analogue era record labels were the only truly feasible route to success for a budding artist. The proposition for the artist was crystal clear: signing to a record label was success. Success was measured squarely in terms of albums sold and chart positions, with labels often expected to spend lavishly in pursuit of those targets. David Byrne recalled the peak years' opulent practices: "I was around when labels were extremely flush. They had in house art departments, pressing and printing plants, in house marketing people and press departments. Madonna had a press person at Warners who pretty much just worked for her. They'd sometimes give lavish tour support to get an act out there. And recording budgets were often irresponsible. Most of those jobs are now farmed out – which is not a bad thing." In the current marketplace though, artists cannot reach millions of fans directly themselves, but success is also measured across a much wider and more diverse range of metrics. The world has changed and what artists and the rest of the music value chain want out of labels has changed also. The exploitation of the rights of the master recording have been at the core of the traditional label model for decades but if music sales are a declining part of the revenue mix then the question that emerges is whether that foundational assumption is as useful as it once was. It is an argument made by Martin Goldschmidt: "The old label view is that you accumulate a bank of copyrights, the new model is that you learn how to sit between the artist and the consumer, serving both and getting music in the most frictionless way possible from one to the other. If you stop thinking of a label as a copyright bank trying to maximize margin you find yourself in far less conflict with artists and fans."

At a highly simplified level record labels have performed three key roles over the last few decades:

1. Discovered and invested in artists

2. Nurtured artists

3. Marketed artists

Each of those are crucial roles needs that still need doing today, the difference is that with a rich portfolio of digital tools at their disposal artists do not always need a label to do all three. One size simply does not fit all for artist-label relationships anymore, instead diversity is the name of the game and this can often translate into labels needing to accept working alongside other partners. As Brian Message put it: "New artists need investment and to be discovered. If you view an artist as a business, with multiple revenue streams working across a global market, then there has to be a case for encouraging new forms of investment into those artist businesses." Though digital tools help artists across all three of the core needs, it is rare that an artist achieves large scale success doing all three without external help, and most often that comes from a label in some form or another. By way of illustration, British Post-Hardcore / Metal act Enter Shikari garnered significant media attention for their self stated intention to never sign with a record label. The band went on to achieve notable critical and commercial success, releasing music via their own Ambush Reality label. But scratch a little under the surface and it emerges that Ambush Reality was once distributed by Warner Music and more recently by PIAS Entertainment Group, a leading international recording, licensing and distribution company. The Enter Shikari example does not belittle the success of post-label models, but instead serves to remind us that even in the self-serve digital age labels can bring a lot of value to the equation, albeit on terms which are more equitable to the artist than would have previously been the case.

Equitability is at the core of why labels need to reconsider what their core attributes are in the digital era. Though there has always been an unhealthy degree of mistrust of labels by artists, many of the underlying misgivings that were tolerated when labels could be counted on to deliver have now become septic open wounds. According to Goldschmidt: "There is a major mistrust of labels by artists. Three things need to happen: 1) more honest and straightforward contracts 2) more straight forward and honest accounting 3) more respect for artists by labels." Labels need artists' trust just as much as the artists need to be able to trust them. This means a recalibrating of relationships that reflects the realities of the digital era, as Cliff Fluet suggested: "Labels are still not in control of their own destiny as they don't control the brand or the platform. They need to let go of control and focus on monetization." The analogue era model was predicated on control and label strategy in the 2000's has had an unhealthy obsession with attempting to regain it. Whether that be fighting Napster, holding back MP3 licenses from Apple, tying artists to 360 deals or lobbying governments on copyright and piracy. The irony in all of this supply side focus is that the grand unifying principle in digital disruption is the consumer. It is the shift of power from the rights owners to the audience that turned the music industry upside down and that must buttress any future vision of what a record label should be. As Roger Faxon observed: "[Labels] are focused on the wrong place, the tension between supplier and retailer. The only way you break that tension and understanding the future is by having an ultimate clear view of the consumer."

The 21st Century Label Manifesto

The role of the label will continue to be a central component of the music value chain. That does not however mean that some or all of the existing labels will perform this role nor that other entities will not come into the mix, but it remains a crucial one nonetheless. The rate of disruption and change in the label space will continue to move relatively slowly because the incumbents own the majority of the recording copyrights, but change will come. Labels and new entrants will compete in an increasingly open sphere for artists and for market mindshare, with each directly fuelling the other. As Sumit Bothra put it: "Labels are now competing with a wider mix of companies and our position has moved from working on a long term commitment to 'let's do it and see if it works, if it does then let's do it again. The landscape is changing so quickly you don't want to tie yourself to any one label for too long." To succeed in this arena labels will need to not only hone their commercial models but also have a clear sense of their raison d'être, of what value they bring to artists in the competitive marketplace. To achieve this labels should pursue the following principles of the 21st Century Label Manifesto. These are:

- Be the bridge from subsistence to sufficiency: The trend of more artists arriving at labels more established, with a clearer sense of autonomy, self belief and control of fan relationships will only intensify. Labels should not attempt to undo this or attempt to assume complete control. Instead they should harness the skills of the artist and the manager, working as a team across all aspects of the artist's recording career. To some degree this already happens in many labels, but it is time for it to become codified and deeply embedded. Even more importantly, labels need to make artists understand that signing with a label does not mean relinquishing their freedom of expression and movement. Instead it means giving that creative and business drive the support of a professional organization to enable artists to hit heights they simply cannot alone. Artists who have worked hard to build their own careers should not have their autonomy entirely taken away from them. Labels have to accept the consequences of investing later in bands than they did ten years ago. If they want more control then they need to start supporting artists sooner in their careers again. Of course a degree of control inherently must be signed away in any label deal but it should be countered with the understanding that a label relationship is the best route for an artist to go from a subsistence existence to sufficiency. Label deals should be the opportunity for artists to forge sustainable careers rather than the get-rich-quick and burn out quicker model that dominated in the CD heyday. The label deal eventually delivering surplus should remain an aspiration, but no longer be the expectation.

- Be responsible investors: Labels of all shapes and sizes have become more sensible investors of resources but there is still a temptation to bet big when the circumstances do not always justify it. Artists will naturally want to have the biggest and best shot at success they can get, but they will also understand and appreciate labels committing to spending prudently. Labels need to help artists understand that a sensibly promoted album will most likely deliver more money back to them than a lavishly promoted one that shifts more units. The approach will not always sit comfortably with a label in search of near term market share and chart positions, but it is far more valuable for a label to have an artist with a long term, sustainable recording career, than a quick hit that rapidly crumbles into obscurity.

- Be transparent: Since time immemorial sceptical artists have assumed that labels take more than their fair share from the equation. This is grounded in multiple factors, not least of which being that the business savvy of the label is always far greater than that of the first time artist signing the first deal. A good lawyer can help but the underlying dynamics remain. Thereafter the typical artist journey of business discovery entails growing dismay at the complexity of accounting procedures and a growing realization that it is going to be a long time, or never, before any royalty income is earned. Even then many artists feel compelled to have their accounts audited, as they are contractually allowed to do. None of this engenders positive, trusting working relationships. Many indies have gone some way to addressing the issue by offering 50/50 net receipt deals to artists and improved reporting. These are good steps but even more needs to be done. Labels have an unprecedented amount of accurate reporting data pouring in from music services and now is the time to use this data as the basis of open, transparent relationships with their artists. Every artist should see, as standard, how many streams and downloads they have had from each service, the income per event and what their streams and revenue represent as a percentage of the label's total for each service, and any details of advance payments from a service to a label as that relates to the artist's catalogue. If such reporting reveals any anomalies then so be it. This will form the foundation for robust long-term relationships where there is a clear and shared vision of the route to success. It is an approach gaining traction in the independent sector as Jeremy Silver observed: "If you are an independent label you realized that the more data you share, the more collaboration you get with artists and the more you both get out of the relationship."

- Be the artist's advocate: In the age of DIY it is tempting for artists to feel there is little they need from a label creatively. But the creative risk of DIY is that the artist lacks a rounded feedback loop, that everything becomes a self-congratulatory echo chamber of pats on the back, begetting creative hubris. The ability of labels to nurture an artist's creativity and career, through A&R sessions, creative input, experience based insights and guidance are priceless but often undervalued assets of the label relationship. Labels need to recognize that in an era when artists can turn to alternative services to do many of the commercial tasks of their business, there is still no compelling alternative to the creative nurturing role that a label plays. Thus labels need to double down and put this creative support front and centre of their proposition to artists.

- Be the window to the world: Facebook, Twitter and YouTube have the potential to deliver millions of fans but breaking out of the background clutter requires more than just creative talent. Being 'good enough' is no guarantee of success. A few artists have self-propelled breakthrough success but most simply do not have the time or skills to build global audiences at scale. Although there are more tools at their disposal than ever before, the same tools are available to every other artist, so the end result is simply to raise the volume of the background noise, not to break through it. Labels need to do an even better job of communicating to artists, and indeed to the wider marketplace, that they have the expertise and resources that can help artists cut through.

- Be an innovation partner: Labels have found themselves bearing the lion's share of criticism in the digital era, principally for holding back innovation. As we have seen some of this has been valid, some not, but labels now need to up their innovation game and act as catalysts for transformation. MusicQubed's Chris Gorman highlights the plight of music start ups: "Everything is difficult, nothing is easy. It is not for the faint hearted as it is so difficult to get in; but the determination to succeed with new, untapped revenue streams should resonate with all." Labels need to work with even more start ups and in an even more flexible manner, which means lessening the dependence on the commercial levers of advances and minimum guarantees, and providing support and access to networks. The start ups that succeed because of above and beyond label support are those that are most likely to bring genuine business benefits and not just cool but ultimately low value features. Similarly labels should embrace and channel the creative ambition of their artists towards technology experimentation. Who better to understand what innovation will work for an artist's fans than the artist themselves? Ultimately the role of the label is less about being an innovator, and instead acting as an innovation enabler. Providing the tools, support and resources for others to do the innovation.

- Be the curator: Music services are falling over themselves to express how central curation is to their respective value propositions. Although there is obviously more new music than ever before there has always been far more music available than any one individual could listen to. The reason that curation emerged as a problem of the digital age is that when media distribution was centralized labels, DJs and retailers did the curating and audiences did the listening. Now audience and channel alike play a hand in curation. Labels have an opportunity to reclaim the mantle of trusted tastemakers. To be clear this does not mean turning back the clock on the social discovery revolution, but instead to act as a quality filter that co-exists with contemporary digital discovery and recommendation tools. As Tony Wadsworth explained: "Something that looks like a record label is more important than ever, to cut through the clutter by selecting what is and what is not good right at the top of the supply chain." When a label signs an artist it is a confirmation of quality, when that label has a reputation for quality signing is a stamp of authority and legitimacy as Martin Mills explained: "Signing to a label like 4AD changes the way the press and public view a band, it is validation."

- Be flexible: Artists have unprecedented power of choice in an ever more competitive marketplace. Labels must have the realism and flexibility to accept that a growing number of artists will only want to engage them for a specific set of duties, working alongside other stand alone services. The all inclusive label relationship will still be a good fit for many artists, but for the rest labels will need to behave more like agencies, tailoring the right mix of services for their clients' needs. This is the natural consequence not just of digital disruption but of labels signing artists later in their careers. Artists now learn just how much they can achieve on their own and arrive at the label negotiating table empowered, confident and with a strong sense of what they want and need from a label.

The Agency Model

Of all the manifesto principles, flexibility is the most impactful, both as a grounding principle and as a way of doing business. In the traditional label model one size, with modest variations, fits all: artists sign away their master recordings to the label and the label then sets about exploiting those rights with a multi-format product strategy underpinned by a concerted marketing effort. There are other standard features, such as focusing on an album, releasing a number of singles to support the album, and working hard to secure radio play. Now though a new approach is emerging that is setting the standards for the next generation of label practices. It is an approach where there is no set model but instead a menu of services that an artist can opt into and, crucially, in which an artist can even retain the rights to their master recordings. This label services approach started to gain significant momentum in the early 2010's, fuelled by the efforts of companies like Cooking Vinyl, Kobalt's AWAL and Believe Digital. Even the major labels have been getting in on the act, paying the greatest compliment to a number of independent label services specialists by poaching some of their staff. The model is predicated on the artist 'renting' services from the label on a similar basis to a distribution deal, with the label becoming part of the artist's team but with the artist retaining their copyright. Cooking Vinyl's Goldschmidt outlined the approach for label services deals in his label group: "The artist gets the lion's share of the money but 100% of the costs are deducted from the artist share. The artist has complete control as they approve all costs. This also gives them financial transparency. If a record does well and the costs are managed well the artist earns far more money, e.g. 70%+ of digital income."

The label services model brings equitability into the artist-label relationship by making the two parties business partners. Artists and label objectives and incentives are aligned, with both incentivized to control the costs and to make the right business decisions. The full label services approach is not the right fit for all artists, but that is the point. Label services represent a greater degree of control and flexibility for artists, one more set of options for them to choose from, not a new single choice model. Labels will have to meet the demand and as Keith Harris put it: "Most business will go towards the label services model as people are increasingly recognizing that money has to be spent more smartly." Some artists will opt for a third party such as PledgeMusic to be part of the mix, others will still opt for a traditional label deal, but as an option among many, not an obligation. With the agency approach the artist is transformed from contracted employee to client. Erik Nielsen suggested that empowered digital era artists need a label partner that is like "a mini-major, offering a full suite of services, such as live support, promotion etc. but with the lowest overheads and at best possible price to the artist. The outlook will be one of a multitude of cottage industries with small but highly effective and multi-skilled teams." Nielsen also made the case that the major label model will buckle under the weight of having tried to add too many extra parts to its core proposition that has arisen from "lots of tunnel vision instead of thinking what an artist career looks like now. Somebody at the top needs to have an ultimate view of the artist." Jenner believes that the innovation in business models is so crucial because: "The traditional label model is broken. That is not to say because of the longevity of sales that they won't be around for a long time yet, but there is a real problem with labels now, that they can't deliver." What is clear is that labels will never be the same again.

Next Generation Labels

Agency models and label services deals will contribute to crucial evolution of the record label in the short to midterm however an even more transformative trend will shape the long term future of the label landscape. Most of today's bigger labels were either born in the analogue era or in the early digital period – i.e. pre-2000 – with reference points and worldviews that still owed a major debut of gratitude to the analogue era. This first wave of digital labels built their businesses, in the main, around the iTunes Store and were thus still squarely focused on selling units, albeit digital ones. As album sales began to grow, as a share of iTunes sales, these same labels became even more like traditional labels, placing ever more importance on releasing and promoting albums. In many respects though, the format is not the most significant analogue era baggage, but instead the broader mindset of acquiring copyrights and selling units. In the words of Keith Harris: "The business is still built around advances and unit sales, traditional label thinking." The stage is set for a new breed of label that plays by a new rulebook, that of the multimedia, on-demand digital era.

An artist is now so much more than the sum of their recorded output. Their social presence, visual imagery and their thoughts and words all constitute what an artist is, especially so in a digital context. Yet labels are poorly equipped to translate this into the core artist proposition, instead most often relying on these elements as marketing tools 'to tell the story' or ignoring them all together. Music fans increasingly rely upon smartphones and tablets for their music experiences yet the balkanization of rights are the unwanted legacy of analogue era peace treaties. The next generation of label will wipe the slate clean, treating the artist as a creative whole, discarding traditional boundaries and business practices. It will be defined by the following characteristics:

- Work across all rights: The division of an artist's rights between recording and song writing copyrights and assigning them separately to a record label and a publisher made absolute sense when the distinction between music product and a license were abundantly clear. Now those distinctions matter less and in fact get in the way of digital product strategy. For example lyrics usually do not appear on digital albums because record labels do not own the rights and would have to pay a fee to the publisher to include them.[32] Next generation labels will work with an artist's rights as a unified whole. This will typically involve obtaining all the rights – recorded and song writing – on a project basis. The labels will utilize these rights to the full to create multimedia product offerings that focus on user experience first rather than having to compromise usability and functionality because the necessary rights are prohibitively fragmented and costly. The artist and the label will have a shared vision and common objectives. In some instances the label will retain those rights; in others they will revert back to the artist after certain income thresholds have been met ensuring that the label is able to cover costs and earn an appropriate margin. Once the rights revert the label will be granted a fixed term revenue share with the artist – between 5 and 10 years – in which the label will be guaranteed a specific percentage of any future revenue arising from the work. When there is a third party songwriter their publishing rights will be pooled into the collective.[33] Where appropriate the songwriter will become an integral member of the team and decision making.

- Be project focused: The traditional three album deal lacks the flexibility and agility required in the digital age. Future artist-label relationships will lean towards specific projects, such as an individual album, a series of EPs, a multimedia app. Any contractual options on future works will be mutual agreements, namely that one party cannot take up the option without agreement of the other. The project approach is not without its challenges, not least of which is reduced opportunities for artists looking to have the security of a multi album deal to develop their careers. It is to be expected that a strata of labels will emerge specializing in developing artists over long periods, but there is no hiding the fact that this will no longer be the norm.

- Be a product innovator: Next generation labels will not acquire the broad suite of rights simply for the traditional rationale of building a bank of rights, but instead will do so with the specific remit of creating multimedia products. These labels will have extensive in-house design and development expertise that will harness and channel the musical creativity of the artists and songwriters into compelling multimedia apps and products. Instead of creating a rich portfolio of non-album assets for helping market the album, these will be built into the core of the

32 Apple oversaw a clever workaround for deluxe edition albums and iTunes LPs, classifying lyrics as 'packaging' and therefore not subject to the full license fee. However this solution inherently precludes the lyrics from becoming a core part of the actual music product experience.
33 Of course many songwriters have long term exclusive contracts with publishers. In the near term as these new models emerge this will likely mean that such songwriters are unlikely to be able to work with next generation labels. But as the model becomes established and proves its worth, publishers and songwriters will find creative ways to be flexible and participate.

product, helping construct an audio-visual narrative to run through the music experience.

Next generation labels will not reach scale quickly, instead they will start small and may even bubble up as skunk works within traditional record labels. Interim transition models will evolve too. One such likely evolutionary step will be streaming agencies that are primarily focused on getting artists listened to more on streaming services. Next generation labels will coexist alongside traditional label models and label agency models, creating a rich array of choices for artists alongside the plethora of D2F and DIY offerings. But unlike any of those alternatives, next generation labels will pull together otherwise disparate threads into a unified whole engendering innovation and equitable revenue models.

Transitioning to the New Models

Labels have been subjected to intense disruption and have undergone dramatic transformation but they remain standing, albeit often in reduced states. As Edgar Berger put it: "No other media industry has been attacked by disruption, turned the corner and still be based upon the same companies." Tony Wadsworth suggested that the squeezed middle concept that is applied to artists applies also to labels: "Labels have been squeezed until they squeaked." Those companies though are markedly different entities to those that existed in 1999, commercially and culturally, and that change will continue apace. Jim Griffin argued that a key contributing factor is the revolution in music marketing strategy: "In the old days it was all about control, it was a very male phenomenon. With the rise of the internet we saw the feminization of marketing, it was less about consummating the relationship with consumers without even knowing their names, and more about establishing valuable relationships that never end." Yet despite all of the added complexities that digital brings, the fundamentals of what a label does remain even more important than they ever were as Goldschmidt described so pithily: "The easier you make it for consumers to get to your music the more you sell."

Labels' monopoly of rights has shielded them from fierce demand side – i.e. music services – competition but on the supply side – i.e. artists – the competition is intense and will only increase. The labels' banks of copyright shielded them from the full impact of demand-side disruption, with any service that wanted to operate legally having to license directly from them or within the relatively narrow constraints of statutory licenses. It is unlikely in the extreme that governments will intervene to compel labels to operate blanket digital licenses so this protection will remain for the foreseeable future. Where labels will feel intensifying disruption however is on the artist side of their business. Labels will evolve but the rate of change in the bigger labels will most likely continue to be moderated by the sense of security that is delivered by enjoying predictable control over the demand side of the market. This of course translates into competitive opportunity for smaller labels, next generation labels and other companies that provide label-like services.

Though we have not yet seen a concerted wave of breakthrough non-label artists maintaining success at scale, this will come. More importantly more artists will look to competitive services to do more of what a label would have traditionally done. This is where the labels will feel the competitive pressure they have been shielded from in the commercial arena and they will need to adapt their businesses accordingly. If they do not the commercial side of their business will be impacted also as more and more of the hot new frontline talent will be breaking through elsewhere. If that goes on for too long the traditional labels will be left looking like little more than licensing vehicles for back catalogue, which is pretty much where EMI was getting to before it got acquired by Universal. What will undoubtedly happen is that however much the big traditional labels adapt, a new generation of digital era labels with flexible, innovative models will become an ever more important part of the landscape, probably helping push the independent label market share up from the c.20% it has been stuck at for years. The last time the independents came to the fore, in the 1980's, the majors went on a shopping spree and assimilated the most successful ones. There is every chance that this could happen again, but the difference this time round is that the majors have to worry about competition from a lot more than just independent labels. So any M&A binge would ultimately prove futile if not backed up with a genuine incorporation of the business practices and cultural ideals of the acquired companies. But let's not wish away the success of the next generation of labels before they have even begun to come to fruition. The future can be truly bright for artist-label relationships, with the balance of power tilting firmly in the direction of the artist. Labels, and label-like companies, will remain the crucial piece of the recorded music business but there will be a renaissance of opportunity for artists with an appetite for adventure. It will take time for many artists to feel the effects, but the change will come and the result will be a more equitable and innovative marketplace for all.

Chapter 17: Artists

Being a recording artist will never be the same again and the future will entail even more change than took place over the last decade. Every artist can build his or her core set of fans but their loyalty cannot be taken for granted. The tools artists have at their disposal give them unprecedented ability to grow global fan bases even if they are not global artists. Yet the efforts associated with maintaining and growing those audiences can quickly become overwhelming, which is why artists will continue to turn to third party specialists, whether they be direct to fan platforms or labels, to outsource many of the nuts and bolts roles necessary for success. The greater control of their destinies artists are developing will be crucial in the near to midterm future as the harsh reality is that they may have to rely even less upon recorded music sales over the coming years, while new business models settle in. Contentious issues of transparency and fairness of payments will take time to resolve but are ultimately details in the much bigger issue of transitioning from sales to monetizing consumption. Ultimately the combination of more equitable deals, more closely aligned stakeholder objectives and increased scale of users will ensure that access based models deliver much more substantial income to artists than is currently the case. Even still it is likely that disparities will remain because:

- Average Revenue Per Artist (ARPA) – a very different thing from Average Revenue Per User (ARPU) – will most likely be smaller from streaming services than for music sales. Although the consumption analysis – see chapter eight – shows us that the discrepancy will be much less than the 200-to-1 ratio of per-stream income compared to per-download income, the 3-to-1 ratio will still leave a pronounced shortfall.

- Annual artist income will be more modest because income from music on streaming services will take longer to realize than the one of income from a sale. It will take time for income to reveal the longer term Life Time Value of a Song.

- Sales, which will still be a crucial part of the revenue mix for the foreseeable future, will nonetheless gradually lessen.

Thus it is crucial that artists become even more effective at making additional income streams work. For some artists this will indeed mean making more from live or selling more t-shirts, but as we have seen their impact should not be overestimated. Instead artists need to focus their energies on learning how to utilize all of the new distribution points on the web to monetize their audiences. Whether they be the D2F platforms, streaming services or social networks. Each and every one of these should be viewed as an opportunity to drive direct spending from their fans, and if any of these do not yet provide the means to drive direct income then artists should apply their collective pressure to ensure they do. In doing so they will find streaming services more willing partners than they might have imagined as this comment from Deezer's Axel Dauchez illustrates: "We are leveraging the revolution in consumer behaviour by becoming a platform. But the innovation has to come from the artists too. The disruption is that one day, instead of selling singles or albums the artist will get compensated from artistic conversation with fans." Artists must continue to become more adept at understanding their audiences and identifying the right product mix for each. They will also have to get even better at prioritizing margin over scale. For example an album might sell a million copies generating the artist perhaps as little as $1 million after label, distributor and retailer costs have been deducted. But selling a t-shirt to 20% of that same audience at $10 mark up for the artist would generate double the income. As Erik Nielsen put it: "If you are selling bread and milk you are never going to make money unless you are a supermarket with vast scale like the labels. Instead you need to be in the business of selling champagne."

Artist Creativity in the Age of Media Mass Customization

The other crucial implication of shrinking music sales is that artists will have to do an even better job of giving their fans a reason to buy their music. This means not just innovating the product but also taking an entirely new approach to creativity by bringing fans into the process. It used to be that playing live was the only regular way of engaging directly with fans on a one-to-many basis. Playing live was also the main way artists could bring fans into the creative process by observing how audiences reacted to new songs and evolving them as they got played throughout a tour.[34] The revolution in social tools and interactive marketing has created a degree of fan engagement previously unimaginable, but digital tools have also enabled fans to start to contribute and participate in the music itself in the shape of cover versions, mash ups, karaoke bootlegs and unofficial remixes. This is the process of Fan-Fuelled Creativity. Despite some stand out experiments and a number of label-led marketing efforts, Fan-Fuelled Creativity is still a largely untapped opportunity. It is also an opportunity to help artists transform a release from a static audio file into a living, evolving creative construct.

The point at which audience and creator meet is no longer a hard break. Affordable digital production technology, user generated content, the remix generation and mash-up culture have all helped create a middle ground that is neither purely audience nor creator. This layer of creator-fans – including also many semi-pro musicians –is increasingly whiting out the creative full stop after a traditional release by creating their own iterations. The late 20th century revolved around mass production and distribution of fixed, physical music formats. But as physical media formats die away to be replaced by modifiable digital alternatives, the early 21st century will become increasingly characterized by the mass customization of music.[35] The creator-fan effectively turns music into open sourced software, where the original song is simply Release Version 1.0. Artists can either embrace it or fight it, either way it will happen, with or without their participation. Though the percentage of fans who add their own creativity to their favourite artist's music will remain relatively small, they will continue to over index in the super fan segments that are so important to labels and artists alike. Their influence is also key, with their creations finding their way in front of mainstream fans via platforms like YouTube, Facebook and Soundcloud.

---

34 The words "here's another new song" uttered by a band during a gig might fill some fans with dread but for others it represents the chance of a priceless experience, of hearing a future classic before anyone else. This fan-engagement dynamic is one of the critical components of Fan-Fuelled Creativity.
35 I am indebted to DJ Spooky for his quote 'the 20th century was about mass production...the 21st century is going to be about mass customization, where you create your own version' http://www.youtube.com/watch?v=1_jtK-WRegA

FIGURE 61

The Three C's of Fan-Fuelled Creativity

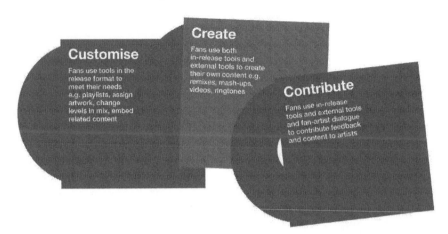

Of course the majority of audiences will not want to become a part of the creative process, they want to remain the audience not the creator. Indeed, most fans of established artists don't even go to their gigs. Similarly most don't regularly visit artists' various social channels, and even of those who do, most don't actively participate, preferring to observe from afar. Put simply, the majority of mainstream music consumers are relatively passive. This is why when artists seek to tap the potential of Fan-Fuelled Creativity they will need to do so with varying degrees of music fan engagement. These are the Three C's of Fan-Fuelled Creativity (see Figure 61):

- Customize. The most mass market and product-centric implementation of Fan-Fuelled Creativity, giving music consumers the ability to customize their music consumption experience.

- Create. For the more creative fans, this encompasses creating mash-ups, bootlegs, ringtones and remixing tracks. There are of course already many good examples of artist and label-led remix competitions and other such initiatives.[36] However for the real potential of Create to be unlocked, such functionality needs to be embedded into recorded music products and formats. In the digital age artists should feel empowered to design at least some of their music with the explicit intention of enabling their fans to create their own content from it.

- Contribute. The most artistically involved of the Three C's, Contribute enables fans to help shape the original music content itself, echoing the wider trend of social co-creation. At a base level this can be simply be a digital extension of the live-gig echo chamber dynamic, testing new songs with online fan communities. At a more involved level it can mean putting fans at the heart of the creative process in the way that Imogen Heap does. Heap regularly turns to her audience, inviting them to participate in the creative process such as contributing lyrics and sound samples.

---

36 Radiohead was an early mover in 2008, making stems of the track 'Nude' available for purchase via iTunes and then allowing fans to upload their own remixes to a specially built remix website and to embed them in their social network pages. The much reported initiative helped push 'Nude' towards becoming Radiohead's first US Billboard Top 40 charting track since 'Creep' 15 years earlier.

The growing portfolio of tools that artists use to communicate with fans have already instigated a change in the artist-fan relationship. Though some artists persist in using social channels as broadcast vehicles rather than genuine, multidirectional conversations, most artists are becoming increasingly cognizant of the value of engagement.[37] This closeness lets artists hear what their fans think about them, though this is not always a comfortable experience as Edgar Berger explained: "It is much more brutal than before. Everyone could always say whatever they liked but now everyone else can see what they say, there is much more of an audience for every single comment. The bad side of this is that comments can be rude, unfair and can discourage artists. The good side is that they can be fantastic for letting artists know what fans really think about their music." Agile Music though, means harnessing this dialogue, cranking the fly wheel of the creative machinery. At its zenith Agile Music delivers a continual iterative process before, during and after the release cycle: a virtuous circle of creativity. Artists can start to think about songs as fluid releases, iteratively evolved works, always evolving. Static, fixed releases were the only viable fit for mass distributed physical media, the only reason they persist in the digital age is the continued adherence to analogue era practices. Of course making every song for every artist a fluid release is not practicable, for just about every element of the digital music value chain. But there is a case for most artists turning some of their music into fluid releases, and indeed some artists will find that they resonate across a majority of their creative output. Business models have been transformed by digital, now it is the turn of the music itself.

---

37 Commercial reach doesn't need to mean a lack of fan interaction, as shown by Lady Gaga who continues to invest time and effort in making her 'Monsters' feel intimately connected with her.

Chapter 18: Revenue Outlook

FIGURE 62

Streaming Will Spur Strong Digital Growth Despite
Helping Decimate the Download Market

Global Digital Music Revenue, Retail Value 2008 to 2019

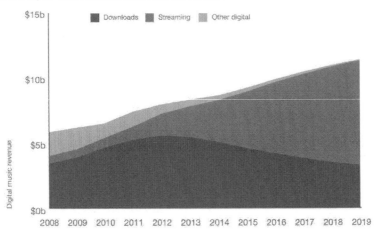

Source: MIDiA Research Music Model (07/14)

If labels, artists, music services and all other music industry stakeholders can overcome
the digital market hurdles and embark on a bold path of innovation and experimentation
then the outlook for digital revenue growth should be strong. Building from the 2008 total
of $5.9 billion (see Figure 62), the global digital music market will nearly double to $11.4
billion by 2019. And it will be a period of pronounced change in the digital landscape:

- Streaming and subscriptions will dominate: Ad supported streaming and subscriptions
  will be the driving force of digital growth generating $8 billion in 2019, 70% of all digital
  revenue, up from 37% in 2014. Premium subscriptions, such as $9.99 services,
  accounted for nearly three quarters of streaming and subscription revenue in 2014 with
  ad supported accounting for the majority of the remainder. By 2019 the streaming
  revenue mix will be more diverse driven by lower priced subscriptions and strong
  growth in ad supported. Ad supported streaming revenue will grow to $2.2 billion in
  2019. Cheaper priced subscriptions will generate $1.1 billion by 2019 and, combined
  with ad supported, will account for 41% of all streaming and subscription revenue.

- Download revenue will shrink as streaming grows: The paid download was always
  a transition technology, a bridge between the analogue world and the digital era.

Swapping ownership for access is not yet a primetime concept but it is not the mainstream that is driving streaming and subscription revenue. Instead it is the most savvy of consumers, those who to date have been the beating heart of download revenues. The combination of streaming services continuing to harvest their subscribers from download buyers and of Apple disrupting itself when it launches its subscription offering, means that streaming will grow at the direct expense of downloads.

- Walking dead music formats and the streaming surge: Over the next five years downloads will decline as quickly as the CD. The problem with this is that these two walking dead music formats will offset the stellar efforts of the streaming sector. Thus global recorded music revenue will continue to decline, only finally returning to modest growth in 2017 by which stage it will grow by less than one percent each year up to 2019. Beneath this less than dazzling global picture though is a diverse mix of country level trends. Japan, currently the world's second biggest music market, shoulders most of the blame for keeping global revenue in check with its revenues set to decline by 27% between 2014 and 2019. Key to this is the absolute dependence on the CD market which is in turn largely a merchandise business in disguise: CDs are often bought for the free gift or ability to get a hand shake with the artist or other such non-music benefits. None of which transfer well to digital. Little wonder then that digital revenues in Japan have actually been in decline since 2008 and only represent 16% of all revenue. Elsewhere though streaming will drive dramatic market growth, not just digitally but lifting the entire market up. We have already seen this happening in Nordic markets like Sweden and others will follow suit, including the Netherlands which will return to a top 10 global ranking, a position it lost some years ago. In fact streaming will help create a recalibration of the global music industry with previously smaller markets becoming digital powerhouses and larger markets seeing their dominance weaken.

- Transition not cannibalization: The shift of digital revenue from downloads to streaming is not a cannibalization story but instead the manifestation of the shift from the distribution era of selling units – physical or digital – to the consumption era where access is monetized. It is a transition process similar to that of the CD to Downloads. The difference though is that whereas the CD was a mature product that had been at the top of its tree for many years, the paid Download was still getting going. The transition of its most valuable customers happened before it had a chance to become a de facto dominant music format.

FIGURE 63

The Long Flash-to-Bang: Download Buyers Will
Still Outnumber Subscribers By 2019
Global Digital Music Customers by Product Type, 2008 to 2019

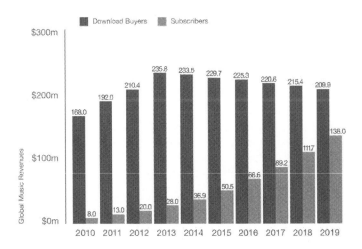

The revenue outlook does not however paint the entire picture. With so much of the future impetus coming from free streaming the growth of audiences is just as important a part of understanding what the future will look like. While streaming and subscriptions will represent a majority of global digital music revenue by 2016 it will take another three years before the installed base of subscribers will outnumber download buyers. As with any new technology there is a long 'flash to bang' from the technology being recognized as being revolutionary to when mainstream consumers adopt in numbers. The fact that subscription spending skews towards the higher spending music consumers, and therefore accentuates the revenue shift, obscures the slower shift in consumer behavior.

Download buyers will remain the largest global premium digital music audience by 2019. By 2019 the number of download buyers will have declined by 10% on 2014 levels, compared to 35% for download revenues. The loss of the higher spending download buyers to subscriptions will pull down headline revenues but the bulk of the installed base of less high spending buyers will remain. Downloads will continue to be a highly accessible digital entry point for mainstream consumers in many markets, meaning that underneath the headline buyer number will be a more complex picture of a steady influx of new digital consumers set against an outflow of others towards subscription services. In some markets though, especially those where downloads never got a foothold, a technology leapfrog effect will take place with digital music consumers going straight to subscriptions, bypassing downloads entirely. This will mirror the trend of many consumers in emerging markets bypassing the desktop web and going straight to mobile broadband.

Conclusion

Throughout the music industry's first digital decade and beyond business models have been turned upside down, revenue streams contracted, worldviews challenged and countless digital milestones passed and forgotten (see Figure 64). The music industry has been reshaped beyond recognition and the rate of change will only accelerate, that much is clear. What remains up for grabs is whether the future will be a brave new world of opportunity or instead an industry Armageddon. Interestingly the strongest positive advocacy positions are emerging from the record labels. For example the RIAA's Cary Sherman said there is: "cause for optimism: our revenue growth has stabilised and digital streaming revenues are growing extremely fast." Other executives pointed to the corner being turned and being 'on the road to recovery.' Meanwhile there is a pervasive theme of fear, uncertainty and doubt among the artist and songwriter community as illustrated by this comment from songwriter Helienne Lindvall: "There is money in the internet but it is just not going to us." While David Byrne said of streaming: "I feel it's the last nail in the coffin."

FIGURE 64

Music's First Digital Decade and Beyond

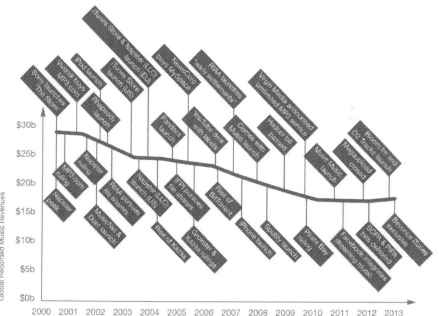

If this was an industry in which the key players did not collectively have exclusive control of the majority of the content then the scale and impact of disruption would have been even more dramatic than what we see now. It took less than five years for Apple and Android to turn Nokia from global smartphone leader into also ran, but after 15 years of disruption the record labels and publishers retain near absolute control of the supply of content in the music business, albeit a much smaller one. Or in the words of Lewis Silkin's Cliff Fluet: "Whilst the triangle is of totally different size it is of exactly the same shape." As we have seen this has had both positive and negative implications but perhaps most important of all it provides a foundation of stability and predictability. The challenge that technology innovators and others must rise to is to ensure that it translates into long term transformative vision rather than retreating into hubris and conservatism.

The most meaningful way of understanding change is looking at how it impacts all of the stakeholders across the business. Throughout this book we have seen that there is no single digital effect. That digital disruption not only has a different bearing on different parts of the industry but also varies markedly within them, and even then the outcome is not determined simply by one party being more innovative. One artist can pursue exactly the same digital strategy as another but have an utterly different experience because their audience or genre of music is different, without even considering the quality of their music. This unpredictability stems from two causes: 1) music is a creative industry that is ultimately dependent upon unpredictable human emotion 2) we are still in the comparatively early days of digital. Though much has happened, the continued strength of the CD across the globe emphasizes just how much distance remains to be travelled. It is a point made by John Irwin: "The disruption of the breaking up of physical music changed everything. But it took 15 years to get some semblance of what the business model is going forward and all that stuff in the middle has been turned on its head by digital." If the late 1990's and 2000's were market immaturity then the 2010's are digital music's adolescence. The changes that will occur in the coming years will not be the end game but they will be the foundational character traits that will underpin the long-term shape of the digital music market.

Measuring the Change

Technology changes quickly, mainstream consumer behaviour follows more gradually, while incumbent industries adapt even more sluggishly. The long flash-to-bang can feel bewildering and frustrating to the digerati and early adopters but this is the nature of digital change. For example the arrival of Spotify's free music service in 2008 represented the first licensed music service that actually tried to embrace the consumer usability principles that Napster had defined nearly an entire decade earlier. In the first 15 years of digital music more questions have been asked than answered but the rate of response absolutely needs to accelerate if the level in the glass is to rise. Notable progress has been made on some counts while depressingly little has been achieved on others:

- Piracy: Piracy was the record labels' obsession in the earliest days of digital and it distracted some of the industry's key resources and best brains when that effort would have been better served building the foundations for the legitimate market. As the 2000's progressed it became clear that no amount of enforcement was going to eradicate piracy, with fragmentation delivering diminishing enforcement ROI. Efforts are now correctly more focused on containment and ultimately file sharing will fade as access progressively trumps ownership. The new threat is the insidious conflation of piracy with copyright reform by elements of the technology lobby, attempting to use the labels' heavy handed, low effectiveness enforcement as a case for copyright change. Thus just as piracy is on the verge of a downward trajectory its impact, albeit indirectly, may be far bigger than it ever was during its peak years.

- Copyright: The global music rights landscape is fragmented and complex. Government intervention has done little except complicate matters further – especially in Europe – and yet the industry itself has proven incapable of getting its own house in order. The reciprocal mesh of collection societies across the globe is simply not fit for digital purpose. The brave efforts of more innovative societies such as the UK's PRS and Sweden's STIM to drive through efforts such as the Hub strategy are swimming against the tide. If the music industry wants a vibrant sector of young, innovative start ups it needs to simplify matters radically. As Larry Miller observed: "I find nothing so disheartening as a young entrepreneur who has got investors for his idea and then finds himself facing the quagmire that is digital music licensing."[38] Currently the complexity skews the market to the big technology companies with deep enough pockets to navigate the complex waters. Cliff Fluet summed up how things can look from a music service's perspective: "There's a big lorry outside and I want a million quid for it but I won't tell you what is inside it. I won't tell you what isn't inside it. I won't tell you precisely what ground it covers. But you have to buy my lorry or you can't launch your services. That is how music rights licensing can feel." In addition the big publishers' push for a 'fairer share', however sound the case may be, will put the still fragile digital music business under huge stress and if labels do not blink first some big music services will pay the ultimate price and fail.

- Copyright reform: That copyright needs reform is clear to most, but there is also a danger that concerted pressure from the technology sectors may skew reform towards weakening rights owners' ability to protect their IP rather than making it easier to innovate. The scene is set for copyright reform of potentially dramatic proportions according to Beggars' Martin Mills: "In the next ten years what happens to the rewriting of copyright laws will be the most important change." The precedents that will be set in music copyright legislation will however go even further than the music industry as the Orchard's Scott Cohen argued: "We have to get copyright right now. We are moving away from a physical age of industrial production to one of intangible goods and services. We are approaching a point where the West is banking on IP. If everything is based on ideas then it is crucial that there is a robust system for remuneration." Whether the technology companies like it or not, sooner or later they will have to recognize that the legal and moral foundations of patents and copyright are remarkably similar and that changes in one will eventually shape the other.

- Innovation: 'Innovation' is a term devalued through overuse yet remains pivotal to the future of the music industry in a way that it never was in the analogue era. However there has too often been tension between digital music innovation and rights owner objectives, as Fluet observed: "There is an obsession with the technology not the behaviour and usage, there is a convergence of technology but a divergence of business needs and rights." Too often the result is music services diluting their user experiences down to the lowest common denominator of rights owner conservatism, with piracy the only clear beneficiary.

- Mobile: Apple was an innovation anomaly and there is nothing to suggest any other company is going to be able to build such a vibrant paid content ecosystem. But it has opened up a new window of mobile opportunity by kick starting the app economy. Music

38   The convolution of a digital license is ironically far removed from the relative simplicity of the analogue model as Peter Jenner noted: "If you were a label all you had to do was clear publishing. If you were a retailer all you had to do was have an account with a maximum of ten distributors who would extend you lines of credit if you got into difficulties."

services will need to harness the unique dynamics of the app economy and connected devices, especially multimedia and in app payments. In app payments may just be the way in which the music industry manages to make the economics of freemium add up.

- The decline of ownership: The first phase of digital music, from Napster through to iTunes, was all about replicating the ownership model in digital contexts. Access based models though go much further, turning half a century's worth of music consumption on its head by removing for ever the need to own music. The outlook is disconcerting for many but the momentum is increasingly irresistible as the NMPA's David Israelite noted: "It is a tremendous mistake to dictate to consumers what they want. It may be that the future is one without ownership of content and we will have to work out how to make that work. If you're focused on the next quarter then this is a concern, but if you focus on the longer term you plan for how to make it work." The change is so fundamental its true impact will be measured not in years but in generational terms. In the interim access models will coexist with ownership, not just in terms of download stores but physical products too.[39]

- Investment: Investment is the life blood of digital music but its flow fluctuates between torrent and trickle, with investors often uncomfortable with many rights holder practices. The investment flowing into the big bets like Spotify, Deezer and Beats Music obscures the fact that less money is flowing into early stage start up licensed music services. The cost of major label advances, 'set up' fees, 'administration fees', minimum revenue guarantees and the technology infrastructure requirements of cloud era services are making digital music a rich man's game. Yet the returns remain in question as Larry Miller observed: "I am hard pressed to think of a digital music start up that achieved true scale via negotiated voluntary licenses with the exceptions of Spotify and Vevo. Statutory licenses have a much better route to scale, and provided Pandora with a licensing framework that enabled the company to get big, fast." Even Spotify proved its model with easier to obtain minor markets licenses before pushing into the big music markets.

- Innovator hegemony: A direct consequence of the major labels' preference for working with companies that have 'scale' has been to skew opportunities towards big established companies, especially Apple, Google and Amazon, and to a lesser degree Sony and Samsung. This coupled with the high investment barriers to entry for small start ups has created a de facto power base for the big technology companies. All of the industry's concerns about companies like Google influencing copyright legislation, and of other partners not doing enough to drive music sales are a direct consequence of the labels' own strategy. Until anti-trust and competition legislation applies more evenly to technology and media companies, labels and publishers will have little meaningful ability to challenge the innovator hegemony. This alone is reason enough for them to double down on their efforts with smaller technology partners.

- Creator empowerment: Artists and songwriters have begun to find their voice, and throughout the next decade they will need to translate mindshare into commercial influence. They are the fuel in the engine without whom everything would come to a grinding halt, and yet in the first 15 years of digital music they have too often been little more than an after thought. The revenue outlook for many is unclear and they will feel the growing pains of new business models far more keenly than big labels and publishers. Artists starting

39 Vinyl sales soared throughout the early 2010's while CD boxsets and collectibles continued to prosper. They did so because once the threshold of having all the music in the world available at the swipe of a fingertip has been passed music fans start looking for something more, something tangible

out on their careers now have to learn to do what ten years prior a record label would have done for them, just to get to a position where a record label might sign them. The resulting two year lag in artist careers makes it difficult for those without economic means to make a go of it as Keith Harris explained: "It is much harder for people who do not have financial means to forge a career in music…So the opposite of what everyone thought was going to happen has taken place." Artists will need to get even better at engaging their core super fans to get through what will be a difficult period for many, while songwriters will have to explore ways they can insert themselves in the DIY value chain.[40]

- Breaking through: Discovery has become the key strategic challenge for streaming music services but the stakeholders who feel the impact most are artists and songwriters. The Tyranny of Choice means that it is harder than ever for artists to break through the clutter – the background noise is drowning out the song. Harris goes as far to argue that: "the next phase of the music business won't come about until the features are significant enough to allow people to skate over the good stuff to find the great stuff that they will feel passionate about."

- Data: The first generation of music services forced labels into a massive digitization process, creating vast databases and new processes. Streaming services have turned up the volume, generating huge, unprecedented tracts of listening data. The industry is only just beginning to come to terms with how to deal with this tidal wave of big data but its potential is clear as Mark Knight explained: "Data is pivotal, data defines everything, it drives what a programme does. Code can be rewritten but data is irreplaceable." More data of course means greater accountability and data will form the backdrop for many of the key debates in the next decade according to Jeremy Silver: "Tech companies, for all their naivety, offered the potential of providing an unprecedented detail of transactional data that threatened, and continues to threaten, to shed too much light on rights holder practices."

- The artist-fan relationship: Artists and fans are closer together than ever before but the intimacy is sometimes uncomfortable. There is also a danger that 'fan engagement strategies' are beginning to erode the value of the new digital interactions because they too often treat tools such as Facebook and Twitter in the same way as traditional marketing tools i.e. as platforms to shout marketing messages from, not as venues for genuine conversation and dialogue. A fundamental shift has taken place in the artist-fan relationship and it is crucial that the underlying principles of the new relationships are not forgotten in a rush to drive 'engagement metrics'. Sumit Bothra summarized the key change that has taken place: "The relationship has moved from 'buy my music' to 'we kind of know each other now'".

- The wider industry: The oft-used argument that the recorded music business should be considered entirely separately from live and other industry revenues misses the point that all aspects of the industry have intimately intertwined symbiotic relationships. As we have seen again and again throughout this book, the recorded music product is what drives everything else. Unless artists break through the clutter with their recordings they cannot hope to earn income from live, merchandize, branding and the rest. By the same token, those sectors will fail without a vibrant influx of new artists with audiences at scale. If a new generation of superstar platinum selling artists – or superstars in terms of whatever

---

40 This could be pitching songs directly to DiY artists; setting up a songwriter collective where artists can self serve songs and songwriters to work with; running crowd funding campaigns for a body of work that will be written just for DIY artists. The unifying strand throughout these concepts is of songwriters targeting artists who might not normally turn to third party songwriters and who control all of their rights. So a songwriter can both open up new opportunities and strike innovative commercial terms geared at enabling the songwriter to share in D2F revenue and, ideally, some portion of the other income streams of early stage DIY artists. Additionally should the artist then get picked up by a label and / or publisher the songwriter is part of the team.

will be the streaming era equivalent measure of success – does not break through, super sized stadiums may have to look for other ways to fill their seats once the current wave of headliners retire. For all the pop stardom of the likes of Justin Beiber and Miley Cyrus, big venues need artists who can expect to hold onto their audiences twenty years from now, something that few pop sensations achieve.[41] However it is clear that the equation is rebalancing and that recorded music is settling towards a new level of importance. With so many established artists reporting that music sales – and streaming – can be up to ten times smaller than live and other income the wider music industry is no longer the ancillary component, but the core. A 2013 UK Music study suggested recorded music was just 18% of the total UK music industry. Though that number is deflated by a broad definition of music revenue streams it nonetheless gives us an indication of the changing industry landscape.[42]

In many respects the fundamentals of the music business, namely the music itself, remain intact, as Sony's Edgar Berger explained: "Nothing changed and everything did. It is still entirely about the song. It was everything else – the business – that changed." Nonetheless the first 15 years of digital music laid the foundations for what will be an even more transformative phase. The rate of change will accelerate because of improving technology and growing consumer sophistication but also because the next generation of music executives will be digital natives who have never known an analogue-era music business as Barney Wragg described: "We are now getting kids at labels who have had iTunes for 10 years. You are going to need this generation of digital natives running labels for the next transformative stage of change to happen." Many of the challenges this new generation will face are the same ones the current generation has been trying to solve, not least of which is learning how to make business work when everything is infected with free as Martin Goldschmidt observed: "We have the same challenge as water – it is freely and widely available. Our biggest weapons are convenience, curation and credibility." But to succeed this next generation will need to blend first hand experience of the technology and start up world with music industry experience as Paul Hitchman suggested: "You have to have been through this to understand how the new music business works."

FIGURE 65

The Balance Of Revenue Power In The Music Industry Has Firmly Shifted

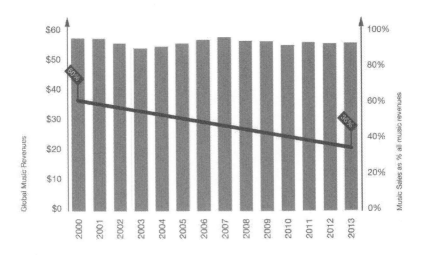

The seismic shockwaves that continue to rip through the recorded music business coincided with a renaissance in the live music business. Compare and contrast the 60% growth in live revenue between 2000 and 2013 with the 42% decline in recorded income. The net effect is that the share of total revenues accounted for by recorded income fell from 60% in 2000 to just 36% in 2013. The balance of power has firmly shifted away from labels to the live value chain. And yet recorded music is still the main way people interact with music. Whether it be on the radio, YouTube, Spotify, iTunes or a CD, the vast majority of consumers spend the vast majority of their music consumption time with the recorded product not the live product. So labels are faced with the paradox of making less money from artists yet those same artists still needing the recording in order to make all their other income streams work.

The realignment of revenue is merely a precursor to the new business models, products and career paths that will emerge to capitalize on the new world order. We are probably about half way through a huge period of transition for the music industry. It is in this next phase that the real 'fun' will start. Expect every traditional element of the industry to be challenged to its core, expect dots to be joined and old models to be broken. But be in no doubt that what we will end up with will be an industry set up for success in the digital era.

The next 15 years are drenched with promise and potential and they will leave the music industry virtually unrecognizable from how it was in that innocent summer of 1999 before Napster changed everything. Many of the underlying principles and structures of that music industry are still here now because the CD remains the number one source of recorded music income. But new structures and principles are also in place to ensure that the next stage of transition is both faster and smoother than the first. Change is never easy but this time round the music industry, if it can rise to the challenge, has the opportunity to ensure that the glass is undisputedly half full.

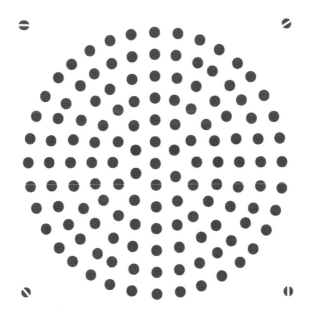

Appendices

Awakening by Mark Mulligan

Publishing Rights Deep Dive

Publishing rights are the most complex component of the music industry and warrant at least a whole book in their own right. The complexity is probably more detail than most readers of this book need. So in order to help ensure the Songwrriter's Story chapter did not become too dense a read I have taken some of the detail out of there and included it here as an appendix. Though even this is little more than a cursory overview of some of the key complexities.

With at least one PRO in every country the publishing side of the rights equation has a huge amount of inherent complexity. When there are multiple PROs in a single market, such as in the US, the situation can become problematic for licensees. This was particularly true in the earliest days of digital when PRO databases and systems had not even begun the long path to digitization. Former Geffen CTO Jim Griffin recalled the difficulty of trying to secure the publishing rights for Geffen's early forays into digital: "It quickly became clear to me that we didn't know who owned most of the rights. And I equally quickly realized that an NMPA (National Music Publishers' Association) license was simply a license to hunt for licenses. When you went to a Harry Fox they would say 'we're going to get you 30-40% of the rights you want, we're not going to tell you who, how or where." As the digital market progressed some collection societies rose to the challenge and started developing innovative licensing frameworks to try to help the market move forward. One of these was the UK's MCPS-PRS Alliance – now called PRS for Music – striking partnership deals with other societies to provide a 'one stop' digital license for Anglo-American and Anglo-Latin repertoires across Europe. The Alliance was also an early licensor to digital services in the UK as PRS for Music CEO Robert Ashcroft explained: "PRS was the first collecting society to license a digital service [OD2 in 2001], the first to license iTunes, the first to license YouTube and the first to license iTunes Match. We have always acted commercially to support the development of the online market." The more innovative approach of the UK's PRS contrasts strongly with a less dynamic approach from some other European PROs, most notably Germany's GEMA which in 2013 had still not licensed to YouTube and has earned a reputation for licensing intransigence. However Tom Frederikse, partner at law firm Clintons, made the case that inconvenience for digital services from the other side of the negotiating table can often be the manifestation of standing firm for songwriters' rights: "GEMA may seem intransigent and their rates may appear higher than most others', but they are ballsy and determined. In some ways they are like the secret fantasy of publishers, and perhaps in the long run may end up looking like the greatest champion of songwriters."

Even if all of the global PROs had similar commercial strategies, the inescapable fact would remain that the system is a complex one that is in clear need of stronger, faster and more ambitious innovation if it is to avoid slowing the digital music market. The global PRO landscape evolved over successive decades in the analogue era, building a complex interconnected web of bilateral reciprocal relationships. Each society agreed individual deals with each other individual society to collect in their local market on behalf of the other when music from their country is played in the other's, and vice versa. It is a model that made sense in the analogue era but is incongruous in the digital age. Launching a digital service can often mean negotiating deals with every single PRO in every market that service wants to launch in. Recently some major publishers withdrew their digital rights from some societies which means negotiation is now often a vast undertaking for a would be digital music service, having to license both from the publishers directly and with the PROs for the smaller publishers' rights. All of which can be as confusing for the songwriters themselves as it can the music services as Lindvall observed: "When I was only working as a songwriter I didn't understand half the complexity that I do now. All I used to know I was limited to what I learned from royalty statements." It took Lindvall becoming a music industry journalist to be in a position to see the bigger picture that songwriters most often are not aware of. Complexity is particularly pronounced in Europe where licensing across 28 territories with multiple publishers and dozens of PROs to reach a combined population of 740 million compares unfavourably with a handful of publishers and PROs to reach 314 million people in the US. Lewis Silkin's Cliff Fluet argued that: "Europe now has a 48 stop license." One global digital service said that it was able to accommodate the complexity because it had a sizeable licensing team with local licensing experts in each market. This however is clearly not feasible for early stage start ups with scarce resources. A number of senior label-side executives made the case that this is simply a reflection of the costs of doing business in digital music and that start ups can instead focus on launching in a smaller number of markets and growing from there.

Another approach is to game the system, to agree to play by the rules but bend them slightly, a sort of misbehaving Rights Ally approach as law firm' Wiggin's Alexander Ross explained: "When I advise music services I say 'if you want to operate across all territories on a fully licensed business it is practically impossible. The best thing to do is acquire the key major rights and work onwards from there'. Apple and Google have resources for negotiating terms in all territories, small start ups don't. In practice you will never get all the rights on board before launching so if you must launch you need to launch with good intent, making it clear that you want to get all the licenses you need." Although labels and publishers make it clear to music services that this approach will prevent them from 'getting off on the right foot' many start ups see it as the only way to try to mitigate some of the tech super powers' distinct advantage. Paul Hitchman suggested that this 'creative' approach to licensing was key to Spotify's success: "Spotify could never have launched without having started in a small market like Sweden. They launched with local licenses and advantageous collection society legislation. By the time they had momentum they could use that as a proof of concept to get licenses for major markets."

The disjointed PRO environment differs markedly from the label side of the equation with major labels, who over the years have been increasingly willing to sign global deals thus making it more straightforward for music services to build global strategies around the recorded rights. For years the anomaly was the independent label sector, an intrinsically fragmented arena, but this was addressed with the formation of the Merlin Network in 2007 that pulled together the rights of 120,000 independent labels, across 35 countries, representing three million tracks.[1] Similar moves have started to be put into motion among PROs, most notably with the emergence of a 'Hub' strategy whereby groups of smaller PROs assign their rights into a regional grouping, often administered by a single larger PRO. The Hub approach builds upon previous collaborative efforts such as the Joint Nordic/Baltic Online License that since early 2009 saw the eight Nordic and Baltic collection societies pooling their rights. One of the key architects of the Hub strategy was the PRS's Ashcroft who tried to apply to the PRO world some of the business strategy learned during his days at Sony. It was something of a baptism of fire for Ashcroft as he grappled with the complexities: "I remember standing with my laptop open on the bonnet

1   Numbers refer to June 2013 as reported by the Merlin Network.

of my old Land Rover at 1 o'clock in the morning one day during the summer of 2010. The scene was the station car park at Effingham Junction and I was consulting one of our major publisher members on the final details of my Hubs paper. He was still in the office, I was new to the industry and I was trying to apply business logic and strategy to an incredibly complex rights landscape. I'd consulted with multiple parties by then and was finalizing the document; so far it seems to have stood the test of time and I don't think I'd change a word of it."

As of 2013 a number of key European licensing hubs have emerged including Armonia[2] and PRS for Music's collaboration with STIM in Sweden and GEMA, and Ashcroft is confident of the model's potential: "The European rights landscape will evolve into a single repertoire database with a few processing hubs and multiple local front offices. This model will eventually go global." The approach certainly has plenty of advocates who can clearly see the progress from the previous situation as Frederikse explained: "Hub licensing has already provided very helpful efficiencies in the European rights landscape by creating what is effectively something like a '4-stop-shop' for nearly all repertoire." Though he also maintains that "it is not sustainable to have 27 independent and separate national societies in Europe; it is an anachronism in the 21st century." Thus Hubs bring much needed efficiency and effectiveness but many of the underlying dynamics still seem inconsistent with the concept of a single global digital marketplace. Hubs are a step on the journey but not the destination.

Hub licensing was in part a response to the continued threat of governmental intervention into the licensing arena, particularly in Europe. The European Commission on multiple occasions expressed an interest in bringing competition and efficiency to the European licensing landscape. Unfortunately the result has too often been an unworkable fudge that, according to Frederikse, complicated matters further: "Digital music publishing changed in Europe in 2005 when the European Commission meddled and introduced three options intended to drive competition. European politicians were hopelessly confused by how songwriting rights work." It is a view shared by Lindvall who argued that although there needs to be more oversight: "when the EU tried to sort out PROs they only succeeded in making the issue more complicated." Fluet echoed the view that European decision making has been hampered by a lack of understanding of the music publishing business: "The EU has always struggled with copyright because it is a monopoly right. But just because it is a monopoly right does not inherently mean it is an abuse of monopolistic position." One of the outcomes that the EU's approach enabled was for major publishers to withdraw some of their rights from PROs and to compel music services to strike deals directly with them, thus adding to the complexity, not reducing it. From the publishers' perspective this was an opportunity to take more control over their digital destinies and to get larger shares of the income by cutting out the PRO middleman. The trigger point for the withdrawal of rights was the Dutch PRO BUMA STEMRA attempting to strike an ambitious pan European license. Frederiske picks up the story: "Two services were responsible for bringing the next big change to the European rights landscape: eMusic and Beatport. eMusic went to BUMA STEMRA and asked if they could do a pan-European deal for them as they were the society they had the best working relationship with. BUMA said 'yes, we're going to interpret our reciprocal relationships as a mandate for licensing all repertoire for all territories'. Few took notice when this first happened because eMusic was small in Europe… but then BUMA offered a pan-European blanket license to Beatport – who signed up and announced the deal. PRS promptly sued BUMA and won an injunction declaring that BUMA did not have the right to license PRS' rights outside of Holland. The repercussions were huge: the industry thought BUMA was trying to do a 'land

2   Armonia includes the repertoire of SACEM, SGAE, SIAE, UMPI, SONY Latino, PEER Latino and SPA.

grab' that would make it disproportionately powerful and many worried that other PROs might follow suit. So the four major publishers withdrew their digital mechanical rights." The net result of which is that publishers were able to negotiate higher rates by licensing directly to music services.

While all this took place in Europe a parallel scenario began to play out on the other side of the Atlantic with some publishers withdrawing their mechanical rights from US PROs, though the stated rationale was very different. In the US publishers sought to remove their rights because they felt constrained by government regulation and fixed price regimes that dated back decades as the NMPA's CEO David Israelite explained: "Where we find ourselves today is a historical anomaly. Consent decrees put us at a disadvantage with other rights holders. Many publishers are withdrawing their rights so that they are no longer treated as a monopolist and can negotiate better rights." Many songwriters voiced concern that music services that are able to operate under statutory rates and consent decrees do not pay enough back in royalties. Pandora, which operates under statutory rates that publishers cannot negotiate directly,[3] found itself the main target of this criticism. These royalty rates for Pandora's so called semi-interactive radio are significantly lower than services like Spotify pay because the listener cannot chose what they listen to. Pandora actually pays more to recording artists than terrestrial US radio – though that is not too fantastic an achievement considering terrestrial radio pays artists nothing in the US. By actively lobbying Congress for lower statutory songwriter royalties Pandora quickly made an enemy of much of the songwriter community. The very fact Pandora was able to seek Congressional intervention strikes at the heart of much of the growing discontent as David Lowery explained: "Consent decrees and compulsory statutory rates mean that the playing field is totally uneven. The ironic and unintended consequence of the situation is that the most vibrant part of the economy – the tech sector – is effectively subsidized."

Whether there was coordination between the US and European publisher withdrawal processes or not, the combined effect was major publishers in both regions being in a position to license directly with music services rather than relying on PROs. Though big publishers are now in a position to secure higher license fee rates, songwriters are not universally convinced they will feel the benefits as Lindvall explained: "As a songwriter I am not confident that a publisher's ability to negotiate better rates will benefit me. Publishers have different priorities than PROs such as having lots of shareholders to pay." There is also a question of whether the same commercial licensing principles that apply to the recording rights should be applied to publishing. Frederikse for one does not believe so: "The notion of a 'market rate' for publishing rights is a non-sequitur, as it suggests applying a capitalist dynamic to a non-capitalist market. When a service licenses a sound recording in any event it is choosing which catalogues and/or tracks it wants. Any service can safely/legally launch without having licensed all recording catalogues – and in each instance when a recording licence is concluded, the service actually receives the recordings for ingestion (by FTP or other system). With publishing, a service cannot know which titles it is getting from which licensor, so it has the stark choice of: (a) license every composition from every publisher and every society in the world; or (b) operate anxiously and nervously with ever-present exposure to litigation. Therefore music publishing licensing is essentially an involuntary process, and is not subject to normal market dynamics."

Apple's iTunes Radio emerged as an early success story for the direct licensing model, resulting in Apple paying better rates to major publishers for the service launched in late 2013. A cynic however might question whether there was ulterior motive for Apple

3   Under terms of the DMCA interactive radio services do not need to seek commercially negotiated licenses from rights holders as long as they comply with clearly specified limits on user interactivity.

setting a higher rate precedent for interactive radio, making it harder for standalone services like Pandora and Slacker to operate while it of course can afford to run a radio service at break-even, or even at a loss in order to help sell more iOS devices.

Glossary of Terms

UMG (Universal Music Group) – The world's largest major label record group

Sony Music – One of the world's three largest major labels

WMG (Warner Music Group) – One of the world's three largest major label groups

MP3 (MPEG-2 Audio Layer III) – The world's most common
digital music file format and encoding format.

AIM (Association of Independent Music) – Trade body for the independent recorded music sector

DPI (Deep Packet Inspection) – A method of assessing the content of data
passing across computer networks. Used by ISPs to monitor P2P activity

ARPU (Average Revenue Per User) – The average amount of
money spent / generated by an individual consumer

CAGR (Compound Annual Growth Rate) – The average growth rate over a period
of time, which in this book exclusively refers to the average growth each year

File Sharing – The sharing of usually, but not always, unlicensed music files.

P2P (Peer-to-Peer) – The underlying technology used in
networked music file sharing / music piracy

Centralized File Sharing – A network where files are distributed from a central server e.g. Napster

De-Centralized File Sharing – A network where files are distributed
using the computers of the network itself e.g. BitTorrent

DRM (Digital Rights Management) – Technology used to protect music files
by locking it with an encryption key served from a central server

Tethered Stream / Cached Stream – A temporary copy of a music file that resides on the
device of the listener so that stream can be listened to even without an internet connection

3G – The most prevalent mobile data network, currently being superseded
by 4G which is also referred to as Long Term Evolution (LTE)

IFPI (The International Federation of the Music Industry) – The
global recorded music industry trade body

RIAA (The Recording Association of America) – The US recorded music industry trade body

PRO (Performing Rights Organization) – The organizations that collect royalties for
the public performance of music. These are often also collection societies.

BPI (British Phonographic Industry) – UK recorded music industry trade body

Collection Societies – The organizations that license copyrighted works and collect royalties as part of compulsory and/or individual licences negotiated on behalf of its members. Members are typically songwriters while board members are typically publishers.

FAC (The Featured Artists Coalition) – A Trade body for artists.

MPAA (The Music Publishers' Association of America) – A trade body for US music publishers.

MMF (Music Managers Forum) – A trade body for music managers.

PRS for Music – The UK performing rights organization and collection society

ASCAP (The American Society of Composers, Authors and Publishers) – One of the four US PROs

BMI (Broadcast Music, Inc) – One of the four US PROs

Sound Exchange – One of the four US PROs. Set up as a result of the Digital Millennium Copyright Act, Sound Exchange is a statutory organization that collects revenues for statutory digital licensed services. The other US PROs are SESAC, Harry Fox Agency, BMI.

DMCA (the Digital Millennium Copyright Act) – The landmark US digital copyright legislation passed in 1998 that has provided the global standard for digital copyright across the globe.

Warez – This term is used to describe copyrighted works that are distributed and shared without paying royalties, usually in violation of copyright law. Warez sites are websites that host and distribute these sorts of files.

Bibliography

How Music Works. David Byrne. Canongate Books 2013

Diffusion of Innovations. Everett M Rogers. Simon & Schuster International 2003

The Innovator's Dilemma: When New Technologies Cause Great Firms to Fail (Management of Innovation and Change). Clayton M Christensen. Harvard Business Review Press; Reprint edition 2013

Crossing the Chasm: Marketing and Selling Technology Products to Mainstream Customers. Geoffrey A Moore. Capstone 1998

Copyright and Creation: A Case for Promoting Inclusive Online Sharing. Cammaerts, Mansell, Meng. London School of Economics 2013

The UK Music Consumer: A presentation for UK Music prepared by Oliver & Ohlbaum Associates. Copyright research 2012

The Economic Contribution of the Core UK Music Industry. UK Music 2013

IFPI Recording Industry in Numbers. IFPI Editions 2012, 2011, 2010, 2009, 2008, 2007, 2006, 2005, 2004, 2003, 2002, 2001

BPI Yearbook. BPI Editions 2013, 2012, 2011.

BPI Statistical Handbook. BPI Editions 2010, 2009, 2008, 2007.

Rockonomics: The Economics of Popular Music Alan Krueger 2006

AIM Membership Survey 2011 Results. Association of Independent Music

Collective Management of Copyright and Related Rights. Daniel J. Gervais Kluwer Law International 2010

In Rainbows, On Torrents. Will Page and Eric Garland. PRS 2008

Music to the M Power. MTV 2013

What's it worth? Calculating the economic value of live music. Dave Laing. Live Music Exchange. June 2012

Developer Economics. Vision Mobile 2013

Statistics and Social Network of YouTube Videos. Xu Cheng, Cameron Dale, Jiangchuan Liu, School of Computing Science Simon Fraser University

Burnaby, BC, Canada 2007

TED Talk: Eli Pariser: Beware online "filter bubbles". TED May 2011

TED Talk: Amanda Palmer: The Art of Asking. TED March 2013

The Music Format Bill Of Rights: A Manifesto for the Next Generation of Music Products. Mark Mulligan, Music Industry Blog 2013

Agile Music: Music Formats and Artist Creativity In The Age of Media

Mass Customization. Mark Mulligan, Music Industry Blog 2011

Making Freemium Add Up: An Assessment of Content Monetization.

Mark Mulligan, MIDiA Research 2013

360-Degree Music Experiences: Use The Cloud To Target Device-

Use Orbits. Mark Mulligan, Forrester Research 2010

Digital Natives: The Generation That Music Product Strategy Forgot. Mark Mulligan, Forrester Research 2011

Disruptive Renewal. Mark Mulligan, Forrester Research 2010

European Next-Generation Digital Music Services: Remove Consumer Barriers to Drive Mass-Market Adoption. Mark Mulligan, JupiterResearch 2008

Music Product Manifesto: The Product Features That Will Save Recorded Music. Mark Mulligan, Forrester Research 2009

How Digital Licensing Will Help Save The Music Industry. Mark Mulligan, Forrester Research 2009

Music Release Windows: The Product Innovation That The Music Business Can't Do Without. Mark Mulligan, Forrester Research 2009

Music Industry Meltdown: Recasting The Mold. Mark Mulligan, Forrester Research 2010

Taking Digital Music To The Mainstream: The Music Product Features For The Living Room. Mark Mulligan, Forrester Research 2009

Which Device Offers The Best: Music Experience? Mark Mulligan and Sonal Ghandi, Forrester Research 2009

Paying For Success: When Audiences Grow More Quickly Than Ad Revenue. Mark Mulligan, Forrester Research 2009

The Future of Digital Music: Fighting Free with Free. Mark Mulligan, JupiterResearch 2007

European Digital Music Consumer Survey, 2006: Legitimate Market Remains in File Sharing Shadow. Mark Mulligan, JupiterResearch 2006

European Digital Music: Converting Nonbuyers. Mark Mulligan, JupiterResearch 2008

European Music Discovery: Using Social Networks to Sell Music. Mark Mulligan, JupiterResearch 2007

European Music File Sharing: Addressing the Non-Network Threat. Mark Mulligan, JupiterResearch 2007

European PC Digital Music Forecast, 2007 to 2012. Mark Mulligan, JupiterResearch 2007

Apple and EMI DRM-free Initiative to Change Shape of Digital Music Distribution. Mark Mulligan, JupiterResearch 2007

Subsidized Mobile Music Subscriptions: Target Entry-Level Offerings to Drive Mass-Market Appeal. Mark Mulligan, JupiterResearch 2008

"The Death of the Long Tail: The Superstar Music Economy". Mark Mulligan, MIDiA Research 2014

Global Music Forecasts 2014 to 2019: The Shift To The Consumption Era. Mark Mulligan, MIDiA Research 2014

The Superstar Artist Economy: Artist Income and the Top 1% Mark Mulligan, MIDiA Research 2014

Unlocking YouTube: How YouTube's Music Key Will Impact Subscriptions. Mark Mulligan, MIDiA Research 2014

The Streaming Effect: Assessing The Impact Of Streaming Music Behaviour. Mark Mulligan, MIDiA Research 2014

Table of Figures

Printed in Great Britain
by Amazon

UNIVERSITY OF CHESTER. WARRINGTON CAMPUS